Taxation

Supporting resources

Visit **www.pearsoned.co.uk/melville** to find valuable online resources

For instructors

- Complete, downloadable Instructor's Manual

For more information please contact your local Pearson Education sales representative
or **visit www.pearsoned.co.uk/melville**

We work with leading authors to develop the
strongest educational materials in accounting,
bringing cutting-edge thinking and best learning
practice to a global market.

Under a range of well-known imprints, including
Financial Times Prentice Hall, we craft high
quality print and electronic publications which
help readers to understand and apply their content,
whether studying or at work.

To find out more about the complete range of our
publishing please visit us on the World Wide Web at:
www.pearsoned.co.uk

Taxation

Finance Act 2009

Fifteenth edition

Alan Melville
FCA, BSc, Cert. Ed.

**Financial Times
Prentice Hall
is an imprint of**

Harlow, England • London • New York • Boston • San Francisco • Toronto • Sydney • Singapore • Hong Kong
Tokyo • Seoul • Taipei • New Delhi • Cape Town • Madrid • Mexico City • Amsterdam • Munich • Paris • Milan

Pearson Education Limited
Edinburgh Gate
Harlow
Essex CM20 2JE
England

and Associated Companies throughout the world

Visit us on the World Wide Web at:
www.pearsoned.co.uk

First published 1995
Fifteenth edition published 2010

© Pearson Professional Limited 1995, 1996
© Financial Times Professional Limited 1997, 1998
© Pearson Education Limited 1999, 2010

ISBN: 978-0-273-73015-6

British Library Cataloguing-in-Publication Data
A catalogue record for this book is available from the British Library

Library of Congress Cataloging-in-Publication Data
A catalog record for this book is available from the Library of Congress

10 9 8 7 6 5 4 3 2 1
13 12 11 10 09

Printed and bound by Ashford Colour Press Ltd, Gosport

Website
A website to accompany the fifteenth edition of *Taxation* can be found at
www.pearsoned.co.uk/melville

The publisher's policy is to use paper manufactured from sustainable forests.

Contents

Preface

The main aim of this book is to describe the UK taxation system in sufficient depth and with sufficient clarity to meet the needs of those undertaking a first course of study in taxation. The book has not been written with any specific syllabus in mind but will be useful to students who are preparing for any of the following examinations:

Examining body	Level	Examination title(s)
Institute of Chartered Accountants in England and Wales	Professional Stage	Principles of Taxation; Taxation
Association of Chartered Certified Accountants	Fundamentals Level Technician Scheme	Taxation Preparing Taxation Computations
Chartered Institute of Public Finance and Accountancy	Diploma Stage	Taxation
Association of Taxation Technicians	Certificates	Personal Taxation; Business Taxation and Accounting Principles
Association of Accounting Technicians	Technician Stage	Preparing Personal and Business Taxation Computations
Association of International Accountants	Foundation Level	Auditing and Taxation
Institute of Financial Accountants	Technician Level	Personal and Business Taxation

The book will also be of value to those studying taxation as part of a university or college course in accounting, finance or business studies and may be used as an introductory text for a study of taxation at an advanced level.

Every effort has been made to explain the tax system as clearly as possible. There are numerous worked examples and each chapter (except Chapter 1) concludes with a set of exercises which thoroughly test the reader's grasp of the new topics introduced in that chapter. The book also contains four sets of review questions which are drawn from the past examination papers of the professional accounting bodies. The solutions to most of these exercises and review questions are to be found at the back of the book but the solutions to the exercises and questions which are marked with an asterisk (*) are provided in a separate Instructor's Manual.

This fifteenth edition incorporates the provisions of the Finance Act 2009.

Alan Melville
July 2009

Acknowledgements

I would like to thank the following accounting bodies for granting me permission to use their past examination questions:

- Association of Chartered Certified Accountants (ACCA)
- Chartered Institute of Management Accountants (CIMA)
- Chartered Institute of Public Finance and Accountancy (CIPFA)
- Association of Accounting Technicians (AAT).

I must emphasise that the answers provided to these questions are entirely my own and are not the responsibility of the accounting body concerned. I should also point out that the questions which are printed in this textbook have been amended in some cases so as to reflect changes in taxation law which have occurred since those questions were originally published by the accounting body concerned.

I would like to thank the Office for National Statistics for granting me permission to reproduce the table of Retail Price Indices given in Chapter 23.

Finally, I would like to express my gratitude to Mrs Margaret Cooper, who has again checked the arithmetic accuracy of every calculation in this book and in the accompanying Instructor's Manual.

Alan Melville
July 2009

Summary of Tax Data

Income Tax

	2009-10	2008-09
TAX RATES AND BANDS		
Starting rate for savings	10%	10%
Basic rate	20%	20%
Higher rate	40%	40%
Starting rate limit for savings	£2,440	£2,320
Basic rate limit	£37,400	£34,800

Notes:
(a)   The dividend ordinary and upper rates are 10% and 32.5%.
(b)   Special rates of tax apply to certain trusts.
(c)   An additional rate of 50% will be introduced in 2010-11.

	2009-10	2008-09
ALLOWANCES	£	£
Personal allowance		
Age 0 to 64	6,475	6,035
Age 65 to 74	9,490	9,030
Age 75 or over	9,640	9,180
Blind person's allowance	1,890	1,800
Married couple's allowance†		
Age under 75 and born before 6 April 1935	-	6,535
Age 75 or over	6,965	6,625
Minimum amount	2,670	2,540
Income limit for age-related allowances	22,900	21,800

†*This allowance is relieved at 10%.*

	2009-10	2008-09
PROPERTY INCOME		
Rent-a-room relief limit	£4,250	£4,250
CAR AND FUEL BENEFIT		
Emission rating qualifying for 10% charge	120g/km	120g/km
Emission rating qualifying for 15% charge	135g/km	135g/km
Set figure used in car fuel benefit calculation	£16,900	£16,900
PENSION SCHEMES	£	£
Annual allowance	245,000	235,000
Lifetime allowance	1,750,000	1,650,000

Capital Allowances

Writing Down Allowance (WDA):

Main pool of plant and machinery	20%
Special rate pool of plant and machinery	10%
Industrial buildings and agricultural buildings (2009-10)	2%

Annual Investment Allowance (AIA):

AIA rate	100%
AIA annual limit	£50,000

First Year Allowance (FYA) on qualifying plant and machinery:

Acquired 6 April 2009 to 5 April 2010†	40%
Very low emission cars	100%
Energy saving or water efficient technology	100%

† *Dates are 1 April 2009 to 31 March 2010 for companies.*

National Insurance Contributions

	2009-10	2008-09
CLASS 1 (Not contracted out)		
Primary threshold (weekly)	£110	£105
Upper accruals point (weekly)	£770	-
Upper earnings limit (weekly)	£844	£770
Employee contributions		
Rate on earnings between primary threshold and UEL	11%	11%
Rate on earnings beyond UEL	1%	1%
Employer contributions		
Secondary threshold (weekly)	£110	£105
Rate on earnings beyond secondary threshold	12.8%	12.8%
CLASS 1A		
Rate	12.8%	12.8%
CLASS 2		
Weekly contribution	£2.40	£2.30
Small earnings exception	£5,075	£4,825
CLASS 3		
Weekly contribution	£12.05	£8.10
CLASS 4		
Lower profits limit	£5,715	£5,435
Upper profits limit	£43,875	£40,040
Rate on profits between lower and upper limit	8%	8%
Rate on profits beyond upper limit	1%	1%

Capital Gains Tax

	2009-10	2008-09
CGT rate	18%	18%
Annual exemption - individuals and disabled trusts	£10,100	£9,600
- other trusts	£5,050	£4,800
Chattels exemption	£6,000	£6,000

Corporation Tax

Financial Year	FY2009	FY2008	FY2007	FY2006
Main rate	28%	28%	30%	30%
Small companies rate (SCR)	21%	21%	20%	19%
SCR lower limit	£300,000	£300,000	£300,000	£300,000
SCR upper limit	£1,500,000	£1,500,000	£1,500,000	£1,500,000
Marginal relief fraction	7/400	7/400	1/40	11/400

Notes:
(a) The main rate for FY2010 will be 28%.
(b) The small companies rate for FY2010 is expected to be 22%.

Inheritance Tax

Date of transfer	0% Band	Rate on chargeable lifetime transfers	Rate on death
6 April 2002 to 5 April 2003	0 - £250,000	20%	40%
6 April 2003 to 5 April 2004	0 - £255,000	20%	40%
6 April 2004 to 5 April 2005	0 - £263,000	20%	40%
6 April 2005 to 5 April 2006	0 - £275,000	20%	40%
6 April 2006 to 5 April 2007	0 - £285,000	20%	40%
6 April 2007 to 5 April 2008	0 - £300,000	20%	40%
6 April 2008 to 5 April 2009	0 - £312,000	20%	40%
6 April 2009 to 5 April 2010	0 - £325,000	20%	40%

Value Added Tax

Standard rate†	17.5%	(from 1 April 1991)
Registration threshold	£68,000	(from 1 May 2009)
Deregistration threshold	£66,000	(from 1 May 2009)

†*Standard rate 15% from 1 December 2008 to 31 December 2009*

Part 1

INCOME TAX AND NATIONAL INSURANCE

Chapter 1

Introduction to the UK tax system

Introduction

The purpose of this first chapter is to provide an overview of the UK tax system. The principal UK taxes are introduced and classified and the main sources of tax law are explained. This chapter also outlines the structure and the functions of Her Majesty's Revenue and Customs (the organisation which is responsible for the administration of the UK tax system) and describes the procedure which is used to assess the tax liability of an individual in each tax year. The chapter concludes by distinguishing between tax evasion and tax avoidance.

UK taxes

The UK taxation system is composed of a number of different taxes, some of which are *direct* taxes and some of which are *indirect* taxes:

(a) Direct taxes are charged on income, profits or other gains and are either deducted at source or paid directly to the tax authorities. The main direct taxes which are payable by individuals are income tax, capital gains tax and inheritance tax. The main direct tax payable by companies is corporation tax. All of these taxes are administered by HM Revenue and Customs (HMRC), which was formed in April 2005 when the Inland Revenue and HM Customs and Excise were merged. National Insurance contributions, which can also be looked upon as a form of direct taxation, are administered by the National Insurance Contributions Office (NICO) of HMRC.

(b) Indirect taxes are taxes on spending. They are charged when a taxpayer buys an item and are paid to the vendor as part of the purchase price of the item. It is then the vendor's duty to pass the tax on to the tax authorities. Indirect taxes include value added tax (VAT), stamp duty, customs duties and the excise duties levied on alcohol, tobacco and petrol. The only indirect tax considered in this book is VAT, which is now also administered by HM Revenue and Customs.

Sources of tax law

There is no single source of UK tax law. The basic rules are laid down in Acts of Parliament but it is left to the courts to interpret these Acts and to provide much of the detail of the tax system. In addition, HMRC issues a variety of statements, notices and leaflets which explain how the law is implemented in practice. These statements have no legal backing but they explain the tax authorities' interpretation of the law and will be adhered to unless successfully challenged in the courts.

Statute law

The basic rules of the UK tax system are embodied in a number of tax *statutes* or Acts of Parliament. The main statutes currently in force for each tax are as follows:

Tax	Statute	Abbreviation
Income tax	Income and Corporation Taxes Act 1988	ICTA 1988
	Capital Allowances Act 2001	CAA 2001
	Income Tax (Earnings and Pensions) Act 2003	ITEPA 2003
	Income Tax (Trading and Other Income) Act 2005	ITTOIA 2005
	Income Tax Act 2007	ITA 2007
Capital gains tax	Taxation of Chargeable Gains Act 1992	TCGA 1992
Inheritance tax	Inheritance Tax Act 1984	IHTA 1984
Corporation tax	Income and Corporation Taxes Act 1988	ICTA 1988
	Taxation of Chargeable Gains Act 1992	TCGA 1992
	Capital Allowances Act 2001	CAA 2001
	Corporation Tax Act 2009	CTA 2009
National Insurance	Social Security Contributions & Benefits Act 1992	SSCBA 1992
Value added tax	Value Added Tax Act 1994	VATA 1994
Administration of } the tax system }	Taxes Management Act 1970 Customs and Excise Management Act 1979	TMA 1970 CEMA 1979

These statutes are amended each year by the annual Finance Act, which is based upon the Budget proposals put forward by the Chancellor of the Exchequer. Some of the tax statutes provide for the making of detailed regulations by *statutory instrument*. A statutory instrument (SI) is a document which is laid before Parliament and then automatically becomes law within a stated period unless any objections are raised to it.

Tax Law Rewrite project

The Tax Law Rewrite project was established in 1996 with the aim of rewriting the primary direct tax legislation of the UK in such a way that it is clearer and easier to understand. The project's output so far includes CAA 2001, ITEPA 2003, ITTOIA 2005, ITA 2007 and CTA 2009.

Two further Acts are expected in 2010. The first of these will complete the rewrite of corporation tax. The second Act will be concerned with international aspects of taxation.

European Union law

Membership of the European Union (EU) involves adherence to EU law and if there is a conflict between EU law and the law of a member state then EU law takes priority. This applies as much to tax law as to any other category of law and the EU's influence on UK tax law is likely to increase over time. At present, the main impact is on VAT, where the prevailing legislation takes the form of EU Directives. These Directives are binding on the UK and they dictate the results which the internal legislation of the UK must bring about.

Case law

Over the years, taxpayers and the tax authorities have frequently disagreed over the interpretation of the tax Acts. As a result, many thousands of tax cases have been brought before the courts. The decisions made by judges in these cases form an important part of the tax law of the UK and some of the more significant cases are referred to in this book.

Statements made by the tax authorities

The main statements and other documents produced by HM Revenue and Customs as a guide to the law on taxation are as follows:

(a) **Statements of Practice**. A Statement of Practice (SP) sets out the HMRC interpretation of tax legislation and clarifies the way in which the law will be applied in practice. For example, SP 2/02 (the second SP issued in 2002) deals with the taxation treatment of exchange rate fluctuations.

(b) **Extra-Statutory Concessions**. An Extra-Statutory Concession (ESC) consists of a relaxation which gives taxpayers a reduction in liability to which they are not entitled under the strict letter of the law. In general, concessions are made so as to resolve anomalies or relieve hardship. For example, ESC B10 is concerned with the income of contemplative religious communities and their members.

  A process of giving statutory effect to certain ESCs is currently underway. This is being done by means of statutory instruments.

(c) **Press releases**. These are issued throughout the year on a variety of tax-related subjects. Of especial interest are the press releases and notes which are issued on Budget day and which provide a detailed explanation of the Budget proposals.

(d) **Internal Guidance Manuals**. HMRC produces a comprehensive set of internal tax manuals for the guidance of its own staff. These manuals may be inspected at HMRC Enquiry Centres or accessed via the Internet.

(e) **Leaflets**. These are aimed at the general public and explain the tax system in non-technical language. For example, HMRC leaflet IR121 is a guide to tax and national insurance contributions for those approaching retirement.

Most of the information produced by the tax authorities is now available on the HMRC website, the address of which is *www.hmrc.gov.uk*.

The tax year

The amendments to the taxation system which are proposed in the annual Budget speech are usually intended to take effect as from the start of the next tax year, although some of the proposals may have a more immediate effect. For individuals, a *tax year*, also known as a *fiscal year* or a *year of assessment*, runs from 6 April to the following 5 April. For instance, the tax year referred to as 2008-09 began on 6 April 2008 and ended on 5 April 2009. This book takes into account the provisions of the Finance Act 2009 (based on the April 2009 Budget proposals) and describes the UK tax system for tax year 2009-10.

It is worth noting that the tax year for corporation tax purposes is slightly different from the fiscal year. A corporation tax *financial year* runs from 1 April in one year to 31 March in the following year and is identified by the year in which it begins. This book describes the corporation tax system for Financial Year 2009, which runs from 1 April 2009 to 31 March 2010 inclusive.

Structure of HM Revenue and Customs

HM Revenue and Customs (HMRC) consists of a large body of civil servants headed by the *Commissioners for Revenue and Customs*. The Commissioners are appointed by the Queen in accordance with recommendations made by the *Treasury*. This Government department is managed by the *Chancellor of the Exchequer* and has overall responsibility for the public finances of the UK. The main duties of the Commissioners for Revenue and Customs are as follows:

(a) to implement the law relating to direct and indirect taxation

(b) to provide advice to the Chancellor of the Exchequer on taxation matters

(c) to administer the many divisions and offices into which HMRC is organised.

The routine work of HMRC is carried out by officials known as *Officers of Revenue and Customs*. With regard to direct taxation, the main function of these officials is to calculate or "assess" a taxpayer's tax liability and then to ensure that the correct amount of tax is paid. Under the Self Assessment system (see later in this chapter) a taxpayer may calculate his or her own tax liability, in which case HMRC officials will check that the taxpayer's self-assessment is correct.

At one time, tax assessment was the responsibility of *Inspectors of Taxes* whilst tax collection was handled separately by *Collectors of Taxes*. However, this separation of assessment and collection is now seen as outdated and the two functions have been combined. In consequence, the terms "Inspector" and "Collector" have been dropped in favour of the above-mentioned "Officer of Revenue and Customs".

The functions of HMRC with regard to indirect taxation (and VAT in particular) are explained later in this book (see Chapter 30).

HMRC has specialist offices which deal with such matters as pension schemes, charities, trusts and so forth but most of the day-to-day work relating to direct taxation takes place in local area offices. These local offices are responsible for routine assessment and collection and for ensuring that taxpayers comply with tax regulations. There is also a network of HMRC Enquiry Centres. These provide a first point of contact for taxpayers with general queries and carry stocks of tax forms and leaflets.

Administration of the tax system

The remainder of this chapter describes the system which is used each year to assess an individual's liability to income tax and capital gains tax. Later chapters explain the equivalent systems which are used for corporation tax, inheritance tax and VAT.

For tax years up to and including 1995-96, the assessment of an individual's tax liability was entirely the responsibility of the tax authorities and it was possible for taxpayers to delay the assessment (and payment) of tax by withholding information from the authorities for as long as possible. The introduction of the Self Assessment system in 1996-97 shifted the responsibility for assessment to the taxpayer and made it much more likely that tax is assessed and paid on time.

Self Assessment

If an individual's tax liability for a tax year cannot be collected entirely by deduction at source (see Chapter 2) or via the PAYE system (see Chapter 7), then the liability must be formally assessed. The amount of tax which is due for the year may be calculated by the taxpayer (or by the taxpayer's accountant) and then checked by HMRC. Alternatively, if the taxpayer prefers not to perform the calculation, the amount of tax due is calculated by HMRC. In either case, the first step is the completion of a *tax return*. The annual procedure is as follows:

(a) Tax returns are normally issued in April each year to those taxpayers who are likely to need them. Each tax return is accompanied by a formal notice requiring a return to be made and delivered to HMRC. The main tax return consists of a basic six-page form together with a four-page "additional information" form which covers some of the less common types of income and tax reliefs. The additional information form need not be submitted to HMRC if none of these types of income or tax reliefs apply to the taxpayer concerned.

There are also several sets of supplementary pages, each dealing with a different type of income or gains (e.g. income from self-employment). Taxpayers are sent only those supplementary pages which are thought to be relevant to their circumstances but can request further supplementary pages if necessary.

(b) A short tax return (STR) is available for taxpayers with simpler tax affairs.

(c) Rather than completing a paper tax return, taxpayers and their agents can file tax returns electronically by means of the Internet and are encouraged to do so. In fact, approximately two-thirds of the 9.5 million tax returns for tax year 2007-08 were filed electronically.

(d) The information requested in a tax return relates to the tax year just ended. For example, the tax returns which were issued in April 2009 required taxpayers to declare their income and gains for tax year 2008-09 and to claim allowances and reliefs (see Chapters 3 and 4) for the same year.

(e) A tax return must be completed in full. It is not permissible to omit figures or to make entries such as "see accounts" or "as submitted by employer". Unless asked to submit accounts or other supporting documentation with the return, a taxpayer is under no obligation to do so. However, it is necessary to retain all supporting documentation in case HMRC enquires into the accuracy of a return.

(f) If a main tax return is submitted on paper, the taxpayer has the option of calculating his or her own tax liability (using extra "tax calculation summary" pages) and then submitting this calculation to HMRC as part of the return. HMRC will calculate the tax liability for taxpayers who do not take up this option or for those who submit the short tax return (which does not include a self-calculation facility). If a tax return is filed electronically, the tax liability is calculated automatically by computer software. In all cases, the resulting assessment is referred to as a "self-assessment".

(g) Self assessment tax returns must normally be filed (i.e. submitted to HMRC) on or before the following dates:
- for paper returns, 31 October following the end of the tax year
- for returns filed electronically, 31 January following the end of the tax year.

However, if the return notice is issued after 31 July following the end of the tax year (but not after 31 October) the taxpayer has three months from the date of the notice to submit a paper return. The deadline for electronic filing in such a case remains at 31 January. If the notice is issued after 31 October, the taxpayer has three months from the date of the notice to submit the return either on paper or electronically.

(h) Penalties are imposed if a return is filed late. Furthermore, the submission of a late return may mean that the tax liability for the year is not determined until after the due date of payment (see below). This could result in the taxpayer becoming liable to surcharges and interest on overdue tax (see Chapter 14).

(i) The 31 January which follows the end of a tax year is known as the "filing date" for that year. For example, the filing date for tax year 2008-09 is normally 31 January 2010. However, if a return notice is issued after 31 October, the filing date becomes the date which falls three months after the issue date of the notice.

(j) HMRC is empowered to correct a tax return (so as to rectify obvious errors or omissions or anything else that is believed to be incorrect) within nine months of the date on which the return is filed. Similarly, the taxpayer has the right to amend his or her tax return within 12 months of the filing date for that return. Taxpayers who believe that an error in their return has resulted in an excessive self-assessment may make an "error or mistake" claim no later than five years after the 31 January which follows the end of the tax year to which the return relates. HMRC will then determine the amount (if any) that is just and reasonable to repay in the circumstances.

As from 1 April 2010, error or mistake claims must be submitted within four years of the end of the tax year to which they relate. At the same time, the requirement that the excessive self-assessment must be caused by a mistake in a return is removed. This allows a claim to be made in relation to any overpayment, however caused.

(k) The tax due in relation to a self-assessment is normally payable as follows:

   (i)   A first payment on account (POA) is due on 31 January in the tax year to which the self-assessment relates.

   (ii) A second POA is due on the following 31 July.

   (iii) A final balancing payment is due on the following 31 January.

   For example, the tax due in relation to a 2009-10 self-assessment would normally be payable on 31 January 2010 (first POA), 31 July 2010 (second POA) and 31 January 2011 (balancing payment). Further information regarding the payment of tax is given in Chapter 14 of this book.

(l) A taxpayer who is entitled to a repayment of tax may make an entry on his or her tax return nominating a charity to receive all or part of that repayment. The taxpayer may also indicate on the tax return that Gift Aid (see Chapter 4) should apply to this charitable donation.

Notification of chargeability to tax

Individuals who have not received a tax return, but have taxable income or gains of which HMRC is not aware, must notify HMRC of their chargeability to tax within six months of the end of the tax year in which the income arises. However, notification of chargeability is *not* required if *all* of the following conditions are satisfied:

(a) the individual has no capital gains

(b) the individual is not a higher-rate taxpayer (see Chapter 2)

(c) all of the individual's income has been subject to deduction of income tax at source (see Chapter 2) or has been dealt with via the PAYE system (see Chapter 7).

An individual who fails to notify chargeability within the permitted six-month period will incur a penalty (see Chapter 14).

Enquiries

HMRC is empowered to "enquire" into any tax return. The usual reason for opening an enquiry is that HMRC suspects that something is wrong with the information provided in the return. However, some enquiry cases are selected entirely at random and HMRC is under no obligation to justify the opening of an enquiry or to state whether or not the case has been chosen randomly. Note that:

(a) If a tax return is filed by the due date, an enquiry cannot usually begin more than 12 months after the date on which the return is filed. This means that the "enquiry window" for a return which is filed early closes correspondingly early.

(b) If a return is filed late or is amended after the date on which the return was due to be filed, the enquiry window is extended until the quarter day which follows the first anniversary of the date on which the return or amendment was filed. For this purpose, the quarter days are 31 January, 30 April, 31 July and 31 October.

EXAMPLE

In April 2009, HMRC issues a notice requiring an individual to submit a tax return for the year 2008-09. The return is submitted electronically to HMRC on 8 December 2009.

(a) State the date by which any enquiry into the above return must begin.

(b) How would the situation differ if a paper return was submitted on 8 December 2009?

(c) How would the situation differ if an electronic return was submitted on 1 March 2010?

Solution

(a) The return is filed before the due date (31 January 2010). Any enquiry must begin within 12 months of the date that the return is filed (i.e. by 8 December 2010).

(b) The return is filed after the due date (31 October 2009). Any enquiry must begin by the quarter day which follows the first anniversary of the date that the return is filed (i.e. by 31 January 2011).

(c) The return is filed after the due date (31 January 2010). Any enquiry must begin by the quarter day which follows the first anniversary of the date that the return is filed (i.e. by 30 April 2011).

Discovery assessments

HMRC may raise a "discovery assessment" if it is discovered that full disclosure has not been made in a tax return and that tax has been lost as a result. The time limits for raising discovery assessments are currently as follows:

(a) 31 January in the sixth tax year following the year to which the assessment relates, in the case of incomplete disclosure of facts without fraud or negligence.

(b) 31 January in the twenty-first tax year following the year to which the assessment relates, in the case of fraudulent or negligent conduct by the taxpayer

Finance Act 2008 includes provisions which will change these time limits. The time limit for making a discovery assessment will normally be four years after the end of the tax year concerned. This will increase to six years if the taxpayer has been negligent and 20 years if the taxpayer has been dishonest. These changes take effect as from 1 April 2010.

Determinations

If an individual fails to submit a tax return by the required filing date for that return, an Officer of Revenue and Customs may make a determination of the tax due, calculated according to "the best of his information and belief". There is no right of appeal against a determination and the tax due cannot be postponed. A determination can be displaced only if the individual files the required return.

Record keeping

Taxpayers are required to keep proper records so that they can make a correct tax return and (if necessary) substantiate the figures entered on the return. A taxpayer who is in business or who lets property must normally preserve these records for five years after the 31 January which follows the end of the tax year concerned. Otherwise, records must be preserved for 12 months after the 31 January which follows the end of the tax year. For example, records for tax year 2009-10 must normally be retained until 31 January 2016 by a taxpayer who is in business or who lets property and until 31 January 2012 otherwise.

Appeals

Under the Self Assessment system, taxpayers have the right of appeal in relation to a number of HMRC decisions. For example, a taxpayer may appeal against a discovery assessment or against an HMRC amendment to a self-assessment.

An appeal may involve an internal review of the decision by an HMRC official and/or a hearing before a tribunal. The main features of the appeals system are as follows:

(a) An appeal must be sent to HMRC in writing within 30 days of the disputed decision.

(b) The taxpayer may also apply to postpone payment of all or part of any tax which is payable as a result of the decision, though interest will continue to accrue on the postponed amount until the appeal is settled. Any non-postponed tax is payable on the due date in the usual way. If the appeal is subsequently settled in the taxpayer's favour, any overpaid tax is refunded.

(c) On receiving an appeal, HMRC considers the taxpayer's reasons for disputing the decision and may discuss the matter with the taxpayer. Most appeals are settled by agreement at this stage.

(d) If the taxpayer and HMRC are unable to agree, the taxpayer will be offered an internal review of the decision. A taxpayer who wishes to accept this offer must normally do so within 30 days. An internal review is carried out by an HMRC officer who has not previously been involved with the disputed decision and is usually completed within 45 days. The review officer then writes to the taxpayer to inform him or her of the review's conclusions.

(e) A taxpayer who rejects the offer of an internal review may appeal to a tribunal within 30 days of the date of the offer letter. Otherwise, an appeal to a tribunal may be made within 30 days of the date of the review conclusion letter.

(f) Most appeals to a tribunal are dealt with by the Tax Chamber of the First-tier Tribunal. However, very complex appeals may be heard by the Finance and Tax Chamber of the Upper Tribunal. The Upper Tribunal also hears appeals against decisions made by the First-tier Tribunal.

(g) If either HMRC or the person concerned is dissatisfied with a decision made by the Upper Tribunal, a dispute on a point of law may be referred to the Court of Appeal.

(h) The costs of bringing an appeal before the First-tier Tribunal are usually fairly modest. Parties bear their own costs and a taxpayer who loses an appeal is not normally required to pay HMRC's costs (unless the taxpayer has acted wholly unreasonably). The costs of taking an appeal to higher authority can be very high and an unsuccessful taxpayer may be required to pay HMRC's costs in defending the appeal as well as his or her own costs.

The Adjudicator

An independent and impartial Adjudicator considers complaints made by taxpayers who are not satisfied with the quality of the service they have received from HMRC. The Adjudicator writes an annual report and makes recommendations for improvements to HMRC procedures and practices. The Adjudicator is not empowered to hear tax appeals.

Tax evasion

Taxpayers are required to provide information which is correct and complete. Dishonest behaviour (such as concealing a source of income) is known as *tax evasion* and is against the law. The law relating to tax evasion was strengthened by the Finance Act 2000, which introduced a statutory offence of fraudulently evading income tax. On summary conviction in a magistrate's court, offenders may be sentenced to up to six months in prison and may be fined up to £5,000 (the "statutory maximum"). On indictment in a higher court, the penalties are increased to a maximum of seven years in prison and/or an unlimited fine.

Tax avoidance

Taxpayers are entitled to organise their financial affairs in any way they please and may do so in such a way that their tax burden is minimised. This perfectly legal activity is known as *tax avoidance*. For example, a taxpayer might legally avoid income tax by moving funds from a bank account which pays taxable interest to an ISA which pays tax-free interest (see Chapter 6). Tax avoidance (which is legal) should be contrasted sharply with tax evasion (which is not).

Tax avoidance is acceptable within limits but, over the years, tax advisors have shown great ingenuity in devising very complex and highly artificial tax avoidance schemes to exploit "loopholes" in the tax system. These schemes often result in a significant loss of tax revenue until eventually blocked by anti-avoidance legislation. In an attempt to limit the effectiveness of tax avoidance schemes, a disclosure regime has been introduced which requires certain disclosures by those who devise such schemes or use them. A summary of the requirements is as follows:

(a) Those who promote and market schemes which bear certain "hallmarks" of tax avoidance (e.g. the creation of tax losses to offset income or capital gains) are required to provide HMRC with details of each scheme. Promoters must provide a description of the scheme, including details of its tax consequences and the statutory provisions on which it relies. The scheme is then registered by HMRC and is allocated a registration number.

(b) Taxpayers using such a scheme are required to quote the registration number of the scheme in their tax returns. Taxpayers who develop their own "in-house" tax avoidance schemes must provide details of each scheme directly to HMRC.

These rules are intended to provide HMRC with advance warning of tax avoidance schemes, so enabling swifter and more effective investigation and counteraction.

Summary

▸ Direct taxes are charged on income, profits and other gains. The main direct taxes are income tax, capital gains tax, inheritance tax and corporation tax. National Insurance contributions are also a form of direct taxation. Indirect taxes are taxes on spending and are paid as part of the price of a bought item. Indirect taxes include VAT, stamp duty, customs duties and excise duties.

▸ Taxation law is a combination of statute law and case law. Statements made by the tax authorities have no legal force but provide information on the authorities' interpretation of the law.

▸ The fiscal year runs from 6 April to the following 5 April. The corporation tax financial year runs from 1 April to the following 31 March.

▸ HM Revenue and Customs (HMRC) calculates a taxpayer's tax liability or checks the taxpayer's own calculation of the liability. The calculation is based upon the information provided in an annual tax return.

▸ Paper tax returns must normally be filed by 31 October following the end of the tax year to which they relate. Returns submitted electronically must be filed by the following 31 January.

▸ A taxpayer who has not received a tax return, but has taxable income or gains of which HMRC is not aware, must notify HMRC of his or her chargeability to tax within six months of the end of the tax year in which the income arises.

▸ If a tax return is submitted on or before the required filing date for that return, HMRC cannot initiate an enquiry into the return more than 12 months after the date on which the return is submitted. Discovery assessments may be made after the enquiry window has closed if it is discovered that the taxpayer has not made full disclosure of all relevant facts.

▸ Taxpayers have the right of appeal against certain HMRC decisions. Appeals which cannot be settled by agreement between the taxpayer and HMRC are dealt with by a two-tier tribunals system.

▸ Tax evasion should be distinguished from tax avoidance. The former involves dishonest conduct by the taxpayer and is illegal. The latter involves the sensible arrangement of the taxpayer's affairs so as to minimise the liability to tax and is perfectly legal.

Chapter 2

Introduction to income tax

Introduction

Income tax assessments are computed for a tax year (or "year of assessment") and are based on the taxpayer's total income for the year from all sources, ignoring any income which is exempt from income tax. This chapter explains the main features of an income tax computation, in preparation for the much more detailed information which is provided in subsequent chapters.

Most of the primary legislation relating to income tax used to be located in the Income and Corporation Taxes Act 1988, but this legislation has been rewritten in recent years and moved to new statutes. Income tax legislation can now be found mainly in the Income Tax (Earnings and Pensions) Act 2003, the Income Tax (Trading and Other Income) Act 2005 and the Income Tax Act 2007, as amended by subsequent Finance Acts.

Taxable persons

Individuals who are resident in the UK for a tax year are generally charged to income tax on all of their income for that year, including both income arising in the UK and income arising overseas. However, there are two main exceptions to this general rule:

(a)   Some forms of income are exempt from income tax altogether (see below).

(b)   UK residents who are not UK-domiciled (i.e. whose permanent home is not the UK) may claim that their overseas income should be subject to UK income tax only to the extent that the income is remitted to the UK. However, this may lead to an additional £30,000 tax charge in some cases (see Chapter 32).

Individuals who are not UK residents are liable to pay income tax on their UK income only (see Chapter 32). Income tax is payable by:

(a)   adults, on their own income and on their share of the income of a partnership

(b)   children, if they have sufficient income to pay tax

(c)   trustees, on the income of a trust or settlement

(d)   personal representatives, on income arising from the estate of a deceased person.

Exempt organisations and individuals

Most organisations are generally exempt from income tax, subject to various restrictions and exceptions. Certain individuals are also exempt. Exempt organisations and individuals include the following:

(a) companies, which are liable to corporation tax rather than income tax

(b) clubs and societies, which are also liable to corporation tax

(c) registered pension schemes

(d) registered charities (on income used for charitable purposes)

(e) local authorities and local authority associations

(f) representatives of foreign countries (e.g. ambassadors)

(g) visiting members of foreign armed forces (on their service pay and on income arising from a source outside the UK).

Classification of income

Income is classified for income tax purposes into a number of types or categories, each with its own set of rules for calculating the amount of income of that type arising in a tax year. These rules are located in the Income Tax (Earnings and Pensions) Act 2003 and in the Income Tax (Trading and Other Income) Act 2005. The main classes of income which are subject to income tax are as follows:

Statute	Type of income	Chapter of this book
ITEPA 2003	Employment income	Chapter 7
	Pensions	Chapter 7
	Social security income	Chapter 7
ITTOIA 2005	Trading income	Chapters 8-12
	Property income	Chapter 5
	Interest	Chapter 6
	Dividends	Chapter 6
	Miscellaneous income	Chapter 6

As indicated above, each of these classes of income is considered in some detail in later chapters of this book.

The schedular system

Until income tax law was rewritten into ITEPA 2003 and ITTOIA 2005, income was classified for income tax purposes into a number of "Schedules", each identified by a letter of the alphabet. However, the schedular system has now been abolished and is considered no further here.

Exempt income

Certain types of income are specifically exempt from income tax and should be completely ignored when preparing an income tax computation. Some of the more important sources of exempt income are as follows:

(a) Exempt savings and investment income (see Chapter 6):

- income from Individual Savings Accounts
- income from National Savings Certificates
- interest arising from a certified SAYE (Save As You Earn) arrangement
- income from investments held in a Child Trust Fund account
- dividends received on shares held in a Venture Capital Trust, so long as certain conditions are satisfied

(b) Exempt employment income (see Chapter 7):

- certain minor benefits provided by employers for their employees
- statutory redundancy pay and the first £30,000 of compensation received for loss of employment
- certain lump sums payable under registered pension schemes (e.g. a lump sum payable at the commencement of a pension)
- the operational allowance paid to UK armed forces serving in specified locations

(c) Exempt property income (see Chapter 5):

- income of up to £4,250 per annum received under the "rent-a-room" scheme

(d) Other exempt income:

- winnings from betting, competition prizes and premium bond prizes
- maintenance payments (see Chapter 4)
- income from scholarships
- wound and disability pensions
- certain social security benefits (e.g. child benefit and housing benefit)
- most commissions, discounts and cashbacks received by ordinary retail customers when purchasing goods, investments or services
- damages or compensation received for personal or professional injury and compensation received for mis-sold personal pension schemes
- foster care receipts not exceeding specified limits and financial support provided to adopters by local authorities or adoption agencies
- income from the sale of electricity generated by home microgeneration systems.

Structure of an income tax computation

In order to calculate a taxpayer's income tax liability for a tax year it is necessary to bring together *all* of the taxpayer's income into a single income tax computation. The structure of an income tax computation is specified in the Income Tax Act 2007 and a typical computation for the year 2009-10 might appear as follows:

	£
Business profits	42,410
Income from property	8,479
Building society interest taxed at source (pre-tax equivalent)	700
Total income	51,589
Less: Tax reliefs	1,200
Net income	50,389
Less: Personal allowance	6,475
Taxable Income	43,914

Income tax

37,400 @ 20%	7,480.00
6,514 @ 40%	2,605.60
43,914	10,085.60
Less: Tax reductions	0.00
Tax borne	10,085.60
Add: Tax withheld on payments	240.00
Tax liability for the year	10,325.60
Less: Tax paid by deduction at source	140.00
Tax payable	10,185.60

All of the terms used in this computation are explained in great detail in this chapter and in later chapters. For the time being it is sufficient to understand the main features of the computation, which are as follows:

(a) The taxpayer's "total income" for the year is calculated by adding together income from all sources, including the pre-tax equivalent of any income from which tax has already been deducted at source. However, any income which is exempt from income tax is excluded.

(b) Relief for certain payments made by the taxpayer (see Chapter 4) together with certain loss reliefs (see Chapters 5 and 11) and relief for certain pension contributions (see Chapter 13) are deducted from total income, giving "net income".

(c) The taxpayer's personal allowance (see Chapter 3) is deducted from net income to give "taxable income". The personal allowance for tax year 2009-10 is £6,475 and this acts as a tax threshold, ensuring that those on very low incomes do not have to pay income tax.

(d) Income tax is charged on the taxable income, using the rates of tax in force for the year. The amount of tax calculated in this way is then subject to a number of adjustments and the result is the tax payable to HM Revenue and Customs.

(e) The *tax borne* by the taxpayer is the amount of income tax suffered for the year. This may be different from the *tax liability*, which is the amount of tax which must be accounted for to HMRC and the *tax payable* which is the tax remaining to be paid after deducting any tax already paid for the year. These distinctions will become clearer in the course of the next two chapters.

A formal tax computation is not required for every taxpayer. For example, a computation is not usually required for an individual whose income is derived entirely from employment, since the correct amount of tax is normally deducted automatically by the PAYE system (see Chapter 7). However, the only way to calculate the tax liability in more complex cases is to prepare a computation and this approach should always be adopted when answering examination questions.

Married couples and civil partners

Married couples are taxed independently, which means that the husband's income and the wife's income are taxed completely separately. This is also the case for same-sex civil partners who have entered into a legally-recognised civil partnership.

If a married couple (or civil partners) receive joint income, such as interest on a joint bank account, the amount of that income will normally be divided between them equally for tax purposes. But if the source of income is genuinely held between them in some other proportion, the couple may make a declaration to that effect and the income will then be divided between them as appropriate.

Dividends from jointly owned shares in close companies (see Chapter 27) are always taxed according to the actual proportions of ownership of the shares, rather than automatically being divided equally between the couple concerned.

Rates of income tax for 2009-10

An individual's taxable income is taxed according to the rates of income tax in force for the year in question. For 2009-10, the main rates of income tax are as follows:

First £37,400 of taxable income	20% (the "basic rate")
Remaining taxable income after the first £37,400	40% (the "higher rate")

Note that:

(a) The point at which basic rate tax gives way to higher rate tax is referred to as the "basic rate limit". For 2009-10, this is £37,400. The first £37,400 of taxable income is often referred to as the "basic rate band".

(b) Calculations are made to the nearest pound when calculating taxable income. The amount of tax due on that income is calculated to the nearest penny in this book but HMRC will generally accept calculations made to the nearest pound.

(c) Savings income and dividend income are treated specially, as explained below.

(d) The Scottish Parliament has the power to increase or decrease (by up to 3%) the basic rate of income tax set by the UK Parliament. The resulting "Scottish variable rate" applies to Scottish taxpayers only. The examples and exercises in this book all assume that the taxpayers referred to are liable to tax at unvaried UK rates.

EXAMPLE 1

Calculate the 2009-10 income tax liability of a taxpayer with taxable income (i.e. income remaining after deducting the personal allowance) of:

(a) £1,250   (b) £37,400   (c) £48,106

Assume that none of the income is derived from savings or dividends.

Solution

(a) £1,250 @ 20% = £250.00.
(b) £37,400 @ 20% = £7,480.00.
(c) £37,400 @ 20% + 10,706 @ 40% = £11,762.40.

Income taxed at source

Certain types of income are *taxed at source*, which means that income tax is deducted from the income before the taxpayer receives it. Typical examples are wages and salaries and most forms of bank and building society interest. Income which has been taxed at source must still be included in the taxpayer's income tax computation, despite the fact that tax has already been paid. This may seem unnecessary but there are two good reasons for including the income in the tax computation:

(a) It is important to derive correct figures for the taxpayer's "total income" and "net income", as will become clearer in later chapters.

(b) The amount of income tax which has already been deducted might not be the correct amount. The only way to check this is to aggregate the income concerned with all of the taxpayer's other income in a single computation.

In a tax computation, all income must be shown "gross". In other words, the amount of income shown must be the amount of the income *before* any income tax was deducted at source. When the tax liability has been calculated, tax paid by deduction at source is subtracted and the taxpayer is then required to pay only the balance of the liability. A tax refund is given if tax deducted at source exceeds the tax liability for the year.

Income which is taxed at source is often referred to as "income received net" and the amount actually received by the taxpayer after tax has been deducted is then referred to as the "net" amount of the income. This usage of the term "net" is very common but it must be carefully distinguished from the entirely different usage of the same term in the Income Tax Act 2007. As indicated earlier in this chapter, ITA 2007 defines "net income" as being equal to a taxpayer's total income less tax reliefs.

Grossing up

If income is received net of basic rate (20%) income tax, the gross amount of that income can be ascertained by multiplying the net amount received by 100/80. This calculation is known as "grossing-up" and the 100/80 fraction may be referred to as the "grossing-up fraction". The amount of income tax deducted at source is equal to the net amount multiplied by 20/80 (or 20% of the gross income). The main types of income which are received by individuals net of basic rate tax are:

(a) most forms of bank and building society interest (apart from interest on a National Savings Bank (NSB) investment account, which is received gross)

(b) debenture and other loan interest paid by UK companies

(c) the income element of a purchased life annuity (i.e. an annuity for life provided by an insurance company in exchange for a lump sum payment)

(d) patent royalties.

Interest on most UK Government securities ("gilt-edged" securities or "gilts") used to be received net of 20% tax but anyone receiving such interest may now choose whether to receive the interest gross or net.

When wages and salaries are received net of income tax, the gross pay and the amount of tax deducted can be ascertained by examining the end-of-year certificate supplied by the taxpayer's employer (see Chapter 7).

EXAMPLE 2

In 2009-10, an individual receives net building society interest of £1,248. Compute the equivalent gross income and the amount of tax deducted at source.

Solution

The equivalent gross income is £1,248 x 100/80 = £1,560 and the tax deducted at source is £1,248 x 20/80 = £312 (or 20% of £1,560).

Savings income

The tax liability on a taxpayer's "savings income" is calculated differently from the tax liability on non-savings income. The main categories of savings income are:

(a) interest from banks and building societies

(b) interest from gilt-edged securities and corporate bonds (i.e. debentures)

(c) the income element of purchased life annuities

(d) certain foreign income (see Chapter 32).

The important difference between the taxation of savings income and the taxation of non-savings income is that savings income which falls into the first £2,440 (for 2009-10) of the basic rate band is taxed at the *starting rate for savings* of 10% rather than at the basic rate of 20%. Therefore, if a taxpayer has both savings income and non-savings income, it is necessary to split taxable income between these two categories before the tax liability can be calculated. Note that:

(a) Non-savings income is regarded as the bottom layer or "slice" of taxable income and savings income is regarded as a higher layer. This means that the basic rate band is made available to non-savings income in priority to savings income.

(b) Tax reliefs and the personal allowance are set against income in the order which will result in the lowest tax liability. The best approach in 2009-10 is to make these deductions from non-savings income in priority to savings income, since non-savings income cannot benefit from the starting rate.

(c) The figure of £2,440 (for 2009-10) is known as the *starting rate limit for savings*. If a taxpayer's taxable income includes non-savings income of at least this amount, then the 10% rate will not be available for savings income at all. Otherwise, some or all of the taxpayer's savings income (if any) will fall into the first £2,440 of the basic rate band and will be taxed at 10%.

(d) Dividends from UK companies used to be regarded as savings income but this is no longer the case. The special tax regime which now applies to UK dividends is explained later in this chapter.

EXAMPLE 3

In 2009-10, Robert has business profits of £17,080 and net bank interest of £360. He claims the personal allowance of £6,475. Calculate the income tax payable for the year.

Solution

	Total £	Non-savings £	Savings £
Business profits	17,080	17,080	
Bank interest £360 x 100/80	450		450
Total income	17,530	17,080	450
Less: Personal allowance	6,475	6,475	
Taxable income	11,055	10,605	450

Income tax due					
Non-savings income	: Basic rate	10,605	@ 20%	2,121.00	
Savings income	: Basic rate	450	@ 20%	90.00	
		11,055			

Tax borne	2,211.00
Less: Tax deducted at source	90.00
Tax payable	2,121.00

Taxable income includes non-savings income of more than £2,440 and so the starting rate is not available for savings income, all of which is taxed at the basic rate.

EXAMPLE 4

In 2009-10, Roberta has rental income of £8,175, net building society interest of £4,000 and net bank interest of £6,080. She claims the personal allowance of £6,475. Calculate the income tax payable for the year.

Solution

	Total £	Non-savings £	Savings £
Income from property	8,175	8,175	
BSI £4,000 x 100/80	5,000		5,000
Bank interest £6,080 x 100/80	7,600		7,600
Total income	20,775	8,175	12,600
Less: Personal allowance	6,475	6,475	
Taxable income	14,300	1,700	12,600

Income tax due

Non-savings income	: Basic rate	1,700	@ 20%	340.00
Savings income	: Starting rate	740	@ 10%	74.00
	: Basic rate	11,860	@ 20%	2,372.00
		14,300		

Tax borne	2,786.00
Less: Tax deducted at source	2,520.00
Tax payable	266.00

Non-savings income occupies £1,700 of the basic rate band. This allows £740 (£2,440 − £1,700) of the savings income to be taxed at the starting rate. The remaining £11,860 of savings income is taxed at the basic rate.

EXAMPLE 5

In 2009-10, Philip has business profits of £46,710 and net bank interest of £4,000. He claims the personal allowance of £6,475. Calculate the income tax payable for the year.

Solution

	Total £	Non-savings £	Savings £
Business profits	46,710	46,710	
Bank interest £4,000 x 100/80	5,000		5,000
Total income	51,710	46,710	5,000
Less: Personal allowance	6,475	6,475	
Taxable income	45,235	40,235	5,000

Income tax due

Non-savings income	: Basic rate	37,400	@ 20%	7,480.00
	: Higher rate	2,835	@ 40%	1,134.00
Savings income	: Higher rate	5,000	@ 40%	2,000.00
		45,235		

Tax borne	10,614.00
Less: Tax deducted at source	1,000.00
Tax payable	9,614.00

Non-savings income occupies the whole of the basic rate band so savings income (and the balance of non-savings income) is taxed entirely at the higher rate.

EXAMPLE 6

In 2009-10, Philippa has business profits of £5,880, National Savings Bank investment account interest (received gross) of £380 and net debenture interest of £41,880. She claims the personal allowance of £6,475. Calculate the income tax payable for the year.

Solution

	Total £	Non-savings £	Savings £
Business profits	5,880	5,880	
NSB interest	380		380
Debenture interest £41,880 x 100/80	52,350		52,350
Total income	58,610	5,880	52,730
Less: Personal allowance	6,475	5,880	595
Taxable income	52,135	nil	52,135

Income tax due

Savings income	: Starting rate	2,440	@ 10%	244.00
	: Basic rate	34,960	@ 20%	6,992.00
	: Higher rate	14,735	@ 40%	5,894.00
		52,135		

Tax borne	13,130.00
Less: Tax deducted at source	10,470.00
Tax payable	2,660.00

Taxable income includes no non-savings income, so the first £2,440 of savings income is taxed at the starting rate. The next £34,960 (£37,400 – £2,440) is taxed at the basic rate and the remaining £14,735 is taxed at the higher rate.

Note that NSB investment account interest is received gross (i.e. without deduction of tax at source) and therefore should not be grossed-up.

Dividends from UK companies

At one time, dividends received from UK companies were regarded as savings income and were treated in a similar way to income received net of tax. However, a special tax regime now applies to UK dividends. The main points of this regime are as follows:

(a) UK dividends have an attached "tax credit" which is equal to *one-ninth* of the amount of the dividend received. A taxpayer's dividend income for a tax year is equal to the amount of the UK dividends received in that year plus the attached tax credits. For example, a taxpayer who receives UK dividends of £720 has dividend income for tax purposes of £800 (£720 plus the tax credits of £80).

(b) UK dividends are not classed as savings income or non-savings income. Dividends constitute a third layer which is treated as the top slice of taxable income, ranking above both non-savings and savings income.

(c) Dividends which fall into the basic rate band are taxed at the "dividend ordinary rate" of 10%. Any dividends which lie above this band are taxed at the "dividend upper rate" of 32.5%.

(d) Tax reliefs and the personal allowance should be set against non-savings income in priority to savings income and against savings income in priority to dividends.

(e) Tax credits relating to dividends which are charged to tax (i.e. dividends which are part of taxable income) may be deducted from the taxpayer's income tax liability on those dividends. However, it is *not* possible to claim payment of any tax credits which exceed this liability. Nor is it possible to deduct tax credits from the income tax which is due on other forms of income. Tax credits that relate to dividends which are not charged to tax are lost.

As from 6 April 2008, the tax regime described above also applies to dividends received from non-UK companies (subject to certain conditions). The tax treatment of dividends received from non-UK companies is explained in Chapter 32 of this book.

Dividends from UK-REITs

A UK company which is a property investment company may elect to become a UK Real Estate Investment Trust (UK-REIT). Dividends received from a UK-REIT, to the extent that they derive from the company's tax-exempt property income or gains, are subject to a different tax regime than the one which is described above. Such dividends are received net of basic rate (20%) income tax and are treated as property income (see Chapter 5).

The examples and exercises in this book all assume that any dividends received are received from companies other than UK-REITs. A fuller description of the tax regime which relates to UK-REITs is given in Chapter 22.

EXAMPLE 7

In 2009-10, Ewan has rental income of £36,825, net bank interest of £3,240 and UK dividends of £3,690. Calculate the income tax payable for the year, assuming that he claims a personal allowance of £6,475.

Solution

	Total £	Non-savings £	Savings £	Dividends £
Income from property	36,825	36,825		
Bank interest £3,240 x 100/80	4,050		4,050	
UK dividends £3,690 + £410	4,100			4,100
Total income	44,975	36,825	4,050	4,100
Less: Personal allowance	6,475	6,475		
Taxable income	38,500	30,350	4,050	4,100

Income tax due

Non-savings income	: Basic rate	30,350	@ 20%	6,070.00
Savings income	: Basic rate	4,050	@ 20%	810.00
Dividend income	: Ordinary rate	3,000	@ 10%	300.00
	: Upper rate	1,100	@ 32.5%	357.50
		38,500		

Tax borne	7,537.50
Less: Tax credits on dividends	410.00
Tax payable	7,127.50
Less: Tax deducted at source	810.00
Tax payable	6,317.50

The dividends are treated as the top slice of income and are taxed at 10% to the extent that they occupy the basic rate band and at 32.5% in the higher rate band. The total tax due on dividends is £657.50, so the tax credits of £410 (i.e. the tax credits relating to dividends which are charged to tax) may be deducted in full.

EXAMPLE 8

Imagine now that Ewan (in the previous example) has no rental income but that all of the other figures remain unchanged. Calculate the income tax payable for the year.

Solution

	Total £	Non-savings £	Savings £	Dividends £
Bank interest £3,240 x 100/80	4,050		4,050	
UK dividends £3,690 + £410	4,100			4,100
Total income	8,150		4,050	4,100
Less: Personal allowance	6,475		4,050	2,425
Taxable income	1,675		-	1,675

Income tax due

Dividend income : Ordinary rate	1,675 @ 10%	167.50
Tax borne		167.50
Less: Tax credits on dividends		167.50
Tax payable		0.00
Less: Tax deducted at source		810.00
Tax repayable		(810.00)

The dividends all fall into the basic rate band and are taxed at the dividend ordinary rate of 10%. Tax credits relating to dividends which are charged to tax are £167.50. The tax due on these dividends is also £167.50, so these tax credits may be deducted. However, Ewan cannot claim payment of the remaining £242.50 of tax credits which relate to the dividends covered by the personal allowance.

Rates of income tax for 2010-11

It has been announced that a 50% "additional rate" of income tax will be introduced in tax year 2010-11. This additional rate will apply to taxable income (non-savings or savings) above £150,000. Dividends which lie above the first £150,000 of taxable income will be taxed at a new "dividend additional rate" of 42.5%.

Summary

▶ In general, income tax is chargeable on all of the income of UK residents and on the UK income of non-residents.

▶ Income is classified into a number of categories, each of which has its own rules for determining the amount of assessable income in a tax year.

▶ Certain types of income are specifically exempt from income tax.

▶ To calculate a taxpayer's income tax liability it is necessary to bring together all of the taxpayer's income into a single computation. The gross equivalent of income received net of income tax must be included in the computation.

▶ Husbands, wives and civil partners are assessed to income tax independently.

▶ In 2009-10, the main rates of income tax are the basic rate of 20% and the higher rate of 40%. Savings income which occupies the first £2,440 of the basic rate band is taxed at the starting rate for savings of 10%.

▶ UK dividends are accompanied by tax credits which generally may be set against the tax liability on those dividends. In 2009-10, this tax liability is calculated at 10% (the dividend ordinary rate) and 32.5% (the dividend upper rate).

▶ If the tax credit attached to a UK dividend exceeds the tax liability with regard to that dividend, the excess tax credit cannot be paid to the recipient under any circumstances.

▶ In 2010-11, the additional rate of 50% will apply to taxable income (non-savings or savings) above £150,000. Dividends which lie above the first £150,000 of taxable income will be taxed at 42.5%.

Exercises

2.1   Calculate the income tax payable in 2009-10 on a taxable income (i.e. income remaining after deducting the personal allowance) of:

(a)   £1,830   (b)   £32,300   (c)   £71,103.

Assume in each case that none of the income is derived from savings or dividends.

2.2   Calculate the income tax payable in 2009-10 on the following incomes, assuming that a personal allowance of £6,475 is claimed in each case:

(a)   Business profits of £22,080 and net bank interest of £720.

(b)   Business profits of £31,610, net building society interest of £8,000 and net bank interest of £2,300.

(c)   Net building society interest of £35,784.

2.3   Stephanie has the following income in 2009-10:

	£
Income from employment	28,755
Rents received	14,730
Bank interest (net)	144
NSB investment account interest, received gross	20
UK dividends	225

Compute the income tax payable by Stephanie for the year (before deducting any tax paid under the PAYE system) assuming that the rents received are not within the "rent-a-room" scheme and that Stephanie is entitled to the personal allowance of £6,475.

2.4   Ernest has a retirement pension in 2009-10 of £5,865. He also receives net bank interest of £416. Compute the income tax payable by Ernest for the year, assuming a personal allowance of £6,475.

What difference would it make if Ernest had received UK dividends of £468 instead of the bank interest?

*2.5   Ivan's income for the tax year 2009-10 is as follows:

	£
Part-time salary	7,840
Building society interest (net)	9,360
Premium bond prize	50
NSB investment account interest, received gross	60

Compute the income tax payable by Ivan for the year (before deducting any tax paid under the PAYE system) assuming a personal allowance of £6,475.

*2.6   Mary's income for the tax year 2009-10 is as follows:

	£
Business profits	38,155
Rents received	3,750
UK dividends	1,890

Compute the income tax payable by Mary for the year, assuming that the rents received are not within the "rent-a-room" scheme and that Mary is entitled to a personal allowance of £6,475.

Chapter 3

Personal allowances

Introduction

One of the factors which must be taken into account when preparing an income tax computation is the taxpayer's entitlement to *personal allowances*. Most taxpayers can claim only the basic personal allowance but there are higher allowances for older taxpayers and extra allowances for blind taxpayers and for older married couples. The purpose of this chapter is to describe the allowances available in tax year 2009-10 and to explain the way in which each allowance is dealt with in a tax computation.

It is important to appreciate that personal allowances are indeed "personal". If all or part of a personal allowance cannot be used by the person to whom it is available, then any unused part of the allowance is generally lost. Excess allowances cannot normally be transferred to anyone else and cannot be carried back to previous years or forward to future years. However, some limited provisions exist for transferring excess allowances between spouses or civil partners (see later in this chapter).

Personal allowances for 2009-10

Personal allowances may be claimed by UK residents and by some non-residents. The main classes of non-resident who may claim personal allowances are:

(a) Commonwealth citizens (but not after tax year 2009-10)

(b) nationals of the European Economic Area (EEA), which comprises all EU states plus Norway, Iceland and Liechtenstein

(c) residents in the Isle of Man or the Channel Islands

(d) persons who used to reside in the UK but now reside abroad for health reasons

(e) Crown servants, ex-Crown servants and their widows/widowers

(f) missionaries.

The personal allowances for 2009-10 are as follows:

Allowances which are deducted from net income:	£
Personal allowance:	
Basic (age 0-64)	6,475
Age 65-74	9,490
Age 75 and over	9,640
Blind person's allowance	1,890
Income limit for age-related allowances	22,900
Allowances which are "tax reducers":	
Married couple's allowance:	
Born before 6 April 1935	6,965
Minimum amount	2,670
Income limit for MCA	22,900

The personal allowance (PA)

Anyone who is entitled to claim personal allowances may claim at least the basic personal allowance (£6,475 in 2009-10). This allowance is deducted from the taxpayer's net income (i.e. total income less tax reliefs) when computing his or her tax liability. The personal allowance is given in full in the tax year in which a taxpayer is born or dies.

If an unmarried minor child receives investment income which is derived from a parent, this income is treated for tax purposes as the income of the parent, not the child, unless the amount involved does not exceed £100 (per parent per child) in the tax year. This prevents parents from transferring income-bearing assets to a child so as to take advantage of the child's personal allowance. Income derived from parental contributions to a Child Trust Fund account (see Chapter 6) does not count towards the £100 limit.

Older taxpayers

As can be seen from the list of allowances given above, the amount of the personal allowance depends upon the taxpayer's age:

(a) A taxpayer who is over 65 years old, or who reaches the age of 65 during the tax year, is entitled to an increased personal allowance (£9,490 in 2009-10), and

(b) the allowance is higher still (£9,640 in 2009-10) for taxpayers who are over 75 years old or who reach the age of 75 during the tax year.

These higher personal allowances are granted *instead* of the usual personal allowance, not in addition to it. A taxpayer who dies in the tax year in which he or she would have reached the age of 65 or 75 is granted the higher allowance for the year of death.

Age-related personal allowances are reduced if the taxpayer's "adjusted net income" exceeds a specified limit (£22,900 in 2009-10). Adjusted net income is defined as the taxpayer's net income for the year less the grossed-up amount of any Gift Aid donations made in the year (see Chapter 4) and the gross amount of any pension contributions which have been relieved at source during the year (see Chapter 13).

If adjusted net income exceeds the specified limit, the personal allowance is reduced by one-half of the excess. However, the allowance is never reduced to less than the personal allowance for those aged 0-64.

EXAMPLE 1

Calculate the personal allowance due in 2009-10 to each of the following taxpayers:

(a) Born 31 July 1944, income £14,600   (b) Born 31 July 1934, income £13,950

(c) Born 22 April 1941, income £23,500   (d) Born 2 May 1940, income £30,900

(e) Born 22 April 1931, income £23,100   (f) Born 2 May 1930, income £30,150.

In each case, the stated income figure is the taxpayer's adjusted net income for the year.

Solution

(a) This taxpayer reaches the age of 65 during 2009-10 and is therefore entitled to a PA of £9,490 for the year.

(b) This taxpayer reaches the age of 75 during 2009-10 and is therefore entitled to a PA of £9,640 for the year.

(c) This taxpayer is in the 65-74 age group and has an income which exceeds the limit by £600, giving a PA of £9,190 (£9,490 – 1/2 x £600).

(d) This taxpayer is in the 65-74 age group and has an income which exceeds the income limit by £8,000. This would give a PA of £5,490 (£9,490 – 1/2 x £8,000) but the allowance is never reduced to less than the PA for those aged 0-64 so the taxpayer will claim £6,475.

(e) This taxpayer is over 75 and has an income which exceeds the limit by £200, giving a PA of £9,540 (£9,640 – 1/2 x £200).

(f) This taxpayer is over 75 and has an income which exceeds the limit by £7,250. This would give a PA of £6,015 (£9,640 – 1/2 x £7,250) so the taxpayer will claim £6,475.

Blind person's allowance (BPA)

The blind person's allowance (£1,890 in 2009-10) may be claimed by registered blind persons. This allowance is deducted from the taxpayer's net income (i.e. total income less tax reliefs). The allowance is given in full in the tax year in which the taxpayer is first registered as a blind person.

   If a husband or wife who is granted the blind person's allowance cannot make full use of the allowance, the unused part can be transferred to the other spouse, even if that spouse is not a registered blind person. Surplus BPA may also be transferred between same-sex civil partners who have entered into a legally-recognised civil partnership.

Tax reducers

The personal allowance and the blind person's allowance are both deducted from net income when calculating taxable income and so automatically save tax at the taxpayer's highest rate. For instance, the personal allowance for 2009-10 saves a basic rate taxpayer who is under 65 years old the sum of £1,295 (£6,475 @ 20%). For higher rate taxpayers the amount of tax saved is £2,590 (£6,475 @ 40%).

By contrast, the married couple's allowance (the only other allowance which is available in 2009-10) is ignored until the amount of tax due on the taxpayer's taxable income has been calculated. The MCA is then relieved by reducing this tax liability by *10% of the amount of the allowance*. For this reason, the MCA is sometimes referred to as a "tax reducer". Note that:

(a) Certain payments and some types of investments made by a taxpayer also act as tax reducers (see Chapters 4 and 6).

(b) The amount of tax borne can never be reduced to less than zero as a result of the tax reduction process. If available tax reductions exceed the tax due on taxable income, there is no repayment of the excess. Any unused part of a tax reduction is generally lost. However, the tax reduction relating to the MCA may be transferred between spouses or civil partners in certain cases (see below).

Married couple's allowance (MCA)

The married couple's allowance is available to a legally married couple who live together for at least part of the tax year, *so long as at least one of the spouses was born before 6 April 1935*. MCA is also available to same-sex civil partners who have entered into a legally-recognised civil partnership, so long as at least one of the partners was born before 6 April 1935. Note the following points:

(a) The allowance is not available to a married couple (or civil partners) who are separated for the whole of the tax year. A couple are regarded as "separated" for tax purposes if they are legally separated or if they are separated in circumstances which make it likely that separation will be permanent.

(b) The amount of the MCA for 2009-10 is £6,965, giving a maximum tax reduction of £696.50 (£6,965 @ 10%).

(c) For couples who were married before 5 December 2005, MCA is generally claimed by the husband. However, the couple may elect that the MCA should instead be claimed by the spouse with the higher net income. Such an election must be made before the start of the first tax year in which it is to have effect and then applies to all subsequent tax years. The election is irrevocable.

(d) For couples who marry on or after 5 December 2005 (and for civil partners) the MCA is claimed by the spouse or partner with the higher net income.

(e) In the same way as the age-related personal allowance is reduced if a taxpayer's adjusted net income exceeds a specified limit, the MCA is reduced if the *claimant's* adjusted net income exceeds the same limit (£22,900 in 2009-10). However, the allowance is never reduced to less than a specified minimum amount (£2,670 in 2009-10). It is noteworthy that the other spouse's (or other partner's) income is not taken into account for this purpose, even if the MCA is being given because of that spouse's or partner's age rather than because of the claimant's age.

(f) The procedure which is adopted if a taxpayer's adjusted net income needs to be taken into account when computing both that taxpayer's own PA (because he or she is over 65) and the MCA (because of the above rules) is as follows:

   (i) The excess of the person's adjusted net income over the income limit is divided by two, giving the required reduction in allowances.

   (ii) The person's own PA is reduced first, but never to an amount which is less than the personal allowance for those aged 0-64.

   (iii) If the reduction made in the personal allowance has not fully achieved the required reduction in allowances, the MCA is reduced next, but never to less than the specified minimum amount.

EXAMPLE 2

Calculate the allowances available in 2009-10 to the following husbands and wives:

Husband	*Wife*
(a) Born 5 July 1938, income £18,000	Born 1 March 1935, income £12,000.
(b) Born 12 April 1945, income £nil	Born 6 August 1934, income £29,700.
(c) Born 3 May 1930, income £23,050	Born 7 September 1936, income £nil.
(d) Born 4 June 1936, income £29,260	Born 8 October 1933, income £13,500.
(e) Born 5 July 1946, income £31,700	Born 9 November 1934, income £nil.

In each case, the stated income figure is the adjusted net income. All of the couples were married before 5 December 2005 and none of them have elected that MCA should be claimed by the spouse with the higher net income.

Solution

(a) The husband is over 65 and is entitled to a PA of £9,490. His wife is over 75 and is entitled to a PA of £9,640. An MCA of £6,965 is available because the wife was born before 6 April 1935.

(b) The husband is under 65 and is therefore entitled to a PA of £6,475, all of which is unused. His wife is over 75 but her income exceeds the limit by £6,800. This would give her a PA of £6,240 (£9,640 – 1/2 x £6,800) but the allowance is never reduced to less than the PA for those aged 0-64 so she will claim a PA of £6,475.

An MCA of £6,965 is available since the wife was born before 6 April 1935. The MCA is not reduced at all since the husband's income does not exceed the income limit.

(c) The husband is over 75 but his income exceeds the limit by £150. This gives him a PA of £9,565 (£9,640 – 1/2 x £150). His wife is over 65 and she is entitled to a PA of £9,490, all of which is unused.

An MCA of £6,965 is available because the husband was born before 6 April 1935. This is not reduced at all since the reduction required because of the size of his income has already been made in full against his own PA.

(d) The husband is over 65 but his income exceeds the limit by £6,360. Therefore he must lose a total of £3,180 in allowances. His PA is first reduced from £9,490 to the minimum of £6,475 (a reduction of £3,015). The remaining £165 is deducted from the MCA of £6,965 (available because of his wife's date of birth). So MCA is £6,800.

The wife is over 75 and she is entitled to a PA of £9,640.

(e) The husband is under 65 and is therefore entitled to a PA of £6,475. His wife is over 75 and so she is entitled to a PA of £9,640, all of which is unused.

The wife was born before 6 April 1935 so an MCA of £6,965 is available. However, this must be reduced because the husband's income exceeds the limit by £8,800. None of the required reduction in allowances (£4,400) can be subtracted from his own PA as he is claiming only the basic £6,475. Therefore the whole of the reduction must be set against the MCA. This would give an MCA of £2,565 (£6,965 – £4,400) but the allowance is never reduced to less than the minimum amount (£2,670) so an MCA of £2,670 is available.

Allocation of the MCA

The tax reduction relating to the MCA is normally set against the tax liability of the *claimant*, but note that:

(a) The couple may elect jointly that the tax reduction relating to the MCA minimum amount (£2,670 for 2009-10) should be set against the tax liability of the claimant's spouse or partner.

(b) The claimant's spouse or partner may elect unilaterally that the tax reduction relating to 50% of the MCA minimum amount (£1,335 for 2009-10) should be set against his or her tax liability.

(c) If either spouse or partner is unable to use their MCA-related tax reduction in full or in part, the unused part may be transferred to the other spouse or partner.

The elections described in (a) and (b) must normally be made before the start of the tax year to which they relate, but they can be made during the tax year if this is the year of marriage or the year in which a civil partnership is registered. If either of these elections is made, any remaining part of the MCA is dealt with in the claimant's tax computation.

The transfer described in (c) may be claimed at any time up to 31 January in the sixth tax year following the year to which it relates. As from April 2010, such a claim will have to be made within four years of the end of the tax year concerned.

CHAPTER 3: PERSONAL ALLOWANCES

Year of marriage and year of separation or death

In the tax year in which a marriage occurs or a civil partnership is registered, MCA is reduced by one-twelfth for each full tax month which elapses between the start of the year and the date of the marriage or registration. A tax month runs from the 6th of one month to the 5th of the next month. An election to transfer all or 50% of the MCA minimum amount to the claimant's spouse or partner in the year of marriage or registration applies to that amount reduced in the same proportion as the MCA itself.

MCA is available in full in the tax year in which a couple separate or in which one of them dies.

EXAMPLE 3

Calculate the MCA available in 2009-10 to a husband and wife (both born in September 1934) who each have an adjusted net income not exceeding £22,900 and who marry on:

(a) 5 April 2009   (b) 9 April 2009   (c) 23 June 2009   (d) 4 April 2010

Solution

(a) A couple who marry on 5 April 2009 are already married by the start of 2009-10, so the MCA of £6,965 is available in full.

(b) A couple who marry on 9 April 2009 are not married for the whole of 2009-10 but no full tax months have passed between the start of the tax year and the date of the marriage. Therefore the full MCA of £6,965 is available.

(c) If the marriage takes place on 23 June 2009, two full tax months have passed since the start of the tax year (6 April 2009 to 5 May 2009 and 6 May 2009 to 5 June 2009). The MCA is reduced by two-twelfths, giving an MCA of £6,965 x 10/12 = £5,804.

(d) If the marriage takes place on 4 April 2010, eleven full tax months have passed since the start of the tax year. Therefore the MCA is reduced by eleven-twelfths, giving an MCA of £6,965 x 1/12 = £580.

EXAMPLE 4

Calculate the tax borne in 2009-10 by a husband and wife (both born in May 1934) given the information shown below. In each case, an election has been made for 50% of the tax reduction relating to the MCA minimum amount to be set against the tax of the claimant's spouse. None of the income is derived from savings or dividends.

(a) Married July 1960; husband's income £24,380, wife's income £20,730.

(b) Married 1 October 2009; husband's income £18,765, wife's income £14,835.

(c) Married July 1960 but husband dies 12 October 2009; husband's income £11,225, wife's income £21,395. The couple have not elected that MCA should be claimed by the spouse with the higher net income.

In each case, the stated income figure is the taxpayer's net income (i.e. total income less tax reliefs) and adjusted net income is the same as net income.

Solution

	(a) £	(b) £	(c) £
HUSBAND			
Net income	24,380	18,765	11,225
Less: Personal allowance	8,900	9,640	9,640
Taxable income	15,480	9,125	1,585
Income tax			
£15,480 @ 20%	3,096.00		
£9,125 @ 20%		1,825.00	
£1,585 @ 20%			317.00
Less: MCA £5,630 @ 10%	563.00		
MCA £3,284 @ 10%		328.40	
MCA £5,630 @ 10% = £563.00			317.00
Tax borne	2,533.00	1,496.60	nil
WIFE			
Net income	20,730	14,835	21,395
Less: Personal allowance	9,640	9,640	9,640
Taxable income	11,090	5,195	11,755
Income tax			
£11,090 @ 20%	2,218.00		
£5,195 @ 20%		1,039.00	
£11,755 @ 20%			2,351.00
Less: MCA £1,335 @ 10%	133.50		
MCA £779 @ 10%		77.90	
MCA £1,335 @ 10% + £246.00			379.50
Tax borne	2,084.50	961.10	1,971.50

Notes:

(i) In case (a), the husband's income is £1,480 over the income limit, therefore his PA is reduced to £8,900 (£9,640 − 1/2 x £1,480). The MCA is available in full. £1,335 (one-half of the minimum amount) is claimed by the wife, leaving £5,630 for the husband.

(ii) In case (b), the available MCA is 7/12 x £6,965 = £4,063. The wife claims 7/12 x £1,335 = £779, leaving £3,284 for the husband.

(iii) In case (c), the MCA is available in full in the year of the husband's death. £1,335 is claimed by the wife, leaving £5,630 for the husband. The tax reduction that he cannot use (£246.00) is transferred to his wife.

Personal allowances for 2010-11

It has been announced that, as from tax year 2010-11, the basic personal allowance will be reduced for taxpayers with adjusted net incomes of more than £100,000. If a taxpayer's adjusted net income exceeds £100,000, the amount of the basic personal allowance will be reduced by £1 for every £2 of the excess.

If a taxpayer's adjusted net income exceeds £100,000 by at least twice the amount of the basic personal allowance, the allowance will be reduced to £nil.

Summary

▸ All UK residents and some non-resident taxpayers are entitled to claim at least the basic personal allowance.

▸ Older taxpayers are entitled to a higher personal allowance but this is reduced if adjusted net income exceeds a specified limit. The reduction is generally equal to one-half of the amount by which this limit is exceeded, but the allowance is never reduced to less than the basic personal allowance.

▸ The blind person's allowance is granted to registered blind persons. If a person who is entitled to this allowance cannot make full use of it, any unused part of the allowance may be transferred to that person's spouse or civil partner.

▸ The married couple's allowance is available to a legally married couple who live together for at least part of the tax year, so long as at least one of the spouses was born before 6 April 1935. MCA is also available to civil partners.

▸ For couples married before 5 December 2005, MCA is normally claimed by the husband but an election may be made for MCA to be claimed by the spouse with the higher net income. For couples married on or after 5 December 2005 (and for civil partners) MCA is claimed by the spouse with the higher net income.

▸ MCA is reduced if the claimant's adjusted net income exceeds a specified limit.

▸ All or part of the MCA may be transferred to the claimant's spouse or partner if an appropriate election is made.

▸ The personal allowance and the blind person's allowance are deducted from the taxpayer's net income when computing taxable income. The MCA reduces tax borne by 10% of the amount of the allowance.

▸ Personal allowances which cannot be used in the tax year to which they relate are lost. There is no provision for carrying unused allowances back to previous years or forward to subsequent years.

▸ As from tax year 2010-11, the basic personal allowance will be restricted for those taxpayers with an adjusted net income exceeding £100,000.

Exercises

3.1 Calculate the personal allowance due in 2009-10 to each of the following taxpayers:

(a) Born on 28 August 1942, adjusted net income £16,100

(b) Born on 25 May 1933, adjusted net income £23,900

(c) Born on 2 February 1945, adjusted net income £31,500.

3.2 Calculate the allowances available to a husband and wife in 2009-10 (assuming that they were married before 5 December 2005 and that they have not elected for MCA to be claimed by the spouse with the higher net income) given the following information:

(a) Husband born 1932, income £17,400; wife born 1937, income £23,200

(b) Husband born June 1934, income £23,600; wife born July 1934, income £9,050

(c) Husband born August 1934, income £29,300; wife born 1940, income £18,900.

In each case, the stated income figure is the adjusted net income.

3.3 Calculate the tax borne in 2009-10 by a husband and wife (both born in 1933), given the information shown below. No elections have been made in relation to the married couple's allowance and none of the income is derived from savings or dividends.

(a) Married in 1956; husband's income £16,280, wife's income £17,580

(b) Married 17 August 2009; husband's income £9,500, wife's income £13,515

(c) Married in 1956 but husband dies on 16 September 2009; husband's income to date of death £9,975, wife's income for the year £17,445.

In each case, the stated income figure is the taxpayer's net income (i.e. total income less tax reliefs) and adjusted net income is the same as net income.

3.4 Calculate the married couple's allowance available in 2009-10 to a married couple who marry on each of the following dates:

(a) 4 May 2009 (both born 1988)

(b) 14 February 2010
     (husband born 1938, income £15,300; wife born 1934, income £10,300)

(c) 25 December 2009
     (husband born 1946, income £24,500; wife born 1934, income £11,700).

In each case, the stated income figure is the adjusted net income.

3.5 Toby is a widower. He was born in August 1933 and his income for 2009-10 is as follows:

	£
Retirement pension	8,620
Bank interest (net)	912

Calculate the amount of income tax repayable to Toby for 2009-10.

3.6   What personal allowances may be claimed by each of the following taxpayers in tax year 2009-10?

(a)   John is single, 45 years old and registered blind.

(b)   June is 28 years old. Her husband died in September 2008.

(c)   James is 14 years old. He earns about £20 per week from his paper round.

3.7   Richard was born on 5 October 1945. His wife, Patricia, was born on 5 April 1935. They were married in 1968. Their income for 2009-10 is as follows:

	£
Richard:	
Business profits	22,930
Patricia:	
UK dividends	3,600

Calculate their tax borne and tax payable in 2009-10.

*3.8   A married man (born 3 November 1934) died on 8 July 2009. He received a retirement pension of £10,870 between 6 April 2009 and the date of his death. His wife (born 12 August 1944) had no income whilst her husband was alive but received a pension of £16,675 between 8 July 2009 and 5 April 2010. They were married in 1970 and made no elections in relation to the married couple's allowance.

Calculate their tax borne in 2009-10.

*3.9   Bill was born in 1970. He is married to Hazel who was born in 1974. In 2009-10, Bill received business profits of £45,930 and UK dividends of £4,680. Hazel received a salary of £20,570 and net bank interest of £2,432.

Calculate their tax payable for the year (before deducting any tax paid under the PAYE system).

Chapter 4

Payments and gifts eligible for tax relief

Introduction

Certain payments and gifts made by a taxpayer are eligible for tax relief in the tax year in which they are made. Some of these are subtracted from the taxpayer's total income when computing his or her tax liability. Others act as tax reducers and are relieved by reducing the amount of tax payable on the taxpayer's taxable income. A special tax regime applies to donations which fall within the "Gift Aid" scheme.

The purpose of this chapter is to identify the main types of payments and gifts which attract tax relief in these ways and to explain how relief is given for each. However, this chapter does *not* deal with:

(a) payments and gifts which are deductible when computing a taxpayer's income from employment (see Chapter 7)

(b) payments and gifts which are deductible when computing a taxpayer's income from self-employment (see Chapter 8)

(c) pension contributions (see Chapter 13).

Payments and gifts deductible from total income

The following payments and gifts are deductible from a taxpayer's total income for the tax year in which the payment or gift is made:

(a) eligible interest payments

(b) certain "annual payments" and patent royalties

(c) gifts of listed shares or securities to a charity

(d) gifts of land or buildings to a charity.

Each of these is explained later in this chapter. As indicated in Chapter 2, the income which remains after these items (and certain other reliefs) have been subtracted from total income is referred to by Income Tax Act 2007 as the taxpayer's "net income".

Tax relief for these payments and gifts is given at the highest rates of tax to which the taxpayer is liable. Deducting them from total income will automatically give the right amount of relief, since the effect of the deduction is to reduce the amount of taxable income which falls into the upper tax bands.

Note that the payments and gifts which are deductible from total income were known until fairly recently as "charges on income". However, the concept of charges on income was abolished for income tax purposes by Income Tax Act 2007.

Payments made gross or net

Some of the payments which are deductible from total income are made gross (without deduction of income tax). Others are required by law to be paid net, after deduction of income tax calculated at the basic rate.

Payments made gross are deducted from the taxpayer's total income when computing his or her income tax liability, but it is tempting to ignore any payments made net since the taxpayer has already taken tax relief at source. However, the tax deducted at source is always calculated at the basic rate (20% for 2009-10) and this will not give the right amount of relief to a taxpayer whose highest rate of tax is not the basic rate. The only way to be sure that the right amount of tax relief is given for a payment made net is to:

(a) calculate the gross amount of the payment (net payment × 100/80)

(b) subtract the gross figure from the taxpayer's total income, thus giving the correct amount of tax relief

(c) increase the taxpayer's income tax liability by the amount of basic rate tax which was deducted from the payment when it was made.

In effect, the person making the payment is regarded as having collected basic rate income tax from the recipient on behalf of HM Revenue and Customs and must therefore account to HMRC for this tax as part of his or her income tax liability. Note the following points:

(a) This treatment of payments made net of tax is entirely consistent with the treatment of income received net of tax (see Chapter 2). Income received net is shown gross in the taxpayer's income tax computation and the amount of tax deducted at source is subtracted when calculating tax payable. Similarly, payments made net are shown gross in the taxpayer's income tax computation and the amount of tax deducted at source is added when calculating tax payable.

(b) Basic rate tax must be deducted at source from certain payments which are allowable when computing a taxpayer's income from self-employment (see Chapter 8). In this case, to ensure that tax relief is not given twice, these payments are not also deducted from total income. However, the amount of tax deducted at source must still be accounted for to HMRC and this is achieved by adding this amount to the taxpayer's income tax liability for the year.

EXAMPLE 1

Bob has total income of £16,420 in 2009-10. None of his income is derived from savings or dividends and he claims only the basic personal allowance. He makes a deductible payment of £200 during the year (paid gross).

Cathy's circumstances are precisely the same as Bob's except that her deductible payment is made net of basic rate tax, so that she pays a net amount of £160.

Compute Bob and Cathy's income tax liabilities for 2009-10. Does it seem to make any difference whether a deductible payment is made gross or net?

Solution

	Bob £	Cathy £
Total income	16,420	16,420
Less: Payment	200	
Payment £160 x 100/80		200
Net income	16,220	16,220
Less: Personal allowance	6,475	6,475
Taxable income	9,745	9,745
Income tax		
£9,745 @ 20%	1,949.00	
£9,745 @ 20%		1,949.00
Tax borne	1,949.00	1,949.00
Add: Tax deducted from payment	0.00	40.00
Tax liability	1,949.00	1,989.00

Note:

Bob has made a payment of £200 and has a tax liability of £1,949.00, a total of £2,149.00. Cathy has made a payment of £160 and has a tax liability of £1,989.00, again a total of £2,149.00. Apart from the timing of the cash flows involved, it makes no difference whether a deductible payment is made gross or net and this is evidenced by the fact that tax borne is the same for both taxpayers.

Higher rate taxpayers

A payment or gift which is deductible from total income costs a higher rate taxpayer less than a basic rate taxpayer, since relief is given at the highest rate of income tax to which the taxpayer is liable. However, there is no need to adjust the method of computation to deal specially with such taxpayers. The method described above will give the correct result for all taxpayers.

EXAMPLE 2

Derek's total income for 2009-10 is £31,620 (all non-savings income). He makes a net deductible payment of £240 during the year and claims only the basic personal allowance. Show his income tax computation:

(a) with the deductible payment   (b) as it would have been without the payment.

How much has the payment effectively cost him? How much would it have cost him if his total income for the year had been £20,000 higher?

Solution

			Income £31,620		Income £51,620	
			(a)	(b)	(a)	(b)
			£	£	£	£
Total income			31,620	31,620	51,620	51,620
Less: Payment £240 x 100/80			300		300	
Net income			31,320	31,620	51,320	51,620
Less: Personal allowance			6,475	6,475	6,475	6,475
Taxable income			24,845	25,145	44,845	45,145
Income tax						
24,845	25,145	@ 20%	4,969.00	5,029.00		
37,400	37,400	@ 20%			7,480.00	7,480.00
7,445	7,745	@ 40%			2,978.00	3,098.00
44,845	45,145					
Tax borne			4,969.00	5,029.00	10,458.00	10,578.00
Add: Tax deducted from payment			60.00		60.00	
Tax liability			5,029.00	5,029.00	10,518.00	10,578.00

Notes:

(i) With total income of £31,620, Derek's tax liability is the same whether or not he makes the payment. This is to be expected since he is a basic rate taxpayer and he has taken basic rate relief at source. The cost of the payment to him is just £240.

(ii) With total income of £51,620, Derek is a higher rate taxpayer. His income tax liability is reduced by £60 (£10,578.00 - £10,518.00) if he makes the payment, so in fact the payment costs him only £180 (£240 – £60). In effect, the gross payment of £300 has been reduced by tax relief at 40%, leaving £180 as the cost to Derek. An alternative way of looking at the situation is to say that he takes 20% tax relief when making the payment but is entitled to 40% tax relief. The extra 20% is automatically given via his tax computation (20% of £300 = £60).

Starting rate and dividend ordinary rate taxpayers

A taxpayer whose highest rate of income tax is the starting rate for savings (10%) or the dividend ordinary rate (10%) is entitled to tax relief on deductible payments and gifts at 10% only. But there is no need to adjust the method of computation to deal specially with such taxpayers. The method described above will automatically ensure that tax relief is given at the correct rate.

EXAMPLE 3

Esmé has total income of £7,030 in 2009-10 (all savings income) and she makes a net deductible payment of £128.00 during the year. She claims only the basic personal allowance. Show her income tax computation:

(a)   with the deductible payment

(b)   as it would have been without the payment.

How much has the payment effectively cost her?

Solution

	(a)	(b)
	£	£
Total income	7,030	7,030
Less: Payment £128.00 x 100/80	160	
Net income	6,870	7,030
Less: Personal allowance	6,475	6,475
Taxable income	395	555
Income tax		
Tax borne @ 10%	39.50	55.50
Add: Tax deducted from payment	32.00	
Tax liability	71.50	55.50

Notes:

(i)   Esmé's highest rate of income tax is the starting rate for savings and her tax liability is increased by £16 (£71.50 – £55.50) if she makes the payment. This is logical since she takes 20% tax relief when making the payment but is actually entitled to relief at only 10%. The difference of 10% is automatically "clawed back" by the tax system (10% of £160 = £16).

(ii)   The cost of the payment to her is £144 (£128 plus tax increase of £16). In effect, the gross payment of £160 is reduced by tax relief at 10% (£16) which leaves £144 as the cost to Esmé.

Non-taxpayers

Non-taxpayers (whose taxable income is zero) are not entitled to any tax relief at all on deductible payments and gifts. Once again, there is no need to adjust the method of computation to deal specially with non-taxpayers. The method described above will automatically ensure that no relief is given.

If deductible payments and gifts obtain no tax relief in the year in which they are made, the opportunity for tax relief is permanently lost. It is not possible to carry the payments (or gifts) back to previous years or forward to future years.

EXAMPLE 4

Glenda has total income of £6,350 in 2009-10. She makes a net deductible payment of £40 during the year and claims only the basic personal allowance. Show her income tax computation:

(a)   with the deductible payment

(b)   as it would have been without the payment.

How much has the payment effectively cost her?

Solution

	(a)	(b)
	£	£
Total income	6,350	6,350
<u>Less</u>: Payment £40 x 100/80	50	
Net income	6,300	6,350
<u>Less</u>: Personal allowance (restricted)	6,300	6,350
Taxable income	0	0
Income tax		
Tax borne	0.00	0.00
<u>Add</u>: Tax deducted from payment	10.00	
Tax liability	10.00	0.00

Notes:

(i)   Glenda's tax liability is increased by £10.00 if she makes the payment. This is logical since she takes 20% tax relief when making the payment but is entitled to no tax relief at all. Therefore the tax relief which she deducts at source is automatically clawed back by the tax system.

(ii)   The cost of the payment to her is £50 (£40 plus increase in tax liability £10). In effect, she bears the full gross amount of the payment, with no reduction for tax relief.

Eligible interest payments

The interest paid on certain loans is deductible from a taxpayer's total income. This interest is generally paid gross. The main types of eligible loan are:

(a) A loan to purchase plant or machinery which is necessarily acquired for use in the taxpayer's employment. Interest on such a loan is eligible for relief in the tax year in which the loan is taken out and the next three years. This relief is not available in relation to the purchase of a mechanically propelled vehicle or a cycle.

(b) A loan to purchase plant or machinery for use in the business of a partnership in which the taxpayer is a partner. Interest on such a loan is eligible for tax relief if it is paid no later than three years after the end of the period of account in which the loan was made.

(c) A loan to purchase ordinary shares in a close company (see Chapter 27), so long as the taxpayer owns at least 5% of the company's ordinary share capital or works for the greater part of his or her time in the management of the company.

(d) A loan to purchase shares in an employee-controlled company or to purchase an interest in a partnership.

(e) A loan to pay inheritance tax. The interest on such a loan is eligible for tax relief if it is paid no more than 12 months after the loan was made.

Note that interest which is paid wholly and exclusively for business purposes is treated as a business expense and is deducted when calculating the business profits charged to income tax as trading income (see Chapter 8). In this case, the interest is not deductible from total income.

Annual payments and patent royalties

A number of "annual payments" must usually be paid net of basic rate income tax. One example is copyright royalties that are paid to an individual who holds the copyright as an investment. Patent royalties must also be paid net of basic rate tax. Tax relief on qualifying annual payments and patent royalties may be obtained in one of two ways:

(a) If annual payments or patent royalties are paid wholly and exclusively for business purposes (which is the most likely case), then they are taken into account when calculating the taxpayer's business profits which are charged to income tax as trading income (see Chapter 8).

(b) Otherwise, the gross amount of the payments made during a tax year is deducted from the taxpayer's total income for the year.

In either case, the amount of tax deducted at source during the tax year is added to the taxpayer's income tax liability for that year.

Gifts of shares or property to charity

A gift of listed shares or securities made to a charity attracts tax relief in the same way as a deductible payment. The amount of the gift is taken to be the market value of the shares on the date of the gift, plus any incidental costs borne by the donor and less the value of any benefits received by the donor in consequence of making the gift. Gifts of land or buildings to a charity are also eligible for relief.

This income tax relief is in addition to the relief from capital gains tax which arises when assets are given to charities (see Chapter 16).

EXAMPLE 5

In 2009-10, a taxpayer who pays income tax at 40% and capital gains tax at 18% gives listed shares with a market value of £20,000 to a charity. There are no incidental costs of disposal and the taxpayer receives no benefit in consequence of making the gift. A capital gain of £15,000 would have been charged to capital gains tax if the shares had been sold. In effect, how much does this gift cost the taxpayer?

Solution

Assuming that the taxpayer would have paid 40% income tax on at least £20,000 of his or her taxable income if the gift had not been made, the income tax saving is £8,000 (40% of £20,000). Capital gains tax of £2,700 (18% of £15,000) is also saved. The total tax saving is £10,700. This amounts to tax relief at a rate of 53.5% and the gift has effectively cost the taxpayer only £9,300.

Payments which are tax reducers

The following payments are granted tax relief by means of a reduction in the tax due on the taxpayer's taxable income:

(a) certain maintenance payments made to an ex-spouse (so long as either the payer or the recipient was born before 6 April 1935)

(b) interest on a loan secured on the taxpayer's main residence and used to purchase a life annuity (so long as the loan was taken out before 9 March 1999).

If such a payment is made gross, a tax reduction at the appropriate rate (see below) is given in the payer's income tax computation. This tax reduction takes priority over the tax reduction for the married couple's allowance (see Chapter 3). No tax refund is available if available tax reductions exceed the tax due on the payer's taxable income.

If such a payment is made net, it should be *entirely omitted* from the taxpayer's income tax computation, since precisely the right amount of tax relief has already been given at source and there is nothing more to be done.

Maintenance payments

Maintenance payments consist of periodical payments made:

(a) by one of the parties to a marriage (or civil partnership) for the maintenance of the other party, at a time when:

    (i) the couple are no longer living together, and

    (ii) the party for whose benefit the payment is made has not entered into a new marriage (or civil partnership)

(b) by one parent of a child to the other parent, made for the child's maintenance and at a time when the two parents are not living together.

Tax relief is available to a person making maintenance payments only if at least one of the parties or parents was born before 6 April 1935 and the payments are made under a court order or under a legally binding agreement (or have been assessed by the Child Support Agency). The income tax regime which applies to payments made under maintenance agreements is as follows:

(a) Maintenance payments are made gross, without any deduction of tax at source.

(b) In 2009-10, a taxpayer making qualifying maintenance payments is entitled to a tax reduction equal to 10% of the *lower* of:

    (i) the payments falling due and made in the tax year, and

    (ii) the minimum married couple's allowance (£2,670).

(c) The recipient of maintenance payments is not liable to pay income tax on them.

Loans used to purchase a life annuity

Tax relief is available in relation to the interest paid on the first £30,000 of a loan taken out *before 9 March 1999* and which was:

(a) made to a taxpayer aged 65 or over at the time that the loan was made, and

(b) used to purchase a life annuity, and

(c) secured on the taxpayer's main residence.

Such arrangements are often referred to as *home income plans*.

Tax relief takes the form of a tax reduction equal to 23% of the qualifying interest. This rate of relief remains at 23% (the basic rate of income tax for tax year 1998-99) even though the basic rate has now fallen to only 20%. If the interest is paid gross, relief is given in the payer's tax computation. If the interest is paid net it should be entirely omitted from the payer's tax computation (as explained above).

Gift Aid

The Gift Aid scheme provides a tax incentive for individuals and companies to make charitable donations. The way in which the scheme applies to individuals is explained below. The way in which the scheme applies to companies is explained in Chapter 22.

Gift Aid scheme for individuals

The Gift Aid scheme applies to any charitable donation (including donations made to community amateur sports clubs) so long as:

(a) the donor is either UK resident or is a Crown servant working overseas or a non-resident with income or gains charged to UK tax

(b) the donation takes the form of a gift of money and this gift is not repayable to the donor, is not covered by the payroll giving scheme (see Chapter 7) and is not deductible when computing the donor's income from any source

(c) the donor receives no benefit at all from making the gift, or receives a benefit which does not exceed the following limits:

    (i)   25% of the amount of the gift, if the gift does not exceed £100

    (ii)   £25, if the gift exceeds £100 but does not exceed £1,000

    (iii) 5% of the amount of the gift, if the gift exceeds £1,000

    subject to a limit of £500 on the value of the benefits which the donor may receive in any one tax year as a consequence of donations to any one charity

(d) the donor makes a Gift Aid declaration with regard to the donation.

If all of these conditions are satisfied, the gift is treated as if it had been made net of basic rate income tax and the charity can recover the tax which is deemed to have been deducted at source. For instance, a £20 gift would be treated as a gross gift of £25 (£20 × 100/80) less tax deducted of £5. In this case, the charity would receive £20 from the donor and a further £5 from HM Revenue and Customs. For tax years 2008-09 to 2010-11, charities are also eligible to receive an extra 2% "transitional relief" from HMRC to compensate for the fact that the basic rate of income tax fell from 22% to 20% in 2008-09.

Gift aid donations are *not* shown in the donor's tax computation, but the following provisions apply:

(a) The donor must pay income tax and capital gains tax equal to at least the amount of tax deemed to have been deducted from the gift. If this is not the case, then the donor's entitlement to personal allowances is restricted to ensure that this amount of tax is in fact paid. If the restriction of personal allowances does not give the required result, the donor is charged to income tax at the basic rate on as much of the gift as is necessary to ensure that the required amount of tax is paid.

(b) The donor's basic rate band is extended by the gross amount of the gift, so ensuring that relief at the higher rate is automatically given to higher rate taxpayers.

(c)   The donor may elect that a qualifying Gift Aid donation should be treated for tax purposes as if paid in the previous tax year. Such an election must be made on or before the date that the tax return for the previous tax year is submitted and no later than the 31 January which follows the end of that year.

EXAMPLE 6

In 2009-10, Owen makes qualifying Gift Aid donations totalling £360. He claims only the basic personal allowance and he has no capital gains tax liability for the year. Show his income tax computation if his only income for the year consists of business profits of:

(a)   £22,800

(b)   £6,590

(c)   £46,090.

Solution

	(a) £	(b) £	(c) £
Business profits	22,800	6,590	46,090
Less: Personal allowance	6,475	6,475	6,475
Taxable income	16,325	115	39,615

Income tax

(a)	(b)	(c)				
16,325	115	37,850	@ 20%	3,265.00	23.00	7,570.00
		1,765	@ 40%			706.00
16,325	115	39,615				

Tax borne				3,265.00	23.00	8,276.00

Notes:

(i)   The donations of £360 are grossed-up to £450 (£360 x 100/80) and are treated as if paid net of 20% tax. Deemed tax deducted is £90.

(ii)   In case (a), Owen's income tax liability far exceeds £90 so there is no more to be done.

(iii) In case (b), Owen's income tax liability falls short of £90 by £67. Therefore he must pay a further £67 of income tax. This is achieved by reducing his personal allowance by £335, so increasing his tax liability by £335 x 20% = £67.

(iv)   In case (c), Owen's basic rate band is extended by £450 from the normal figure of £37,400 to £37,850. This moves £450 of taxable income from the higher rate to the basic rate and saves tax of £90 (£450 x 20%). Together with the £90 deemed to have been deducted at source, total tax relief is now £180 (i.e. £450 x 40%).

Summary

▶ Certain payments and gifts made by a taxpayer are either deducted from total income or act as tax reducers.

▶ Payments which are deducted from total income must always be shown gross in the tax computation. Any tax deducted when the payment was made is added to the tax liability of the payer.

▶ If a payment which ranks as a tax reducer is made gross, the appropriate tax reduction is given in the payer's income tax computation. But payments made net should be omitted from the computation entirely.

▶ The main deductible payments are eligible interest payments and certain annual payments and patent royalties. A charitable gift consisting of listed shares or securities (or land and buildings) may also be deducted from total income.

▶ Qualifying maintenance payments of up to the amount of the minimum married couple's allowance are relieved at 10%. This relief is available only if either the payer or the recipient was born before 6 April 1935.

▶ Subject to certain conditions, the interest paid on a home loan which is used to buy a life annuity is relieved at 23%. This relief is available only if the loan was taken out before 9 March 1999.

▶ The Gift Aid scheme covers charitable donations which satisfy certain conditions. Qualifying donations are deemed to have been made net of basic rate tax.

▶ A taxpayer making a Gift Aid donation must pay income tax and capital gains tax equal to at least the amount of tax deemed to have been deducted from the donation. Higher rate taxpayers obtain higher rate relief on such donations.

Exercises

4.1 Mabel has total income of £21,180 in 2009-10, none of which is derived from savings or dividends. During the year she makes a net deductible payment of £200. Show her income tax computation for the year.

4.2 Paul has total income of £47,980 in 2009-10, none of which is derived from savings or dividends. During the year he makes a net deductible payment of £1,280. Show his income tax computation:

(a) with the payment   (b) as it would have been without the payment.

How much has the payment effectively cost him?

4.3 Rose has total income of £6,465 in 2009-10. During the year she makes a net deductible payment of £20. Show her income tax computation for the year.

4.4   At what rate of income tax is each of the following types of payment relieved in tax year 2009-10?

   (a)   interest on a qualifying home loan used to buy an annuity

   (b)   interest on a loan used to buy an interest in a partnership

   (c)   qualifying maintenance payments

   (d)   patent royalties.

4.5   A taxpayer with no capital gains tax liability makes a qualifying Gift Aid donation of £960 in tax year 2009-10. Explain:

   (a)   why this donation is worth more than £960 to the charity which receives it

   (b)   why this donation might cost the taxpayer more than £960

   (c)   why this donation might cost the taxpayer less than £960.

4.6   Raj was born in 1942 and is single. In 2009-10, he has business profits of £23,900 and no other income. He makes a qualifying Gift Aid donation of £280 during the year. Show his 2009-10 income tax computation.

4.7   Geoffrey is aged 48 and lives with his wife (aged 47) and their two children. Geoffrey's income for 2009-10 consists of a salary of £42,455 and UK dividends of £3,780. He makes a qualifying Gift Aid donation of £320 during the year. Show Geoffrey's 2009-10 income tax computation.

*4.8   Pauline (born March 1935) marries Adrian (born May 1937) on 17 October 2009. Their income for 2009-10 is as follows:

	£
Pauline:	
Retirement pension	10,930
Net building society interest	2,420
Adrian:	
Business profits	32,130
UK dividends	1,575

During 2009-10, Adrian pays maintenance of £3,000 to his former wife, as required by a court order. She was born in February 1935 and has not remarried.

Show Pauline and Adrian's income tax computations for 2009-10.

*4.9   Matthew dies on 23 December 2009, leaving a widow aged 63. He was born on 1 June 1934. His only income in 2009-10 is a retirement pension of £24,010. His wife has income from property of £16,270 and no other income. She makes a net deductible payment of £400 during the year and she also makes a Gift Aid donation of £100.

They were married for many years and made no elections with regard to the married couple's allowance. Calculate their tax liabilities for 2009-10.

Chapter 5

Income from property

Introduction

An individual's income from property is charged to income tax in accordance with the rules of the Income Tax (Trading and Other Income) Act 2005. The main purpose of this chapter is to explain those rules and to show how a taxpayer's UK property income for a tax year is calculated. Income from property situated overseas is considered separately in Chapter 32.

Definition of property income

Section 268 of ITTOIA 2005 states that income tax is charged on the profits of a property business. The Act also states that a person's UK property business consists of a business which is carried on for generating income from land which is situated in the UK and that "generating income from land" means "*exploiting an estate, interest or right in or over land as a source of rents or other receipts*". This is a broad definition but, in practice, the main classes of property income are:

(a) rents

(b) lease premiums (if the length of the lease does not exceed 50 years)

(c) amounts receivable in respect of rights of way, sporting rights etc.

(d) income from the letting of fixed caravans or permanently moored houseboats.

Dividends received from a UK Real Estate Investment Trust (UK-REIT) are also treated as property income to the extent that they are derived from the company's tax-exempt property income or gains (see Chapter 22). Such dividends are received net of basic rate income tax and do not carry an attached tax credit (see Chapter 2).

Despite the use of the word "business" above, income from property is almost always treated as *unearned* income. The only occasion on which property income is treated as earned income is when the income derives from the commercial letting of furnished holiday accommodation (see later in this chapter). The distinction between earned and unearned income may be especially important if the taxpayer is hoping to obtain tax relief on pension contributions (see Chapter 13).

Basis of assessment and allowable expenditure

A taxpayer's property income for a tax year is normally calculated on the accruals basis, in accordance with generally accepted accounting principles. However, short lease premiums are subject to a special tax regime (see below) and dividends received from UK-REITs are taxed on the receipts basis.

Expenditure which is incurred wholly and exclusively for the purposes of a property business is deducted when computing property income. This "wholly and exclusively" rule is copied directly from the rules relating to trading income and is considered more fully in Chapter 8 of this book, but the types of expenditure which are likely to be deductible when computing property income include the following:

(a) repairs and maintenance to the property (excluding improvements)

(b) insurance of the property and/or its contents

(c) the cost of providing services to tenants

(d) administrative and management costs, including bad debts incurred

(e) rent paid to a superior landlord (if the property is sub-let)

(f) business rates, water rates or council tax (which are the legal responsibility of the occupier of premises, not the owner, but may be paid by a landlord on behalf of a tenant and then recouped via an increased rent)

(g) interest paid on a loan to buy or improve the property concerned.

If a property is partly let and partly owner-occupied, it is necessary to apportion the expenditure accordingly.

When a taxpayer derives income from two or more properties it is *not* necessary to calculate the amount of profit (or loss) arising on each property individually. In each tax year, total property expenditure is deducted from total property income, giving a single profit (or loss) figure for the year. However, dividends received from UK-REITs are *not* aggregated with other property income but are treated instead as income arising from a separate property business.

EXAMPLE 1

Ryan owns a house which he lets to a tenant. Rent is payable monthly in advance on the 6th day of each month. For some years the rent has been fixed at £7,200 per annum but this was increased to £7,800 per annum with effect from 6 December 2009. The rent due on 6 March 2010 was not paid until 7 April 2010. Compute Ryan's property income for 2009-10, given that his allowable expenditure for the year is £2,350.

Solution

The rent for 2009-10 is £7,400 ((£7,200 x 8/12) + (£7,800 x 4/12)). So property income for the year is £5,050 (£7,400 − £2,350). The fact that some of the rent was not received until early in the following year is irrelevant, since rents are assessed on the accruals basis.

Capital expenditure

Capital expenditure is normally not deductible when computing property income but tax relief may be obtained on certain types of capital expenditure as follows:

(a) Allowances for depreciation known as "capital allowances" are available in relation to capital expenditure on:

    (i) plant and machinery which is used in the repair, maintenance or management of let property

    (ii) qualifying industrial buildings let for industrial use

    (iii) the renovation or conversion of vacant or underused space above shops and other commercial premises to provide flats for rent

    (iv) the renovation of business premises in disadvantaged areas.

    Capital allowances are considered in Chapter 10 of this book.

(b) A "wear and tear allowance" may be available in relation to expenditure on furniture and other equipment let to a tenant. The wear and tear allowance is commonly calculated as 10% of the rent for the year, net of any council tax or rates borne by the landlord on behalf of the tenant.

(c) An alternative to the wear and tear allowance is the "renewals basis". If this basis applies, no tax relief is available for the initial cost of providing furniture or equipment, but subsequent expenditure on replacements (not improvements) is allowed as a deduction when computing property income for the year in which the expenditure is incurred.

Capital expenditure on the acquisition and installation of certain energy-saving items in let residential property (e.g. loft insulation) may be deducted when calculating the landlord's income from property. This deduction is known as the "landlords energy saving allowance" (LESA) and cannot exceed £1,500 per dwelling per tax year. No deduction may be claimed for expenditure incurred after 5 April 2015.

EXAMPLE 2

Ursula owns a flat which she lets furnished. In 2009-10 the flat was let for 46 weeks at £100 per week. For the remaining 6 weeks of the year, Ursula occupied the flat herself. Her expenditure during the year was as follows:

	£		£
Council tax and water rates	1,240	Cleaning (whilst property let)	592
Minor repairs	270	Painting and decorating	500
Advertising for tenants	76	Insurance	240

Compute Ursula's property income for 2009-10, assuming that the wear and tear allowance is claimed.

Solution

	£	£	£
Rents for the year £100 x 46			4,600
Less: Expenses allowed in full:			
Advertising for tenants		76	
Cleaning		592	
Apportioned expenses:			
Council tax and water rates	1,240		
Minor repairs	270		
Painting and decorating	500		
Insurance	240		
$\frac{46}{52}$ x 2,250	1,990		
Wear and tear allowance (see note)		350	3,008
Property income			1,592

Note:

The wear and tear allowance is calculated at 10% of the rents, less any part of those rents which are deemed to reimburse Ursula for expenses incurred by her which are legally the tenants' responsibility (i.e. council tax and water rates). The tenants were in occupation for 46 weeks, so 46/52ths of the council tax and water rates were their responsibility. The wear and tear allowance is therefore 10% of (£4,600 – 46/52 x £1,240) = £350.

Losses

If a taxpayer's gross property income for a tax year is exceeded by the allowable expenditure, then the taxpayer has incurred a loss and taxable property income for the year is £nil. The loss is carried forward and relieved against the first available property income arising in subsequent tax years. Strictly speaking, relief is given by deduction from the taxpayer's total income (see Chapter 2), but the amount of relief given in any tax year cannot exceed the property income for that year.

Any loss incurred on an individual property in a tax year will automatically be set against profits arising on other properties in the same year, since property income and expenditure is generally pooled to give an overall profit or loss for the year. However (as explained earlier) dividends from UK-REITs are *not* pooled with other property income but are treated instead as income arising from a separate property business. Losses arising from a general property business cannot be set against such dividends.

EXAMPLE 3

Sandra's entire income is derived from the letting of property. She has the following income and expenditure in tax years 2007-08 through to 2009-10:

	2007-08	2008-09	2009-10
	£	£	£
Total rental income	29,320	31,400	31,100
Total allowable expenditure	38,510	25,430	7,540

Compute her net income for each year.

Solution

	2007-08	2008-09	2009-10
	£	£	£
Total rental income	29,320	31,400	31,100
Total allowable expenditure	38,510	25,430	7,540
Property income/(loss)	(9,190)	5,970	23,560
Total income	0	5,970	23,560
Less: Losses b/f	-	(5,970)	(3,220)
Net income	0	0	20,340

Note:

The 2007-08 loss must be set against the first available property income in subsequent years. This means that Sandra's net income for 2008-09 is reduced to £nil and (since this is her only source of income) her personal allowance for that year is wasted. However, it is not possible to restrict the amount of loss relief claimed in 2008-09.

Lease premiums

A premium is a lump sum paid by a tenant to a landlord on the grant of a lease. The income tax treatment of lease premiums is as follows:

(a) Premiums arising on the grant of a "long lease" (a lease of more than 50 years) are not charged to income tax at all.

(b) Premiums arising on the grant of a "short lease" (a lease of 50 years or less) are charged to income tax in the tax year in which the lease is granted. However, the amount of the premium is reduced for this purpose by 2% for each year of the lease except for the first year.

Note that the above provisions relate only to the *grant* of a lease, not the *assignment* of a lease. The grant of a lease occurs when a new lease is created. The assignment of a lease occurs when an existing lease is sold to a new owner.

Note also that lease premiums arising on the grant of a lease may give rise to a capital gains tax liability (see Chapter 18).

EXAMPLE 4

In tax year 2009-10, a landlord receives a premium of £36,000 when granting a 25-year lease to a tenant. How much of this premium is assessable to income tax?

Solution

For income tax purposes, the lease premium is reduced by 2% for each year of the lease except for the first year. Therefore 48% (24 x 2%) of the premium is not charged to income tax. The remaining 52% is taxable, so the assessable amount of the premium is £18,720 (52% of £36,000).

Relief for premiums paid

A tenant who pays a premium on being granted a short lease may obtain tax relief on the premium paid in one of two ways:

(a) If the tenant uses the property for business purposes then, throughout the duration of the lease, the tenant may claim an annual deduction from his or her trading profits which are charged to income tax (see Chapter 8). This annual deduction is equal to the amount of the premium on which the landlord is assessable to income tax, divided by the number of years of the lease.

(b) If the tenant sub-lets the property to someone else and receives a premium from the sub-lessee, then the assessable amount of the premium received is reduced by virtue of the premium paid. The reduction is equal to:

$$\text{Landlord's income tax assessment on premium paid} \times \frac{\text{Duration of sub-lease}}{\text{Duration of head-lease}}$$

If this reduction cannot be made in full (either because the premium received is too small or because no premium was received at all) the excess is spread evenly over the period of the sub-lease and set against the rents due from the sub-lessee.

EXAMPLE 5

Susan is granted a 20-year lease on a property, paying a premium of £76,000. Explain how tax relief will be given in relation to this premium if:

(a) she uses the property for trading purposes, or

(b) she grants a sub-lease to Timothy for five years, receiving a premium of:

    (i) £25,000

    (ii) £10,000.

Solution

(a) The amount assessable to income tax on Susan's landlord is £47,120 (£76,000 less 38% of £76,000). If Susan uses the premises for trading purposes she will be able to claim an annual deduction of £2,356 from her trading profits for each of the next 20 years (£47,120 divided by 20 = £2,356).

(b)

	(i) £	(ii) £
Premium received	25,000	10,000
Less: 2% x 4 x £25,000	2,000	
2% x 4 x £10,000		800
	23,000	9,200
Less: Premium paid £47,120 x $\frac{5}{20}$	11,780	11,780
Assessable premium	11,220	nil

In case (ii), the reduction available in relation to the premium paid cannot be made in full. The amount unrelieved is £2,580 (£11,780 – £9,200).

There will be no income tax assessment on the premium received in this case and a deduction of £516 will be made from Susan's property income for each of the five years of the sub-lease (£2,580 divided by 5 = £516).

Reverse premiums

It is not uncommon for a landlord to pay a so-called "reverse premium" to a potential tenant so as to induce that tenant to take out a lease. This arises most frequently when commercial premises are let to business tenants. The amount of any reverse premium paid by a landlord will usually be treated as enhancement expenditure for capital gains tax purposes when the landlord disposes of the property (see Chapter 17). But if the landlord is a property developer or dealer, the premium may be an allowable expense when computing the landlord's trading income (see Chapter 8).

From the point of view of a tenant who receives a reverse premium, this premium is chargeable to income tax (or to corporation tax for a corporate tenant). If the rented premises are used for business purposes, the amount received is treated as trading income (see Chapter 8). Otherwise the amount received is assessable as property income. In both cases, the timing of the tax charge will usually follow accepted accountancy practice, so that the tax liability arising on the receipt of a reverse premium will probably be spread over the period of the lease.

"Rent-a-room" relief

If an individual lets furnished accommodation which is part of his or her only or main residence, gross annual rents not exceeding a specified limit (£4,250 for 2009-10) are exempt from income tax. However, the taxpayer may elect to ignore this exemption and to be assessed instead according to the usual property income rules. This might be beneficial if the rents were exceeded by expenses, so that a loss could be claimed.

If gross rents for the year exceed the limit, the exemption does not apply and rents less expenses will be assessed to income tax in the normal way. However, the taxpayer may elect to be assessed instead on the excess of gross rents over the limit, without deducting expenses of any kind.

Both of the elections referred to above must be made by 31 January in the second tax year following the tax year to which the election relates. The election to ignore the exemption applies only to the year for which it is made. The election to be assessed on the excess of gross rents over the limit applies to all subsequent tax years until a year arises in which gross rents do not exceed the limit (or until the election is withdrawn).

EXAMPLE 6

In 2009-10, Victor rents out two rooms in his house and receives rents totalling £4,900. He incurs allowable expenses of £820. No "rent-a-room" elections are currently in force. What elections (if any) should he make?

Solution

The rent-a-room exemption does not apply since gross rents exceed £4,250.

If Victor does nothing, he will be charged to income tax on property income of £4,080 (£4,900 − £820). If he elects to be assessed on the excess of gross rents over the rent-a-room relief limit, his property income for tax purposes will be only £650 (£4,900 − £4,250). He should make this election and he has until 31 January 2012 to do so.

Furnished holiday lettings

Income derived from the "commercial letting of furnished holiday accommodation" is treated for income tax purposes as if it were trading income. The main beneficial effects of this treatment are as follows:

(a)   The income is regarded as earned income when determining the extent to which tax relief is available in relation to pension contributions (see Chapter 13).

(b)   Losses are treated as trading losses and may be relieved as such (see Chapter 11).

(c)   Capital allowances may be claimed in respect of the furniture (see Chapter 10).

(d)   Business-related capital gains tax reliefs may be available (see Chapter 21).

Letting qualifies as the commercial letting of furnished holiday accommodation if the property is let furnished with a view to profit and is:

(a)   available for letting to the general public as holiday accommodation for at least 140 days in the tax year, and

(b)   actually let to the general public as holiday accommodation for at least 70 days in the tax year, and

(c)   not normally in the same occupation for more than 31 consecutive days in the tax year (with no more than 155 days of longer-term occupation).

If a taxpayer owns two or more properties, each of which satisfies the 140-day rule and the 31-day rule but which do not all satisfy the 70-day rule, these properties will all be regarded as satisfying the 70-day rule if their average number of days let is at least 70.

Repeal of the furnished holiday lettings rules

It should be noted that the furnished holiday lettings rules are to be repealed as from tax year 2010-11. Income derived from such lettings will then be treated in the same way as any other property income and will no longer be regarded as trading income.

EXAMPLE 7

Yvonne owns four cottages, all of which she lets furnished with a view to profit. None of the cottages is normally in the same occupation for more than 31 consecutive days. In 2009-10 the number of days for which each cottage was available for letting and the number of days actually let were:

	Days available	Days actually let
Cottage A	150	80
Cottage B	170	56
Cottage C	120	113
Cottage D	180	68

Show Yvonne's potential averaging claims.

Solution

Cottage C cannot be regarded as furnished holiday accommodation since it does not pass the 140-day test. Cottages A, B and D all pass this test but only Cottage A also passes the 70-day test. Without any averaging claims, therefore, only Cottage A will be regarded as furnished holiday accommodation. Possible averaging claims are:

(a)   Average Cottage A with Cottage B. This is no use since the average number of days let is only 68.

(b)   Average Cottage B with Cottage D. This is no use since the average number of days let is only 62.

(c)   Average Cottage A with Cottage D. This would be beneficial since the average number of days let is 74.

(d)   Average Cottage A with Cottage B and Cottage D. This is no use since the average number of days let is only 68.

Therefore, Yvonne should claim that Cottage A should be averaged with Cottage D, in which case both cottages would qualify as furnished holiday accommodation.

Summary

▸   Income tax is charged on the profits of a business which is carried on for the purpose of generating income from land situated in the UK.

▸   Property income is usually treated as unearned income unless it arises from the commercial letting of furnished holiday accommodation.

▸   A taxpayer's property income for a tax year is generally calculated on the accruals basis. Expenditure incurred wholly and exclusively for the purposes of a property business is deducted when computing property income.

▸   Capital allowances are available in relation to certain types of capital expenditure incurred in relation to a property business.

▸   Losses incurred by a property business are carried forward and set against the first available property income arising in subsequent years.

▸   A premium received on the grant of a lease is charged to income tax if the lease does not exceed 50 years. The assessable amount is the amount of the premium less 2% for each year of the lease except the first.

▸   A tenant paying a lease premium will receive tax relief on the premium if the property is sub-let or is used for the purposes of a trade.

▸   Rent-a-room relief is available if a taxpayer receives rents of up to £4,250 p.a. from the letting of furnished rooms in his or her main residence.

▸   Under certain conditions, the letting of furnished property qualifies as the commercial letting of furnished holiday accommodation and income from the property is treated as trading income. This offers a number of benefits to the taxpayer. However, the furnished holiday lettings rules will be repealed as from tax year 2010-11.

Exercises

5.1 Andrew owns a house which he lets to tenants. Rent is payable quarterly in advance on 1 January, 1 April, 1 July and 1 October. The rent was £8,000 per annum until it was increased to £8,800 per annum with effect from 1 January 2010. Rent received by Andrew during 2009-10 was as follows:

	£
2 July 2009	2,000
30 September 2009	2,000
3 January 2010	2,200
	6,200

Andrew did not receive the payment due on 1 April 2010 until 7 April 2010. Compute his property income for 2009-10, assuming that he incurred no allowable expenditure during the year.

5.2 Simon owns a country cottage which he uses as a holiday home for 4 weeks per year and lets furnished at £220 per week for the remaining 48 weeks of the year. Simon's expenses in relation to the cottage in 2009-10 were as follows:

	£
Council tax	1,400
Advertising	35
Repairs to furniture (damaged by tenant)	50
Gardener's wages (£20 per week)	1,040
Insurance	230

Compute Simon's property income for 2009-10.

5.3 In 2009-10, a landlord receives a premium of £12,000 when granting a lease to a tenant. Compute the amount of this premium which is chargeable to income tax if the length of the lease is:

(a) 60 years

(b) 50 years

(c) 20 years

5.4 In 2009-10, Jasper is granted a 10-year lease on a property, paying a premium of £15,000. He uses the property for trading purposes. Compute the tax relief which he will be allowed in respect of the lease premium.

5.5   Georgina owns three holiday flats, all of which she lets furnished with a view to profit. None of the flats is normally in the same occupation for more than 31 consecutive days. In 2009-10 the number of days for which each flat was available for letting, and the number of days actually let, were:

	Days available	*Days actually let*
Flat 1	140	64
Flat 2	150	72
Flat 3	182	74

Show Georgina's potential averaging claims.

*5.6   In 2009-10, Peter is granted a 12-year lease on a property, paying a premium of £40,000 to his landlord. He immediately grants a 4-year sub-lease to Paula, receiving a premium of £14,000. Calculate the income tax assessment on the premium received by Peter.

*5.7   Melissa is single and was born in 1940. She owns a house which she lets unfurnished at a rent of £200 per week. Her allowable expenditure in 2009-10 was £4,100 and she had property losses brought forward from 2008-09 of £6,550. Her other income in 2009-10 was as follows:

	£
Retirement pension	11,284
Net building society interest	9,680

Compute the income tax payable by Melissa for the year.

Chapter 6

Income from savings and investments

Introduction

The main purpose of this chapter is to explain the tax treatment of income arising from savings and investments. The main options available to a taxpayer who wishes to save or invest are to deposit money in bank and building society accounts or to invest in shares and securities. Each of these courses of action has its taxation implications and this chapter explains those implications.

This chapter also briefly considers the taxation of income from trusts and settlements and the tax treatment of certain miscellaneous sources of income.

Interest received

Interest received by a taxpayer is charged to income tax by the Income Tax (Trading and Other Income) Act 2005. This Act states that tax is charged on the full amount of interest arising in the tax year and that interest "arises" when it is paid to the taxpayer or when it is credited to the taxpayer's account. Therefore, any interest which has accrued at the end of a tax year but has not yet been paid or credited to the taxpayer is ignored when computing the income for that year.

Interest ranks as savings income (see Chapter 2) and so any interest falling into the first £2,440 (for 2009-10) of the basic rate band is taxed at the starting rate for savings of 10%. No expenses are allowed against this form of income.

Interest received net

Interest is generally received net of 20% income tax. Some investments do pay gross interest but these are comparatively few (see later in this chapter).

The gross equivalent of any interest received net by a taxpayer during a tax year is included in the taxpayer's total income. The tax suffered by deduction at source is then subtracted when calculating tax payable.

Self-certification

Individuals resident in the UK who are unlikely to be liable to income tax for a given tax year may supply a certificate to this effect to their bank or building society. Interest is then paid to such individuals without deduction of tax at source, so avoiding the need for repayment claims at the end of the year. As might be expected, there are penalties for supplying such certificates fraudulently or negligently.

EXAMPLE 1

Alfred is single and 66 years old. He receives the following income in 2009-10:

	£
Retirement pension	8,620
Building society interest (net)	352

Calculate the amount of income tax reclaimed by Alfred at the end of 2009-10. Could the need to make a repayment claim have been avoided?

Solution

Alfred's total income for the year is £9,060 (£8,620 + (£352 x 100/80)). This is less than his over-65 personal allowance of £9,490, resulting in a zero income tax liability for the year. He may reclaim the £88 tax deducted at source from the interest.

Since it was probably evident at the beginning of the year that Alfred was going to be a non-taxpayer in 2009-10, he could have supplied his building society with a certificate to that effect. He would then have received his interest without deduction of tax.

Interest received gross

Certain types of interest are received gross (without deduction of tax at source). The amount of any such interest received by a taxpayer during a tax year is included in the taxpayer's total income. The main types of interest received gross are:

(a) National Savings Bank (NSB) investment account interest

(b) interest on gilt-edged securities unless the recipient has opted for net interest.

Interest on a National Savings Bank ordinary account also used to be received gross (and the first £70 a year of such interest was exempt from income tax). However, it has not been possible to open an NSB ordinary account since 2004 and any outstanding balances on these accounts were transferred to NSB investment accounts in 2008. Therefore NSB ordinary account interest cannot arise after tax year 2008-09.

Accrued income scheme

The accrued income scheme exists in order to prevent a form of tax avoidance known as "bond washing". Bond washing involves selling securities "cum interest" (so that the buyer of the securities will receive the next interest payment) just before an interest payment is due. The price paid by the buyer reflects the fact that the sale is cum interest and so the seller of the securities is not disadvantaged. However, the effect of the transaction from the tax point of view is that the seller has converted what would have been income into a capital gain. Since capital gains arising on the disposal of certain securities are exempt from capital gains tax (see Chapter 19) the seller appears to have avoided tax.

The accrued income scheme overcomes this potential loss of tax by charging the seller income tax on the interest which has accrued up to the date of the sale. The buyer of the securities is entitled to tax relief on the same amount and this is given by deduction from the next interest payment the buyer receives. Similar arrangements apply if securities are transferred "ex interest" (so that the seller will receive the next interest payment). In this case, the buyer is taxed on the interest accruing from the date of the sale to the date of the next interest payment and the seller is entitled to tax relief on the same amount.

The accrued income scheme applies to securities such as gilt-edged stocks, local authority bonds and company debentures. It does not apply to ordinary or preference shares in a company. Transfers made by individuals who have not held securities with a total nominal value exceeding £5,000 in the current tax year or in the preceding tax year are excluded from the scheme.

Dividends received

Dividends received by an individual from a UK resident company are charged to income tax by the Income Tax (Trading and Other Income) Act 2005. This Act states that tax is charged on the amount of dividends actually received in the tax year, with no adjustment for any accrued dividends. UK dividends have an attached tax credit which is equal to one-ninth of the amount of the dividend received (see Chapter 2) and an individual's dividend income for a tax year is equal to the UK dividends received in that year plus the attached tax credits. No expenses are allowed against dividend income.

Dividends falling into the basic rate band are taxed at the dividend ordinary rate of 10%. Dividends which lie above this band are taxed at the dividend upper rate of 32.5% (see Chapter 2). Tax credits relating to dividends which are charged to tax are set against the income tax liability on those dividends. Tax credits exceeding this liability cannot be paid to the taxpayer or set against the tax liability on any other income. Note also that:

(a) As from 6 April 2008 (subject to certain conditions) the tax regime described above also applies to dividends received from overseas companies (see Chapter 32).

(b) Any capital gain arising on the disposal of shares or securities is generally subject to capital gains tax (see Chapter 19).

Tax-efficient investments

A taxpayer who is seeking an alternative, tax-efficient means of investing in an interest-bearing account or in shares and securities may invest in any of the following:

(a) an Individual Savings Account (ISA)

(b) the Enterprise Investment Scheme

(c) a Venture Capital Trust

(d) a Community Development Finance Institution.

Each of these forms of investment is explained below. A further investment opportunity is offered by Child Trust Funds, which provide a tax-efficient means of building up an investment fund on behalf of a young person. Child Trust Funds (CTFs) are explained later in this chapter.

Individual Savings Accounts

Tax-free Individual Savings Accounts (ISAs) were introduced on 6 April 1999. The main features of these accounts are currently as follows:

(a) Individuals who are resident and ordinarily resident in the UK (see Chapter 32) and at least 16 years old may hold an ISA. The residence requirement is waived in the case of Crown servants serving overseas and their spouses (or civil partners).

(b) ISAs are of two types. These are "cash ISAs" and "stocks and shares ISAs". Money invested in a cash ISA is deposited with a bank or building society and is held in a savings account. Money invested in a stocks and shares ISA is used by the ISA provider to acquire stocks and shares on the saver's behalf. These stocks and shares may be listed on a stock exchange anywhere in the world. Savers under the age of 18 may invest in a cash ISA only.

(c) Each tax year, a saver may invest in a single cash ISA and/or a single stocks and shares ISA. Savers may start fresh ISAs each year or may continue to invest in ISAs started in previous years.

(d) The maximum amount which a saver under the age of 50 may invest in ISAs during tax year 2009-10 is £7,200. No more than £3,600 of this may be saved in a cash ISA. The remainder of the £7,200 may be invested in a stocks and shares ISA, which could be managed by the same provider as the cash ISA or by a different provider.

As from 6 October 2009, the ISAs limit for savers aged 50 or over is increased to £10,200, of which no more than £5,100 may be saved in a cash ISA. The ISAs limit will be raised to this level for all savers in 2010-11.

(e) There is no cumulative limit on the total amount which an individual can save in ISAs during his or her lifetime. Nor is there a specified minimum level of saving.

(f) Interest and dividends arising from ISAs are exempt from income tax. Capital gains (and losses) arising from ISAs are exempt from capital gains tax.

(g) Withdrawals may be made from an ISA without loss of tax relief. But once the maximum amount has been subscribed to an ISA for a tax year, no further subscriptions will be allowed in that year, regardless of how much is withdrawn.

(h) Some or all of the money saved in cash ISAs in previous tax years may be transferred to stocks and shares ISAs without affecting the current year's ISA investment limit. Savers may also transfer money saved in a cash ISA in the current tax year to a stocks and shares ISA. Such a transfer must be for the whole amount saved in the cash ISA during the current year up to the date of the transfer. If money saved in the current year is transferred in this way, it is treated as if it had been invested directly in a stocks and shares ISA in the current year.

(i) Personal Equity Plans (PEPs) held at 6 April 2008 were automatically redesignated as stocks and shares ISAs. Therefore PEPs ceased to exist as from that date.

EXAMPLE 2

(a) An individual who is aged 37 saves £500 in a cash ISA on 6 April 2009. What further investments in ISAs may the individual make during 2009-10?

(b) An individual who is aged 58 saves £6,000 in a stocks and shares ISA on 21 May 2009. What further investments in ISAs may the individual make during 2009-10?

(c) An individual who is aged 25 saves £1,000 in a cash ISA on 30 June 2009. A further £800 is saved in the cash ISA on 31 July 2009. On 31 December 2009, the individual decides to make a transfer from the cash ISA to a stocks and shares ISA. Is there any restriction on the amount that can be transferred? How will the transfer affect further ISA investments during 2009-10?

Solution

(a) A further £6,700 may be saved during the year. Up to £3,100 of this may be saved in the same cash ISA and the remainder may be saved in a stocks and shares ISA.

(b) A further £4,200 may be saved during the year. This could all be saved in the same stocks and shares ISA or in a cash ISA or in a combination of both. No more than £1,200 may be saved before 6 October 2009.

(c) The entire £1,800 must be transferred. A further £5,400 may then be saved in ISAs during the year. Up to £3,600 of this may be saved in a cash ISA and the remainder may be saved in the stocks and shares ISA to which the £1,800 was transferred.

Enterprise Investment Scheme

The Enterprise Investment Scheme (EIS) was established in 1994 to provide a means of encouraging investment in industry. The main features of the EIS are as follows:

(a) Income tax relief is available to taxpayers who subscribe for newly-issued shares in certain "qualifying companies". Essentially, these are unlisted trading companies with less than 50 employees which operate wholly or mainly in the UK and which have gross assets not exceeding £7m immediately before the share issue and not exceeding £8m immediately after it.

(b) For an investment to qualify for EIS relief, the company concerned must have raised no more than £2m under the EIS and other venture capital schemes in the previous 12 months.

(c) Relief takes the form of a reduction in the amount of tax due on the taxpayer's taxable income, equal to 20% of the amount invested in qualifying companies during the tax year. This reduction takes priority over the tax reductions relating to certain payments made by the taxpayer (see Chapter 4) and the tax reduction relating to the married couple's allowance (see Chapter 3).

(d) A taxpayer's EIS investments of up to £500,000 in each tax year are eligible for tax relief. Any of the EIS investments made in a tax year may be carried back and treated as if made in the previous year, but the total EIS investment that can attract income tax relief in any one tax year is subject to the £500,000 limit.

(e) The taxpayer must not be connected with the company at any time during the two years prior to the date of the investment and the three years following that date. Broadly speaking, an individual is connected with a company for this purpose if he or she is an employee of the company or, together with associates, owns more than 30% of the company's ordinary shares.

(f) Dividends received on the shares are subject to income tax in the usual way.

(g) Any capital gain arising on the eventual disposal of the shares is exempt from capital gains tax but any loss arising on the disposal is eligible for relief. A loss may be relieved either:

(i) as a capital loss, in the usual way (see Chapter 16), or

(ii) against the taxpayer's total income of the year in which the loss is incurred or the previous year (see Chapter 11).

When calculating the loss arising on disposal, the shares are deemed to have been acquired for their issue price, less the tax reduction obtained by the taxpayer when the shares were purchased.

(h) The taxpayer must retain the shares for a minimum holding period of at least three years or both the income tax and capital gains tax reliefs are lost.

Venture Capital Trusts

A Venture Capital Trust (VCT) is a company which is approved as such by HM Revenue and Customs. The main conditions which must be satisfied before HMRC approval can be obtained are as follows:

(a)   The company's ordinary shares must be listed on the UK Stock Exchange.

(b)   Its income must be derived wholly or mainly from shares or securities and no more than 15% of this income may be retained by the company.

(c)   At least 70% of its total investments must consist of "qualifying holdings" and at least 30% must consist of ordinary shares. Broadly, shares or securities owned by a VCT rank as qualifying holdings if they were newly issued to the VCT and if they are shares or securities of a company which would be a qualifying company for the purposes of the EIS (see earlier in this chapter).

   If a VCT acquires shares in a company and this acquisition brings the VCT's total investment in that company to more than £1m in the previous six months (or since the start of the tax year, if earlier) then the excess over £1m does not count as a qualifying holding.

(d)   No holding in any one company (other than in another VCT) can represent more than 15% of a VCT's investments. At least 10% of a VCT's investment in any one company must be held in the form of ordinary shares.

Income tax relief is available to taxpayers who subscribe for newly-issued shares of a VCT. This takes the form of a tax reduction equal to 30% of the amount invested, subject to an investment limit of £200,000 per tax year. This reduction takes priority over the tax reductions relating to certain payments made by the taxpayer (see Chapter 4) and the tax reduction relating to the MCA (see Chapter 3). To qualify for income tax relief, the taxpayer must hold the shares for a minimum holding period of at least five years.

   Dividends on the first £200,000 of VCT shares acquired in each tax year are exempt from income tax and any capital gain or loss arising on the disposal of these shares is exempt from capital gains tax, regardless of whether or not the shares have been held for the minimum holding period.

Community investment tax credit

Community investment tax credits provide tax relief to individuals who make an investment in an accredited Community Development Finance Institution (CDFI). The objective of a CDFI is to provide finance to support enterprises in disadvantaged communities. The main features of this scheme are as follows:

(a) The investment may take the form of a loan to a CDFI or a subscription for the shares or securities of a CDFI. The investor must not control the CDFI or be a partner in it (if it is a partnership).

(b) A loan must be for at least five years. No repayment can be required within the first two years of the loan and required repayments cannot exceed 25% of the loan amount before the end of the third year, 50% before the end of the fourth year and 75% before the end of the fifth year.

(c) Shares or securities must be subscribed for wholly in cash and must not be redeemable within five years of the investment date.

(d) Tax relief may be claimed for the tax year in which the investment is made and for each of the four subsequent tax years. In each year, relief is given by means of a tax reduction equal to the *lower* of:

(i)   5% of the "invested amount", and
(ii) the amount which reduces the investor's tax liability to nil.

(e) In the case of a loan the "invested amount" for the tax year in which the loan is made is defined as the average capital balance during the first 12 months of the loan. For subsequent tax years, the invested amount is normally equal to the average capital balance for the 12 months beginning with the anniversary of the investment date which falls into the tax year concerned.

(f) In the case of shares or securities, the invested amount is equal to the amount subscribed by the investor.

(g) If the investment takes the form of a loan, relief is denied for a tax year if the loan is disposed of, or repaid in excess of the permitted amount, before the "qualifying date" for that year. The qualifying date for a tax year is the anniversary of the investment date which falls into the subsequent tax year.

(h) For shares and securities, relief is denied for a tax year if the shares or securities are disposed of before the qualifying date for that year.

A similar relief is available to *companies* which invest in a CDFI.

Child Trust Funds

Tax-free Child Trust Fund (CTF) accounts became available as from April 2005. The intention of these accounts is to build up a stock of assets for a young person to use or reinvest at the age of 18, so giving the young person added security and opportunity in adulthood. The main features of CTF accounts are as follows:

(a) A CTF account is automatically awarded to each child who is born on or after 1 September 2002 and who lives in the UK.

(b) A voucher for £250 is sent to the person who claims Child Benefit in relation to the child (usually the parent) and this person is then responsible for using the voucher to open a CTF account with a provider of their choice.

(c) Children from families with a gross income not exceeding the level at which Child Tax Credit begins to be tapered away receive an additional £250.

(d) The Government makes a further payment into each child's CTF account when the child reaches his or her seventh birthday. This further payment is £250 (or £500 for children from lower-income families).

   The Government also pays £100 a year into the CTF account of a disabled child and £200 a year into the CTF account of a severely disabled child.

(e) The child's family and friends (and the child himself or herself, when older) may make additional contributions into the CTF account of up to a total of £1,200 a year between them. These additional contributions do not attract tax relief.

(f) Although any income derived from parental gifts is generally treated as that of the parent (not the child) unless the amount of the income does not exceed £100 for the tax year, income derived from parental contributions to a CTF account does not count towards this £100 limit (see Chapter 3).

(g) No money may be withdrawn from a CTF account until the account matures on the child's eighteenth birthday. Income and gains arising from CTF investments are not taxable and there will be no tax liability when the account matures.

(h) There are several different types of CTF account available, including cash deposit accounts, stocks and shares accounts and life policies.

The first Child Trust Funds will mature in 2020. The Government will then allow the funds held in these accounts to rollover into ISAs, with the aim of encouraging young people to maintain a saving habit into adulthood.

Income from trusts and settlements

A trust or settlement is an arrangement whereby property is held by persons known as *trustees*, for the benefit of other persons known as *beneficiaries*. Trusts fall into two main categories, as follows:

(a) If one or more persons are entitled to receive all of the income which is generated by the trust property, then those persons are "life tenants" and the trust is a "trust with an interest in possession".

(b) If there is no life tenant and the trustees have the discretion to distribute as much or as little of the trust income to the beneficiaries as they see fit, then the trust is a "discretionary trust".

Trust taxation is a very complex matter and a full study of the subject is beyond the scope of this book. However, an introduction to trust taxation is given below.

Trusts with an interest in possession

For tax year 2009-10, the trustees of a trust with an interest in possession are liable to income tax at the dividend ordinary rate (10%) on the trust's dividend income and at the basic rate (20%) on all of its other income. Note that:

(a) The tax liability of the trustees is never calculated at the starting rate for savings income, the higher rate or the dividend upper rate.

(b) The general expenses of administering the trust are *not* allowed when computing the income tax liability of the trustees. However, expenses which relate to specific items of trust income (e.g. expenses normally deductible from property income) are set against that income.

(c) The trustees' tax liability is calculated without deduction of personal allowances.

(d) Relief is given for income tax deducted at source and tax credits on dividends.

The income which remains after tax and all expenses have been deducted (including general administration expenses) is paid to the life tenants and is dealt with in their personal tax computations. In those computations:

(a) trust non-savings income is treated as income received net of basic rate tax

(b) trust savings income is also treated as income received net of basic rate tax

(c) trust dividend income is treated as dividend income with an attached tax credit.

The general administration expenses of the trust are deemed to have been paid first out of dividend income, then out of savings income and then out of non-savings income.

EXAMPLE 3

An interest in possession trust with one life tenant has the following income in 2009-10:

	£
Rents receivable	30,200
Bank interest (net)	7,200
UK dividends	1,350

Expenses were incurred in the year as follows:

	£
Property expenses	6,900
Administration expenses	1,990

(a) Compute the trustees' income tax liability for 2009-10.

(b) How much income does the life tenant receive from the trust in 2009-10 and how will this be treated in his or her personal tax computation?

Solution

	Total £	Non-Savings £	Savings £	Dividends £
Property income £30,200 – £6,900	23,300	23,300		
Bank interest £7,200 x 100/80	9,000		9,000	
UK dividends £1,350 + tax credit £150	1,500			1,500
	33,800	23,300	9,000	1,500
Income tax @ 20%	(4,660)	(4,660)		
Income tax @ 20%	(1,800)		(1,800)	
Income tax @ 10%	(150)			(150)
Income after tax	27,190	18,640	7,200	1,350
Administration expenses	(1,990)		(640)	(1,350)
Income after tax and expenses	25,200	18,640	6,560	0

(a) The trustees' tax liability for the year is £6,610 (£4,660 + £1,800 + £150). The £1,800 of tax deducted at source and the £150 of tax credits are deducted, leaving tax payable by the trustees of £4,660.

(b) The income of the life tenant is:

	Gross £	Tax deducted £
Non-savings £18,640 x 100/80	23,300	4,660
Savings £6,560 x 100/80	8,200	1,640
Total	31,500	6,300

This income will be included in the life tenant's tax computation for 2009-10 and the tax deducted at source of £6,300 will be subtracted when computing tax payable for the year.

Discretionary trusts

In general, the income tax liability of the trustees of a discretionary trust is calculated at the "dividend trust rate" on dividend income and at the "trust rate" on all other income. For tax year 2009-10, these rates are 32.5% and 40% respectively. However, these special rates do not apply to income which has been used to fund the expenses of administering the trust. Such income is taxed at the dividend ordinary rate (10%) or the basic rate (20%), depending upon the type of income involved.

Also, the first £1,000 of the income of a discretionary trust is not taxed at the special trust rates but is instead charged to tax at the income tax rate which generally applies to the class of income concerned (i.e. the dividend ordinary rate or the basic rate). When identifying the first £1,000 of a trust's income, non-savings income is considered first, then savings income, then dividends.

Any payments which are made to beneficiaries are deemed to have been made net of tax at the trust rate of 40% and must therefore be grossed-up at 100/60 in their personal income tax computations. The tax which is deemed to have been deducted from such payments is assessable on the trustees, but only to the extent (if any) that the amount of this tax exceeds the trustees' tax liability on the trust income. For this purpose, the tax liability of the trustees is deemed to exclude any tax which is satisfied by deduction of tax credits on dividends.

Trust rates for 2010-11

It has been announced that the trust rate for 2010-11 will be 50% and that the dividend trust rate for 2010-11 will be 42.5%.

Trusts with vulnerable beneficiary

A special tax regime applies to trusts with a vulnerable beneficiary. This tax regime ensures that the tax liability of this type of trust is reduced to the amount of tax that would have been payable if the trust income and gains had accrued directly to the beneficiary concerned.

A "vulnerable beneficiary" may be either a disabled person or (in certain instances) a minor. Trustees who wish to claim the special tax treatment available under this regime must make an appropriate election to HM Revenue and Customs. Once made, such an election is irrevocable.

EXAMPLE 4

Assume that a discretionary trust has the same income and expenses in 2009-10 as the trust described in the above example. Assume also that a payment of £4,500 was made to a beneficiary during the year.

(a) Compute the trustees' income tax liability for 2009-10.

(b) Show how the £4,500 received by the beneficiary will be treated in his or her personal tax computation.

Solution

	Total £	Non-Savings £	Savings £	Dividends £
Property income £30,200 – £6,900	23,300	23,300		
Bank interest £7,200 x 100/80	9,000		9,000	
UK dividends £1,350 + tax credit £150	1,500			1,500
	33,800	23,300	9,000	1,500
First £1,000 of trust income:				
Income tax at 20% on £1,000	(200)	(200)		
Remainder of trust income:				
Income tax @ 10% on £1,500	(150)			(150)
Income tax @ 20% on £800	(160)		(160)	
Income tax @ 40% on £8,200	(3,280)		(3,280)	
Income tax @ 40% on £22,300	(8,920)	(8,920)		
Income after tax	21,090	14,180	5,560	1,350
Administration expenses	(1,990)		(640)	(1,350)
Income after tax and expenses	19,100	14,180	4,920	0

Note:

The administration expenses of £1,990 are deemed to have been paid out of the trust's after-tax income, first out of dividends (£1,350) and then out of savings income (£640). As £640 of net savings income has been used for this purpose, gross savings income of £800 is taxed at only 20% and not at the special rate of 40%.

(a) The trustees' tax liability is £12,710 (£200 + £150 + £160 + £3,280 + £8,920). The tax deducted at source of £1,800 and tax credits of £150 are subtracted, leaving tax payable by the trustees of £10,760. This consists of £9,120 payable on the non-savings income and an extra 20% (40% – 20%) on the £8,200 of savings income which is taxed at the trust rate.

(b) The payment of £4,500 is grossed-up at 100/60, giving gross income of £7,500. This income is included in the beneficiary's tax computation for 2009-10 and the £3,000 of tax deducted at source is subtracted when computing tax payable for the year. The trustees' tax liability on the trust income (excluding the £150 which is satisfied by tax credits on dividends) is £12,560. This exceeds £3,000 so there is no further assessment on the trustees in relation to this payment.

Miscellaneous income

ITTOIA 2005 charges income tax on certain items of miscellaneous income to the extent that these items are not already taxed under another heading. The Act also provides rules for computing the amount of such income arising in the tax year.

Examples of miscellaneous income include certain royalties, receipts from the sale of patent rights and income from any source which is not otherwise charged to tax.

Summary

▶ Income tax is payable on the amount of interest received by a taxpayer during the tax year. Most interest is received net of tax but non-taxpayers may receive their interest gross if they certify themselves as non-taxpayers. The main source of gross interest is the National Savings Bank.

▶ Income tax is payable on UK dividends received. Such dividends have an attached tax credit. Tax credits relating to dividends which are charged to income tax are set against the tax liability on those dividends.

▶ Individual Savings Accounts (ISAs) provide a tax-free means of saving cash or investing in stocks and shares.

▶ The Enterprise Investment Scheme provides tax incentives for those who subscribe for the newly-issued shares of unlisted trading companies which operate wholly or mainly in the UK.

▶ Subject to certain conditions, tax relief is available in relation to an investment in a Venture Capital Trust.

▶ Community investment tax credits provide tax relief for those who subscribe for the shares or securities of a Community Development Finance Institution (CDFI) or who make loans to a CDFI.

▶ Child Trust Fund (CTF) accounts provide a tax-free means of building up a stock of assets for a young person to use or reinvest at the age of 18.

▶ Trustees must account for income tax on the income of a trust. The administration expenses of the trust are not allowed when computing the trustees' income tax liability. Special rates of tax apply to the income of a discretionary trust.

▶ Certain forms of miscellaneous income are charged to income tax.

Exercises

6.1 Edward has the following income in 2009-10:

	£
Building society interest (net)	15,772
UK dividends	36,468

Compute the income tax payable by Edward for the year, assuming that he claims only the basic personal allowance.

Chapter 8

Income from self-employment: Computation of income

Introduction

This is the first of five chapters which deal with income from self-employment. The profits of a self-employed person are charged to income tax by the Income Tax (Trading and Other Income) Act 2005 and the main purpose of this chapter is to show how those profits are calculated for tax purposes. Subsequent chapters deal with related topics such as tax relief for capital expenditure, the tax consequences of making a loss and the taxation of partnerships.

A self-employed person may be conducting a trade or may be exercising a profession or vocation. However, the profits of trades, professions and vocations are all taxed in accordance with the same set of rules. Therefore, in this chapter and in subsequent chapters, references to "trades" and "trading" should be assumed to include professions and vocations. Similarly, the terms "trader" and "sole trader" will be used to refer to any self-employed person, regardless of whether that person is actually conducting a trade or is in fact exercising a profession or vocation.

The badges of trade

ITTOIA 2005 states that the trading profits of a person who is resident in the UK are chargeable to income tax wherever the trade is carried on. The trading profits of a non-UK resident are chargeable to income tax only if the trade is carried on wholly or partly in the UK (see Chapter 32). When deciding whether or not a person is trading it is necessary to make two important distinctions:

(a) the distinction between employment and self-employment (see Chapter 7)

(b) for a taxpayer who sells goods or other assets, the distinction between trading activities (which give rise to trading profits) and non-trading activities (which will usually fall within the scope of capital gains tax).

Section 989 of the Income Tax Act 2007 states that a "trade" includes "*any venture in the nature of trade*". This circular definition replaces a similar definition in ICTA 1988 and is of little real help. Therefore it has been left largely to the courts to decide whether or not a given activity constitutes trading. The main criteria which have arisen from case law decisions and which may be used to distinguish between trading and non-trading activities are known as the "badges of trade". They are as follows:

(a) **Subject matter of the transaction**

If a taxpayer sells assets of a type which might normally be acquired for personal enjoyment or held as a source of income, this may suggest that any profit arising on their sale should be treated as a capital gain rather than a trading profit.

But if the assets concerned do not provide personal enjoyment and do not yield income, it would seem that the only way in which they could be turned to advantage is by selling them. In these circumstances, any profit arising on their sale might be treated as a trading profit. In *Martin* v *Lowry* (1926), the taxpayer bought and sold a huge quantity of war surplus linen. In *Rutledge* v *CIR* (1929), the taxpayer bought and sold one million toilet rolls. In both of these cases, it was held that the subject matter of the transaction was such that the activity must be construed as trading.

(b) **Length of the period of ownership**

Trading stocks are normally retained for only a short period before being sold, whereas assets acquired for personal use or as a source of income are generally retained for longer. Therefore, if assets are bought and sold within a short space of time it is more likely that any profit made will be treated as a trading profit.

(c) **Frequency of transactions**

The more often that a taxpayer repeats a certain type of transaction, the more likely it is that the activity will be construed as trading. In *Pickford* v *Quirke* (1927), the taxpayer bought a cotton mill and sold off its assets at a profit. This was the fourth time that the taxpayer had carried out this particular type of transaction and therefore he was held to be trading.

(d) **Supplementary work**

A taxpayer who buys an asset, performs work on the asset so as to make it more saleable and then sells the asset is more likely to be regarded as trading than someone who simply buys and sells an asset without performing any supplementary work. In *Cape Brandy Syndicate* v *CIR* (1921), a group of individuals bought a large quantity of brandy which they first blended and then sold. They were held to be trading.

(e) **Reason for the sale**

The circumstances which have prompted the sale of an asset might be taken into account when deciding whether trading has occurred. A sale necessitated by a sudden urgent need for cash is less likely to be regarded as a trading activity than a sale made in the normal course of events.

(f) **Motive**

The presence of a profit motive in the mind of the taxpayer when acquiring an asset provides strong evidence of trading. In *Wisdom* v *Chamberlain* (1969), the taxpayer acquired silver bullion with the intention of selling it at a profit and eventually did so. He was held to be trading.

However, this test is not always conclusive. After all, many investments are bought at least partially with a view to their long-term sale at a profit and yet such profits are generally treated as capital gains. This point emphasises the need to consider the evidence provided by *all* of the badges of trade (not just one) when trying to decide whether or not trading has occurred.

Since trading requires the presence of a profit motive when the asset was acquired, the sale of an asset originally acquired by inheritance or by gift (or in any way otherwise than by purchase) is very unlikely to be construed as trading.

The calculation of trading profits

The computation of a self-employed person's trading profit begins with the net profit shown by that person's accounts. For tax purposes, trading profits must be calculated in accordance with generally accepted accounting practice, which means that income and expenditure must be measured on the accruals basis. Self-employed professionals were allowed at one time to calculate their profits for tax purposes on a cash basis but this is no longer permissible, except for new barristers in their first seven years of practice.

It is usually necessary to make a number of adjustments to the net profit shown by the accounts in order to arrive at the trading profit for tax purposes These adjustments can be summarised as follows:

		£	£
Net profit shown by the accounts			XXX
Add:	Expenditure shown in the accounts but not deductible for tax purposes	XXX	
	Trading income not shown in the accounts	XXX	XXX
			XXX
Less:	Expenditure deductible for tax purposes but not shown in the accounts	XXX	
	Non-trading income shown in the accounts	XXX	XXX
Trading profit adjusted for tax purposes			XXX

Each of these adjustments is explained below.

Deductibility of expenditure

In general, expenditure is deductible (allowable) when computing trading profits only if it is incurred *wholly and exclusively for the purposes of the trade*. This rule is not as restrictive as the "wholly, exclusively and necessarily" rule applied to the expenses of an employee (see Chapter 7) but it does have the following implications:

(a) Expenditure which has no connection with the trade is disallowed (the "remoteness test"). In *Strong & Co of Romsey Ltd* v *Woodifield* (1906), damages paid by a brewery to a hotel guest injured by a falling chimney were disallowed. These damages were incurred by the brewery in its capacity as a property owner, not in its capacity as a trader, and therefore failed the remoteness test.

(b) Expenditure which serves both a business purpose and a private purpose cannot be allowed in full (the "duality test"). If the expenditure can be apportioned with reasonable accuracy, then the private element is disallowed. However, in *Mallalieu* v *Drummond* (1983), the cost of black clothing worn in court by a lady barrister was wholly disallowed, since it was not possible to apportion the cost of the clothing between the part which satisfied professional standards of dress and the part which simply provided warmth and decency.

Even if expenditure passes both of these tests it may still be disallowed by statute.

Disallowed expenditure

Certain classes of expenditure are disallowed (either by statute or by case law) when computing trading profits. If any of these types of expenditure have been deducted in the accounts of a self-employed person, then the amount of the expenditure must be "added back" to the profit shown by the accounts in order to arrive at the trading profit for tax purposes. The main classes of disallowed expenditure are identified below.

Capital expenditure

Capital expenditure is specifically disallowed by ITTOIA 2005 but the Act does not provide a definition of the term "capital". Consequently, there is a great deal of case law on this subject, much of which is concerned with distinguishing between repairs (which are allowable) and improvements (disallowed as capital expenditure). In *Atherton* v *British Insulated & Helsby Cables Ltd* (1926), it was stated that capital expenditure is such that it brings an "enduring benefit" to the business, and this test is still widely used. The following capital-related expenses are also disallowed:

(a) legal or professional fees incurred in relation to an item of capital expenditure

(b) depreciation and amortisation charges, although capital allowances may be available instead (see Chapter 10)

(c) losses on the disposal of non-current assets.

Even repairs may be disallowed if they relate to a newly acquired asset and if the repairs are required in order to put the asset into usable condition. In *Law Shipping Co Ltd* v *CIR* (1923), the costs of putting a newly acquired ship into seaworthy condition were disallowed for this reason. However, repairs to a newly acquired asset which was usable before the repairs were carried out are generally allowed. In the case of *Odeon Associated Theatres Ltd* v *Jones* (1971), repairs to cinemas which had been bought in a state of disrepair (but were nonetheless usable) were allowed.

Appropriations of profit

Appropriations of profit made by the owner of a business (whether these are described as drawings, owner's salary or anything else) are disallowed. The owner's personal income tax payments and personal National Insurance contributions are also disallowed.

Provisions

Provisions are allowed so long as they are in respect of revenue expenditure and are made in accordance with generally accepted accounting practice. However, a provision will be disallowed if it cannot be estimated with sufficient accuracy.

Transfers to a general provision for doubtful debts (which is perhaps more correctly referred to as an "allowance" rather than a "provision") are usually disallowed when computing trading profits, since the amount involved is insufficiently accurate. The same is true of transfers to other general provisions. For example, a transfer to a general stock (or inventory) provision would usually be disallowed.

Entertainment and gifts

The cost of entertaining customers is disallowed. Staff entertaining costs are allowable but the employees concerned may incur an income tax liability if the amount involved is excessive (see Chapter 7). The cost of gifts is also disallowed, other than:

(a)   gifts to employees, if made wholly and exclusively for trade purposes

(b)   gifts to customers costing no more than £50 per customer per year, displaying a conspicuous advertisement for the business and not consisting of food, drink or tobacco

(c)   gifts of trading stock (or inventory) or used plant and machinery to designated UK educational establishments, charities or community amateur sports clubs

(d)   reasonably small gifts to local charities, if made wholly and exclusively for trade purposes (e.g. a charitable gift which attracts favourable publicity and enhances the firm's public image)

(e)   contributions made to local enterprise agencies, training and enterprise councils and urban regeneration companies.

Charitable donations made within the Gift Aid scheme are given tax relief under the Gift Aid rules and are disallowed when computing trading profits (see Chapter 4).

Political donations

Political donations and subscriptions are usually not allowed. But political donations which result in a definite benefit to the trade may be allowed. In *Morgan* v *Tate & Lyle Ltd* (1954), the costs of a political campaign against nationalisation were allowed on the grounds that the campaign was waged for the survival of the trade.

Non-trade bad debts

Bad debts incurred in the course of trade are allowable. But loans written off are generally not allowable unless:

(a) the taxpayer is in the business of lending money and the loan concerned was made in the course of trade, or

(b) the loan was to an employee and was made by reason of the employment and for trade purposes; in this case, the written-off loan will usually be taxable on the employee as income from employment (see Chapter 7).

Transfers to a *specific* bad debts provision (or allowance) are allowable but transfers to a *general* provision are usually disallowed, as stated earlier. Bad debts recovered and reductions in a specific bad debts provision are both treated as trading income.

EXAMPLE

A sole trader's nominal ledger contains the following bad and doubtful debts account for the year ended 30 June:

	£	£		£	£
Trade debts w/o		812	Allowances b/f at 1 July:		
Staff loan w/o		50	General	432	
			Specific	312	744
Allowances c/f at 30 June:					
General	459		Trade debt recovered		42
Specific	288	747	Income statement		823
		1,609			1,609

The staff loan written off was not made for trade purposes. How much of the £823 charged to the income statement for the year should be added back when computing trading profits for tax purposes?

Solution

The figure of £823 charged to the income statement can be analysed as follows:

	£
Trade debts written off, less trade debts recovered (£812 – £42)	770
Staff loan written off	50
Increase in general allowance (£459 – £432)	27
Decrease in specific allowance (£312 – £288)	(24)
	823

The £50 staff loan written off and the £27 increase in the general allowance for doubtful debts are disallowed, so a total of £77 should be added back when calculating the trading profits for tax purposes.

Fines and penalties

Fines or penalties incurred because of infringements of the law are not regarded as trading expenses and are disallowed. An exception occurs if an employer pays parking fines incurred by employees whilst on their employer's business. Such payments are usually allowed when computing trading profits but may then be assessed on the employees as income from employment.

Criminal payments

A payment is disallowed if the making of the payment in itself constitutes a criminal offence (e.g. a bribe). Payments to blackmailers or extortionists are also disallowed.

Allowable expenditure

As explained earlier, expenditure is allowable when computing trading profits if it has been incurred wholly and exclusively for the purposes of the trade and is not specifically disallowed by statute. Apart from the disallowed items listed above, most of the expenditure shown in a typical income statement (or profit and loss account) will probably be allowable but the following points should be noted:

(a) **Interest**. Interest, including credit card and overdraft interest, is allowable if it is incurred for trade purposes. But interest paid on overdue tax is disallowed.

(b) **Legal and professional fees**. Legal and professional fees relating to capital expenditure are specifically disallowed (see above), but fees incurred for other trade purposes are normally allowable. For example, fees are allowed if incurred in connection with such matters as the collection of trade debts, the raising of loan finance, the renewal of a short lease (a lease of up to 50 years), a legal action for breach of contract or the preservation of trading rights.

Audit and accountancy fees incurred in relation to the preparation of accounts and the agreement of tax liabilities are normally allowed. Fees incurred in relation to a tax investigation by HMRC are incurred in the role of taxpayer rather than trader and are generally disallowed unless no profit adjustment arises from the investigation. The cost of tax appeals is disallowed, even if successful.

(c) **Short lease premiums**. A premium paid for the grant of a short lease of business premises (50 years or less) is discounted according to the length of the lease and is then allowed in equal annual instalments over the period of the lease (see Chapter 5). A reverse premium received by a tenant using premises for business purposes is taxable as trading income.

(d) **Damages**. Damages and compensation payments are allowed if incurred for the purposes of the trade.

(e) **Value added tax**. If a trader pays VAT in relation to an item of expenditure and is unable to reclaim that VAT (see Chapter 30), the amount of VAT suffered will be allowable so long as the item of expenditure is itself allowable.

(f) **Trade subscriptions**. Subscriptions payable to professional and trade associations are generally regarded as having been incurred for the purposes of the trade and are allowable. Political subscriptions are generally disallowed.

(g) **Employees' remuneration**. Remuneration paid to employees is allowable so long as it is genuinely expended for business purposes. In the case of *Copeman* v *Flood (William) & Sons Ltd* (1941), it was held that large salaries paid to family members could be allowed only to the extent that they were expended for trading purposes.

Remuneration which is not actually paid to employees within nine months of the end of the period of account in which it is accrued is disallowed in that period but allowed in the period of payment.

Employers' contributions to registered pension schemes (see Chapter 13) are allowed in the *period of account in which they are paid*.

Redundancy payments and compensation payments made for loss of employment are usually allowable, as are lump sum payments made to employees on retirement. On a cessation of trade, contractual redundancy payments, statutory redundancy payments and non-contractual redundancy payments of up to three times the statutory amount are all allowed.

The cost of educational courses provided for employees is allowable if incurred for trade purposes. The cost of retraining employees who are about to leave (or have recently left) is allowed subject to certain conditions. The cost of temporarily seconding an employee to a charity or educational establishment is allowable.

(h) **Staff defalcations**. Losses caused by the dishonesty of an employee are normally allowable. But, following the decision in *Curtis* v *J & G Oldfield Ltd* (1925), the defalcations of a person having control over the business (e.g. a business partner) are not allowed.

(i) **Travel expenses**. The cost of business travel is allowable but the cost of travelling between home and work is generally disallowed. In *Newsom* v *Robertson* (1952), the travelling expenses of a barrister between his home and his chambers were disallowed. But in *Horton* v *Young* (1971), the travelling expenses of a self-employed bricklayer between his home and the sites at which he worked was allowed, on the grounds that his business was conducted from his home.

Traders whose annual turnover does not exceed the VAT registration threshold (see Chapter 29) may use the HMRC approved mileage rates to calculate their motor expenses (see Chapter 7) rather than keeping records of their actual expenses.

(j) **Leased cars**. As from 6 April 2009, the amount of lease rental payments allowed in relation to a leased motor car is restricted if the car has an emission rating of more than 160g/km. The restriction consists of a flat-rate disallowance of 15% of the lease rental payments. This restriction does not apply if the car has an emission rating of 160g/km or less. Nor does it apply if a car is leased for no more than 45 days.

These rules replace a set of "old rules" which restricted relief on the cost of leasing "expensive" cars (those with a retail price exceeding £12,000). Although the old rules do not apply to leases that begin on or after 6 April 2009, any lease that began before that date continues to be subject to the old rules until the end of the lease. The old rules restrict the allowable amount of the cost of leasing an expensive car to:

$$\text{Lease rental payments} \times \frac{£12,000 + 1/2(\text{Retail price} - £12,000)}{\text{Retail price}}$$

For example, if lease rental payments of £3,600 are incurred in relation to the lease of a car with a retail price of £18,000 (and the lease began before 6 April 2009), the allowable expense is restricted to:

$$£3,600 \times \frac{£12,000 + 1/2(£18,000 - £12,000)}{£18,000} = £3,000.$$

This restriction does not apply to the lease of a low-emission car (currently defined as a car with an emission rating of 110g/km or less).

It should be noted that neither the new rules nor the old rules apply to cars which are acquired under hire purchase agreements (see Chapter 10).

(k) **Patent royalties**. At one time, patent royalties were specifically disallowed when computing trading profits, but the section of ITTOIA 2005 which disallowed patent royalties was repealed by ITA 2007. In consequence, patent royalties paid for trade purposes are now allowable when computing trading profits.

(l) **Pre-trading expenditure**. Expenditure incurred during the seven years before starting to trade is treated as if incurred on the first day of trading and is allowable so long as the expenditure is of a type which would normally be allowable.

(m) **Registration of patents and trademarks**. The cost of registering a patent or trademark is allowable.

Trading income not shown in the accounts

The most common example of trading income being omitted from the accounts of a business occurs when the owner of the business appropriates trading stock (or inventory) for his or her personal use. This is referred to as "own consumption".

In this situation, generally accepted accounting practice (GAAP) suggests that the cost of the goods concerned, less any contribution made by the owner, should be credited to the income statement. But ITTOIA 2005 requires that own consumption of trading stock is accounted for at *market value*. This means that the profit of the business for tax purposes should be increased by the *selling price* of the goods, less any contribution made by the owner. For this purpose, "trading stock" consists of goods that are sold in the ordinary course of trade (including partially manufactured stock), but does not include:

- materials used in the manufacture, preparation or construction of trading stock
- services performed in the ordinary course of trade.

These items continue to be accounted for at cost price rather than selling price.

The above rule in ITTOIA 2005 puts onto a statutory basis the view that was originally expressed in the famous case of *Sharkey* v *Wernher* (1955). In this case, horses were transferred from a farm to the owner's private stables and it was held that the profits of the farm should be increased, for tax purposes, by the full market value of those horses.

Non-trading income shown in the accounts

Any non-trading income which is shown in the accounts of a business must be deducted when computing trading profits. The main categories of non-trading income which might be found in the accounts of a business are:

(a) income which is taxed under another heading (e.g. interest, property income)

(b) profits made on the disposal of non-current assets; these are normally depreciation adjustments but a genuine gain may be chargeable to capital gains tax

(c) decreases in general provisions or allowances.

Expenditure not shown in the accounts

The most common example of allowable expenditure not being shown in the accounts of a business is the trader's claim (if any) to capital allowances. The types of expenditure which attract capital allowances and the way in which capital allowances are calculated are considered in Chapter 10.

Another instance of allowable expenditure not shown in the accounts is a premium paid for the grant of a short lease. As explained earlier, part of such a premium is deductible from trading income in equal annual instalments over the lease period. If the premium is being amortised in the accounts, the amortisation charges are added back and the allowable amount of the premium (see Chapter 5) is deducted instead.

Post-cessation receipts

Post-cessation receipts are sums received after a person permanently ceases trading and which arise from the carrying on of the trade prior to cessation. Such receipts fall within the scope of ITTOIA 2005 and are treated as trading income.

Deductions are allowed for any expenses incurred which would have been deductible in calculating the profits of the trade if it had not ceased.

Summary

▶ A set of criteria known as the "badges of trade" may be used to distinguish between trading activities and non-trading activities.

▶ The net profit shown in the accounts of a self-employed person has to be adjusted in order to arrive at the trading profit for tax purposes.

▶ Expenditure is deductible when computing trading profits if it is wholly and exclusively incurred for the purposes of the trade. Expenditure which is not so incurred is disallowed. Certain categories of expenditure are disallowed by statute.

▶ The amount of any disallowed expenditure which is shown in the accounts of a self-employed person must be added back to the profit shown by those accounts when computing the trading profit for tax purposes.

▶ If the owner of a business takes trading stock for personal use, the full market value of that stock (less any amount paid by the owner) must be added to the net profit shown by the accounts when computing the trading profit.

▶ Non-trading income included in the accounts of a business must be deducted from the net profit shown by those accounts when computing the trading profit.

▶ Any allowable expenditure not shown in the accounts (e.g. the deductible part of a premium paid for the grant of a short lease) must be deducted from the net profit shown by the accounts when computing the trading profit.

▶ Post-cessation receipts are treated as trading profits for tax purposes.

Exercises

8.1   List the six badges of trade.

8.2   State the general rule which governs whether or not expenditure is deductible when computing trading profits.

8.3   Which of the following items of expenditure would be allowed when computing trading profits?

      (a)   the salary paid to a sole trader's wife

      (b)   a Gift Aid donation

      (c)   a new lathe bought by an engineering business

      (d)   diaries costing £3 each given to customers

      (e)   the cost of the annual staff outing to Blackpool

      (f)   the black suit worn at work by a self-employed undertaker

      (g)   the legal costs of acquiring new freehold premises

      (h)   a subscription to the local chamber of commerce

      (i)   cases of wine costing £49.99 each given to customers at Christmas

      (j)   the legal costs of suing a trade debtor for non-payment.

8.4   Julian, a self-employed shopkeeper, takes goods costing £30 from his trading stock for his own personal use. If he had sold the stock to a customer he would have charged £45. When computing his trading profit, what adjustment would need to be made to the net profit shown by his accounts if:

      (a)   he pays nothing for the goods?

      (b)   he puts £30 of his own money into the till so as to pay for the goods?

      (c)   he puts £45 of his own money into the till?

8.5   (a)   A motor car with a retail price of £21,000 is leased for six months at a total cost of £2,940. The car is used for trade purposes and has an emission rating of 182g/km. How much of the £2,940 should be disallowed when calculating trading profits if:

           (i)   the lease began on 1 July 2009?

           (ii)   the lease began on 1 January 2009?

      (b)   A sole trader is granted a 15-year lease on premises which he uses for business purposes. He pays a premium of £15,000 and writes off £1,000 per year in his business accounts. How much of the £1,000 should be disallowed each year when calculating trading profits?

8.6 Linda's profit and loss account (or income statement) for the year ended 31 March 2010 is as follows:

	£	£
Sales		82,500
Less: Cost of sales		37,200
Gross profit		45,300
Add: Rents receivable	1,200	
Bank interest receivable	80	
Profit on sale of non-current asset	310	1,590
		46,890
Less: Wages and salaries	22,620	
Business rates and insurance	1,750	
Heating and lighting	2,170	
Repairs and renewals	4,280	
Telephone	880	
Motor expenses	3,250	
Sundry expenses	1,650	
Bad and doubtful debts	640	
Credit card interest	120	
Loss on sale of non-current asset	70	
Depreciation	2,500	39,930
Net profit for the year		6,960

Notes:

(a) Linda draws a salary of £200 per week from the business. This is included in the wages and salaries figure.

(b) Repairs and renewals are as follows:

	£
Decoration of business premises	400
Installation of new improved heating system	3,800
Minor repair	80
	4,280

(c) It has been agreed with HMRC that one-quarter of telephone costs and one-fifth of motor expenses relate to private use.

(d) Sundry expenses include business entertaining of £520.

(e) Trade debts written off in the year amount to £440 and £200 has been set aside as a general provision or allowance for bad and doubtful debts.

Compute Linda's trading profit (before deduction of capital allowances) for the year ended 31 March 2010.

*8.7   A sole trader's bad and doubtful debts account for the year ended 31 March 2010 is as follows:

	£	£		£	£
Trade debts written off		638	Allowances b/f		
Allowances c/f			General	200	
General	150		Specific	231	431
Specific	317	467			
			Staff loan recovered		500
			Income statement		174
		1,105			1,105

The staff loan recovered was not allowable as a trade expense when it was originally written off. How much of the £174 charged to the income statement for the year should be added back when calculating trading profit?

*8.8   Imran owns a business which operates from rented premises. He has a 10-year lease on the premises and paid a premium of £7,000 in order to obtain the lease. His profit and loss account (or income statement) for the year ended 31 December 2009 is as follows:

	£	£
Gross profit for the year		52,618
Add: Interest receivable	212	
Surplus on sale of office equipment	300	512
		53,130
Less: Wages (see Note 1)	19,280	
Rent, rates and insurance (see Note 2)	6,915	
Electricity	4,328	
Telephone (see Note 3)	1,650	
Repairs (see Note 4)	2,286	
Printing and advertising	1,250	
Motor expenses (see Note 5)	5,712	
Legal and professional expenses (see Note 6)	3,000	
Sundry expenses (see Note 7)	4,777	
Bad and doubtful debts (see Note 8)	860	
Bank charges and interest	2,765	
Lease premium amortisation	700	
Depreciation	8,749	62,272
Net loss for the year		(9,142)

Notes:

1. Wages include £5,800 for Imran's wife (who works part-time for the business) and £1,000 for his son (a student who does not work for the business at all). Also included is Imran's personal income tax of £3,394 and personal National Insurance contributions of £121.

2. Insurance includes Imran's private medical insurance premium of £414.

3. It has been agreed that one-sixth of telephone costs relate to private use.

4. Repairs include £750 for the cost of essential repairs to a newly-acquired second-hand forklift truck which could not be used until the repairs had been carried out.

5. Motor expenses are as follows:

	£
Vehicle servicing and repairs	1,165
Fuel and oil	2,815
Loss on disposal of motor vehicle	422
Road fund licences and insurance	610
Fine for speeding by Imran	700
	5,712

It has been agreed that one-tenth of motor expenses relate to private use.

6. Legal and professional expenses consist of:

	£
Fees relating to renewal of lease	500
Debt collection	1,500
Accountancy fees	1,000
	3,000

7. Sundry expenses are:

	£
Business entertaining	3,320
Staff Christmas dinner	312
Subscription to trade association	350
Donation to political party	200
Miscellaneous small items (all allowable)	595
	4,777

8. Trade debts of £500 were written off during the year. The general allowance for doubtful debts was reduced by £100 and the specific allowance for doubtful debts was increased by £460.

9. During the year, Imran appropriated trading stock costing £220 from the business for personal use, paying £220 of his own money into the business bank account. His gross profit percentage on turnover is 20%.

Compute Imran's trading profit (before deduction of capital allowances) for the year ended 31 December 2009.

Chapter 9

Income from self-employment: Basis periods

Introduction

Income tax is charged for tax years (or "years of assessment") which run from 6 April to the following 5 April. Therefore it would be convenient if all traders were required to choose 5 April as their annual accounting date, so that the trading income for each tax year could be readily identified. However, traders are free to choose any annual accounting date that they wish and so it is necessary to devise some means of establishing a link between the periods of account for which trading profits are calculated and the tax years in which those profits are charged to tax.

The trading profits charged to tax in a tax year are the profits that are earned during the *basis period* for that year and the purpose of this chapter is to explain the rules which are used to determine the basis period for any given tax year. The basis period rules which are now in use were originally introduced by Finance Act 1994 and the old rules which these rules replaced no longer apply. However, one aspect of the transition to the FA1994 rules which is sometimes still relevant is considered towards the end of this chapter.

The current year basis

The main principle of the self-employment basis period rules is that the basis period for a tax year is *the accounting year ending in that tax year*. This is known as the "current year basis" (CYB). However, special rules apply when a business starts trading, ceases trading or changes its accounting date (see below).

EXAMPLE 1

(a) A trader prepares accounts annually to 31 December. Identify the basis period for tax year 2009-10.

(b) A trader prepares accounts annually to 30 April. For which tax year will the accounting year to 30 April 2010 form the basis period?

Assume in both cases that the special rules which are used on commencement, cessation or change of accounting date do not apply in any of the years concerned.

Solution

(a) The accounting year to 31 December 2009 ends during 2009-10 and therefore forms the basis period for 2009-10. This means that the profits of the year to 31 December 2009 are charged to income tax in tax year 2009-10.

(b) The accounting year to 30 April 2010 ends during 2010-11 and therefore forms the basis period for 2010-11. This means that the profits of the year to 30 April 2010 are charged to income tax in tax year 2010-11.

Commencement of trade

Special rules are used to determine basis periods for the first three tax years when a business starts trading. The first tax year in which trading profits are taxed is the tax year in which trade commences and basis periods for the opening years are determined in accordance with the following rules:

Tax year			Basis period
1			Date of commencement to the following 5 April (the "actual basis")
2	*either*	(a)	12 months to the accounting date in the second tax year (if possible)
	or	(b)	The first 12 months of trading (if the accounting date in the second tax year is less than 12 months after commencement)
	or	(c)	The actual tax year from 6 April to 5 April (if there is no accounting date in the second tax year)
3	*either*	(a)	Current year basis (if possible)
	or	(b)	12 months to the accounting date in the third tax year
4 etc.			Current year basis.

Note the following points:

(a) The basis period for the first tax year will often be less than 12 months long but the basis period for each of the remaining opening years will always be exactly 12 months long.

(b) Basis periods for the opening tax years may overlap to some extent and therefore some of the profits made in the early years of trading may be the subject of more than one tax assessment (see below).

(c) If necessary, the trading profits for early periods of account are apportioned on a time basis in order to compute the amount of profit arising in each basis period.

(d) ITTOIA 2005 states that apportionments should be made by reference to the number of *days* in the period concerned, but adds that any other reasonable method of apportionment will be accepted so long as it is applied consistently. In practice, such calculations are usually made to the nearest month and this is the approach adopted in this book. However, some examining bodies may require exact daily apportionments. Therefore the reader is advised to find out whether his or her examining body requires apportionments to be made in days or in months.

EXAMPLE 2

(a) Vera commences trading on 1 January 2008, preparing accounts annually to 31 December. Identify the basis periods for the first four tax years.

(b) Wilbur commences trading on 1 October 2008. He chooses 30 June as his annual accounting date and prepares his first accounts for the 9 months to 30 June 2009. Identify the basis periods for the first four tax years.

(c) Yasmin commences trading on 1 February 2008 and chooses 30 April as her annual accounting date. She prepares her first accounts for the 15 months to 30 April 2009. Identify the basis periods for the first four tax years.

Solution

(a)

2007-08	Actual	1 January 2008 to 5 April 2008
2008-09	12 months to a/c date in year 2	year to 31 December 2008
2009-10	CYB	year to 31 December 2009
2010-11	CYB	year to 31 December 2010

(b)

2008-09	Actual	1 October 2008 to 5 April 2009
2009-10	First 12 months	1 October 2008 to 30 September 2009
2010-11	CYB	year to 30 June 2010
2011-12	CYB	year to 30 June 2011

(c)

2007-08	Actual	1 February 2008 to 5 April 2008
2008-09	Actual	6 April 2008 to 5 April 2009
2009-10	12 months to a/c date in year 3	1 May 2008 to 30 April 2009
2010-11	CYB	year to 30 April 2010

Overlap profits

If a business chooses 5 April as its annual accounting date, the basis periods used in the opening tax years will not overlap at all. Otherwise, the opening basis periods will overlap and some profits will form the basis of more than one tax assessment. Such profits are known as "overlap profits".

ITTOIA 2005 states that accounts prepared to 31 March or to the 1st, 2nd, 3rd or 4th of April will normally be treated as if prepared to 5 April, so as to avoid very short overlap periods and very small amounts of overlap profits.

EXAMPLE 3

Albert begins trading on 1 May 2008 and has the following results:

	Adjusted trading profit £
15 months to 31 July 2009	16,800
year to 31 July 2010	21,600

Compute Albert's trading income for each of the first three tax years and also calculate the amount of any overlap profits.

Solution

Albert's first period of account contains 15 months and his first basis period comprises the 11 months from 1 May 2008 to 5 April 2009. Trading income for the first three tax years is as follows:

Year	Basis	Basis period	Workings	Trading income £
2008-09	Actual	1/5/08 to 5/4/09	£16,800 x 11/15	12,320
2009-10	12 months to a/c date in year 2	1/8/08 to 31/7/09	£16,800 x 12/15	13,440
2010-11	CYB	y/e 31/7/10		21,600

The overlap period consists of the 8 months from 1 August 2008 to 5 April 2009, which are common to the basis periods for 2008-09 and 2009-10. The overlap profits are therefore £8,960 (£16,800 x 8/15).

Overlap relief

In general, overlap profits which arise in the opening years of a business are relieved by deduction from the trading profits that are charged to tax in the final tax year when trade ceases. Note the following points regarding "overlap relief":

(a) Overlap relief ensures that, over the entire lifetime of a business, the total of the trading profits which are charged to tax is equal to the total of the adjusted trading profits for each period of account.

(b) Overlap profits are not index-linked. The real value of overlap relief is eroded by inflation, especially in the case of businesses which trade for many years.

(c) If overlap profits exceed the trading profits which are charged to tax in the final tax year, the resulting loss is eligible for tax relief (see Chapter 11).

However, if a business changes its accounting date at some point during its lifetime, it is possible that some of the overlap profits arising in the opening years may be relieved by deduction from the trading profits which are taxed in the year of the change. It is also possible that further overlap profits might arise on a change of accounting date (see later in this chapter).

Cessation of trade

A cessation of trade occurs when the owner of a business retires or sells the business or dies. The final tax year in which trading profits are taxed is the tax year in which the cessation occurs. The basis period for this final tax year is determined as follows:

(a) If a business commences trading and ceases trading in the same tax year, the basis period for that year consists of the entire lifespan of the business.

(b) If a business ceases trading in its second tax year, the basis period for that year runs from 6 April at the start of the year up to the date of cessation. This rule overrides the usual commencement rules for the second tax year.

(c) Otherwise, the basis period for the final tax year runs from the end of the basis period for the previous tax year up to the date of the cessation. This basis period may be less than, equal to or more than 12 months in length. The usual commencement rules for the third year are overridden if a business ceases trading in its third tax year.

If the final set of accounts prepared for a business covers a period which is of more than 12 months, it is possible that no accounting date at all falls into the penultimate tax year (the last year but one). This makes it impossible to apply the usual current year basis in that year. In these circumstances, the basis period for the penultimate tax year is the 12 months up to the normal accounting date falling in that year.

It is important to appreciate that income tax is charged on the owner of a business and not on the business itself. Therefore a change in the ownership of a business is treated for tax purposes as a cessation of one business followed by the commencement of another.

EXAMPLE 4

Carmen starts trading on 1 July 2009 and chooses 30 June as her annual accounting date. Identify the basis periods for her last two tax years if she ceases trading as follows:

	Date of cessation	Final set of accounts
(a)	31 March 2010	9 months to 31 March 2010
(b)	30 June 2010	year to 30 June 2010
(c)	30 June 2014	year to 30 June 2014
(d)	31 May 2014	11 months to 31 May 2014
(e)	30 April 2014	22 months to 30 April 2014

Solution

(a) Trade both commences and ceases in 2009-10. The basis period for this single tax year is the entire lifespan of the business i.e. 1 July 2009 to 31 March 2010.

(b) The cessation occurs in the second tax year. Basis periods are:

2009-10	Actual	1 July 2009 to 5 April 2010
2010-11	6 April to date of cessation	6 April 2010 to 30 June 2010

(c)	2013-14	CYB	y/e 30 June 2013
	2014-15	End of previous basis period up to date of cessation	y/e 30 June 2014

(d)	2013-14	CYB	y/e 30 June 2013
	2014-15	End of previous basis period up to date of cessation	1 July 2013 to 31 May 2014

(e)	2013-14	12 months to normal a/c date	1 July 2012 to 30 June 2013
	2014-15	End of previous basis period up to date of cessation	1 July 2013 to 30 April 2014

EXAMPLE 5

Damien starts trading on 1 July 2004 and chooses 31 December as his annual accounting date. He ceases trading on 30 September 2009 and has the following results:

	Adjusted trading profit £
6 months to 31 December 2004	8,400
year to 31 December 2005	9,200
year to 31 December 2006	10,500
year to 31 December 2007	7,500
year to 31 December 2008	6,400
9 months to 30 September 2009	5,800

Compute Damien's trading income for each tax year and show that the total of this income is equal to the total of the adjusted trading profits listed above.

Solution

Year	Basis period	Workings	Trading income £
2004-05	1/7/04 to 5/4/05	£8,400 + 3/12 x £9,200	10,700
2005-06	y/e 31/12/05		9,200
2006-07	y/e 31/12/06		10,500
2007-08	y/e 31/12/07		7,500
2008-09	y/e 31/12/08		6,400
2009-10	1/1/09 to 30/9/09	£5,800 – overlap relief £2,300	3,500
			47,800

The overlap period is from 1 January 2005 to 5 April 2005 (3 months) and the overlap profits are £2,300 (£9,200 x 3/12). The total of the trading income which is charged to tax is £47,800, the same as the total of the adjusted trading profits.

Change of accounting date

If a business changes its accounting date from one date (the "old date") to another (the "new date"), special rules are used to determine the basis period for the year of change. The year of change is defined as the first tax year in which accounts are *not* made up to the old date or *are* made up to the new date (or both). There will be a change of basis period for a year of change so long as the following conditions are satisfied:

(a) The first set of accounts made up to the new date does not cover a period of more than 18 months.

(b) Notice of the change of accounting date is given to HM Revenue and Customs in a tax return on or before the due filing date for that return.

(c) Either:

  (i) None of the previous five tax years has been a year of change resulting in a change of basis period, or

  (ii) HMRC is satisfied that the change of accounting date has been made for genuine commercial reasons and not for tax avoidance purposes.

If all of these conditions are satisfied, the basis period for the year of change is determined as follows:

(a) The "relevant period" is identified as the period beginning immediately after the end of the basis period for the previous tax year and ending with the new date in the year of change.

(b) If the length of the relevant period is less than 12 months, the basis period for the year of change is the 12 months to the new date in the year of change.

(c) If the length of the relevant period is not less than 12 months, the basis period for the year of change is the relevant period itself.

(d) In consequence, the basis period for a year of change will always be of at least 12 months' duration.

If all of the required conditions are *not* satisfied, the basis period for the year of change is the 12 months to the old date in that year. However, the following tax year is then regarded as a year of change (the taxpayer being treated as though this were the first year in which the new date had been used) and a change of basis period will occur in that year if all of the conditions are satisfied in relation to that year. A change of accounting date can be carried forward indefinitely in this way until such time as the necessary conditions for a change of basis period are satisfied.

If a taxpayer regularly prepares accounts to a particular *day* in the year (e.g. the last Saturday in June) rather than a particular *date*, the fact that the accounting date will change slightly in each year does not trigger the change of accounting date rules.

EXAMPLE 6

(a) Gary began trading many years ago, preparing accounts to 30 September each year. He decided to change his accounting date to 30 June and the first accounts made up to the new date were for the period from 1 October 2008 to 30 June 2009. The conditions necessary for a change of basis period were all satisfied. Identify the basis periods for years 2007-08 to 2010-11 inclusive.

(b) Audrey began trading on 1 January 2006, preparing accounts to 31 December each year. She decided to change her accounting date to 31 March and the first accounts made up to the new date were for the period from 1 January 2008 to 31 March 2009. The conditions necessary for a change of basis period were all satisfied. Identify the basis periods for years 2005-06 to 2010-11 inclusive.

(c) Grant began trading many years ago, preparing accounts to 30 June each year. He decided to change his accounting date to 31 December and the first accounts made up to the new date were for the period from 1 July 2009 to 31 December 2009. The conditions necessary for a change of basis period were all satisfied. Identify the basis periods for years 2008-09 to 2011-12 inclusive.

(d) Clare began trading on 1 March 2005, preparing accounts to 31 January each year. Her first accounts were for the period to 31 January 2006. She decided to change her accounting date to 30 April and the first accounts made up to the new date were for the period from 1 February 2008 to 30 April 2009. The conditions necessary for a change of basis period were all satisfied. Identify the basis periods for years 2004-05 to 2010-11 inclusive.

Solution

(a) The year of change is 2009-10 (the first year in which the old date was not used and the new date was used). The basis period for 2008-09 ended on 30 September 2008, so the relevant period is from 1 October 2008 to 30 June 2009. This is less than 12 months in length so the basis period for 2009-10 is the 12 months to 30 June 2009. Basis periods for 2007-08 to 2010-11 are:

2007-08   year to 30 September 2007
2008-09   year to 30 September 2008
2009-10   year to 30 June 2009
2010-11   year to 30 June 2010

Note that there is an overlap between the basis periods for 2008-09 and 2009-10. The treatment of overlap profits on a change of accounting date is explained below.

(b) The year of change is 2008-09 (the first year in which the old date was not used and the new date was used). The basis period for 2007-08 ended on 31 December 2007, so the relevant period is from 1 January 2008 to 31 March 2009. This is not less than 12 months in length so the basis period for 2008-09 is the same as the relevant period. Basis periods for 2005-06 to 2010-11 are:

2005-06   1 January 2006 to 5 April 2006
2006-07   year to 31 December 2006
2007-08   year to 31 December 2007
2008-09   1 January 2008 to 31 March 2009
2009-10   year to 31 March 2010
2010-11   year to 31 March 2011

(c) The year of change is 2009-10 (the first year in which the new date was used). The basis period for 2008-09 ended on 30 June 2008, so the relevant period is from 1 July 2008 to 31 December 2009. This is not less than 12 months in length so the basis period for 2009-10 is the same as the relevant period. Basis periods are:

2008-09   year to 30 June 2008
2009-10   1 July 2008 to 31 December 2009
2010-11   year to 31 December 2010
2011-12   year to 31 December 2011

(d) The year of change is 2008-09 (the first year in which the old date was not used). The basis period for 2007-08 ended on 31 January 2008, so the relevant period is from 1 February 2008 to 30 April 2008. This is less than 12 months in length so the basis period for 2008-09 is the 12 months to 30 April 2008, even though this accounting date was not used in 2008-09. Basis periods for 2004-05 to 2010-11 are:

2004-05   1 March 2005 to 5 April 2005
2005-06   1 March 2005 to 28 February 2006
2006-07   year to 31 January 2007
2007-08   year to 31 January 2008
2008-09   year to 30 April 2008
2009-10   year to 30 April 2009
2010-11   year to 30 April 2010

There is an overlap between the basis periods for 2007-08 and 2008-09 (as well as the usual overlaps arising on the commencement of trade).

Overlap profits on a change of accounting date

If a change of accounting date results in profits being taxed more than once, these overlap profits are added to any earlier overlap profits which arose in the opening years or on a previous change of accounting date. The total overlap profits are then carried forward for relief on cessation or on a subsequent change of accounting date.

On the other hand, if the basis period for a year of change exceeds 12 months, a part of the overlap profits brought forward from previous years may be relieved in the year of change. The amount to be relieved is calculated according to the following formula:

$$\text{Amount relieved} = A \times \frac{B - C}{D}$$

where: A = Total overlap profits brought forward and not yet relieved

B = Length of the relevant period

C = 12 (or 365 if daily apportionments are being used)

D = Total length of the overlap period(s) to which the total overlap profits brought forward relate.

EXAMPLE 7

(a) Byron began trading on 1 November 2005, preparing accounts to 31 October each year. He decided to change his accounting date to 31 August and the first accounts made up to the new date were for the period from 1 November 2007 to 31 August 2008. The conditions necessary for a change of basis period were all satisfied. The adjusted trading profits for Byron's first five periods of account were as follows:

	£
Year to 31 October 2006	12,000
Year to 31 October 2007	18,000
Period to 31 August 2008	16,000
Year to 31 August 2009	21,000
Year to 31 August 2010	24,000

Compute Byron's trading income for years 2005-06 to 2010-11.

(b) Michelle began trading on 1 January 2006, preparing accounts to 31 December each year. She decided to change her accounting date to 28/29 February and the first accounts made up to the new date were for the period from 1 January 2009 to 28 February 2010. The conditions necessary for a change of basis period were all satisfied. The adjusted trading profits for Michelle's first five periods of account were:

	£
Year to 31 December 2006	4,560
Year to 31 December 2007	5,250
Year to 31 December 2008	11,680
Period to 28 February 2010	14,390
Year to 28 February 2011	16,270

Compute Michelle's trading income for years 2005-06 to 2010-11.

Solution

(a) The year of change is 2008-09 (the first year in which the old date was not used and the new date was used). The basis period for 2007-08 ended on 31 October 2007, so the relevant period is from 1 November 2007 to 31 August 2008. This is less than 12 months in length so the basis period for 2008-09 is the 12 months to 31 August 2008. Trading income for 2005-06 to 2010-11 is:

Year	Basis period	Workings	Trading income £
2005-06	1/11/05 to 5/4/06	£12,000 x 5/12	5,000
2006-07	y/e 31/10/06		12,000
2007-08	y/e 31/10/07		18,000
2008-09	y/e 31/8/08	(£18,000 x 2/12) + £16,000	19,000
2009-10	y/e 31/8/09		21,000
2010-11	y/e 31/8/10		24,000

There are overlap profits of £5,000 (5 months) on the commencement of trade and a further £3,000 (2 months) on the change of accounting date. Total overlap profits carried forward are £8,000 (7 months).

(b) The year of change is 2009-10 (the first year in which the old date was not used and the new date was used). The basis period for 2008-09 ended on 31 December 2008, so the relevant period is from 1 January 2009 to 28 February 2010. This is not less than 12 months in length so the basis period for 2009-10 is the relevant period itself. Trading income for 2005-06 to 2010-11 is:

Year	Basis period	Workings	Trading income £
2005-06	1/1/06 to 5/4/06	£4,560 x 3/12	1,140
2006-07	y/e 31/12/06		4,560
2007-08	y/e 31/12/07		5,250
2008-09	y/e 31/12/08		11,680
2009-10	1/1/09 to 28/2/10	£14,390 – overlap relief £760	13,630
2010-11	y/e 28/2/11		16,270

There are overlap profits of £1,140 (3 months) on the commencement of trade. The relevant period is 14 months long, which exceeds 12 months by 2 months. Overlap relief in the year of change is calculated as £1,140 x 2/3 = £760. Overlap profits carried forward are £380 (1 month).

Transitional overlap relief

The basis period rules now in use were introduced by Finance Act 1994. Businesses which existed before 6 April 1994 used to be assessed on the *preceding year basis*, which meant that the basis period for a tax year was the accounting year ending in the *previous* tax year. The switch to the current year basis for these businesses occurred as from 1997-98 with a special transitional rule for 1996-97. Broadly, the basis period for 1996-97 was the 24 months to the accounting date in that year and the assessment for the year was computed as 50% of the profits occurring during this 24-month period.

An aspect of this transition which will remain relevant for many years to come is that the period between the end of the basis period for 1996-97 and 5 April 1997 is treated as an overlap period. Ordinary overlap relief is not available to these older businesses but the profits of this special overlap period are eligible for *transitional overlap relief* on a subsequent change of accounting date or on a cessation of trade.

EXAMPLE 8

Norman began trading in 1976 preparing accounts to 31 October each year. He ceases trading on 31 October 2009. Recent adjusted trading profits have been as follows:

	£
year to 31 October 2008	26,490
year to 31 October 2009	28,100

Adjusted trading profit for the year to 31 October 1997 was £28,560. Compute Norman's trading income for 2009-10.

Solution

Norman's trading income for 1996-97 would have been 50% of the profits for the 24 months to 31 October 1996. Transitional overlap relief is available in relation to the profits of the period from 1 November 1996 to 5 April 1997 (£28,560 x 5/12 = £11,900).

The business ceases in 2009-10 so the basis period for 2009-10 runs from the end of the basis period for 2008-09 to the date of cessation (from 1 November 2008 to 31 October 2009). Trading income for 2009-10 is therefore £16,200 (£28,100 less transitional overlap relief of £11,900).

Averaging of trading profits for farmers, market gardeners and creative artists

Certain trades, professions and vocations are more likely than others to experience profits which fluctuate considerably from one period of account to the next, leading to corresponding fluctuations in the trading income which is charged to tax. In particular, this problem may affect:

(a) farmers and market gardeners (who are at the mercy of the weather)

(b) creative artists.

The income tax system allows farmers, market gardeners and creative artists to smooth out fluctuating profits by making a claim for *averaging*. Trading income for two consecutive tax years may be averaged if the difference between the two income figures is at least 30% of the higher figure. The effect of an averaging claim is to replace the normal trading income for each of these two tax years by the average of the two figures. Note the following points in relation to the averaging process:

(a) If a loss has been incurred in either of the two years which are involved in a claim for averaging, this loss counts as zero in the averaging calculations. The loss is then eligible for tax relief, as described in Chapter 11.

(b) An averaging claim may not be made for the tax year in which trade commences or for the tax year in which trade ceases.

(c)   If an averaging claim has been made for two tax years, the revised trading income for the second year may subsequently be used in another averaging claim. For example, if a claim has already been made for 2007-08 and 2008-09, then another claim may be made for 2008-09 and 2009-10. Overlapping claims of this nature must be made in chronological order.

(d)   An averaging claim must be made by the first anniversary of the 31 January which follows the end of the second tax year to which the claim relates. For example, an averaging claim which relates to 2008-09 and 2009-10 must be made by 31 January 2012.

EXAMPLE 9

The recent adjusted trading profits of a self-employed farmer who began trading many years ago are as follows:

	£
year to 30 November 2008	46,200
year to 30 November 2009	10,640

He has no other income. May an averaging claim be made and would the farmer benefit from such a claim?

Solution

The tax years in question are 2008-09 and 2009-10. The difference between the trading income of the two years is £35,560, which exceeds 30% of £46,200 so an averaging claim may be made. If such a claim is made, trading income for both 2008-09 and 2009-10 is revised to £28,420 (the average of £46,200 and £10,640). The farmer benefits from this claim in the following ways:

(a)   the likelihood of paying 40% tax for 2008-09 is removed, so reducing the total tax liability for the two years, and

(b)   the farmer's cash flow situation is improved, since the 2008-09 tax liability is reduced and the 2009-10 tax liability is increased.

EXAMPLE 10

A market gardener who began trading many years ago has the following recent results:

	Adjusted trading profit/(loss) £
year to 31 December 2005	21,500
year to 31 December 2006	14,200
year to 31 December 2007	(5,400)
year to 31 December 2008	6,900
year to 31 December 2009	10,800

Compute the trading income for 2005-06 to 2009-10 inclusive, assuming that all possible averaging claims are made.

Solution

2005-06 and 2006-07

	£
Original trading income for 2005-06 (y/e 31/12/05)	21,500
Original trading income for 2006-07 (y/e 31/12/06)	14,200
Difference (more than 30% of £21,500)	7,300

Averaging gives revised trading income of £17,850 in 2005-06 and 2006-07.

2006-07 and 2007-08

	£
Revised trading income for 2006-07	17,850
Original trading income for 2007-08 (y/e 31/12/07)	0
Difference (more than 30% of £17,850)	17,850

Averaging gives revised trading income of £8,925 in 2006-07 and 2007-08.

2007-08 and 2008-09

	£
Revised trading income for 2007-08	8,925
Original trading income for 2008-09 (y/e 31/12/08)	6,900
Difference (less than 30% of £8,925)	2,025

No averaging is possible so trading income is unaltered.

2008-09 and 2009-10

	£
Original trading income for 2008-09 (y/e 31/12/08)	6,900
Original trading income for 2009-10 (y/e 31/12/09)	10,800
Difference (more than 30% of £10,800)	3,900

Averaging gives revised trading income of £8,850 in 2008-09 and 2009-10.

The final trading income for all years concerned is as follows:

	£
2005-06	17,850
2006-07	8,925
2007-08	8,925
2008-09	8,850
2009-10	8,850 (which may perhaps be averaged with 2010-11).

Marginal relief

As explained above, an averaging claim may not be made if the difference between the trading income figures for the two tax years concerned is less than 30% of the higher figure. However, if the difference is at least 25% of the higher figure, a form of averaging known as "marginal relief" may be claimed. The effect of marginal relief is to reduce the higher income figure (H) and increase the lower income figure (L) by an amount given by the following formula:

$$3 \times (H - L) - 0.75 \times H$$

If the difference between H and L is exactly 30% of H, this formula has the same effect as an ordinary averaging claim. If the difference between H and L is exactly 25% of H, this formula has no effect at all.

EXAMPLE 11

A farmer's trading income for 2008-09 is £12,000. What averaging claims (if any) can he make if his 2009-10 trading income is:

(a) £7,600?

(b) £8,600?

(c) £9,600?

Solution

(a) The difference between the two income figures is £4,400, which is more than 30% of £12,000 so a normal averaging claim can be made, revising both of the income figures to £9,800 (the average of £12,000 and £7,600).

(b) The difference between the two income figures is £3,400, which is between 25% and 30% of £12,000 so marginal relief may be claimed. The adjustment to each figure is:

$$3 \times (£12,000 - £8,600) - 0.75 \times £12,000 = £1,200.$$

The income for 2008-09 is reduced by £1,200 to £10,800. The income for 2009-10 is increased by £1,200 to £9,800.

(c) The difference between the two income figures is £2,400, which is less than 25% of £12,000 so no averaging is possible at all.

Summary

▸ Trading profits are charged to income tax on the current year basis. Special basis period rules apply in the opening and closing years of a business and on a change of accounting date.

▸ Overlap profits arising in the opening years of a new business are relieved either on the cessation of trade or on a change of accounting date.

▸ Further overlap profits may arise on a change of accounting date.

▸ Transitional overlap relief may be available when a business which commenced before 6 April 1994 ceases trading.

▸ In certain cases, farmers, market gardeners and creative artists may claim that the trading income of two consecutive tax years should be averaged.

Exercises

9.1   Under the *current year basis*, for which tax years would the following accounting years form the basis period?

(a)   year to 31 October 2009   (b)   year to 31 March 2010

(c)   year to 30 April 2011   (d)   year to 5 April 2011

9.2   Frank began trading on 1 July 2007. Identify the basis periods for his first four tax years if he:

(a)   chooses 30 June as his annual accounting date and prepares his first accounts for the year to 30 June 2008

(b)   chooses 30 April as his annual accounting date and prepares his first accounts for the 22 months to 30 April 2009

(c)   chooses 30 April as his annual accounting date and prepares his first accounts for the 10 months to 30 April 2008.

Also identify any overlap periods which arise in each case.

9.3   Greta commences trading on 1 January 2008 and chooses 30 June as her annual accounting date. Her first accounts are made up for the 18 months to 30 June 2009 and show an adjusted trading profit of £27,300. Compute Greta's trading income for the first three tax years and calculate the amount of any overlap profits.

9.4   Hitesh has been trading for many years, preparing accounts to 31 January each year. His last full year of trading is the year to 31 January 2009. Identify the basis periods for the last three tax years in each of the following cases:

	Date of cessation	*Final set of accounts*
(a)	31 May 2009	4 months to 31 May 2009
(b)	31 March 2010	14 months to 31 March 2010
(c)	30 April 2010	15 months to 30 April 2010

9.5   Larry began trading in 1981, preparing accounts to 31 July each year. He ceases trading on 31 July 2009 and his adjusted trading profits in the closing years are as follows:

	£
year to 31 July 2007	14,660
year to 31 July 2008	12,150
year to 31 July 2009	11,200

Adjusted trading profits for the year to 31 July 1997 were £15,900. Calculate Larry's trading income for 2009-10.

*9.6   Ivy begins trading as a market gardener on 1 January 2007, making up annual accounts to 31 December. Her adjusted trading profits in the opening years are as follows:

	£
year to 31 December 2007	7,200
year to 31 December 2008	5,010
year to 31 December 2009	4,570

(a)   Compute Ivy's trading income for the first four tax years, assuming that no averaging claims are made.

(b)   Compute Ivy's revised trading income for the first four tax years, assuming that all possible averaging claims are made.

*9.7   Ken starts trading on 1 October 2004 and chooses 30 April as his accounting date. He ceases trading on 31 January 2010 and has adjusted trading profits as follows:

	£
7 months to 30 April 2005	3,500
year to 30 April 2006	6,480
year to 30 April 2007	7,700
year to 30 April 2008	7,900
year to 30 April 2009	8,200
9 months to 31 January 2010	7,300

Compute Ken's trading income for all tax years.

*9.8   Belinda began trading on 1 March 2005 and chose 31 December as her accounting date. Her first accounts were for the period to 31 December 2005. She eventually decided to change her accounting date to 31 May and the first accounts made up to the new date were for the 17 months to 31 May 2009. The conditions necessary for a change of basis period were all satisfied. The adjusted trading profits for her first five periods of account were as follows:

	Adjusted trading profit
	£
1 March 2005 to 31 December 2005	43,700
year to 31 December 2006	52,590
year to 31 December 2007	54,300
1 January 2008 to 31 May 2009	71,060
year to 31 May 2010	68,200

Compute Belinda's trading income for 2004-05 to 2010-11 inclusive, showing the amounts of any overlap profits or overlap relief.

*9.9   Roger began trading on 1 January 2003, preparing accounts to 30 April each year. His first accounts were for the 16 months to 30 April 2004. In 2006 he decided to change his accounting date to 30 June. The first accounts made up to the new date were for the 14 months to 30 June 2006 and the conditions necessary for a change of basis period were all satisfied. Roger ceased trading on 31 May 2009. His adjusted trading profits were as follows:

	Adjusted trading profit
	£
1 January 2003 to 30 April 2004	33,920
year to 30 April 2005	29,700
1 May 2005 to 30 June 2006	33,300
year to 30 June 2007	41,600
year to 30 June 2008	37,900
1 July 2008 to 31 May 2009	23,500

Compute Roger's trading income for all tax years.

Chapter 10

Income from self-employment: Capital allowances

Introduction

Capital expenditure is generally not deductible when computing trading income but certain types of capital expenditure attract tax relief in the form of standardised depreciation allowances known as *capital allowances*. The purpose of this chapter is to define the categories of capital expenditure which are eligible for capital allowances and to explain how capital allowances are calculated.

Eligible expenditure

In order to be eligible for capital allowances, capital expenditure must usually fall into one of the following categories:

(a) plant and machinery

(b) industrial buildings and agricultural buildings

(c) patents, know-how and research and development

(d) mineral extraction, dredging and crematoria.

Each of these categories (other than the last) is considered in this chapter.

Chargeable periods

Capital allowances are calculated in respect of *chargeable periods*. For income tax purposes, each period of account generally ranks as a chargeable period and so there is usually one capital allowances computation per period of account. The only exception occurs if a period of account lasts for more than 18 months. In this case, the period of account is subdivided into one or more 12-month chargeable periods with (possibly) a short chargeable period at the end. Capital allowances are then calculated separately for each of these chargeable periods and are aggregated to give the capital allowances due for the whole period of account.

The capital allowances for a period of account are treated as a trading expense and are deducted when computing the adjusted trading profit for that period. The basis period rules which are explained in Chapter 9 are applied to the trading profit *after* deduction of capital allowances.

It is worth noting at this early stage that the chargeable periods of *companies*, which pay corporation tax on their profits rather than income tax, are determined according to a different set of rules (see Chapter 22).

EXAMPLE 1

Lee begins trading on 1 January 2009 preparing accounts to 31 December each year. His adjusted trading profit for the year to 31 December 2009 (before deduction of capital allowances) is £9,000 and capital allowances of £1,200 are claimed for that year. Compute his trading income for 2008-09 and 2009-10.

Solution

The adjusted trading profit for the year to 31 December 2009 (after deduction of capital allowances) is £7,800. Therefore trading income for the first two tax years is as follows:

Year	Basis	Basis period	Workings	Trading income £
2008-09	Actual	1/1/09 to 5/4/09	£7,800 x 3/12	1,950
2009-10	12 months to a/c date in year 2	y/e 31/12/09		7,800

Plant and machinery

Capital Allowances Act 2001 (the main statute concerned with capital allowances) does not provide a definition of the term "plant and machinery". Therefore it has been left mainly to case law to decide whether or not any given item should qualify as plant and machinery and so attract capital allowances. In *Yarmouth* v *France* (1887) it was stated that plant and machinery includes:

"whatever apparatus is used by a businessman for carrying on his business, not his stock in trade which he buys or makes for sale, but all goods and chattels, fixed or moveable, live or dead, which he keeps for permanent employment in his business".

It is fairly clear that machinery of all types, motor vehicles and items such as office furniture and equipment all qualify as plant and machinery but difficulties arise in connection with expenditure on buildings and fixtures to buildings. Much case law has been concerned with the distinction between:

(a) assets which perform an *active function* in the carrying on of the business i.e. the apparatus *with which* the business is carried on, and

(b) assets which perform a *passive function* in the carrying on of the business i.e. the setting *in which* the business is carried on.

Assets in the first of these categories qualify as plant and machinery whilst assets in the second category do not, but the distinction between the categories can be a very fine one. Some of the more important case law decisions are as follows:

Held to be plant and machinery:

(a) a dry dock built for the repair and the maintenance of ships, in *CIR* v *Barclay Curle & Co Ltd* (1969)

(b) a swimming and paddling pool, in *Cooke* v *Beach Station Caravans Ltd* (1974)

(c) a concrete grain silo, in *Schofield* v *R & H Hall Ltd* (1975)

(d) decorative screens placed in the window of a building society's offices and incorporating the name of the building society, in *Leeds Permanent Building Society* v *Proctor* (1982)

(e) moveable office partitions, in *Jarrold* v *John Good & Sons Ltd* (1962)

(f) display lighting in a store window, in *Cole Brothers Ltd* v *Phillips* (1982)

(g) light fittings, plaques and pictures on the walls of an hotel, in *IRC* v *Scottish and Newcastle Breweries Ltd* (1982)

(h) storage platforms built in a warehouse, in *Hunt* v *Henry Quick Ltd* (1992)

(i) a barrister's law books, in *Munby* v *Furlong* (1977).

Held *not* to be plant and machinery:

(a) prefabricated school buildings, in *St John's School* v *Ward* (1974)

(b) a moored ship used as a restaurant, in *Benson* v *The Yard Arm Club Ltd* (1979)

(c) a petrol station forecourt canopy, in *Dixon* v *Fitch's Garage Ltd* (1975)

(d) a football stand, in *Brown* v *Burnley Football and Athletic Co Ltd* (1980)

(e) a false ceiling built to hide electrical conduits, in *Hampton* v *Fortes Autogrill Ltd* (1979)

(f) a false ceiling, mezzanine floors, staircases, decorative floor and wall tiles all used to create ambience in a restaurant, in *Wimpey International Ltd* v *Warland* (1988).

In an attempt to clarify the distinction between buildings and plant, Capital Allowances Act 2001 provides a detailed list of types of expenditure on buildings or structures which are statutorily excluded from qualifying as plant. The Act also provides a detailed list of types of expenditure on buildings or structures which are not statutorily excluded from qualifying as plant and may therefore qualify if permitted by case law.

Expenditure statutorily deemed to be plant and machinery

By statute, expenditure of the following types always qualifies as plant and machinery:

(a)   expenditure on the thermal insulation of a building

(b)   expenditure incurred so as to comply with safety regulations at sports grounds

(c)   expenditure on assets necessary to safeguard personal security

(d)   expenditure on computer software

(e)   expenditure on building alterations, incidental to installation of plant and machinery.

Capital allowances on plant and machinery

With some exceptions (see later in this chapter) capital allowances are not calculated individually for each item of plant and machinery acquired by a business. Instead, expenditure on plant and machinery is pooled and capital allowances are calculated with reference to the value of the pool. In fact there are two pools to consider. These are:

(a)   **Main pool**. This is the pool to which most general plant and machinery is allocated (e.g. factory machines, office equipment etc.). Motor vans, motor cycles and lorries are also allocated to this pool. The situation with regard to motor cars is as follows:

   (i)   **Cars acquired before 6 April 2009**. Cars costing £12,000 or less are allocated to the main pool. Cars costing more than £12,000 are deemed "expensive" and are dealt with individually (see later in this chapter).

   (ii) **Cars acquired on or after 6 April 2009**. Cars with emissions of 160g/km or less are allocated to the main pool. Cars with higher emissions are allocated to the special rate pool (see below).

   These rules do not apply to motor cars with emissions of 110g/km or less acquired on or before 31 March 2013. Such cars are eligible for a 100% first year allowance and do not join any pool (see later in this chapter).

(b)   **Special rate pool**. This is a pool of assets arising from any or all of the following:

   (i)   the acquisition on or after 6 April 2009 of motor cars with emissions exceeding 160g/km

   (ii) the acquisition or replacement of certain "integral features" of a building; these are listed in CAA 2001 as electrical systems, water systems, heating and cooling systems, lifts, escalators/moving walkways and external solar shading

   (iii) expenditure on the thermal insulation of a building

   (iv) expenditure on assets with a working life of 25 years or more ("long-life" assets) but only if the business spends more than £100,000 a year on such assets.

The rate of capital allowances to which a business is entitled in relation to an item of plant and machinery depends upon the pool to which the item is allocated, as explained below.

Writing down allowance (WDA)

In general, a business may claim a *writing down allowance* for each of its pools of plant and machinery in each chargeable period. The procedure for computing the amount of the writing down allowance for each pool is as follows:

(a) The written down value (WDV) of the pool at the end of the previous chargeable period is brought forward.

(b) The cost of any relevant plant and machinery acquired during the chargeable period but not subject to a claim for either first year allowance or annual investment allowance (see below) is added to the pool. Items of plant and machinery owned by the trader personally and then brought into the business at a later date are treated as if purchased at their market value on that date.

   Plant and machinery acquired by hire purchase is treated as if bought for its cash price. A similar treatment applies to assets acquired under "long funding leases". In broad terms, these are finance leases with a term of more than five years.

(c) If any pool items have been disposed of during the chargeable period a disposal value is subtracted from the pool, equal to:

   (i)   sale proceeds, if the asset is sold in the open market

   (ii) market value on the date of disposal, if the asset is given away or sold for less than market value (unless the new owner will be claiming capital allowances, in which case the sale proceeds are used)

   (iii) scrap value or compensation received, if the asset is scrapped or destroyed.

But if the disposal value exceeds the original cost of the item, only the original cost is subtracted from the pool. The profit on the disposal may give rise to a capital gains tax liability (see Chapter 18).

(d) The available writing down allowance (WDA) is then calculated as a percentage of the pool balance. The applicable percentages are currently as follows:

Main pool   20% per annum
Special rate pool   10% per annum

Note that WDA is calculated at a percentage rate *per annum*. This refers to the length of the chargeable period for which capital allowances are being claimed and WDA is scaled up or down accordingly if the length of this period is not 12 months.

(e) The WDA claimed for the chargeable period is subtracted from the pool, leaving a WDV which is carried forward to the next period. This WDV will then attract WDAs in future chargeable periods (even if all the plant and machinery has now been sold).

It is not mandatory to claim the maximum WDA available for a chargeable period and a trader with low profits (or a loss) may wish to claim less than the maximum, usually to avoid wasting personal allowances. The effect of such a claim is to increase the WDVs carried forward, thus increasing the allowances available in future chargeable periods.

EXAMPLE 2

Joanne started a business on 1 August 2008, preparing accounts to 31 July each year. During the year to 31 July 2009 she bought plant and machinery as follows:

		£
1 August 2008	Bought motor car (emissions 180g/km)	8,600
27 May 2009	Bought motor car (emissions 150g/km)	10,400

During the year to 31 July 2010, she bought and sold plant and machinery as follows:

		£
31 October 2009	Sold motor car bought in August 2008	6,400
31 October 2009	Bought motor car (emissions 175g/km)	14,200

Prepare her capital allowances computation for the years to 31 July 2009 and 2010.

Solution

	Main pool £	Special rate pool £	Allowances £
y/e 31/7/09			
Additions (£8,600 + £10,400)	19,000		
WDA @ 20%	3,800		3,800
WDV c/f	15,200		
Total allowances			3,800
y/e 31/7/10			
WDV b/f	15,200		
Additions		14,200	
Disposals	(6,400)		
	8,800		
WDA @ 20%	1,760		1,760
WDA @ 10%		1,420	1,420
WDV c/f	7,040	12,780	
Total allowances			3,180

Notes:

(i) The car bought for £8,600 goes into the main pool because it was bought before 6 April 2009 and was not "expensive".

(ii) The car bought for £10,400 goes into the main pool because it was bought on or after 6 April 2009 and has emissions not exceeding 160g/km.

(iii) The car bought for £14,200 goes into the special rate pool because it was bought on or after 6 April 2009 and has emissions exceeding 160g/km.

Hybrid rate of WDA (periods spanning 6 April 2008)

The annual rate of WDA in the main pool (currently 20%) was 25% until 6 April 2008. This means that a special rule is required to deal with chargeable periods which span that date. This rule states that WDA in such periods should be calculated at a "hybrid rate" which is calculated as follows:

$$\text{Main pool hybrid rate} = (25 \times \frac{\text{BRD}}{\text{CP}}) + (20 \times \frac{\text{ARD}}{\text{CP}})$$

where: BRD is the number of days in the chargeable period before 6 April 2008

ARD is the number of days in the chargeable period on or after 6 April 2008

CP is the number of days in the chargeable period.

If a hybrid rate is a figure with more than 2 decimal places, it is rounded up to the nearest second decimal place.

EXAMPLE 3

A trader prepares accounts to 31 December each year. Calculate the hybrid rate of WDA available in the main pool for the year to 31 December 2008.

Solution

The hybrid rate in the main pool is (25 x 96/366) + (20 x 270/366) = 21.32%.

Small pools of plant and machinery

If the balance in the main pool or in the special rate pool before calculating writing down allowance is £1,000 or less, the business concerned may claim a WDA of any amount up to the amount of that balance. This rule means that it is not necessary for businesses to carry forward very small pool balances for many years, claiming ever diminishing WDAs in each chargeable period.

Businesses with a balance of £1,000 or less in the main pool or special rate pool can claim a WDA of less than the full balance if they so wish.

Annual investment allowance (AIA)

The first £50,000 per annum of expenditure on plant and machinery (other than motor cars) qualifies for a 100% annual investment allowance (AIA). The availability of this allowance greatly simplifies the capital allowances computations of many smaller businesses whose annual expenditure on general plant and machinery does not exceed £50,000. The main features of the AIA are as follows:

(a) If the qualifying expenditure of a business in a 12-month chargeable period does not exceed £50,000, a 100% AIA may be claimed in relation to all of that expenditure. If the qualifying expenditure exceeds £50,000, the expenditure beyond £50,000 enters either the main pool or the special rate pool and is eligible for WDAs (or possibly a first year allowance). First year allowances are explained later in this chapter.

(b) As mentioned above, AIA is not available in relation to motor cars.

(c) A business is free to allocate the AIA between items of qualifying expenditure in any way that it sees fit. For example, a business which invests £30,000 in main pool items and £40,000 in special rate pool items in a 12-month period might allocate £10,000 of the AIA to the main pool expenditure and the remaining £40,000 to the special rate pool expenditure. This would maximise allowances for the period, since the main pool attracts WDA at 20% whilst the special rate pool attracts WDA at only 10%. A business which spends no more than £50,000 a year on special rate items might use this approach to avoid having a special rate pool at all. However, a special rate pool is unavoidable if the business acquires cars with emissions exceeding 160g/km, since cars are not eligible for the AIA.

(d) The maximum AIA of £50,000 is increased or reduced proportionately for chargeable periods of more or less than 12 months.

(e) A business is not required to claim the full AIA to which it is entitled. Any qualifying expenditure which is not the subject of a claim for AIA enters the appropriate pool and is eligible for WDAs (or possibly a first year allowance).

(f) If a person controls more than one business, these businesses are entitled to only one AIA between them if they are "related". For this purpose, businesses are deemed to be related if they are conducted from shared premises or if their activities are within the same EU classification. This is an anti-avoidance rule, aimed at persons who might consider splitting a single business into two or more separate businesses, in the hope of qualifying for more than one AIA.

Periods spanning 6 April 2008

AIA was introduced on 6 April 2008. If a chargeable period spans 6 April 2008, the maximum allowance is calculated as if the period began on 6 April 2008 and ended at the end of the period. For example, the maximum AIA for a chargeable period comprising the year to 31 December 2008 would be 9/12ths of £50,000 = £37,500.

First year allowance (FYA)

At various times in the past, expenditure on general plant and machinery has qualified for a first year allowance, usually of 40% or 50%. First year allowances (FYAs) are intended to encourage businesses to invest in items of plant and machinery by providing increased allowances in the period in which the items are acquired. However, the introduction of the 100% annual investment allowance on 6 April 2008 meant that FYAs generally ceased to be available for expenditure incurred on or after that date.

In an attempt to further encourage investment in plant and machinery, Finance Act 2009 has re-introduced FYA in relation to expenditure incurred between 6 April 2009 and 5 April 2010. The main features of this "temporary" FYA are as follows:

(a) Expenditure on plant and machinery allocated to the main pool and in excess of the £50,000 AIA limit is eligible for a 40% FYA, so long as the expenditure is incurred between 6 April 2009 and 5 April 2010 inclusive.

(b) If FYA is claimed in relation to an item of plant and machinery, it is given *instead* of WDA in the chargeable period in which the item is acquired. The balance of the asset's cost then enters the pool (after WDA for that period has been calculated) and is eligible for WDAs in subsequent chargeable periods.

(c) It is not mandatory to claim FYA on the full amount of the qualifying expenditure. Any part of this expenditure on which FYA is not claimed is added into the pool and is immediately eligible for WDAs.

(d) Unlike WDA and AIA, FYA is not scaled up or down in accordance with the length of the chargeable period in which it is being given.

(e) The temporary FYA is not available in relation to expenditure on motor cars, plant and machinery allocated to the special rate pool or assets acquired for leasing.

100% FYAs

A first year allowance of 100% is available in relation to certain classes of expenditure on plant and machinery. The main 100% FYAs are as follows:

(a) Expenditure on a low emission motor car is eligible for a 100% FYA so long as the expenditure is incurred on or before 31 March 2013. The current definition of a low emission car for this purpose is one with an emission rating not exceeding 110g/km.

(b) Expenditure on plant and machinery for use in the refuelling of vehicles with natural gas, biogas or hydrogen fuel is eligible for a 100% FYA so long as the expenditure is incurred on or before 31 March 2013.

(c) Expenditure incurred on certain classes of energy-saving and water-efficient plant and machinery also qualifies for a 100% FYA.

EXAMPLE 4

(a)   Sharon started a business on 1 January 2009 and chose 31 March as her accounting date. Her first accounts covered the period from 1 January 2009 to 31 March 2010. During this period she bought plant and machinery as follows:

		£
1 January 2009	Bought plant	3,000
19 May 2009	Bought car (emissions 142g/km))	7,840
17 June 2009	Bought plant	6,000

She claims maximum capital allowances in all chargeable periods. Prepare a capital allowances computation for the 15 months to 31 March 2010.

(b)   Sharon's purchases and sales of plant and machinery during the year to 31 March 2011 are:

		£
1 April 2010	Bought plant	5,990
30 June 2010	Sold plant (original cost £3,500 on 17/6/09)	2,630

Prepare a capital allowances computation for the year to 31 March 2011.

Solution

(a)

		Main pool £	Allowances £
1/1/09 - 31/3/10			
Additions not eligible for AIA or FYA		7,840	
WDA @ 20% x 15/12		1,960	1,960
		5,880	
Additions qualifying for AIA	9,000		
AIA @ 100%	9,000	-	9,000
WDV c/f		5,880	
Total allowances			10,960

Notes:

(i)   The motor car is allocated to the main pool since it has emissions not exceeding 160g/km. Cars are not eligible for AIA or the temporary FYA.

(ii)   WDA is scaled up by 15/12 for a 15-month period.

(iii)   The maximum AIA for a 15-month period is £62,500 (£50,000 x 15/12). Sharon's AIA of £9,000 is well within this maximum.

(iv)   Total capital allowances for the period are £10,960.

(b)		Main pool £	Allowances £
y/e 31/3/11			
WDV b/f		5,880	
Disposals		(2,630)	
		3,250	
WDA @ 20%		650	650
		2,600	
Additions eligible for AIA	5,990		
AIA @ 100%	5,990	-	5,990
WDV c/f		2,600	
Total allowances			6,640

Notes:

(i) The maximum AIA for a 12-month period is £50,000. Sharon's AIA of £5,990 is well within this maximum.

(ii) Total capital allowances for the year are £6,640.

EXAMPLE 5

Ian is self-employed and prepares accounts to 31 December each year. The written down value of his main pool of plant and machinery after deducting capital allowances for the year to 31 December 2008 was £116,250. There was no special rate pool. Purchases and sales of plant and machinery for the year to 31 December 2009 were as follows:

		£
3 January 2009	Bought plant	72,000
5 May 2009	Bought car (emissions 105g/km)	8,400
17 July 2009	Bought plant	25,800
25 August 2009	Sold plant (bought in 2008 for £1,000)	1,100
31 October 2009	Bought car (emissions 163g/km)	13,500

Prepare a capital allowances computation for the year to 31 December 2009, assuming that maximum allowances are claimed.

Solution

		Main pool	Special rate pool	Allowances
		£	£	£
y/e 31/12/09				
WDV b/f		116,250		
Additions not eligible for AIA or FYA		22,000	13,500	
Disposal		(1,000)		
		137,250		
WDA @ 20%		27,450		27,450
WDA @ 10%			1,350	1,350
		109,800	12,150	
Additions eligible for AIA	50,000			
AIA @ 100%	50,000	-		50,000
Additions eligible for 40% FYA	25,800			
FYA @ 40%	10,320	15,480		10,320
Additions eligible for 100% FYA	8,400			
FYA @ 100%	8,400	-		8,400
WDV c/f		125,280	12,150	
Total allowances				97,520

Notes:

(i) Maximum AIA for the year is £50,000. This could be allocated in any way between the expenditure of £72,000 in January 2009 and the expenditure of £25,800 in July 2009. Capital allowances are maximised if the AIA is allocated to the expenditure in January, since this is not eligible for the 40% FYA. The expenditure in July is incurred between 6 April 2009 and 5 April 2010 and so qualifies for the 40% FYA.

(ii) Setting the AIA against the expenditure of £72,000 leaves a balance of £22,000 which is not eligible for AIA or FYA.

(iii) The disposal value of the plant sold in August 2009 is restricted to original cost.

(iv) The car bought in May 2009 has emissions not exceeding 110g/km and is therefore eligible for a 100% FYA.

(v) The car bought in October 2009 has emissions exceeding 160g/km and is allocated to the special rate pool.

Balancing allowances and charges

If the disposal value of the plant and machinery disposed of during a chargeable period exceeds the balance of expenditure in the relevant pool before disposals are deducted, this is evidence that the capital allowances given to date exceed the depreciation which has actually occurred. In these circumstances, the written down value of the pool is set to zero and a *balancing charge* is made, equal to the amount of the excess. A balancing charge is a negative capital allowance which is *added* to trading profits for tax purposes.

It may be possible to avoid (or reduce) this balancing charge by not claiming AIA or FYA in relation to items acquired during the period. Such items become eligible for WDA in the period and are added to the pool before deducting disposal values, thus reducing the likelihood of a balancing charge. A similar effect might be achieved by not making a de-pooling election in relation to a short-life asset acquired during the period (see below).

Balancing adjustments may also be required when a business ceases trading (see later in this chapter) or when a non-pooled asset is disposed of. Non-pooled assets are assets which are treated individually for capital allowances purposes (see below). When a non-pooled asset is disposed of, a balancing adjustment is required to ensure that the total capital allowances granted in respect of the asset are exactly equal to its depreciation. If the asset's disposal value exceeds its WDV brought forward, a *balancing charge* is made, equal to the excess. If WDV brought forward exceeds disposal value, a *balancing allowance* is given, equal to the excess.

Non-pooled assets

Certain items of plant and machinery are not brought into the main pool or the special rate pool. Instead, these items are treated individually for capital allowances purposes, each item having its own "single asset pool". The items in question are:

(a) expensive motor cars acquired before 6 April 2009

(b) assets with some private use

(c) short-life assets.

The treatment of each of these items is explained below.

Expensive motor cars

Motor cars acquired before 6 April 2009 and costing more than £12,000 are dealt with on an individual basis. WDA is calculated at an annual rate of 20%, subject to a maximum of £3,000 per car per annum. This rule does not apply to low-emission motor cars which qualify for the 100% FYA (see earlier).

Any unrelieved expenditure remaining in relation to an expensive car will be transferred to the main pool at the beginning of the first chargeable period starting on or after 6 April 2014. But this transfer will not occur if there is any private use of the car (see below).

EXAMPLE 6

Bianca began trading on 1 September 2008. Her first accounts covered the 16 months to 31 December 2009 and she prepared accounts to 31 December thereafter. On 21 October 2008 she bought a motor car (not eligible for the 100% FYA) costing £19,600. Compute the capital allowances available on this car for the first three chargeable periods.

Solution

	£
1/9/08 - 31/12/09	
Addition	19,600
WDA (£19,600 @ 20% = £3,920, restricted to £3,000) x 16/12	4,000
WDV c/f	15,600
y/e 31/12/10	
WDA (£15,600 @ 20% = £3,120, restricted to £3,000)	3,000
WDV c/f	12,600
y/e 31/12/11	
WDA @ 20% (no restriction necessary)	2,520
WDV c/f	10,080

Assets with some private use

Any asset which is used partly for private purposes by the owner of a business is dealt with in a single asset pool. Capital allowances in relation to the asset are calculated in the usual way, with AIA or FYA as appropriate and WDAs at either 20% or 10% (depending on the type of asset concerned). But only the business proportion of the allowances which have been calculated may then be claimed.

Note that capital allowances are available in full on assets used for private purposes by an *employee* of the business, but the employee may then be assessed to income tax on a benefit in kind (see Chapter 7).

EXAMPLE 7

Allan prepares accounts to 31 October. In August 2007 he bought an Audi motor car for £23,000. His acquisitions and disposals of plant and machinery in the years to 31 October 2009 and 2010 included the following:

		£
12 June 2009	Bought computer system (private use 25%)	2,500
27 August 2010	Sold Audi motor car	14,600
27 August 2010	Bought BMW motor car (emissions 181g/km)	24,400

Private use of both cars was agreed to be 30%. Compute the capital allowances available in relation to these items for the years to 31 October 2009 and 2010, assuming that Allan's entitlement to AIA in both years has been fully used against other assets.

Solution

	Audi (30% p.u.)	Computer (25% p.u.)	BMW (30% p.u.)		Allces
	£	£	£		£
y/e 31/10/09					
WDV b/f (£23,000 - £3,000 - £3,000)	17,000				
WDA (restricted)	3,000			x 70%	2,100
Addition eligible for 40% FYA		2,500			
FYA @ 40%		1,000		x 75%	750
WDV c/f	14,000	1,500			
Total allowances					2,850
y/e 31/10/10					
Addition			24,400		
Disposal	(14,600)				
Balancing charge	(600)			x 70%	(420)
WDA @ 20%		300		x 75%	225
WDA @ 10%			2,440	x 70%	1,708
WDV c/f		1,200	21,960		
Total allowances					1,513

Notes:

(i)   The Audi motor car was acquired in the year to 31 October 2007. Maximum WDAs of £3,000 would have been deducted in that year and in the following year.

(ii) The computer was acquired between 6 April 2009 and 5 April 2010 and is eligible for the temporary FYA of 40%.

(iii) The BMW motor car has emissions which exceed 160g/km and so WDAs on this car are calculated at 10% per annum.

Short-life assets

A trader may elect that an asset (other than a car) which would normally join the main pool should instead be treated as a "short-life asset". This has the following consequences:

(a)   The asset is treated on an individual basis. For this reason, the election is sometimes known as a "de-pooling" election.

(b)   If the asset is not disposed of within four years of the end of the chargeable period in which it is acquired, it joins the main pool at its written down value and the short-life election will have had no effect.

(c)   If the asset is disposed of within the four-year period, a balancing allowance will be given (or a balancing charge will be made).

Making a short-life election in relation to an asset which is likely to be sold for less than its WDV within four years will generate a balancing allowance on disposal, so ensuring that capital allowances are given as quickly as possible. There is (of course) no point in making such an election if a 100% AIA is available in relation to the asset.

A short-life election in relation to expenditure incurred during a chargeable period must be made by 31 January in the second tax year following the tax year in which the chargeable period ends.

EXAMPLE 8

Anita starts trading on 1 July 2009, preparing accounts to 30 June each year. On 1 July 2009 she buys general plant costing £70,000 and a machine costing £40,000. She sells the machine on 31 May 2012 for £10,000. Compute capital allowances for the first three chargeable periods if:

(a) she does not make a short-life election with regard to the machine

(b) she does make the short-life election, assuming that her AIA for the year to 30 June 2010 is set against the £70,000 expenditure on general plant.

Solution

(a) Total expenditure in the year to 30 June 2010 is £110,000, all of which is dealt with in the main pool. Deducting AIA (£50,000) leaves £60,000 which is eligible for FYA at 40% (£24,000). Total allowances for the year are £74,000. WDV c/f is £36,000.

In the year to 30 June 2011, WDA at 20% is £7,200. WDV c/f is £28,800.

In the year to 30 June 2012, the disposal proceeds of £10,000 are deducted from the WDV b/f of £28,800, leaving £18,800. WDA at 20% is £3,760. WDV c/f is £15,040.

(b) Main pool expenditure is £70,000. Deducting AIA (£50,000) leaves £20,000 which is eligible for FYA at 40% (£8,000). WDV c/f is £12,000. The short-life expenditure of £40,000 is dealt with separately. This is eligible for FYA at 40% (£16,000) leaving a WDV c/f of £24,000. Total allowances for the year are £74,000.

In the year to 30 June 2011, WDA at 20% in the main pool is £2,400 and WDV c/f is £9,600. WDA at 20% on the short-life asset is £4,800 and WDV c/f is £19,200. Total allowances for the year are £7,200.

In the year to 30 June 2012, WDA at 20% in the main pool is £1,920 and WDV c/f is £7,680. There is a balancing allowance of £9,200 (£19,200 − £10,000) in relation to the short-life asset. Total allowances for the year are £11,120.

The short-life election makes no difference to the total allowances for the years to 30 June 2010 (£74,000) and 2011 (£7,200). But total allowances for the year to 30 June 2012 are increased by £7,360 (£11,120 − £3,760) if the short-life election is made. However, this is at the expense of reducing WDVs c/f by the same amount and so reducing future capital allowances.

Allowances on cessation of trade

When a business ceases trading and all of the plant and machinery is disposed of, capital allowances for the final chargeable period are computed as follows:

(a) Any items acquired in the final period are added into the relevant pool.

(b) No WDA, FYA or AIA is given in the final chargeable period.

(c) The disposal value of each pool (including single asset pools) is subtracted from the balance of unrelieved expenditure, giving rise to balancing allowances or balancing charges. Assets taken over personally by the trader are treated as if sold for their market value on the date they are taken over.

The balancing adjustments normally made on a cessation of trade can be avoided if the business is taken over by a connected person (e.g. the trader's spouse, civil partner or other relative) so long as an election to this effect is made by both parties. In this case, the final chargeable period is treated in exactly the same way as any other chargeable period and the assets are then transferred to the new owner at their WDVs.

EXAMPLE 9

Jake has been trading for many years, preparing accounts to 30 September each year. The written down value of his plant and machinery at 30 September 2008 was:

	£
Main pool	11,350
Motor car (20% private use by Jake)	13,200

Jake bought plant costing £1,150 in October 2008. This was his only transaction in plant and machinery until 30 June 2009, when he ceased trading. On that date, all of the items in his main pool were sold for a total of £12,850 (all items sold for less than cost) and his car was sold for £12,000. Prepare Jake's capital allowances computation for the 9 months to 30 June 2009.

Solution

	Main pool	Motor car (20% private)	Allowances
	£	£	£
1/10/08 - 30/6/09			
WDV b/f	11,350	13,200	
Additions	1,150		
	12,500		
Disposals	(12,850)	(12,000)	
Balancing allowance/(charge)	(350)	1,200 x 80% = 960	610

Industrial buildings allowances

Capital allowances known as *industrial buildings allowances* (IBAs) have been available for many years in relation to expenditure on industrial buildings and certain hotels. These allowances will cease to exist as from 6 April 2011, but they may still be claimed until that date. The term "industrial buildings" includes buildings such as:

(a) factories and ancillary buildings associated with factories (e.g. warehouses for the storage of raw materials or finished goods)

(b) staff welfare buildings provided for the welfare of those working in factories and ancillary buildings (e.g. canteens)

(c) sports pavilions provided for the welfare of employees in *any* trade.

The term does *not* include dwellings, shops, showrooms or offices (other than drawing offices attached to an industrial building). If a building is used partly as a qualifying industrial building and partly for non-qualifying purposes, the whole building will attract IBAs so long as the cost of the non-qualifying part does not exceed 25% of the building's total cost. Otherwise, only the qualifying part of the building attracts IBAs.

Hotels

IBAs may be claimed in relation to an hotel which satisfies the following conditions:

(a) It offers sleeping accommodation consisting of at least ten "letting bedrooms" which are available to the general public and are not normally occupied by the same person for more than one month.

(b) It offers ancillary services including (at least) breakfast, evening meals, cleaning of rooms and bed-making.

(c) It is open for at least four months between April and October.

Accommodation for hotel staff is qualifying expenditure but accommodation for the proprietor's own use is not. For the remainder of this chapter, references to industrial buildings should be taken to include qualifying hotels.

Qualifying expenditure

The IBAs available in relation to an industrial building are based on the "qualifying expenditure" of the person who first uses the building. This is either:

(a) the cost of constructing the building, if constructed by the user

(b) the price paid for the building, if bought unused from a builder

(c) the lower of the price paid for the building and the building's construction cost, if bought unused from someone other than a builder.

In all cases, the cost of land is excluded but the costs of land preparation are allowed, as are professional fees such as those paid to an architect.

EXAMPLE 10

(a) Smith (who does not trade as a builder) buys a building site for £100,000 and then incurs the following costs on the erection of an industrial building on that site:

	£
Levelling the site and preparing foundations	95,000
Architect's fees	50,000
Building costs	650,000

What is Smith's qualifying expenditure for IBAs purposes?

(b) If the building is sold unused to Brown for £1,000,000 (including £120,000 for the land), what is Brown's qualifying expenditure?

(c) If (instead of buying Smith's building) Brown buys a similar unused building for the same price from a firm of builders, what is Brown's qualifying expenditure?

Solution

(a) The cost of construction (excluding land) amounts to £795,000. This is Smith's qualifying expenditure.

(b) Brown's qualifying expenditure is also £795,000 (the lower of the price paid by Brown and the building's construction cost).

(c) If Brown purchases an industrial building from a firm of builders, the price paid to the builder is fully eligible for IBAs. So Brown's qualifying expenditure is £1,000,000 less the part of that price which is allocated to the land.

Writing down allowance

A *writing down allowance* (WDA) is available in relation to an industrial building so long as the building is in industrial use at the end of the chargeable period in which IBAs are claimed. Until fairly recently, this WDA was calculated as 4% of the qualifying expenditure, but the rate of WDA is being reduced as IBAs are gradually phased out. Note that:

(a) WDA is available to the holder of the "relevant interest" in a building. This is the interest of the person who first acquired the building (usually the freehold) and is transferred to the new owner when the building is sold.

(b) The relevant interest is *not* transferred when a building is leased, so that WDA is normally given to the landlord of a leased building, not the tenant. However, the landlord and tenant may jointly elect that the grant of a long lease (a lease of more than 50 years) should be treated as a sale for capital allowances purposes, in which case WDA will be given to the tenant.

(c) Industrial buildings are treated on an individual basis and are not pooled.

(d) The annual rate of WDA was 4% for 2007-08 and earlier years. This was reduced to 3% for 2008-09 and reduces again to 2% for 2009-10 and 1% for 2010-11. IBAs will cease entirely as from 6 April 2011. If a chargeable period falls into more than one tax year, the amount of WDA available for that period is calculated according to the number of days in the period that fall into each tax year.

(e) WDA is calculated on the straight line basis (as opposed to the reducing balance basis used for plant and machinery) and is given in proportion to the length of the chargeable period for which allowances are claimed.

(f) A building has a "tax life" of 25 years, as from the date on which it is first used for any purpose. If a building is used initially for non-industrial purposes and is put to industrial use later, WDA may be claimed for the remainder of its tax life. The period between the date of first use and the date of first industrial use is covered by "notional allowances" (see below).

EXAMPLE 11

Brian began trading on 1 April 2007, preparing accounts annually to 31 December. His first accounts were for the nine months to 31 December 2007. On 12 May 2007, he bought a new factory building for £250,000 (excluding the cost of land) and immediately put the building to industrial use.

Calculate the IBAs available for Brian's first four chargeable periods.

Solution

(i) IBAs for the nine months to 31 December 2007 are £7,500 (4% of £250,000 x 9/12).

(ii) IBAs for the year to 31 December 2008 are (4% of £250,000 x 96/366) + (3% of £250,000 x 270/366) = £8,156.

(iii) IBAs for the year to 31 December 2009 are (3% of £250,000 x 95/365) + (2% of £250,000 x 270/365) = £5,651.

(iv) IBAs for the year to 31 December 2010 are (2% of £250,000 x 95/365) + (1% of £250,000 x 270/365) = £3,151.

Non-industrial use

A building which is not in industrial use at the end of a chargeable period will either be disused or will be in use for a non-industrial purpose. IBAs may be claimed during a period of temporary disuse following a period of industrial use but IBAs may *not* be claimed if a building is being used for a non-industrial purpose.

A "notional WDA" is calculated for a building which is in non-industrial use at the end of a chargeable period and this notional WDA is deducted from the WDV of the building in the usual way. However, notional WDAs are *not* available to the trader.

EXAMPLE 12

Carole prepares annual accounts to 5 April. On 1 July 2005, she buys a new building for £200,000 (excluding the cost of land) and immediately puts it to industrial use. This use continues until 1 October 2008, when she starts using the building for a non-industrial purpose. Industrial use recommences on 1 March 2010. Show the capital allowances computation for all years up to and including the year ending 5 April 2010.

Solution

	Building £	Allowances £
y/e 5/4/06, 07 & 08		
Cost	200,000	
WDA @ 4% of £200,000 for 3 years	24,000	24,000
WDV c/f	176,000	
y/e 5/4/09		
Notional WDA @ 3% of £200,000	6,000	
WDV c/f	170,000	
y/e 5/4/10		
WDA @ 2% of £200,000	4,000	4,000
WDV c/f	166,000	

Note: The notional WDA of £6,000 is not available to Carole.

Sale of an industrial building

If an industrial building is sold during its 25-year tax life, then:

(a) No WDA is available to the seller of the building in the final chargeable period and no balancing adjustments are made.

(b) The buyer of the building may then claim an annual WDA, which is calculated by dividing the building's "residue of expenditure" by the number of years remaining of its tax life and then multiplying this amount by a percentage (see below). Residue of expenditure is equal to the WDV of the building prior to the sale.

(c) The percentage referred to in (b) above is as follows:

Tax year	Percentage
2007-08 and earlier years	100%
2008-09	75%
2009-10	50%
2010-11	25%
2011-12 and later years	0%

(d) If a chargeable period falls wholly into a tax year, the percentage used is taken from the above table. Chargeable periods that fall into more than one tax year are apportioned between the years and the available WDA is calculated according to the number of days in the period that fall into each tax year.

If an industrial building is sold after the expiry of its tax life, no balancing adjustments are made and the second-hand buyer is unable to claim any WDA.

EXAMPLE 13

Christopher and Dean both prepare accounts to 31 December each year. On 21 February 2005, Christopher bought a new building for £150,000 (excluding land) and started using it immediately for an industrial purpose. He sold the building to Dean on 21 August 2008.

Calculate the IBAs available to Christopher and to Dean for all chargeable periods.

Solution

Christopher may claim a WDA of £6,000 (4% x £150,000) for each of the three years to 31 December 2007. This leaves a residue of expenditure of £132,000. There are 21.5 years left of the building's tax life on the date of the sale, so Dean's WDA each year is the appropriate percentage of £132,000/21.5 = £6,140. His WDAs are as follows:

year to 31/12/08: (100% x £6,140 x 96/366) + (75% x £6,140 x 270/366) = £5,008

year to 31/12/09: (75% x £6,140 x 95/365) + (50% x £6,140 x 270/365) = £3,470

year to 31/12/10: (50% x £6,140 x 95/365) + (25% x £6,140 x 270/365) = £1,935

year to 31/12/11: (25% x £6,140 x 95/365) = £400.

Commercial buildings in enterprise zones

Enterprise zone allowances (EZAs) are generally available in relation to any commercial building constructed in an enterprise zone. An initial allowance of 100% may be claimed for the chargeable period in which the expenditure is incurred. If the full allowance is not claimed, the remaining expenditure is eligible for an annual WDA of 25%, calculated on the straight-line basis on the cost of the building and beginning when the building is first brought into use. EZAs are to be withdrawn as from April 2011 but are not subject to the phasing-out rules which apply to industrial buildings allowances.

Business premises renovation allowance

A 100% allowance known as the Business Premises Renovation Allowance (BPRA) is available for capital expenditure on the renovation of certain business premises. In order to qualify for BPRA, the premises must be located in a disadvantaged area and must have been vacant for at least a year.

BPRA is available in relation to qualifying expenditure incurred on or after 11 April 2007. The scheme will last for at least five years.

Agricultural buildings allowances

Capital allowances known as *agricultural buildings allowances* (ABAs) have been available for many years in relation to expenditure on the construction of agricultural buildings. These allowances will cease to exist as from 6 April 2011, but they may still be claimed until that date. The term "agricultural buildings" includes farmhouses, farm buildings, fences and drainage works. However, no more than one-third of the expenditure on a farmhouse is eligible for ABAs. The cost of land is always excluded.

The ABAs system is similar to the IBAs system. ABA's begin in the chargeable period in which the qualifying expenditure is incurred and are calculated at the same percentage rates as IBAs. However, the 25-year tax life of an agricultural building begins on the first day of the chargeable period in which ABAs are first given (not the first day of use).

Sale of an agricultural building

If an agricultural building is sold during its 25-year tax life, the buyer simply takes over the right to the ABAs that the seller would have received. The procedure is as follows:

(a) No balancing adjustments are made on the sale and the price paid by the second-hand buyer is totally ignored.

(b) For the chargeable period in which the sale occurs, the vendor receives WDA from the start of the period to the date of the sale.

(c) For the chargeable period in which the purchase occurs, the buyer receives WDA from the date of purchase to the end of the period. This WDA is based upon the building's original cost, not the second-hand price paid by the buyer.

(d) In subsequent chargeable periods, the buyer continues to receive a WDA based upon the building's original cost.

EXAMPLE 14

Bill trades as a farmer, preparing accounts to 31 December each year. On 1 December 2005 he constructed a barn at a cost of £50,000 (excluding land). On 1 August 2007 he sold the barn to Ben for £47,000 (excluding land). Ben also trades as a farmer, preparing accounts to 5 April each year.

Calculate the ABAs available to Bill. Also calculate the ABAs available to Ben for the years to 5 April 2008, 2009 and 2010. Perform all calculations to the nearest month.

Solution

Bill's allowances are: £

y/e 31/12/05	£50,000 x 4%	2,000
y/e 31/12/06	£50,000 x 4%	2,000
y/e 31/12/07	£50,000 x 4% x 7/12	1,167

Ben's allowances are: £

y/e 5/4/08	£50,000 x 4% x 8/12	1,333
y/e 5/4/09	£50,000 x 3%	1,500
y/e 5/4/10	£50,000 x 2%	1,000

Notes:

(a) Bill's sale is made after seven months of the chargeable period have elapsed, so his final WDA is calculated at 7/12ths of 4%.

(b) Ben's purchase is made with eight months of the chargeable period remaining, so his first WDA is calculated at 8/12ths of 4%. The rate of WDA then falls to 3% for the year to 5 April 2009 and to 2% for the year to 5 April 2010.

(c) The price paid by Ben (£47,000) is ignored.

Miscellaneous capital allowances

Capital allowances are available in relation to some miscellaneous categories of capital expenditure. These include expenditure on patent rights, know-how and research and development.

Patent rights

The treatment of purchased patent rights acquired for trade purposes is as follows:

(a) Patent rights are pooled together. There is a separate patent rights pool for each trade carried on by the taxpayer. Patent rights pools are adjusted in each chargeable period for acquisitions and disposals and then WDA is calculated at 25% per annum on the reducing balance.

(b) WDA is proportionately increased or decreased if the chargeable period is of more than 12 months or less than 12 months.

(c) As with plant and machinery, disposal value is restricted to original cost.

(d) If the disposal value of a patent exceeds the balance of unrelieved expenditure in the pool, a balancing charge is made and the pool value is set to zero.

(e) On cessation of trade, there will be a balancing allowance if the patents are sold for less than the balance of unrelieved expenditure in the pool. There will be a balancing charge if the patents are sold for more than the balance of unrelieved expenditure.

Know-how

"Know-how" is defined as industrial information and techniques of use in either:

(a)   manufacturing or the processing of goods or materials

(b)   the working of mineral deposits

(c)   agricultural, fishing or forestry operations.

All expenditure on know-how is pooled and capital allowances are calculated in much the same way as for patent rights. However, if know-how is sold for more than original cost, the disposal value used in the capital allowances computation is the *full sale proceeds*. Depending upon the balance of unrelieved expenditure in the pool prior to the disposal, this will either create a balancing charge or restrict the value of subsequent WDAs. In either case, the profit made on the disposal is (in effect) treated as trading income.

Research and development

Capital expenditure on research and development related to the claimant's trade attracts a first year allowance of 100%. Any proceeds subsequently received on the disposal of a research and development asset are treated as a trading receipt.

Summary

▶   Capital allowances are granted for chargeable periods. For income tax purposes, each period of account usually ranks as a chargeable period, but periods of account of more than 18 months are divided into two or more chargeable periods.

▶   In order to qualify as plant and machinery, an asset must perform an active function in the trade, not merely provide a setting in which the trade is carried on.

▶   WDAs on plant and machinery are granted at 20% per annum in the main pool and at 10% per annum in the special rate pool.

▶   The first £50,000 per annum of expenditure on plant and machinery (other than cars) is eligible for a 100% AIA. FYA at 40% is available in relation to expenditure which is allocated to the main pool (other than cars) but which is not covered by the AIA, so long as that expenditure is incurred between 6 April 2009 and 5 April 2010.

▶   As from 6 April 2009, cars with emissions in excess of 160g/km are allocated to the special rate pool. Cars with lower emissions are generally allocated to the main pool but cars with emissions not exceeding 110g/km attract a 100% FYA.

▶   Expensive cars acquired before 6 April 2009, assets with private use and short-life assets are allocated to single asset pools.

▶   Capital allowances are available in relation to industrial buildings and agricultural buildings but these allowances will cease to exist as from 6 April 2011.

▶   Capital allowances are also available in relation to patent rights, know-how and research and development expenditure.

Exercises

It should be assumed in all of these exercises that maximum capital allowances are claimed.

10.1 Maurice prepares accounts to 31 March each year. The written down value of his main pool at 31 March 2009 was £10,300. There was no special rate pool. His purchases and sales of plant and machinery during the year to 31 March 2010 were as follows:

		£
1 April 2009	Bought plant	600
11 April 2009	Sold machinery (original cost £4,000 in 2008)	4,200
11 July 2009	Bought motor car (emissions 144g/km)	8,000
1 November 2009	Bought machinery	400
12 January 2010	Sold equipment (original cost £7,000 in 2006)	3,000

Compute the capital allowances which may be claimed for the year to 31 March 2010, assuming no private use of any of the assets.

10.2 Laura started a business on 1 July 2009. Her adjusted trading profit for the year to 30 June 2010 (before deduction of capital allowances) was £89,700. Her purchases of plant and machinery during the year were as follows:

		£
1 July 2009	Bought machinery	76,400
1 July 2009	Bought motor car (emissions 178g/km)	15,000
1 August 2009	Bought machinery	4,000
31 May 2010	Bought machinery	6,600

Compute her trading income for the first two tax years, assuming 40% private use of the car by Laura. Also compute the amount of any overlap profits.

10.3 Norma prepares accounts to 31 December each year. The written down value of her plant and machinery at 31 December 2008 was as follows:

	£
Main pool	178,400
Toyota motor car (50% private use by Norma)	18,200

Her purchases and sales of plant and machinery during the year to 31 December 2009 were as follows:

		£
17 April 2009	Bought plant	82,800
1 May 2009	Sold Toyota motor car	15,000
1 May 2009	Bought Saab motor car (emissions 150g/km,)	29,300
30 June 2009	Bought motor van	14,500
12 October 2009	Bought Ford motor car (emissions 105g/km)	11,600
3 November 2009	Bought Peugeot motor car (emissions 166g/km)	13,700
1 December 2009	Sold plant (original cost £10,000)	1,600

There was 50% private use (by Norma) of the Toyota and Saab motor cars. There was no private use of any of the other items. Prepare a capital allowances computation for the year to 31 December 2009.

10.4   Oliver prepares accounts to 5 April each year. On 1 August 2007 he acquired a brand new factory for £100,000 and put the factory to immediate industrial use. The cost of £100,000 included land of £20,000 and general offices of £22,500. Calculate the IBAs available for the years to 5 April 2008, 2009 and 2010.

10.5   Francesco has traded for many years, preparing accounts to 31 December each year. On 1 February 2001 he bought a new workshop for £56,000 (including land £11,000). He began using the workshop on 1 February 2001 and it was in continuous industrial use until 1 August 2008, when he sold it to Maria for £45,000 (including land £15,000). Maria immediately began to use the workshop for an industrial purpose.

Maria began trading on 1 July 2008 and chose 5 April as her annual accounting date. Her first accounts covered the period to 5 April 2009.

(a)   Compute the IBAs available to Francesco for all affected years.

(b)   Compute the IBAs available to Maria for the period from 1 July 2008 to 5 April 2009 and for the year to 5 April 2010.

10.6   Giles has traded as a farmer for many years, preparing annual accounts to 5 April. On 1 July 2007 he constructed a barn at a cost (excluding land) of £30,000. On 1 October 2009, he sold the barn to Pam for £35,000 (excluding land).

Pam also trades as a farmer and began trading on 1 May 2009. She chose 31 December as her annual accounting date and her first accounts covered the period from 1 May 2009 to 31 December 2009.

Calculate the ABAs available to Giles for the years to 5 April 2008, 2009 and 2010 and to Pam for her first two chargeable periods.

*10.7   David has traded for many years, preparing accounts to 31 March annually. On 1 July 2001 he bought a new industrial building for £80,000 (excluding land) and put the building to immediate industrial use. Throughout David's ownership, the building was always in industrial use apart from the period between 1 January 2004 and 31 December 2006 when it was used for a non-industrial purpose. On 1 February 2009, he sold the building to Diana for £120,000 (excluding land).

Diana began trading on 1 July 2008 and chose 5 April as her annual accounting date. Her first accounts covered the period to 5 April 2009.

Calculate the IBAs available to David for all affected years and to Diana for the period to 5 April 2009 and for the year to 5 April 2010.

*10.8   Talat prepares accounts to 31 October each year. The written down value of his plant and machinery after deducting capital allowances for the year to 31 October 2008 was as follows:

	£
Main pool	113,190
Special rate pool	9,900
VW motor car (30% private use by Talat)	14,500

He had the following transactions during the year to 31 October 2009:

		£
1 January 2009	Sold plant (original cost £4,200 in 2004)	1,310
12 March 2009	Bought plant	63,400
5 July 2009	Sold car (original cost £7,500 in 2006)	3,000
5 July 2009	Bought car (emissions 161g/km)	8,200
18 August 2009	Sold plant (original cost £1,000 in September 2008)	1,150
23 August 2009	Bought plant	19,600
6 September 2009	Sold VV motor car	17,200
6 September 2009	Bought BMW motor car (emissions 154g/km)	32,000

Private use of the VW and BMW motor cars by Talat has been agreed at 30%.

There were no capital transactions between 1 November 2009 and 31 March 2010, when Talat ceased trading. On 31 March 2010, the plant and machinery was disposed of as follows:

(i)   All of the plant and machinery other than motor cars was sold for £122,000. This consisted of £110,000 for main pool items and £12,000 for special rate items.

(ii)   Talat took over the BMW car. Its market value on 31 March 2010 was £29,000.

(iii)   The only other car remaining was the one acquired in July 2009 and Talat gave this to his brother, who will be using it for private purposes. The market value of the car on 31 March 2010 was £6,300.

Prepare the capital allowances computations for the year to 31 October 2009 and for the period from 1 November 2009 to 31 March 2010.

Chapter 11

Income from self-employment: Trading losses

Introduction

If the computation of a self-employed person's adjusted trading profit for a period of account produces a negative result, then a trading loss has been incurred. This has two main consequences:

(a) the person's trading income for the relevant tax year is set to £nil

(b) tax relief may be claimed in respect of the loss.

Several forms of tax relief are available and each involves offsetting the trading loss against other income or gains of the person concerned, so reducing the amount of tax payable on that other income or on those gains. The purpose of this chapter is to explain the main features of each form of loss relief.

Relief for trading losses

The rules which grant tax relief in relation to trading losses are now located in the Income Tax Act 2007. This Act provides the following main reliefs:

(a) **Carry-forward trade loss relief**. Section 83 of ITA 2007 allows a trading loss to be carried forward and set against future profits of the same trade.

(b) **Trade loss relief against total income**. Section 64 of ITA 2007 allows a trading loss to be set against the trader's total income for a period of up to two years.

(c) **Early trade losses relief**. Section 72 of ITA 2007 provides a special relief for trading losses incurred in the early years of trading.

(d) **Terminal trade loss relief**. Section 89 of ITA 2007 provides a special relief for any trading losses incurred in the final year of trading.

Each of these forms of loss relief is described below.

Carry-forward trade loss relief

Unless a trader claims any other form of loss relief, a trading loss is automatically carried forward under Section 83 of ITA 2007 and relieved against future trading profits. It is important to note the following points:

(a) Carry-forward relief is given against future *trading profits* only, not against any other form of income.

(b) Furthermore, relief is given only against future trading profits arising from *the same trade* as that in which the loss was incurred. So if a trader ceases one trade and commences another, the losses of the old trade cannot be carried forward and relieved against the future profits of the new trade. Similarly, if a trader carries on two trades simultaneously, a loss incurred in one of the trades cannot be carried forward and relieved against the future profits of the other trade.

(c) Relief must be given against the *first available* trading profits arising in the future. The maximum possible relief must be taken in each year until the loss is fully relieved, even if this leaves insufficient income to absorb personal allowances.

(d) Strictly speaking, relief is given by deduction from the trader's total income when computing his or her net income (see Chapter 2). But the amount of relief given in any tax year cannot exceed the trading profits for that year.

EXAMPLE 1

Carla incurred a trading loss of £12,200 in the year to 30 June 2009. Her trading profits for the following three years (adjusted for tax purposes) are as follows:

	£
year to 30 June 2010	5,500
year to 30 June 2011	6,000
year to 30 June 2012	30,000

Carla's only other income consists of interest received of £500 per annum. Assuming that the trading loss is carried forward, calculate her net income (i.e. total income less reliefs) for tax years 2009-10 to 2012-13 inclusive.

Solution

	2009-10	2010-11	2011-12	2012-13
	£	£	£	£
Trading income	nil	5,500	6,000	30,000
Interest received	500	500	500	500
Total income	500	6,000	6,500	30,500
Less: Trading losses b/f	-	5,500	6,000	700
Net income	500	500	500	29,800

Notes:

(a) Carla's trading income for 2009-10 is £nil since there is a loss in the basis period for that year.

(b) The trading loss carried forward is relieved only against future trading profits (not against the interest received) and maximum relief must be given in each year. This results in a waste of personal allowances in 2010-11 and 2011-12. Carla would probably prefer to carry forward the loss in its entirety to 2012-13, where it can be put to good use, but this is not permissible.

Capital allowances

As explained in Chapter 10, any capital allowances claimed for a period of account are treated as a trading expense of that period. Therefore capital allowances are included automatically in the calculation of a trading loss.

It is important to remember that it is not mandatory to claim the maximum capital allowances available for a chargeable period. If a trading loss has been incurred it may be advisable to claim less than the maximum capital allowances (or even none at all) so as to avoid wasting personal allowances when the trading loss is relieved. Disclaimed capital allowances are not lost permanently, since higher WDVs are carried forward than would otherwise have been the case and this results in higher capital allowances in future years.

EXAMPLE 2

Colin's adjusted trading profits/(losses) for the years to 31 August 2008 and 2009 are:

	Before capital allowances	Capital allowances available	After capital allowances
	£	£	£
year to 31 August 2008	(9,300)	2,100	(11,400)
year to 31 August 2009	15,300	3,700	11,600

He has no other income. If the trading loss is carried forward under s83 ITA 2007, should Colin claim maximum capital allowances in these two years?

Solution

If Colin claims maximum capital allowances in both years, relief in 2009-10 for trading losses carried forward will be £11,400. This will almost entirely absorb the trading profit of £11,600 assessed in that year, leaving only £200 against which to set the personal allowance, most of which will therefore be wasted.

It would be better to claim no capital allowances at all for the two years concerned. The trading loss carried forward would then be £9,300 and this would be relieved in 2009-10 against the trading profit of £15,300, leaving income of £6,000 against which to set Colin's personal allowance. There would be minimal waste of personal allowances and the capital allowances available to Colin in future years would be increased.

Trade loss relief against total income

As illustrated earlier, carrying trading losses forward under Section 83 of ITA 2007 does not always provide the most satisfactory form of loss relief. Problems associated with carry-forward relief include:

(a) Loss relief is delayed until sufficient profits arise from the same trade in future years (if, indeed, they ever do).

(b) The trader has no control over the amount of relief given in each year and therefore personal allowances may be wasted.

(c) If tax rates are falling, relief may be given at a lower rate than the rates which were in force when the loss was incurred.

An alternative form of loss relief which overcomes some of these problems is provided by Section 64 of ITA 2007. This tax relief allows trading losses to be set against the trader's total income for a period of up to two years. It is important to note that:

(a) The trader is under no obligation to make a claim to set trading losses against total income. If no such claim is made, trading losses are automatically carried forward under Section 83.

(b) Any unrelieved losses remaining after a claim has been made to set trading losses against total income are automatically carried forward under Section 83.

(c) Trading losses may be set against the trader's total income only if the business is being carried on "on a commercial basis" and "with a view to the realisation of profits". Furthermore, there is an annual limit of £25,000 on the amount of trading losses which may be set against total income if the trader is not personally engaged in the activities of the trade for at least 10 hours per week (a "non-active trader").

(d) In the case of *farmers and market gardeners*, a loss is usually not eligible for relief against total income if losses (calculated without regard to capital allowances) have also been incurred in each of the previous five tax years.

(e) If a claim is made to set trading losses against total income, relief is given by deducting the amount of the claim from the trader's total income when calculating his or her net income (see Chapter 2). Relief is given against non-savings income, savings income and dividends in the way which results in the lowest tax liability.

(f) ITA 2007 uses the term "sideways relief" to refer to the relief of trading losses against total income. This term is also used in connection with the special relief which is available in relation to trading losses incurred in the early years of trading (see later in this chapter).

Relieving a trading loss against total income

Section 64 of ITA 2007 states that relief against total income is available if a person who carries on a trade makes a trading loss "in the tax year". In most cases, the amount of the trading loss in a tax year is defined as the amount of the loss which was incurred in the basis period for that year. However, in order to prevent double counting, a trading loss incurred in an overlap period is treated as a loss of the earlier tax year only.

A trading loss incurred in a tax year may be set against the total income of:

either (i)   the tax year in which the loss is incurred

  or (ii)   the previous tax year

  or (iii) both of these years (if the loss is large enough for this).

A claim to set a trading loss against total income must be made by 31 January in the second tax year following the year in which the loss was made. For example, a claim in relation to a loss incurred in 2009-10 must be made by 31 January 2012. Note that:

(a)   The trader can decide whether to make a claim under Section 64 for one of the available years, for both of these years, or for neither year. But partial claims are not allowed. A claim to set a trading loss against total income must be for as much of the loss as can be relieved, even if this leaves insufficient income to absorb personal allowances. But if a claim is made for both years, the trader can decide whether to claim maximum relief in the year of the loss (relieving the remainder of the loss in the previous year) or vice versa.

(b)   A trading loss may be set against the total income of the previous tax year whether or not the loss-making trade was being carried on in that year. The £25,000 annual limit on sideways relief for non-active traders (see above) does not affect the giving of such relief against the profits of that same trade in the previous year.

(c)   If a trader claims that two trading losses should be set against the total income of the same tax year (one claim for a loss incurred in that tax year and another claim for a loss incurred in the following tax year) then the claim in respect of the current year's trading loss takes priority.

EXAMPLE 3

Ashok has been trading for many years, preparing annual accounts to 31 July. Recent trading profits/(losses), adjusted for tax purposes, are as follows:

	£
year to 31 July 2007	12,400
year to 31 July 2008	10,450
year to 31 July 2009	(9,500)

He has investment income amounting to £5,000 per annum and claims only the basic personal allowance. Identify the claims which he could make in relation to the trading loss incurred in the year to 31 July 2009. Which of these loss relief claims (if any) might be recommended?

Solution

Ashok's trading income is:

Year	Basis period	Trading income
		£
2007-08	y/e 31/7/07	12,400
2008-09	y/e 31/7/08	10,450
2009-10	y/e 31/7/09	nil

He could make a claim to relieve the trading loss of £9,500 against his total income for 2009-10 only, 2008-09 only, both of these years, or neither year:

(a) A claim for 2009-10 only would relieve £5,000 of the loss against his other income, leaving no tax liability for the year and losses of £4,500 to carry forward against future trading profits. This would be a waste, since the other income of £5,000 would in any case have been covered by the personal allowance.

(b) A claim for 2008-09 only would relieve the entire loss against that year's total income of £15,450 (£10,450 + £5,000), leaving income of £5,950 (£15,450 – £9,500) against which to set the personal allowance. There would be some minor wastage of the personal allowance but the tax liability for 2008-09 would become zero. This seems to be a fairly efficient way of relieving the loss.

(c) A claim for both years is pointless, since:

   (i) a claim giving relief in 2008-09 first would leave no losses to relieve in 2009-10

   (ii) a claim giving relief in 2009-10 first leads to a waste of personal allowances in that year (see above).

(d) A claim for neither year would result in the entire loss being carried forward. This would mean that loss relief would be delayed until such time as sufficient profits of the same trade arose in future years.

On balance, a claim to set the trading loss against total income of 2008-09 might be recommended. This claim combines early relief of the loss with a fairly small wastage of personal allowances. The claim would have to be made by 31 January 2012.

However, this claim would relieve the loss at only 20%. If the first available future profits from the same trade are expected to be very high, it might be better to carry the loss forward and possibly obtain relief at 40%.

Relieving trading losses against capital gains

If a claim is made to set a trading loss against the total income of a tax year (or if no such claim is made because total income for that year is zero) the trader concerned may claim that any unrelieved part of the loss should be set against his or her capital gains. Such a claim must be made by 31 January in the second tax year following the tax year in which the trading loss was incurred. This relief is considered further in Chapter 16.

Temporary extension of carry-back relief

As explained earlier in this chapter, trading losses can generally be carried back and set against the trader's total income of the previous tax year. It is not normally possible to carry back trading losses any further than this. However, Finance Act 2009 has introduced a temporary extension to the carry-back period, allowing trading losses incurred in tax years 2008-09 and 2009-10 to be carried back for three years and relieved against *profits of the same trade*. The details of this temporary extension are as follows:

(a) Extended carry-back relief for a trading loss is unavailable unless a claim has already been made to set that loss against total income (or no such claim can be made because total income for the year of the loss and the previous year are both zero) and some part of the loss remains unrelieved.

(b) For a trading loss incurred in 2008-09:

    (i) If a claim has been made to set the loss against total income of 2008-09 (but only that year) then the unrelieved part of the loss may be carried back and set against profits of the same trade in 2007-08, 2006-07 and 2005-06.

    (ii) Otherwise, the unrelieved part of the loss may be carried back and set against profits of the same trade in 2006-07 and 2005-06.

(c) For a trading loss incurred in 2009-10:

    (i) If a claim has been made to set the loss against total income of 2009-10 (but only that year) then the unrelieved part of the loss may be carried back and set against profits of the same trade in 2008-09, 2007-08 and 2006-07.

    (ii) Otherwise, the unrelieved part of the loss may be carried back and set against profits of the same trade in 2007-08 and 2006-07.

(d) Losses carried back are set against the profits of a later year before those of an earlier year. A claim for extended carry-back relief must be made by 31 January in the second tax year following the tax year in which the trading loss was incurred.

(e) The amount of trading losses that may be carried back to the previous tax year is unlimited. But no more than £50,000 of trading losses may be carried back to the earlier two years (in total). A separate £50,000 limit applies to the extended carry-back of trading losses made in each of the tax years 2008-09 and 2009-10.

EXAMPLE 4

Alexander has trading profits of £39,000 in 2006-07, £45,000 in 2007-08 and £58,000 in 2008-09. He incurs a trading loss of £125,000 in 2009-10. He also has investment income amounting to £6,000 in each tax year.

Alexander claims that the trading loss for 2009-10 should be set against his total income for 2008-09. He also claims extended carry-back relief in relation to the loss. Show how the loss is relieved and calculate the amount of any unrelieved part of the loss.

Solution

Loss relief against total income for 2008-09 is £64,000, leaving £61,000 of the loss still to be relieved. A claim for extended carry-back relief will set the loss against trading profits of 2007-08 and 2006-07 (in that order) but no more than £50,000 may be relieved in this way. Relief is £45,000 in 2007-08 and £5,000 in 2006-07. The remaining £11,000 of the loss is carried forward for relief against future profits of the same trade.

Early trade losses relief

Losses incurred in the early years of trading may (just like other trading losses) be carried forward against future trading profits or set against the trader's total income. But, in addition to these forms of relief, Section 72 of ITA 2007 allows trading losses incurred in *any of the first four tax years* to be set against the trader's total income of the three previous tax years. Note that:

(a) If this relief is claimed in relation to a trading loss, the loss is relieved against the trader's total income of the previous three tax years, *beginning with the earliest year*. For example, an early years trading loss incurred in 2009-10 could be set against the trader's total income of 2006-07, 2007-08 and 2008-09, in that order.

(b) A claim for early trade losses relief applies to *all* of the three years prior to the loss-making year. The trader cannot specify the years in which relief is to be given or the amount of relief to be given in each year. The maximum possible relief is given in each year and this may result in a waste of personal allowances.

(c) Relief is given by deducting the amount of the trading loss from total income when calculating the trader's net income (see Chapter 2). Relief is given against non-savings income, savings income and dividends in the way which results in the lowest tax liability.

(d) Early trade losses relief is not available in relation to a trading loss unless the trade is commercial. This means that the trade is carried on "on a commercial basis" and "in such a way that profits could reasonably be expected to be made in the basis period or within a reasonable time afterwards". The £25,000 annual limit on sideways relief for non-active traders (see above) encompasses early trade losses as well as trade losses relieved against total income under Section 64.

(e) A claim for early trade losses relief must be made by 31 January in the second tax year following the loss-making tax year.

(f) A claim for early trade losses relief *cannot* be extended so as to set any unrelieved trading losses against capital gains.

(g) A loss incurred in an overlap period is treated as *a loss of the earlier tax year only*. This rule ensures that a loss is relieved only once.

EXAMPLE 5

Carl begins trading on 1 July 2007 and chooses 30 June as his accounting date. His adjusted trading profits/(losses) for the first two accounting years are as follows:

	£
year to 30 June 2008	(43,200)
year to 30 June 2009	(12,400)

Now that he is self-employed, Carl has no other income. Prior to becoming self-employed his only income was from employment, as follows:

	£
2004-05	23,900
2005-06	18,760
2006-07	17,920
2007-08 (to 30 June 2007)	5,180

Assuming that Carl makes all possible early trade losses claims, calculate his net income (i.e. total income less reliefs) for years 2004-05 to 2007-08 inclusive.

Solution

The losses which are eligible for early trade losses relief are:

Year	Basis period	Workings	Trading loss £	Early trade losses claim
2007-08	1/7/07 to 5/4/08	£(43,200) x 9/12	(32,400)	04-05 *to* 06-07
2008-09	y/e 30/6/08	£(43,200) – overlap £(32,400)	(10,800)	05-06 *to* 07-08
2009-10	y/e 30/6/09		(12,400)	06-07 *to* 08-09

Trading income for 2007-08 through to 2009-10 is of course £nil. If all possible early trade loss claims are made, net income for years 2004-05 to 2007-08 is:

	2004-05 £	*2005-06* £	*2006-07* £	*2007-08* £
Employment income	23,900	18,760	17,920	5,180
Trading income	-	-	-	0
Total income	23,900	18,760	17,920	5,180
Less: Early trade losses:				
2007-08 loss	(23,900)	(8,500)		
2008-09 loss		(10,260)	(540)	
2009-10 loss			(12,400)	
Net income	-	-	4,980	5,180

Terminal trade loss relief

In normal circumstances, a trader who incurs a trading loss may choose between carrying the loss forward against future profits of the same trade or relieving the loss against total income. But if a trading loss is incurred in the final year of trading, the first of these alternatives is not available since there can be no future profits against which to set the trading loss. In order to remedy this situation, Section 89 of ITA 2007 provides a relief known as "terminal trade loss relief" which permits a trading loss incurred in the last 12 months of trading to be set against the trading profits of the tax year in which the cessation occurs and the previous three tax years.

Calculating the terminal loss

The "terminal loss" eligible for terminal trade loss relief is the trading loss incurred in the final 12 months of trading, excluding any part of that loss which has already been relieved in other ways (i.e. by deduction from total income). The terminal loss is calculated by adding together the following components:

(a) the actual trading loss incurred from 6 April to the date of the cessation

(b) the actual trading loss incurred from a date 12 months before the date of the cessation to the following 5 April

(c) any available overlap relief (see Chapter 9).

If either (a) or (b) is a profit, this counts as a zero in the calculation of the terminal loss.

EXAMPLE 6

Andrea ceases trading on 31 October 2009. Her adjusted trading profits/(losses) for the closing periods of account are as follows:

	£
year to 31 December 2007	6,600
year to 31 December 2008	2,400
10 months to 31 October 2009	(22,500)

Overlap profits of £3,200 arose when Andrea began trading. Calculate the amount of the loss which is eligible for terminal trade loss relief, assuming that no claims are made to set trading losses against total income.

Solution

		£
Trading loss 6/4/09 to 31/10/09	£(22,500) x 7/10	(15,750)
Trading loss 1/11/08 to 5/4/09	£2,400 x 2/12 + £(22,500) x 3/10	(6,350)
Overlap relief		(3,200)
Terminal loss		(25,300)

Relieving the terminal loss

As stated above, the terminal loss may be relieved against the trading profits of the year of cessation and the three tax years preceding the year of cessation. Note that:

(a) Relief is given in later years first. For example, a terminal loss arising as a consequence of a business ceasing to trade during 2009-10 would be set against the trading profits of 2009-10, 2008-09, 2007-08 and 2006-07, in that order.

(b) The maximum possible relief must be given in each tax year even if this results in a wastage of personal allowances.

(c) Strictly speaking, relief is given by deduction from the trader's total income when computing his or her net income (see Chapter 2). But the amount of relief given in any tax year cannot exceed the trading profits for that year.

EXAMPLE 7

Brendan ceases trading on 30 September 2009. His recent trading profits/(losses) are:

	£
year to 31 January 2007	24,700
year to 31 January 2008	12,500
year to 31 January 2009	2,100
8 months to 30 September 2009	(21,840)

He has no other income. Overlap profits of £4,700 arose when Brendan began trading and no claims are made to set Brendan's trading loss against his total income. Calculate the amount of the terminal loss and show how this may be relieved.

Solution

The calculation of the terminal loss is as follows:

		£
Trading loss 6/4/09 to 30/9/09	£(21,840) x 6/8	(16,380)
Trading loss 1/10/08 to 5/4/09	£2,100 x 4/12 + £(21,840) x 2/8	(4,760)
Overlap relief		(4,700)
Terminal loss		(25,840)

The terminal loss may be relieved as follows:

	2006-07 £	2007-08 £	2008-09 £	2009-10 £
Trading income	24,700	12,500	2,100	nil
Less: Terminal trade loss relief:				
(i) in 2008-09			(2,100)	
(ii) in 2007-08		(12,500)		
(iii) in 2006-07	(11,240)			
Net income	13,460	-	-	-

Post-cessation trade relief

As a general rule, post-cessation expenses which were not provided for in the final accounts of a business are relieved against any post-cessation receipts (which are taxed as trading income). If post-cessation receipts are insufficient to absorb all post-cessation expenses, the excess expenses are normally unrelieved.

However, certain categories of unrelieved post-cessation expenses may be set against the taxpayer's total income for the tax year in which the expenses are incurred. The main categories of post-cessation expenses which may be relieved in this way are:

(a) the costs of remedying defective work done whilst the business was operating, together with associated legal costs and insurance premiums

(b) bad debts which were not provided for in the accounts of the business, together with associated debt collection costs.

If the taxpayer's total income for a tax year is insufficient to absorb all of the post-cessation expenses eligible for relief in that year, the excess expenses may be set against the taxpayer's capital gains for the year.

Expenses incurred more than seven years after cessation are not eligible for post-cessation trade relief.

Transfer of a business to a company

If the owner of a business transfers that business to a limited company, there is a change in the legal ownership of the business and the vendor is deemed to have ceased trading. In consequence, any trading losses sustained by the vendor before the date of the transfer cannot be carried forward and set against the company's trading profits.

Relief for such losses might be obtained by deduction from the taxpayer's total income for the year of the loss and/or the previous year. Terminal loss relief might be available if the losses were incurred in the final 12 months of trading. But a further relief is offered by Section 86 of ITA 2007, which provides that:

(a) if a business is transferred to a limited company wholly or mainly in exchange for shares in that company, and

(b) the vendor of the business continues to hold those shares, and

(c) the company continues to carry on the transferred business

then the vendor may set unrelieved trading losses against the first available income that he or she receives from the company.

Losses on shares in unlisted trading companies

A person who subscribes for newly issued shares in certain unlisted trading companies and then incurs a capital loss on the disposal of those shares may claim that this capital loss should be set against his or her total income as if it were a trading loss. This relief is provided by Section 131 of ITA 2007.

Tax relief under this provision is generally available only if the trading company concerned is of a type which would qualify for the purposes of the Enterprise Investment Scheme (see Chapter 6).

Summary

▸ Under Section 83 of ITA 2007, a trading loss may be carried forward and relieved against future profits of the same trade.

▸ Under Section 64 of ITA 2007, a trading loss may be relieved against the trader's total income for a specified two-year period.

▸ Any trading losses remaining unrelieved after a Section 64 claim has been made for a tax year may be set against the trader's capital gains for that year.

▸ Under Section 72 of ITA 2007, a trading loss incurred in any of the first four tax years may be set against the trader's total income of the three previous tax years.

▸ Under Section 89 of ITA 2007, a trading loss incurred during the final 12 months of trading may be set against the trading profits of the tax year in which trade ceases and the previous three tax years.

▸ If a business is transferred to a company, the unrelieved trading losses of the vendor may (subject to certain conditions) be set against the first available income which the vendor receives from the company.

▸ Capital losses incurred on the disposal of shares in certain unlisted trading companies may (subject to certain conditions) be treated as trading losses.

Exercises

11.1   Sally, who has been trading for many years, incurs an adjusted trading loss of £40,000 in the year to 31 December 2009.

(a)   What is her trading income for 2009-10?

(b)   If she makes no claim in relation to her trading loss, how will it be relieved?

(c)   How will the loss be relieved if she does make a claim?

11.2   Jane is self-employed. Her recent adjusted trading profits/(losses) are:

	£
year to 31 May 2006	(18,860)
year to 31 May 2007	4,710
year to 31 May 2008	6,210
year to 31 May 2009	14,810

Jane has other income of £4,800 per annum. Assuming that the trading loss is carried forward and set against future trading profits, calculate her net income (i.e. total income less reliefs) for tax years 2006-07 through to 2009-10.

11.3   Marcus begins trading on 1 January 2008 and has the following results:

	Adjusted trading profits/(losses) before capital allowances	Capital allowances claimed
	£	£
year to 31 December 2008	13,720	3,460
year to 31 December 2009	(7,980)	1,820

He has no other income.

(a)   Compute his trading income (before loss relief) for 2007-08 to 2009-10.

(b)   Identify the claims that could be made in relation to the trading loss, assuming that early trade losses relief is not claimed. Which (if any) of these claims should be recommended?

11.4   Nathan begins trading on 1 October 2007, making up accounts to 31 December each year. His first two sets of accounts show the following adjusted trading losses:

	£
15 months to 31 December 2008	(26,850)
year to 31 December 2009	(25,660)

He has had no other income since becoming self-employed but his income before he started trading was as follows:

	£
2004-05	15,100
2005-06	15,250
2006-07	16,400
2007-08 (to 30 September 2007)	8,450

Assuming that all possible early trade losses relief claims are made, calculate Nathan's net income (i.e. total income less reliefs) for years 2004-05 to 2007-08.

*11.5   Olive ceases trading on 31 May 2009. Her recent adjusted trading profits/(losses) are:

	£
year to 30 June 2005	37,450
year to 30 June 2006	39,190
year to 30 June 2007	16,120
year to 30 June 2008	(6,840)
11 months to 31 May 2009	(36,300)

Overlap relief of £7,140 is available. Calculate the terminal loss and show how this would be relieved, assuming that Olive has investment income of £20,000 per annum and that no claims are made to set trading losses against total income.

*11.6   Craig began trading on 1 August 2007 and has the following results:

	Adjusted trading profits/(losses) before capital allowances	Capital allowances claimed
	£	£
year to 31 July 2008	5,460	1,140
year to 31 July 2009	(27,400)	1,920

Before commencing to trade, Craig had only investment income. He sold all of his investments in July 2008 (realising a large capital gain) so as to raise extra working capital for his own business. His income from investments in recent years has been:

	£
2005-06	4,150
2006-07	4,940
2007-08	2,190
2008-09 (to July 2008)	1,510

(a)   Compute Craig's trading income for 2007-08 to 2009-10.

(b)   Explain the trading loss reliefs available to Craig. Which would you recommend?

Chapter 12

Income from self-employment: Partnerships

Introduction

The purpose of this chapter is to explain the taxation treatment of individuals who are members of a partnership. Most of the information given in the previous four chapters with regard to the computation of trading profit, basis periods, capital allowances and trading loss reliefs is applicable to partners as well as to sole traders. The main new problem which arises when dealing with partnerships is the problem of calculating each partner's share of the partnership profit or loss for taxation purposes and much of this chapter is devoted to that problem.

Note that a Limited Liability Partnership (LLP) which is regulated by the Limited Liability Partnership Act 2000 and which carries on a trade or profession is generally dealt with for tax purposes as a partnership rather than as a company.

Principles of partnership taxation

Under the partnership tax rules, a partnership is not regarded as a separate entity for taxation purposes and the partnership itself is not charged to tax. Instead, the profits of the partnership are allocated between the partners and then each partner is taxed as an individual. In detail, the procedure for each tax year is as follows:

(a) The partnership submits a tax return to HM Revenue and Customs. This return provides information on the profit or loss for the period of account ending in the tax year and gives details of the profit-sharing agreement in force during that period. The return is also used to:

(i)   claim capital allowances for the period of account, both on partnership assets and on individual partners' assets

(ii) claim relief for any business expenses which have been incurred by partners personally.

(b) The adjusted trading profit or loss of the partnership is calculated in the usual manner. Any drawings or other appropriations of profit made by the partners are of course disallowed. Capital allowances on partnership assets are treated as a trading expense.

(c)   The adjusted trading profit or loss is then allocated between the partners according to the profit-sharing agreement in force during the period of account. If the agreement changes during the period of account, it is necessary to time-apportion the profit or loss, applying the old agreement to the pre-change profit or loss and the new agreement to the post-change profit or loss.

(d)   Any capital allowances claimed on an individual partner's assets and any expenses incurred personally by a partner are deducted from the relevant partner's share of the adjusted trading profit or added to that partner's share of the adjusted trading loss.

(e)   Partners are then assessed to tax individually, as if each partner's share of the partnership's trading profit or loss had arisen from a trade carried on by that partner alone. In effect, each partner is treated as a sole trader who:

(i)   begins trading when joining the partnership

(ii)   has the same periods of account as the partnership (except that a partner who joins or leaves the partnership part-way through a period of account will have an individual period of account which begins or ends part-way through a partner-ship period of account)

(iii) ceases trading when leaving the partnership.

(f)   Each partner is solely responsible for the tax due on his or her share of the partnership profit. Partners must include their share of the partnership profit or loss in their own tax returns and in their self-assessment calculations.

EXAMPLE 1

Tom, Dick and Harry begin trading as a partnership on 1 January 2008, sharing profits in the ratio 3:2:1. With effect from 1 January 2009, they agree that Harry should receive a salary of £4,000 per annum, that partners should be entitled to 4% per annum interest on capital and that remaining profits should be shared in the ratio 5:3:2. The adjusted trading profits of the partnership are:

	£
y/e 31 December 2008	18,000
y/e 31 December 2009	22,000

Fixed capitals are Tom £10,000, Dick £12,000, Harry £16,000. Compute each partner's trading income for 2007-08, 2008-09 and 2009-10.

Solution

The allocation of trading profit for each period of account is:

	Tom £	Dick £	Harry £	Total £
y/e 31/12/08				
Profit (shared 3:2:1)	9,000	6,000	3,000	18,000
y/e 31/12/09				
Salary	-	-	4,000	4,000
Interest on capital	400	480	640	1,520
Remainder of profit (shared 5:3:2)	8,240	4,944	3,296	16,480
	8,640	5,424	7,936	22,000

Each partner is treated as a sole trader, commencing trade on 1 January 2008, making up accounts to 31 December and with trading profits for the first two accounting years as shown above. The trading income of each partner is:

Tom

Year	Basis period	Workings	Trading income £
2007-08	1/1/08 to 5/4/08	£9,000 x 3/12	2,250
2008-09	y/e 31/12/08		9,000
2009-10	y/e 31/12/09		8,640

Dick

Year	Basis period	Workings	Trading income £
2007-08	1/1/08 to 5/4/08	£6,000 x 3/12	1,500
2008-09	y/e 31/12/08		6,000
2009-10	y/e 31/12/09		5,424

Harry

Year	Basis period	Workings	Trading income £
2007-08	1/1/08 to 5/4/08	£3,000 x 3/12	750
2008-09	y/e 31/12/08		3,000
2009-10	y/e 31/12/09		7,936

Note:

In each case, the overlap period is from 1 January 2008 to 5 April 2008. Overlap profits are Tom £2,250, Dick £1,500 and Harry £750. These overlap profits will be relieved when the relevant partner leaves the partnership (or on a change of accounting date).

Notional profits and losses

Occasionally, the effect of taking into account partners' salaries and/or interest on capital is to allocate a trading loss to an individual partner, even though the partnership as a whole has made a trading profit. In these circumstances, that partner's share of the trading profit is set to £nil and then his or her "notional loss" is allocated between the remaining partners in proportion to their original profit allocations. A similar procedure is followed if a partner is allocated a "notional profit" in a year in which the partnership as a whole has sustained a trading loss.

EXAMPLE 2

(a) Lock, Stock and Barrel are in partnership, making up accounts to 30 June each year. Their profit-sharing agreement specifies that Lock and Barrel should receive annual salaries of £20,000 and £24,000 respectively and that remaining profits or losses should be divided equally. The partnership has an adjusted trading profit of £26,000 in the year to 30 June 2009. Show how this will be allocated between the partners.

(b) Rod, Pole and Perch are in partnership, also making up accounts to 30 June each year. Their profit-sharing agreement specifies that Perch should receive an annual salary of £25,000 and that remaining profits or losses should be shared in the ratio 3:2:1. The partnership has an adjusted trading loss of £5,000 in the year to 30 June 2009. Show how this will be allocated between the partners.

Solution

(a)

	Lock £	Stock £	Barrel £	Total £
Salaries	20,000	-	24,000	44,000
Remainder (£26,000 – £44,000)	(6,000)	(6,000)	(6,000)	(18,000)
	14,000	(6,000)	18,000	26,000
Stock's notional loss divided in the ratio 14,000:18,000	(2,625)	6,000	(3,375)	-
Allocation of trading profit	11,375	-	14,625	26,000

(b)

	Rod £	Pole £	Perch £	Total £
Salaries	-	-	25,000	25,000
Remainder (£5,000 + £25,000)	(15,000)	(10,000)	(5,000)	(30,000)
	(15,000)	(10,000)	20,000	(5,000)
Perch's notional profit divided 15,000:10,000	12,000	8,000	(20,000)	-
Allocation of trading loss	(3,000)	(2,000)	-	(5,000)

Change in partnership composition

A change in partnership composition occurs if a new partner joins the partnership or if an existing partner dies or leaves the partnership. A change in composition has no effect on those persons who were carrying on the trade before the change (either alone or in partnership) and who continue to carry on the trade after the change (either alone or in partnership). Such persons are taxed on the current year basis as if the change had not taken place. But new partners have commenced trading and are subject to the commencement rules, whilst leaving partners have ceased trading and are subject to the cessation rules.

EXAMPLE 3

Red and White begin trading as a partnership on 1 October 2006, sharing profits equally. On 1 January 2008, they agree to admit Blue as a partner and to share profits in the ratio 3:2:1. The adjusted trading profits of the partnership are:

	£
y/e 30 September 2007	21,000
y/e 30 September 2008	24,000
y/e 30 September 2009	27,000

Compute each partner's trading income for the years 2006-07 through to 2009-10.

Solution

The allocation of trading profit for each period of account is:

	Red	White	Blue	Total
	£	£	£	£
y/e 30/9/07 (shared equally)	10,500	10,500	-	21,000
y/e 30/9/08				
1/10/07 - 31/12/07				
£24,000 x 3/12 (shared equally)	3,000	3,000	-	6,000
1/1/08 - 30/9/08				
£24,000 x 9/12 (shared 3:2:1)	9,000	6,000	3,000	18,000
	12,000	9,000	3,000	24,000
y/e 30/9/09 (shared 3:2:1)	13,500	9,000	4,500	27,000

For tax purposes, each partner is now treated as a sole trader and is assessed on his or her share of the partnership trading profit. The position of each partner is as follows:

(a) Red began trading on 1 October 2006, preparing accounts to 30 September. Each period of account is of 12 months' duration. Profits are £10,500 for the year to 30 September 2007, £12,000 for the year to 30 September 2008 and £13,500 for the year to 30 September 2009.

(b) White began trading on 1 October 2006, preparing accounts to 30 September. Each period of account is of 12 months' duration. Profits are £10,500 for the year to 30 September 2007, £9,000 for the year to 30 September 2008 and £9,000 for the year to 30 September 2009.

(c) Blue began trading on 1 January 2008, preparing accounts to 30 September. The first accounts cover the nine-month period from 1 January 2008 to 30 September 2008 with profits of £3,000. Profits are £4,500 for the year to 30 September 2009.

Each partner's trading income is as follows:

Red

Year	Basis period	Workings	Trading income £
2006-07	1/10/06 to 5/4/07	£10,500 x 6/12	5,250
2007-08	y/e 30/9/07		10,500
2008-09	y/e 30/9/08		12,000
2009-10	y/e 30/9/09		13,500

White

Year	Basis period	Workings	Trading income £
2006-07	1/10/06 to 5/4/07	£10,500 x 6/12	5,250
2007-08	y/e 30/9/07		10,500
2008-09	y/e 30/9/08		9,000
2009-10	y/e 30/9/09		9,000

Blue

Year	Basis period	Workings	Trading income £
2007-08	1/1/08 to 5/4/08	£3,000 x 3/9	1,000
2008-09	1/1/08 to 31/12/08	£3,000 + 3/12 x £4,500	4,125
2009-10	y/e 30/9/09		4,500

Note:

In the case of Red and White, the overlap period is from 1 October 2006 to 5 April 2007 and each partner has overlap profits of £5,250. In the case of Blue, there is an overlap period from 1 January 2008 to 5 April 2008 and another overlap period from 1 October 2008 to 31 December 2008. Blue's overlap profits are £1,000 + (£4,500 x 3/12) = £2,125.

Non-trading income

A partnership which has trading income may also have non-trading income. For partnership tax purposes, non-trading income falls into two categories:

(a) **Taxed income**

For this purpose, "taxed income" is defined as income from which tax has been deducted at source (e.g. most interest) and dividends which have an attached tax credit. The amount of any taxed income arising in a period of account is divided between the partners in profit-sharing ratio and then each partner's share is apportioned between tax years and assessed to tax on the actual basis.

It is acceptable to allocate taxed income between tax years on the receipts basis if this would be more appropriate than time-apportionment.

(b) **Untaxed income**

For this purpose, "untaxed income" is defined as non-trading income which is not taxed income (e.g. income from property or interest received gross). The amount of any untaxed income arising in a period of account is allocated between the partners in profit-sharing ratio and is then assessed to tax using *the same basis periods as those used for the trading income*. The basis periods that would normally be applied if the income were received by an individual rather than a partnership are totally ignored. If this treatment results in non-trading income being taxed twice when a partner starts trading, overlap relief is available.

If a partnership does not carry on a trade or profession, the treatment described at (a) above applies to *all* of the partnership's non-trading income.

EXAMPLE 4

Hook, Line and Sinker begin trading as a partnership on 1 July 2007, sharing profits equally. The chosen accounting date is 30 June and the first accounts are made up for the year to 30 June 2008. In addition to its trading income, the partnership has non-trading income as follows:

	y/e 30/6/08	y/e 30/6/09
	£	£
Income from property	1,500	1,800
Net bank interest	2,400	3,600

(a) Compute each partner's income from property for tax years 2007-08, 2008-09 and 2009-10.

(b) Compute the gross amount of bank interest on which each partner is taxed in tax years 2007-08 and 2008-09.

Solution

(a) Each partner is allocated property income of £500 in the year to 30 June 2008 and £600 in the year to 30 June 2009. Property income per partner for each tax year is as follows:

Year	Basis period	Workings	Property income
			£
2007-08	1/7/07 to 5/4/08	£500 x 9/12	375
2008-09	y/e 30/6/08		500
2009-10	y/e 30/6/09		600

Each partner is entitled to overlap relief of £375.

(b) Each partner is allocated net bank interest of £800 in the year to 30 June 2008 and £1,200 in the year to 30 June 2009. When grossed-up at 100/80, these figures become £1,000 and £1,500 respectively. Therefore the gross amount of bank interest on which each partner is taxed (assuming time-apportionment between the tax years) is as follows:

Year	Workings	Savings income
		£
2007-08	£1,000 x 9/12	750
2008-09	(£1,000 x 3/12) + (£1,500 x 9/12)	1,375

The remaining 3/12ths of the bank interest received during the year to 30 June 2009 will be taxed in 2009-10, along with the first 9/12ths of any bank interest received in the year to 30 June 2010.

Trading losses

As explained above, a trading loss is allocated between the partners in the same way as a trading profit. In general, each partner is then entitled to precisely the same loss reliefs as a sole trader (see Chapter 11) with regard to his or her share of the loss.

EXAMPLE 5

Game, Set and Match begin trading in partnership on 1 August 2007, preparing accounts to 31 January each year and sharing profits equally. With effect from 1 March 2008, they agree to share profits in the ratio 1:2:2. The adjusted trading profits/(losses) of the partnership are as follows:

	£
period to 31 January 2008	8,610
y/e 31 January 2009	4,320
y/e 31 January 2010	(7,420)

Compute each partner's trading income for tax years 2007-08, 2008-09 and 2009-10 and explain how the trading loss incurred in the year to 31 January 2010 will be treated.

Solution

The allocation of trading profit or loss for each period of account is:

	Game	Set	Match	Total
	£	£	£	£
period to 31/1/08 (shared equally)	2,870	2,870	2,870	8,610
y/e 31/1/09				
1/2/08 - 29/2/08				
£4,320 x 1/12 (shared equally)	120	120	120	360
1/3/08 - 31/1/09				
£4,320 x 11/12 (shared 1:2:2)	792	1,584	1,584	3,960
	912	1,704	1,704	4,320
y/e 31/1/10 (shared 1:2:2)	(1,484)	(2,968)	(2,968)	(7,420)

Each partner's trading income is as follows:

Game

Year	Basis period	Workings	Trading income
			£
2007-08	1/8/07 to 5/4/08	£2,870 + 2/12 x £912	3,022
2008-09	y/e 31/1/09		912
2009-10	y/e 31/1/10		nil

Set

Year	Basis period	Workings	Trading income
			£
2007-08	1/8/07 to 5/4/08	£2,870 + 2/12 x £1,704	3,154
2008-09	y/e 31/1/09		1,704
2009-10	y/e 31/1/10		nil

Match

Year	Basis period	Workings	Trading income
			£
2007-08	1/8/07 to 5/4/08	£2,870 + 2/12 x £1,704	3,154
2008-09	y/e 31/1/09		1,704
2009-10	y/e 31/1/10		nil

Notes:

(i)   The basis period for 2007-08 for each partner includes two months out of the year to 31 January 2009. The profit for these two months is calculated by taking 2/12ths of the partner's profit for that year. In the case of Game (for example) it would be wrong to take £120 + (1/11 x £792) as the profit of the period from 1/2/08 to 5/4/08.

(ii) Each partner has overlap profits, calculated in the usual way.

(iii) Each partner may choose individually how to relieve his or her share of the trading loss incurred in the basis period for 2009-10. Possibilities include carrying the loss forward against future trading profits, loss relief against total income or an early trade losses claim.

Treatment of certain interest as a loss

As explained in Chapter 4, certain types of loan interest are deductible from a partner's total income when computing his or her net income. The eligible loans are:

(a) a loan to purchase plant or machinery for use in the business of a partnership

(b) a loan to purchase an interest in a partnership.

If a partner's total income is insufficient to deduct such loan interest in full, the excess interest may be treated as a trading loss for the purposes of carry-forward trade loss relief and terminal trade loss relief (see Chapter 11).

Restrictions on trade loss relief for certain partners

Income Tax Act 2007 contains anti-avoidance rules which restrict the amount of tax relief that may be given for trading losses incurred by certain partners. These rules relate to limited partners, members of a Limited Liability Partnership and "non-active" partners. A non-active partner is one who is not personally engaged in the activities of the trade for at least ten hours per week.

The anti-avoidance rules restrict the amount of sideways relief and capital gains relief that may be claimed by such partners. As explained in Chapter 11, the term "sideways relief" refers to the relief of trade losses against total income, including early trade losses relief. The main restrictions are as follows:

(a) A limited partner or a member of an LLP is denied sideways relief or capital gains relief for a trading loss incurred in a tax year to the extent that the loss exceeds the partner's "contribution to the firm" as measured at the end of the basis period for that year. For this purpose, a partner's "contribution" is broadly equal to the amount of capital which the partner has contributed to the partnership, plus any share of profits that have not been withdrawn.

(b) Similarly, a non-active partner is denied sideways relief or capital gains relief for a trading loss incurred in an "early tax year" to the extent that it exceeds his or her contribution to the firm. For this purpose, an early tax year is defined as the tax year in which the partner began trading or one of the next three tax years.

(c) A further restriction is that the total amount of sideways relief and capital gains relief given in relation to trading losses incurred by a limited partner or non-active partner is capped at £25,000 per tax year.

Note that the restrictions on sideways relief do *not* restrict the extent to which a trading loss may be relieved against the partner's profits from the loss-making trade. For example, if a trading loss is relieved against total income of the previous tax year, there is no restriction on the amount of the loss which may be set against the partner's trading profit from the partnership in that year. The aim of the anti-avoidance rules is to restrict the extent to which losses may be relieved against other forms of income.

Summary

▶ Under the partnership tax rules, each partner is taxed individually on his or her share of the partnership profit and each partner is solely responsible for his or her own tax liability.

▶ The adjusted trading profit of a partnership is allocated between the partners in accordance with the profit-sharing agreement for the period of account in which the profit arises. Notional profits and losses allocated to a partner are redistributed among the remaining partners.

▶ In effect, each partner is treated as a sole trader who begins trading when joining the partnership, has the same accounting dates as the partnership and ceases trading when leaving the partnership.

▶ The tax treatment of the non-trading income of a partnership depends upon whether the income ranks as taxed income or untaxed income and whether or not the partnership also has trading income.

▶ The trading losses of a partnership are allocated between the partners in the same way as trading profits. Each partner may then choose individually how to relieve his or her share of the loss.

Exercises

12.1 Nickleby, Copperfield and Drood have traded as equal partners for many years, making up accounts to 31 December each year. As from 1 April 2009 they agree to share profits in the ratio 1:2:2. The adjusted trading profit for the year to 31 December 2009 is £18,300. Show how this profit is allocated between the partners.

12.2 Pickwick, Snodgrass and Tupman are in partnership, making up accounts to 31 March annually. Each partner receives 6% interest on fixed capital, Pickwick and Tupman each receive an annual salary of £8,000 and remaining profits or losses are divided equally. Fixed capitals are Pickwick £12,000, Snodgrass £20,000 and Tupman £10,000. The adjusted trading profit for the year to 31 March 2010 is £14,500. Show how this profit is allocated between the partners.

12.3 Dodson and Fogg began trading in equal partnership on 1 July 2006. On 1 July 2007, they admitted Jackson as a partner and agreed to share profits in the ratio 5:4:1. The adjusted trading profits of the partnership are:

	£
year to 30 June 2007	17,000
year to 30 June 2008	22,000
year to 30 June 2009	29,000

Compute each partner's trading income for 2006-07 through to 2009-10.

12.4   Wardle, Jingle and Trotter began trading on 1 October 2007, preparing accounts to 30 September each year and sharing profits in the ratio 7:2:1. Results for the first two years of trading are as follows:

	y/e 30/9/08	y/e 30/9/09
	£	£
Trading profit	23,490	27,310
Interest received gross	2,000	2,200
Interest received net (net amount received)	1,000	1,088

(a) Compute each partner's trading income for 2007-08, 2008-09 and 2009-10.

(b) Compute each partner's interest received gross for 2007-08, 2008-09 and 2009-10.

(c) Compute the gross amount of taxed interest on which each partner is charged to tax in 2008-09.

*12.5   Cluppins and Raddle form a partnership on 1 November 2005, preparing accounts to 31 May each year. Bardell is admitted as a partner on 1 January 2007. Cluppins leaves the partnership on 29 February 2008 and Winkle is admitted as a partner on 1 March 2008.

Profits and losses are shared as follows:

Cluppins and Raddle	1:2
Cluppins, Raddle and Bardell	7:8:5
Raddle, Bardell and Winkle	4:3:1

Adjusted trading profits are:

	£
1 November 2005 to 31 May 2006	6,000
year to 31 May 2007	12,000
year to 31 May 2008	3,000
year to 31 May 2009	8,000

Calculate each partner's trading income for 2005-06 through to 2009-10, identifying any overlap periods and profits.

Chapter 13

Pension contributions

Introduction

The most tax-efficient way of providing for a pension is to make contributions into a registered pension scheme. Typically, this might be an occupational pension scheme sponsored by an employer or a personal pension scheme taken out with an insurance company or bank. The main purpose of this chapter is to explain the tax reliefs which are available in relation to contributions made into registered pension schemes.

This chapter concentrates on the tax reliefs available for tax year 2009-10. However, the Government has announced its intention to restrict tax relief on pension contributions for those individuals with taxable incomes of £150,000 or more. This restriction will take effect as from tax year 2011-12 and is explained briefly at the end of the chapter.

Registered pension schemes

The tax regime which now applies to pension schemes has been in effect since 6 April 2006 and was established by Finance Act 2004. This Act defines a pension scheme as "*a scheme ... to provide benefits to or in respect of persons -*

(a)   on retirement,

(b)   on death,

(c)   on having reached a particular age,

(d)   on the onset of serious ill-health or incapacity, or

(e)   in similar circumstances."

A pension scheme may be either a "defined benefits" scheme or a "money purchase" scheme. In a defined benefits scheme, the benefits payable to a member are calculated by reference to earnings or length of service or some other such factor. An example of a defined benefits scheme is an occupational pension scheme in which an employee's pension rights are based upon his or her final salary. In a money purchase scheme, the benefits payable to a member are calculated by reference to the size of the pension fund built up during the member's working life.

Registration

A pension scheme which is registered with HM Revenue and Customs is known as a "registered pension scheme" and qualifies for various tax reliefs and exemptions. An application to register a pension scheme may be made if the scheme satisfies certain conditions and is either:

(a)   an occupational pension scheme, or

(b)   a public service pension scheme, or

(c)   a scheme established by an insurance company, bank or similar institution.

An occupational pension scheme is one established by an employer or employers so as to provide benefits to employees. A public service pension scheme is (broadly) one established by the Government. The tax advantages of registration include:

(a)   The scheme's investment income is exempt from income tax. Any capital gains made on the disposal of scheme investments are exempt from capital gains tax.

(b)   Contributions made by scheme members attract tax relief (see below).

(c)   Contributions made by employers attract tax relief (see below).

(d)   Although pensions are chargeable to income tax, lump sums paid to scheme members are generally exempt from income tax, subject to the operation of the "lifetime allowance" (see below).

Except on ill-health grounds, a registered pension scheme must not allow members to take any pension benefits until they reach normal minimum pension age. This is set to age 50 at present but will rise to age 55 as from 6 April 2010. However, there is no requirement that members should actually retire before benefits are taken. Therefore, a member of an occupational pension scheme could draw a pension from his or her employer's scheme whilst continuing to work for that employer. There is no maximum age by which pension benefits must begin but special rules apply if pension benefits are not taken until after the age of 75.

Unregistered pension schemes

A registered pension scheme must comply with many regulations with regard to its investments, the payments it makes to its members and a number of other matters. A pension scheme which does not wish to register is under no compulsion to do so and therefore these regulations can be avoided. However, unregistered schemes do not qualify for any of the tax reliefs and exemptions enjoyed by registered schemes.

Tax relief for contributions by members

An individual may belong to as many pension schemes as he or she wishes and may make unlimited pension contributions. However, there are limits on the amount of contributions which can attract tax relief.

To be eligible for tax relief, an individual's contributions must be "relievable pension contributions" made into a registered pension scheme and the individual must be a "relevant UK individual" who is an "active member" of that scheme. Note that:

(a) Relievable pension contributions are contributions paid by the scheme member or by a third party on his or her behalf, excluding contributions made after the age of 75 and excluding employer contributions.

(b) An individual is a relevant UK individual for a tax year if *at least one* of a number of conditions is satisfied. The main conditions are that:

(i) the individual has UK earnings that are chargeable to income tax for the year (i.e. income from employment or self-employment)

(ii) the individual is resident in the UK at some time during the year.

Income derived from the commercial letting of furnished holiday accommodation ranks as self-employment income for this purpose. However, the furnished holiday accommodation rules are to be repealed as from tax year 2010-11 (see Chapter 5).

(c) An active member of a registered pension scheme is an individual who is accruing benefits under that scheme.

Tax relief can be claimed for a contribution only in the tax year in which payment is made. There are no provisions for carrying contributions back to previous tax years or forward to subsequent tax years.

Limit on tax relief

The maximum amount of pension contributions on which an individual can claim tax relief in any tax year is the *greater* of:

(a) 100% of the amount of the individual's UK earnings for the year that are chargeable to income tax

(b) the "basic amount", which is currently set at £3,600 (gross).

If the individual's earnings for a tax year are less than £3,600, tax relief on the amount of any contributions beyond the level of earnings up to the £3,600 limit can be given only if these contributions are made to a pension scheme which operates tax relief at source (see below).

EXAMPLE 1

Gordon is self-employed and a member of a registered pension scheme. His trading income for tax year 2008-09 is £31,600 but this falls to only £2,500 in 2009-10.

(a) How much may Gordon contribute to his pension scheme in each year ?

(b) How much of these contributions would attract tax relief?

Solution

(a) Gordon may make unlimited contributions to his pension scheme in both years.

(b) He may claim tax relief on contributions of up to £31,600 in 2008-09 and £3,600 in 2009-10 (assuming that the pension scheme operates tax relief at source).

Refund of excess contributions

If an individual makes pension contributions in a tax year which exceed the maximum amount on which tax relief can be claimed, then the excess contributions may be refunded (if the individual so wishes). Such a refund is known as a "refund of excess contributions lump sum" and must be made within six years of the end of the tax year in which the contributions were made.

A refund of excess contributions lump sum is not subject to income tax. This reflects the fact that the contributions which are being refunded by the pension scheme did not attract tax relief in the first place.

Methods of giving tax relief

There are three methods by means of which tax relief is given on member's pension contributions. The method adopted in any particular case depends upon the type of pension scheme concerned and cannot be chosen by the member. The three methods are as follows:

(a) **Relief at source**. If relief at source applies, the member's pension contributions are paid net of basic rate tax (20%) and the pension scheme administrator recovers the tax deducted at source from HMRC. For higher-rate taxpayers, relief at the higher rate is obtained by extending the member's basic rate band by the gross amount of the contributions. This is similar to the way in which higher-rate relief is given on Gift Aid donations (see Chapter 4). Another similarity with Gift Aid donations is that the "adjusted net income" of individuals who are eligible for age-related personal allowances (see Chapter 3) is reduced by the gross amount of the contributions.

If pension contributions are made in excess of the maximum amount on which tax relief can be claimed (see above) and relief at source applies, the excess net contributions are treated as if they were actually gross contributions on which no tax relief is available.

(b) **Net pay arrangements**. The net pay arrangement applies if an employer deducts an employee's contributions to an occupational pension scheme from the employee's pay before operating the PAYE system. This automatically gives tax relief at the employee's marginal rate of income tax.

(c) **Relief on making a claim**. If it is not possible to use relief at source or the net pay arrangement, tax relief on a member's pension contributions is given by deducting those contributions from total income when computing the member's income tax liability for the year. This might apply (for example) in the case of contributions to a retirement annuity contract. Retirement annuity contracts were at one time an important means of providing for a pension but it has not been possible to take out a new retirement annuity contract since 30 June 1988. However, contributions may still be made in relation to contracts which were in existence at that date and retirement annuity contracts which have now become registered pension schemes are not obliged to operate relief at source.

EXAMPLE 2

(a) Wesley has no income for tax purposes in 2009-10. He belongs to a registered pension scheme which operates relief at source and he makes pension contributions during 2009-10 which are all eligible for tax relief. Compute the maximum amount of his net contributions in the year.

(b) Alana is self-employed and has trading income of £62,000 in 2009-10. She belongs to a registered pension scheme which operates relief at source and she makes contributions of £500 per month (gross) to this scheme during 2009-10. Explain how tax relief will be given in relation to these contributions.

(c) Bruce is self-employed and a member of a registered pension scheme to which he pays net contributions of £320 per month. His trading income for 2009-10 is £2,750 and he has no other earnings. Explain the tax treatment of his pension contributions for the year.

(d) Charlotte is employed at an annual salary of £24,000. She pays 7% of her salary each month into her employer's occupational pension scheme (which is a registered scheme). Explain how tax relief will be given in relation to her pension contributions.

Solution

(a) Gross contributions of up to £3,600 are eligible for tax relief in the year. Deducting basic rate (20%) tax relief at source gives maximum net contributions in the year of £2,880. Wesley is entitled to basic rate tax relief on these contributions even though he is a non-taxpayer.

(b) Alana pays net contributions of £400 per month (80% of £500). Her basic rate band will be extended by £6,000 (12 x £500) so she will pay higher-rate tax on the excess of her taxable income over £43,400 (£37,400 + £6,000).

(c)   Bruce is entitled to tax relief in 2009-10 on contributions of up to £3,600 (the greater of £2,750 and £3,600). This means that his maximum net contributions are £2,880 (80% of £3,600). He has made payments totalling £3,840 (12 x £320) so there are excess contributions of £960. He will be treated as though he had made gross contributions of £4,560 (£3,600 + £960) with basic rate tax of £720 (20% of £3,600) deducted at source, giving net contributions of £3,840. His pension scheme will recover £720 from HMRC.

(d)   Charlotte earns £2,000 per month and makes monthly pension contributions of £140 (7% of £2,000). Her employer will deduct these contributions from her salary before operating the PAYE system, so she will pay income tax on only £1,860 per month.

Tax relief for contributions by employers

In general, contributions made by an employer into a registered pension scheme are deductible when computing the employer's trading profit for tax purposes. This is subject to the overriding condition that the contributions must be made wholly and exclusively for trade purposes. Note the following points:

(a)   The amount of contributions which may be deducted when computing the trading profit for a period of account is usually the amount of the contributions *actually paid* by the employer in that period. However, "spreading" provisions may apply to especially large contributions (see below).

(b)   There is no upper limit on the amount of contributions which may be deducted when computing an employer's trading profits. This is in contrast to the situation with regard to an individual's own contributions, which are subject to a limit on the amount which may attract tax relief in each tax year (see above).

(c)   Contributions made by an employer in respect of an employee are disregarded when computing the employee's income for tax purposes.

Spreading of relief

If there is an unusually large increase in an employer's pension contributions between one period of account and the next, tax relief on excess contributions may be spread over a number of periods. Assuming that the current period and the previous period are of equal length, the required procedure is as follows:

(a)   The contributions made by the employer in the current period are compared with those for the previous period. Certain contributions made in the current period are disregarded when making this comparison (e.g. contributions paid into the scheme so as to fund cost-of-living increases in current pensions).

(b) If the amount of contributions in the current period is more than 210% of the amount for the previous period, then there is an excess and this may need to be spread.

(c) The amount of the excess is calculated as the contributions made in the current period less 110% of the contributions made in the previous period. Spreading does not apply if this amount is less than £500,000. Otherwise, tax relief on the excess contributions is spread as follows:

Amount of the excess	Tax relief spread equally over
£500,000 to £999,999	current period and next period
£1,000,000 to £1,999,999	current period and next two periods
£2,000,000 or more	current period and next three periods

A further adjustment is required if the current period and previous period are of unequal length. Spreading does not apply if the employer made no contributions at all in the previous period (e.g. if a new scheme has been established in the current period).

EXAMPLE 3

During the year to 31 May 2009, an employer made contributions of £400,000 into a registered pension scheme. Explain how tax relief will be given on the contributions made during the year to 31 May 2010 if the amount of these contributions is:

(a) £800,000

(b) £920,000

(c) £1,000,000

(d) £2,640,000

Solution

(a) The current year contributions are 200% of those for the previous year. This does not exceed 210% so spreading does not apply. Tax relief on contributions of £800,000 will be given in the year to 31 May 2010.

(b) Current year contributions are 230% of those for the previous year. This exceeds 210% so spreading may be necessary. However, the excess of current year contributions over 110% of previous year contributions is only £480,000. This is less than £500,000 so spreading does not apply. Tax relief on contributions of £920,000 will be given in the year to 31 May 2010.

(c) Current year contributions are 250% of those for the previous year. This exceeds 210% so spreading may be necessary. The excess of current year contributions over 110% of previous year contributions is £560,000. This is between £500,000 and £999,999 so the excess must be spread equally over the current period and the next period.

Tax relief on contributions of £720,000 (£440,000 + £280,000) will be given in the year to 31 May 2010 and tax relief on the remaining £280,000 of contributions will be given in the year to 31 May 2011.

(d)   Current year contributions are 660% of those for the previous year. This exceeds 210% so spreading may be necessary. The excess of current year contributions over 110% of previous year contributions is £2,200,000. This exceeds £2,000,000 so the excess must be spread equally over the current period and the next three periods.

Tax relief on contributions of £990,000 (£440,000 + £550,000) will be given in the year to 31 May 2010. Relief on contributions of £550,000 will be given in each of the three years to 31 May 2011, 2012 and 2013.

Annual allowance charge

If an individual is a member of one or more registered pension schemes, a charge to income tax (known as the "annual allowance charge") arises if the "total pension input amount" for the individual in a tax year exceeds the annual allowance for the year. The annual allowance figures for tax years 2006-07 to 2010-11 are as follows:

2006-07	£215,000
2007-08	£225,000
2008-09	£235,000
2009-10	£245,000
2010-11	£255,000

The annual allowance will remain at £255,000 for tax years 2011-12 to 2015-16.

If an individual's total pension input amount (see below) for a tax year exceeds the annual allowance for that year, the excess is charged to income tax at 40%. This tax charge falls upon the individual concerned.

Pension input amount

An individual's total pension input amount for a tax year is found by calculating the pension input amount for each registered pension scheme to which the individual belongs and then aggregating these figures. The method of calculating pension input amount in relation to a pension scheme depends upon whether the scheme in question is a money purchase scheme or a defined benefits scheme. The rules are as follows:

(a)   **Money purchase schemes**. Pension input amount for an individual for a tax year in relation to a money purchase scheme is equal to the total relievable contributions made by or in respect of that individual during the "pension input period" which ends during the tax year, together with any employer contributions.

(b)   **Defined benefits schemes**. Pension input amount for an individual for a tax year in relation to a defined benefits scheme is equal to the increase in the value of the individual's pension rights under the scheme during the pension input period which ends during the tax year. For this purpose, the value of an individual's pension rights on a specified date is equal to:

(i)   the amount of any lump sum which would be payable to the individual if he or she became entitled to payment of it on that date, plus

(ii) 10 times the amount of the annual pension which would be payable to the individual if he or she became entitled to payment of it on that date.

If no pension rights accrue to the individual during a pension input period, the value of the individual's pension rights at the start of that period are increased by the greater of 5% and the percentage rise in the Retail Prices Index during the period. This might apply in the case of an occupational pension scheme if the individual no longer works for the employer concerned but will be entitled to a deferred pension at some time in the future.

There is no pension input amount for a tax year in respect of a pension scheme if the individual becomes entitled before the end of that year to all of the benefits which may be provided under the scheme. Nor is there any pension input amount for a tax year if the individual dies before the tax year ends.

Pension input periods

In general, the first pension input period for an individual in relation to a pension scheme begins on the date that the individual joins the scheme and ends on the first anniversary of that date. However, this period could end earlier (e.g. on the date up to which the pension scheme draws up its annual accounts) if this is thought to be more convenient. Each subsequent period then lasts for a year, except that the final period ends when the individual has become entitled to all of the benefits which may be provided under the scheme.

EXAMPLE 4

Diane is a member of three registered pension schemes. Her pension input amounts for the two most recent pension input periods for each of these schemes are as follows:

Scheme A:
year to 30 June 2009	£92,000
year to 30 June 2010	£95,000

Scheme B:
year to 5 April 2009	£71,000
year to 5 April 2010	£86,000

Scheme C:
year to 30 April 2009	£98,000
year to 30 April 2010	£101,000

Compute the annual allowance charge payable by Diane for tax year 2009-10.

Solution

The pension input periods which are relevant when computing total pension input amount for 2009-10 are those which end during 2009-10. Total pension input amount is therefore £276,000 (£92,000 + £86,000 + £98,000). This exceeds the 2009-10 annual allowance of £245,000 by £31,000. The annual allowance charge is £31,000 @ 40% = £12,400.

EXAMPLE 5

Compute the annual allowance charge payable by each of the following individuals for tax year 2009-10, assuming in each case that the individual concerned belongs to only one registered pension scheme:

(a) Jill's scheme is a money purchase scheme. Her relievable contributions for the pension input period which ended during 2009-10 were £130,000. Her employer's contributions on her behalf in the same period were £200,000.

(b) Eric's scheme is a defined benefit scheme. When he retires he will receive an annual pension equal to 1/80th of his final salary for each year of pensionable service. He will also receive a lump sum equal to 3/80ths of final salary for each year of pensionable service. At the start of the pension input period ending during tax year 2009-10, Eric had completed 22 years of pensionable service and his salary was £72,000 per annum. His salary had risen to £80,000 by the end of the period.

Solution

(a) Total pension input amount for the year is £330,000. This exceeds the 2009-10 annual allowance by £85,000. Therefore the annual allowance charge payable by Jill is £34,000 (40% of £85,000).

(b) If Eric became entitled to payment of his pension and lump sum at the start of the period, he would receive an annual pension of £19,800 (£72,000 x 22/80) and a lump sum of £59,400 (£72,000 x 66/80). The value of his pension rights at the start of the period is therefore £257,400 (£59,400 + (10 x £19,800)).

If Eric became entitled to payment of his pension and lump sum at the end of the period, he would receive an annual pension of £23,000 (£80,000 x 23/80) and a lump sum of £69,000 (£80,000 x 69/80). The value of his pension rights at the end of the period is therefore £299,000 (£69,000 + (10 x £23,000)).

Total pension input amount for the year is £41,600 (£299,000 − £257,400). This is less than the annual allowance of £245,000 for 2009-10 and therefore there is no annual allowance charge.

Lifetime allowance charge

There is no limit to the total level of benefits which an individual can receive from registered pension schemes during his or her lifetime. However, a charge to income tax known as the "lifetime allowance charge" will arise if total benefits exceed the lifetime allowance. Whenever pension benefits "crystallise" (e.g. on the commencement of a scheme pension) the value of the crystallised benefits is compared with the proportion of the lifetime allowance which remains unused. Any excess is chargeable to income tax. The lifetime allowance figures for tax years 2006-07 to 2010-11 are as follows:

2006-07	£1,500,000
2007-08	£1,600,000
2008-09	£1,650,000
2009-10	£1,750,000
2010-11	£1,800,000

The lifetime allowance will remain at £1,800,000 for tax years 2011-12 to 2015-16.

Any excess of crystallised benefits over the available lifetime allowance is taxed at 55% if taken as a lump sum and at 25% otherwise. This tax charge falls jointly upon the individual and the scheme administrator. In practice, the tax will usually be paid by the scheme administrator and then deducted from the benefits paid to the individual.

Operation of the lifetime allowance

Whenever a "benefit crystallisation event" occurs, it is necessary to compare the value of the benefits that have crystallised with the proportion of the individual's lifetime allowance which remains unused after any previous such events. The main examples of a benefit crystallisation event are the payment of a lump sum and the commencement of a pension. Note the following points:

(a) The value of a lump sum is the amount paid to the scheme member. The value of a pension is 20 times the amount of the pension which will be paid to the member during the first 12 months.

(b) On the first occasion that a benefit crystallisation event occurs, the value of the benefits that have crystallised is compared with the lifetime allowance as it stands on the date of the event. On a subsequent event, the value of the crystallised benefits is compared with the *proportion* of the lifetime allowance (if any) that remains after previous events. However, this proportion is applied to the lifetime allowance as it stands on the date of the subsequent event.

(c) If an individual becomes entitled to a scheme pension and a pension commencement lump sum from the same scheme on the same date, the payment of the lump sum is considered to be the earlier of the two events.

EXAMPLE 6

Sharon is a member of two registered pension schemes. She receives no benefits from either of these schemes until 19 March 2008, when she takes a lump sum of £960,000 from one of her schemes. On 5 January 2010 she takes a lump sum of £810,000 from her other scheme. Calculate the lifetime allowance charge arising from these two events.

Solution

On 19 March 2008, the crystallised benefits absorb 60% of the lifetime allowance (which is £1,600,000 for events occurring during 2007-08). There is no lifetime allowance charge and 40% of the lifetime allowance remains unused.

On 5 January 2010, the crystallised benefits of £810,000 are compared with 40% of £1,750,000 (the lifetime allowance for events occurring during 2009-10). Benefits exceed the available allowance of £700,000 by £110,000. Therefore there is a lifetime allowance charge of £60,500 (55% of £110,000).

The lifetime allowance has now been fully used, so the full value of any further pension benefits will be subject to the lifetime allowance charge.

EXAMPLE 7

Stuart is a member of a registered pension scheme. He took no benefits from this or any other scheme until February 2010, when he received a lump sum of £600,000 and began to receive a pension of £65,000 per annum. Calculate the lifetime allowance charge arising from these events.

Solution

The value of the pension is £1,300,000 (20 x £65,000) so the total value of the benefits received is £1,900,000. This exceeds the lifetime allowance for 2009-10 by £150,000 and so there will be a lifetime allowance charge.

The lump sum is deemed to be the earlier of the two benefit crystallisation events, so it is the pension which has caused the lifetime allowance to be exceeded. Hence the excess is taxed at 25% and the lifetime allowance charge is £37,500 (25% of £150,000).

Tax relief on pension contributions as from 6 April 2011

As from tax year 2011-12, tax relief on pension contributions made by an individual with a taxable income exceeding £180,000 will be restricted to the basic rate. If taxable income is between £150,000 and £180,000, the rate of relief will be tapered down until it becomes equal to the basic rate at taxable income of £180,000.

Special "anti-forestalling" legislation has been introduced to ensure that individuals who are affected by this change cannot benefit by increasing their pension contributions (in excess of their normal regular pattern) before the restriction takes effect.

Summary

▶ In a defined benefits pension scheme, the benefits payable to members are usually based on final salary and length of service. In a money purchase scheme, the benefits payable to members are based upon the size of the pension fund built up during a member's working life.

▶ Registered pension schemes enjoy certain tax advantages when compared with unregistered schemes. A registered scheme's investment income is exempt from income tax. Any capital gains made on the disposal of scheme investments are exempt from capital gains tax. Tax relief is available in relation to contributions made by members and employers. Tax-free lump sums may be paid to members.

▶ Normal minimum pension age will rise from 50 to 55 as from 6 April 2010.

▶ The maximum amount of pension contributions on which an individual can claim tax relief in any tax year is equal to the greater of the individual's earnings for that year and £3,600.

▶ Basic rate tax relief on a individual's pension contributions may be given by deduction at source. Relief at the higher rate is then given by extending the basic rate band by the gross amount of the contributions. Alternatively, tax relief may be given by deducting contributions from an employee's pay before operating PAYE or (exceptionally) by deduction from total income.

▶ In general, an employer's pension contributions are deducted when computing the employer's trading profit for the period of account in which the contributions are paid. However, tax relief on contributions which are unusually large may be spread over two or more periods.

▶ A tax liability will arise if an individual's total pension inputs for a tax year exceed the annual allowance. The excess is charged to income tax at 40% and this tax charge falls upon the individual concerned.

▶ A tax liability may arise when a benefit crystallisation event occurs. The most common examples of such an event are the payment of a lump sum to a member or the commencement of a pension. The value of the crystallised benefits is compared with the unused proportion of the lifetime allowance and any excess is charged to income tax. The tax charge is at either 55% or 25% (depending on whether the benefits are taken as a lump sum or a pension) and falls jointly upon the scheme administrator and the member concerned.

Exercises

13.1 State the maximum contribution to registered pension schemes on which an individual could obtain tax relief in 2009-10 if the individual's earnings for the year were:

(a)   £120,000   (b)   £1,200.

13.2 Freda is a member of a registered pension scheme which operates tax relief at source. She has income from self-employment of £60,000 in 2009-10 and makes pension contributions of £1,000 (gross) per month. Explain how tax relief will be given in relation to her pension contributions.

13.3 An employer's contributions into a registered pension scheme during the year to 30 June 2009 are £600,000. Explain how tax relief will be given on the contributions of £1,860,000 which the employer makes during the year to 30 June 2010.

13.4 Damon is a member of a defined benefit registered pension scheme. On retirement, he will receive an annual pension equal to 1/60th of final salary for each year of pensionable service. He will also receive a lump sum equal to 3/80ths of final salary for each year of pensionable service.

At the start of the pension input period ending during tax year 2009-10, Damon's annual salary was £360,000 and he had accumulated 20 years of pensionable service. By the end of the period his salary had risen to £450,000. Calculate the annual allowance charge payable by Damon for 2009-10.

13.5 Karen belongs to a number of registered pension schemes. Until tax year 2007-08 she had received no benefits from any of these schemes but in October 2007 she took a lump sum of £1,280,000 from one of her schemes. She received no further benefits until July 2010 when she took a lump sum of £400,000 from another of her schemes.

(a)   Calculate the amount of any lifetime allowance charges arising in relation to either of Karen's lump sums.

(b)   How would the situation change if the lump sum of £400,000 had been received in October 2007 and the lump sum of £1,280,000 had been received in July 2010?

*13.6 Irma is self-employed. She was born in 1951. Her trading income for 2009-10 was £27,490 and during the year she made net contributions to a registered pension scheme of £6,000. Her only other income in 2009-10 comprised net bank interest of £27,208.

(a)   Calculate Irma's income tax liability for 2009-10.

(b)   Re-calculate Irma's income tax liability for 2009-10, now assuming that she was born in 1941.

Chapter 14

Payment of income tax, surcharges, interest and penalties

Introduction

Interest is charged on income tax which is paid late. Conversely, interest may be added to repayments of income tax. The main purpose of this chapter is to identify the dates on which income tax is payable and to explain how the interest due on underpaid or overpaid tax is calculated. This chapter also considers financial penalties to which a taxpayer may become liable as a consequence of non-compliance with tax law.

Payment of income tax

Under the Self Assessment system (see Chapter 1) income tax which is not deducted at source is payable as follows:

(a)   The taxpayer's income tax liability for the tax year in relation to all sources of income is aggregated. This tax liability is increased by the amount of any Class 4 National Insurance contributions (NICs) which are due for the year (see Chapter 15).

(b)   Payments on account of the total liability (POAs) are due on 31 January in the tax year and on the following 31 July. For example, the POAs for 2009-10 are due on 31 January 2010 and 31 July 2010. Each POA is equal to 50% of the taxpayer's liability to income tax and Class 4 NICs for the *previous* tax year, less any tax which was paid by deduction at source. For this purpose, the term "deduction at source" includes tax paid via the PAYE system and any tax satisfied by the set-off of tax credits, as well as tax deducted at source from interest etc. Note that:

(i)   POAs are not required if the taxpayer's total liability to income tax and Class 4 NICs for the preceding year (less tax deducted at source) was under £1,000.

(ii)   POAs are also not required if more than 80% of the taxpayer's liability for the previous year was satisfied by deduction of tax at source.

(iii) A taxpayer who believes that his or her liability for the current year will be less than in the previous year may claim to make reduced POAs. HMRC cannot reject such a claim but there are penalties for making the claim fraudulently or negligently (see below).

(c) A balancing payment (or repayment) is normally due on 31 January following the end of the tax year. For example, the 2009-10 balancing payment is due on 31 January 2011. But note that:

(i) If a tax return is issued late (i.e. after 31 October following the end of the tax year to which it relates) and this has not been caused by the taxpayer's failure to notify his or her chargeability to tax, the balancing payment is due three months after the issue date of the return.

(ii) If a self-assessment is amended by the taxpayer or by HMRC (or if a discovery assessment is raised) any additional amount payable is due 30 days after the date of its notification to the taxpayer or on 31 January following the end of the tax year, whichever is the later. However, this rule does *not* defer the date from which interest accrues on the additional tax.

The amount of the balancing payment is equal to the income tax and Class 4 NICs liability for the year, less any tax deducted at source and less the POAs. Any capital gains tax due for the year (see Chapter 16) is added to this payment.

(d) Finance Act 2009 introduced "Managed payment plans" (MPPs) which will allow taxpayers to spread their tax payments over a period straddling the normal due dates. However, MPPs will not begin until after April 2011.

Interest is charged if any payment is made late and surcharges (see below) may also be imposed. Taxpayers receive regular statements from HMRC showing the amounts due, the amounts paid to date and the amounts of any interest and surcharges.

EXAMPLE 1

Warren's income tax and Class 4 NICs liability for 2008-09 was £17,200, of which £14,500 was satisfied by deduction at source. His liability for 2009-10 is £19,300, of which £16,100 is paid by deduction at source. State the dates on which Warren is required to pay his 2009-10 income tax and Class 4 NICs and compute the amount payable on each date.

Solution

Over 80% of Warren's total liability for 2008-09 was paid by deduction at source and so no POAs are required for 2009-10. His remaining liability of £3,200 (£19,300 − £16,100) for 2009-10 is payable on 31 January 2011.

EXAMPLE 2

In 2008-09, Barbara's income tax and Class 4 NICs liability was £26,000, of which £4,000 was satisfied by deduction at source. Her liability for 2009-10 is £34,000, of which £5,000 is paid by deduction at source. State the dates on which Barbara is required to pay her 2009-10 income tax and Class 4 NICs and compute the amount payable on each date.

Solution

(i)   31 January 2010, POA £11,000 (50% of (£26,000 – £4,000))

(ii) 31 July 2010, POA £11,000

(iii) 31 January 2011, balancing payment £7,000 (£34,000 – £5,000 – POAs £22,000).

Surcharges

In addition to any interest due on tax paid late (see below), the taxpayer may also be required to pay a "surcharge". The surcharges scheme operates as follows:

(a)   If all or part of a balancing payment remains unpaid more than 28 days after the due date, a surcharge arises equal to 5% of the amount unpaid.

(b)   If a self-assessment is amended (or a discovery assessment is raised) and any of the additional amount which becomes payable remains unpaid more than 28 days after the due date, a surcharge arises equal to 5% of the amount unpaid.

(c)   Any amount due under (a) and (b) above which remains unpaid more than six months after the due date is subject to a further 5% surcharge.

(d)   Surcharges are payable 30 days after the date on which they are imposed.

Note that the surcharges scheme does *not* apply to POAs.

EXAMPLE 3

Continuing the above example, Barbara made the following payments for 2009-10:

	£
31 January 2010	11,000
1 September 2010	11,000
31 January 2011	6,000
1 September 2011	1,000

Compute the surcharges (if any) which would be imposed.

Solution

(i)   The first POA is paid in full and on time.

(ii) The second POA is paid 32 days late. However, late POAs do not attract surcharges.

(iii) £1,000 of the balancing payment is paid over six months late. A first surcharge of £50 (5% of £1,000) is imposed on 1 March 2011 (payable 31 March 2011). A second £50 surcharge is imposed on 1 August 2011 (payable 31 August 2011).

Interest on income tax

Under the Self Assessment system, interest is charged on all late payments of tax and Class 4 NICs. Interest is also charged if a surcharge is paid late. However, interest may be paid to the taxpayer when repayments are made of overpaid tax and Class 4 NICs.

Interest on overdue income tax

Interest charged on overdue income tax (and Class 4 NICs) is calculated as follows:

(a) In the case of late POAs and balancing payments, interest runs from the due date of payment up to the date on which the tax is actually paid.

(b) In the case of discovery assessments and amendments to self-assessments, interest runs from the date on which the balancing payment is due for the year to which the assessment relates (normally the 31 January which follows the end of that year) even though the tax itself might not be due for payment until a later date.

(c) Interest on a surcharge runs from the due date of payment of that surcharge (i.e. 30 days after its imposition).

(d) In practice, if a taxpayer submits a paper tax return by 31 October without calculating his or her tax liability (see Chapter 1) and HMRC does not notify the taxpayer of the amount due until after 31 December, interest on this tax starts to run 30 days after the date on which the taxpayer is notified.

(e) Interest is calculated on a daily basis. Apparently it is HMRC practice to use a denominator of 366 in such calculations, whether or not a leap year is involved.

EXAMPLE 4

Again continuing the above example, calculate the total interest payable by Barbara for 2009-10, assuming that the two surcharges are both paid on 29 September 2011 and that interest is charged at 4.5% per annum.

Solution

(i) Interest on the second POA is £43.28 (£11,000 x 4.5% x 32/366).

(ii) Interest on the final £1,000 of the balancing payment (paid 213 days late) is £26.19 (£1,000 x 4.5% x 213/366).

(iii) Interest on the first surcharge (paid 182 days late) is £1.12 (£50 x 4.5% x 182/366).

(iv) Interest on the second surcharge (paid 29 days late) is £0.18 (£50 x 4.5% x 29/366).

Total interest due is £70.77 (£43.28 + £26.19 + £1.12 + £0.18).

Interest on overpaid income tax

Repayments of overpaid income tax and Class 4 NICs attract interest. This is calculated at a lower rate than the rate of interest which is charged on overdue tax but is itself exempt from income tax. Interest on overpaid income tax and Class 4 NICs is known as "repayment supplement" and runs from the "relevant date" to the date on which repayment is made to the taxpayer. The relevant date is:

(a) as regards POAs and any other payments of income tax and Class 4 NICs (other than tax deducted at source), the date of payment

(b) as regards income tax deducted at source, 31 January following the tax year for which the tax is deducted.

Repayments of income tax and Class 4 NICs for a year are attributed first to the balancing payment made for that year, secondly in two equal parts to the POAs for that year and finally to tax deducted at source for the year. Note that:

(a) If a repayment is triggered by a claim to carry back a loss or payment from a later year to an earlier year (e.g. if a trading loss is carried back or a Gift Aid donation is carried back) interest on this repayment runs from 31 January following the later year, *not* the earlier year.

(b) Surcharges and penalties repaid to a taxpayer also attract interest, running from the date of payment to the date of repayment.

(c) Apparently it is HMRC practice to use a denominator of 365 when computing interest on a repayment, whether or not a leap year is involved.

(d) Repayment supplement is not paid in relation to tax that has been deliberately overpaid. This rule prevents taxpayers from using HMRC as a source of tax-free interest.

Penalties

A taxpayer who fails to comply with statutory requirements may become liable to a number of financial penalties, the most important of which are listed below. Some of these penalties are fixed in amount but HMRC often has the power to "mitigate" (i.e. reduce) the amount charged if it sees fit to do so. Whether or not a penalty is mitigated will usually depend mainly upon the seriousness of the taxpayer's offence and the degree to which the taxpayer has co-operated with HMRC. The main penalties are as follows:

(a) **Failure to notify chargeability to tax**. An individual must notify HMRC if he or she is liable to tax for a tax year, even if a return has not been issued for that year. At present, failure to notify within six months of the end of the tax year could render the individual liable to a penalty of up to 100% of the tax remaining unpaid on 31 January following the end of the tax year.

   However, a new penalty regime applies to failures which occur on or after 1 April 2010. This regime is not confined to income tax but covers a range of taxes, including capital gains tax, corporation tax and VAT. Under the new regime, the penalty for a failure to notify liability to income tax for a tax year is expressed as a percentage of the tax remaining unpaid on 31 January following the end of that year. But no penalty is charged if the taxpayer has a reasonable excuse for the failure. The applicable percentage is determined as follows:

   (i)   For a "deliberate and concealed" failure to notify, where the failure is deliberate and the taxpayer has attempted to conceal it, the percentage is 100%.

   (ii) For a failure which is "deliberate but not concealed" the percentage is 70%.

   (iii) Otherwise, the percentage is 30%.

   These penalties may be reduced if the taxpayer discloses the failure. There are greater reductions if the disclosure is "unprompted" than if it is "prompted". A disclosure is unprompted if it is made at a time when the taxpayer has no reason to believe that the irregularity has been discovered or is about to be discovered by HMRC.

(b) **Late submission of a tax return**. A £100 fixed penalty is imposed if a tax return is submitted late and a further £100 fixed penalty is imposed if the return is more than six months late. If the return is more than 12 months late, an additional penalty may be imposed of up to 100% of the tax liability for the year. Furthermore, a tribunal may direct that a penalty of up to £60 per day should be imposed, running from the date of the direction to the date on which the tax return is finally submitted.

   It should be noted that a new penalty regime is to be introduced in relation to the late submission of a return. This regime will apply across a range of taxes and will also cover penalties for late payment. When implemented, the new regime will replace the present penalties for late submission of a self assessment tax return and will also replace the surcharges system explained earlier in this chapter. However, it seems likely that the new penalty regime will not take effect for income tax until at least April 2011.

(c) **Submission of an incorrect tax return**. A single penalty regime applies in relation to the submission of incorrect returns (and certain other documents) for the purposes of income tax and many other taxes. This common regime applies if an incorrect return or other document leads to an understatement of the amount of tax due and the inaccuracy was either careless or deliberate. No penalty is charged if the taxpayer has taken reasonable care. The regime also applies if an assessment issued by HMRC understates the amount of tax due and the taxpayer fails to take reasonable steps to notify HMRC of this fact within 30 days. The amount of any penalty under the regime is expressed as a percentage of the potential lost revenue and is determined as follows:

(i) For a "deliberate and concealed" inaccuracy, the percentage is 100%.

(ii) If an inaccuracy is "deliberate but not concealed" the percentage is 70%.

(iii) Otherwise, the percentage is 30%. The percentage is also 30% in cases where the taxpayer has failed to notify HMRC of an under-assessment.

As with the "failure to notify chargeability" penalties (see above) these penalties may be reduced if the taxpayer discloses the infringement and there are greater reductions if the disclosure is unprompted than if it is prompted.

(d) **Fraud or negligence when claiming reduced POAs**. A taxpayer who makes a claim for reduced POAs and does so fraudulently or negligently may be subject to a maximum penalty equal to the difference between the POAs actually made and the POAs that should have been made.

(e) **Failure to keep required records**. A taxpayer who fails to maintain or retain adequate records in support of the year's tax return may be subject to a penalty of up to £3,000.

In every case, the penalty is *in addition* both to the tax itself and to any surcharges or interest charged in relation to that tax.

Summary

▸ Under the Self Assessment system, income tax not collected at source or via the PAYE system is usually payable by means of two payments on account, followed by a balancing payment.

▸ Surcharges may be levied if a balancing payment is paid late and interest is payable on any tax paid late. Interest usually runs from the due date of payment up to the actual date of payment.

▸ Repayments of overpaid tax also attract interest, usually running from the date on which the tax was paid up to the date of repayment.

▸ Financial penalties may be imposed for various breaches of the tax law.

Exercises

14.1   For each of the following taxpayers, state the dates on which the 2009-10 income tax is due to be paid and calculate the amount payable on each date. (Ignore Class 4 NICs).

(a)   Guy's 2008-09 income tax liability was £1,600, of which £1,150 was paid via the PAYE system and £50 was deducted at source from investment income. His income tax liability for 2009-10 is £1,750, of which £1,250 is paid via PAYE and £60 is deducted at source.

(b)   Marie's 2008-09 income tax liability was £6,730, of which £4,370 was paid via PAYE and £20 was deducted at source. Her 2009-10 liability is £6,580, of which £4,810 is paid via PAYE and £35 is deducted at source.

(c)   Majid's 2008-09 income tax liability was £14,850, of which £11,990 was paid via PAYE and £110 was deducted at source. His 2009-10 liability is £16,110, of which £12,370 is paid via PAYE and £140 is deducted at source.

14.2   Dorothy's income tax and Class 4 NICs liability for 2008-09 was £30,000, of which £6,000 was deducted at source. Her liability for 2009-10 is £35,000, of which £7,000 is deducted at source. She made a first POA in respect of 2009-10 on 27 February 2010 and a second POA on 12 September 2010. She also made a balancing payment for the year on 21 February 2011. All of her payments were for the correct amount.

(a)   Calculate the amount of any surcharges payable by Dorothy in relation to 2009-10.

(b)   Assuming an interest rate of 4.5% per annum, calculate the amount of any interest payable by Dorothy in relation to 2009-10.

14.3   Jabran did not receive a tax return for 2008-09 but he was aware that he had income which had not been assessed to tax. He notified HMRC of this fact on 2 October 2009 and a return was issued to him on 15 November 2009. He completed the return and sent it back with the necessary payment on 7 April 2010.

Explain the penalties, surcharges and interest which Jabran might be required to pay.

*14.4   Frances paid income tax and Class 4 NICs of £43,000 in 2008-09, of which £19,000 was deducted at source. Her total liability for 2009-10 is £63,000, of which £21,000 is deducted at source. Her payments for 2009-10 are as follows:

	£
15 February 2010	12,000
14 September 2010	12,000
3 February 2011	14,000
15 December 2011	4,000

Calculate the surcharges and interest payable for the year, assuming that any surcharges are paid on 15 December 2011 and that interest is charged at 4.5% per annum.

Chapter 15

National Insurance contributions

Introduction

National Insurance contributions (NICs) are payable by employees, by employers and by those who are self-employed. Contributions are collected by the National Insurance Contributions Office (NICO) of HM Revenue and Customs and paid into a National Insurance Fund. This fund, supplemented (if necessary) by a grant from the Treasury, is then used to provide contributory social security benefits such as the state retirement pension. The purpose of this chapter is to explain the circumstances in which NICs are payable and the way in which NICs are calculated.

Class 1 National Insurance contributions

Class 1 NICs are payable in relation to employees aged 16 or over. The employees themselves pay *primary* Class 1 NICs whilst employers pay *secondary* Class 1 NICs on their employees' behalf. Employees who continue to work after reaching state pension age pay no further primary contributions but employers must still pay secondary contributions in relation to such employees.

The amount of Class 1 NICs payable in relation to an employee depends upon the employee's earnings. For National Insurance purposes, an employee's earnings consist of his or her gross pay *before* deducting pension contributions, donations made under the terms of a payroll giving scheme or any other expenses borne by the employee. An employee's earnings for this purpose do *not* include:

(a) tips received directly from customers

(b) mileage allowances received from the employer if these are calculated at a rate which does not exceed the AMAP rate for the first 10,000 miles, regardless of the number of miles actually driven by the employee (see Chapter 7); but any excess forms part of the employee's earnings chargeable to Class 1 NICs

(c) pensions and redundancy pay

(d) employer contributions to a registered pension scheme

(e) business expenses paid for or reimbursed by the employer, including reasonable travel and subsistence expenses

(f)   certain items which are paid for or provided by the employer, to the extent that these items are exempt from income tax; including relocation expenses, personal incidental expenses, workplace car parking, suggestion scheme awards, works buses, the loan of bicycles, up to £55 per week of childcare etc. (see Chapter 7).

Benefits in kind which are not convertible into cash are generally not subject to Class 1 NICs. However, the *employer* may incur a Class 1A NICs liability in relation to such benefits (see below). If an employee's remuneration is paid in the form of non-cash assets such as gold bars, coffee beans, fine wines or assigned trade debts, a liability to Class 1 NICs will arise if the assets are readily convertible into cash. Payments made in shares are also liable to Class 1 NICs, unless they are "own company" shares provided under an approved share scheme or share option scheme (see Chapter 7).

Contribution periods

The main principles of the Class 1 National Insurance system are as follows:

(a)   Primary and secondary Class 1 NICs are calculated according to the amount of an employee's earnings in a "contribution period". For those paid weekly or monthly, each week or month usually constitutes a contribution period. However, special rules apply to company directors (see later in this chapter).

(b)   The liability to Class 1 NICs in a given contribution period is governed solely by the employee's earnings in that period and is totally unaffected by earnings in other periods. This is in contrast to the income tax PAYE system (see Chapter 7) which accumulates earnings over the year and calculates a tax liability each week or month based on the employee's total earnings for the tax year to date.

(c)   If an employee has two or more employments in a contribution period, each of these employments is considered separately for the purpose of calculating the liability to Class 1 NICs. Earnings from two or more employments are aggregated only if the employments are with the same employer or associated employers.

(d)   The percentage rate at which Class 1 NICs are calculated depends upon whether or not the employee is contracted out of the State Second Pension (S2P), formerly known as the State Earnings Related Pension Scheme (SERPS). Those who are not contracted out pay higher Class 1 NICs in return for an earnings-related increase in some of their social security benefits.

Some employees are contracted out because they are members of their employer's contracted-out salary-related (COSR) occupational pension scheme. Others may be members of contracted-out money-purchase (COMP) schemes. The primary and secondary Class 1 NICs payable in relation to a contracted-out employee depend upon the type of pension scheme to which the employee belongs.

Primary Class 1 NICs

The primary Class 1 NICs payable by an employee for a contribution period falling during 2009-10 are calculated as follows:

(a)　The employee's earnings in the period are compared with the *primary threshold*. The primary threshold for 2009-10 is £110 per week or £476 per month. No primary Class 1 NICs are payable for a contribution period if the employee's earnings in the period do not exceed this threshold.

(b)　If earnings in the contribution period exceed the primary threshold, primary Class 1 NICs are generally payable at 11% on earnings between the primary threshold and the upper earnings limit (UEL). The UEL for 2009-10 is £844 per week or £3,656 per month. Any earnings beyond the UEL attract primary Class 1 NICs at 1%.

(c)　However, if the employee is contracted out, the rate of primary Class 1 NICs payable on earnings between the primary threshold and the upper accruals point (UAP) is reduced to 9.4%. The UAP for 2009-10 is £770 per week or £3,337 per month.

(d)　These rules may be summarised as follows:

	Not contracted out	Contracted out (COSR)	(COMP)
Weekly-paid:			
On the first £110	0%	0%	0%
On the next £660 (up to £770)	11%	9.4%	9.4%
On the next £74 (up to £844)	11%	11%	11%
On remaining earnings above £844	1%	1%	1%
Monthly-paid:			
On the first £476	0%	0%	0%
On the next £2,861 (up to £3,337)	11%	9.4%	9.4%
On the next £319 (up to £3,656)	11%	11%	11%
On remaining earnings above £3,656	1%	1%	1%

It is worth noting that the UEL is now aligned with the point at which higher rate income tax becomes payable. This occurs when a taxpayer's total income exceeds the sum of the personal allowance and the basic rate band. For 2009-10, this means that the UEL for the year is £43,875 (£6,475 + £37,400). Thus the UEL for a week is £844 (£43,875 ÷ 52) and the UEL for a month is £3,656 (£43,875 ÷ 12).

EXAMPLE 1

(a)　Compute the primary Class 1 NICs payable by the following weekly-paid employees for the week ending 14 August 2009:

(i)　Employee A has earnings in the week of £500 and is not contracted out.

(ii)　Employee B has earnings in the week of £800 and is not contracted out.

(iii)　Employee C has earnings in the week of £1,000 and is contracted out (COSR).

(b) Compute the primary Class 1 NICs payable by the following monthly-paid employees for the month of August 2009:

  (i) Employee D has earnings in the month of £2,500 and is contracted out (COSR).

  (ii) Employee E has earnings in the month of £3,500 and is contracted out (COSR).

  (iii) Employee F has earnings in the month of £4,500 and is not contracted out.

Solution

(a) (i) 11% x (£500 – £110) = £42.90.

  (ii) 11% x (£800 – £110) = £75.90.

  (iii) 9.4% x (£770 – £110) + 11% x (£844 – £770) + 1% x (£1,000 – £844) = £71.74.

(b) (i) 9.4% x (£2,500 – £476) = £190.26.

  (ii) 9.4% x (£3,337 – £476) + 11% x (£3,500 – £3,337) = £286.86.

  (iii) 11% x (£3,656 – £476) + 1% x (£4,500 – £3,656) = £358.24.

Secondary Class 1 NICs

The secondary Class 1 NICs payable by an employer in relation to an employee for a contribution period falling during 2009-10 are calculated as follows:

(a) The employee's earnings in the contribution period are compared with the *secondary threshold*. This is the same as the primary threshold. No secondary contributions are payable if earnings in a contribution period do not exceed this threshold.

(b) If earnings in the period exceed the secondary threshold, secondary Class 1 NICs are generally payable at 12.8% on earnings above the threshold.

(c) However, if the employee is contracted out, the secondary Class 1 NICs payable on earnings between the secondary threshold and the UAP are calculated at either 9.1% (COSR) or 11.4% (COMP).

(d) These rules may be summarised as follows:

	Not contracted out	Contracted out (COSR)	(COMP)
Weekly-paid:			
On the first £110	0%	0%	0%
On the next £660 (up to £770)	12.8%	9.1%	11.4%
On remaining earnings above £770	12.8%	12.8%	12.8%
Monthly-paid:			
On the first £476	0%	0%	0%
On the next £2,861 (up to £3,337)	12.8%	9.1%	11.4%
On remaining earnings above £3,337	12.8%	12.8%	12.8%

EXAMPLE 2

Refer back to the previous example in this chapter and compute the secondary Class 1 NICs payable in relation to each employee.

Solution

(a) (i)   12.8% x (£500 – £110) = £49.92.

     (ii)   12.8% x (£800 – £110) = £88.32.

     (iii) 9.1% x (£770 – £110) + 12.8% x (£1,000 – £770) = £89.50.

(b) (i)   9.1% x (£2,500 – £476) = £184.18.

     (ii)   9.1% x (£3,337 – £476) + 12.8% x (£3,500 – £3,337) = £281.21.

     (iii) 12.8% x (£4,500 – £476) = £515.07.

Directors' Class 1 NICs

The fact that NICs are calculated for each contribution period separately, without reference to any earnings in other contribution periods, means that employees with identical annual earnings may pay very different amounts of primary contributions in the tax year, depending upon the distribution of their earnings over that year. Consider the following (rather extreme) example:

EXAMPLE 3

During 2009-10, an employee (not contracted out) earns a total of £48,000, paid at the rate of £4,000 each month.

(a)   Calculate the total primary Class 1 NICs payable for the year.

(b)   What would the total primary contributions be for the year if the employee received £48,000 in one month and nothing in the remaining 11 months?

Solution

(a)   Primary contributions each month are equal to 11% x (£3,656 – £476) + 1% x (£4,000 – £3,656) = £353.24. This gives a total of £4,238.88 for the year.

(b)   Primary contributions for the month in which the employee was paid £48,000 would be equal to 11% x (£3,656 – £476) + 1% x (£48,000 – £3,656) = £793.24. Nothing would be payable for the rest of the year.

     Therefore the employee would save £3,445.64 in primary contributions (£4,238.88 – £793.24) if the entire year's salary were received in a single month.

Employees are not normally able to arrange for all of their year's earnings to be paid in one contribution period so as to avoid primary Class 1 NICs. However, company directors may well have sufficient influence to make such an arrangement. To counter this, the Class 1 contributions of company directors are calculated on an *annual* basis, regardless of the distribution of their earnings over the tax year. In effect, the entire year becomes a single contribution period. For 2009-10, the Class 1 NICs of a company director are payable according to the following rules:

(a) The primary threshold, upper accruals point (UAP) and upper earnings limit (UEL) for the year are £5,715, £40,040 and £43,875 respectively.

(b) The total primary contributions payable for the year by a director with earnings which exceed £5,715 are calculated as follows:

	Not contracted out	Contracted out (COSR)	(COMP)
Annual earnings:			
On the first £5,715	0%	0%	0%
On the next £34,325 (up to £40,040)	11%	9.4%	9.4%
On the next £3,835 (up to £43,875)	11%	11%	11%
On remaining earnings above £43,875	1%	1%	1%

(c) The secondary threshold for the year is also £5,715. The total secondary contributions payable for the year in relation to a director with earnings which exceed £5,715 are calculated as follows:

	Not contracted out	Contracted out (COSR)	(COMP)
Annual earnings:			
On the first £5,715	0%	0%	0%
On the next £34,325 (up to £40,040)	12.8%	9.1%	11.4%
On remaining earnings above £40,040	12.8%	12.8%	12.8%

EXAMPLE 4

Rework the previous example, given that the employee in question is a company director.

Solution

Regardless of the distribution of the director's earnings over the tax year, primary contributions would be equal to 11% x (£43,875 − £5,715) + 1% x (£48,000 − £43,875) = £4,238.85.

Class 1A National Insurance contributions

Benefits in kind which are not convertible into cash are generally exempt from Class 1 NICs. However, these benefits give rise to a Class 1A contribution instead, *payable only by the employer* (not by the employee). For 2009-10, this contribution is calculated as 12.8% of the amount of the benefit in kind which is assessed on the employee for income tax purposes (see Chapter 7).

EXAMPLE 5

In 2009-10, George (a P11D employee) is provided with a petrol-engined motor car by his employer who pays for all fuel and other running costs. The car had a list price when new of £11,700 and has an emission rating of 189g/km. George's employer also pays his private medical insurance premium of £600 per annum.

Calculate the Class 1A contribution payable by George's employer for the year.

Solution

The employee benefits assessed on George for income tax purposes are:

	£
Car (15% + 10% = 25% x £11,700)	2,925
Fuel (25% x £16,900)	4,225
Medical insurance premium	600
	7,750

Therefore the Class 1A contribution payable by George's employer is 12.8% x £7,750 = £992.00.

Class 1B National Insurance contributions

From time to time, an employer may enter into a PAYE Settlement Agreement (PSA) with HM Revenue and Customs. The effect of such an agreement is that the employer pays the income tax liability of employees in relation to minor or irregular benefits in kind. In these circumstances, the employer is liable to make a Class 1B National Insurance contribution calculated (in 2009-10) as 12.8% of the sum of the benefits in kind and the associated tax which is payable under the terms of the PSA.

Class 2 National Insurance contributions

Class 2 NICs are payable by self-employed people who are over 16 and under pensionable age. The contributions are payable at a flat rate (for 2009-10) of £2.40 per week. A person whose earnings from self-employment in a tax year are less than the "small earnings exception" (£5,075 for 2009-10) is not required to pay Class 2 NICs for that year but may do so voluntarily so as to maintain a full contributions record. Note that:

(a) For the purposes of Class 2 NICs, a self-employed person's earnings in a tax year are equal to the net profit, *before* adjustment for tax purposes, shown by that person's accounts for the year. The required figure is the actual net profit from 6 April to the following 5 April. Unless accounts are drawn up to 5 April, it will be necessary to apportion the net profits shown in two years' accounts to obtain this figure.

(b) If a self-employed person has two or more businesses, the profits of all of them are aggregated and a Class 2 NICs liability arises unless the aggregate profits are less than the small earnings exception.

EXAMPLE 6

(a) Alison is self-employed. Her accounts for the year to 5 April 2010 show a net profit of £4,770. Is she liable to pay Class 2 NICs for 2009-10?

(b) Amanda is also self-employed. Her accounts for the year to 31 December 2009 show a net profit of £4,880 and her accounts for the year to 31 December 2010 show a net profit of £6,080. Is she liable to pay Class 2 NICs for 2009-10?

Solution

(a) Alison's accounts (which coincide with tax year 2009-10) show a net profit which is less than the small earnings exception. Therefore she is not required to pay Class 2 NICs for 2009-10.

(b) Amanda's accounts do not coincide with the tax year so some apportionment is necessary. Her actual net profit in 2009-10 is £5,180 (£4,880 x 9/12 + £6,080 x 3/12). This is not less than the small earnings exception so she is required to pay Class 2 NICs for 2009-10.

Class 3 National Insurance contributions

Any individual (employed or self-employed) whose earnings are too low in a contribution period to require a National Insurance contribution may make a voluntary Class 3 contribution so as to maintain a full contributions record. For 2009-10, the amount of the Class 3 contribution is £12.05 per week.

Class 4 National Insurance contributions

In addition to the flat rate Class 2 liability described above, self-employed people who are over 16 and under pensionable age may also be liable to pay earnings-related Class 4 contributions. A self-employed person's Class 4 liability for a given tax year is based on the amount of trading income which is charged to income tax for that year. The Class 4 NICs are collected along with the income tax liability (see Chapter 14). Note that:

(a) The Class 4 liability is based on the person's trading income for the tax year *after* adjusting for capital allowances and trading losses but *before* deducting pension contributions. Trading losses which are set against the non-trading income of a tax year for income tax purposes (see Chapter 11) are set against the first available trading income of that year or subsequent years for Class 4 purposes.

(b) If a self-employed person has more than one business, the earnings from all businesses for the year are aggregated.

(c) There is no liability to Class 4 NICs if trading income does not exceed the *lower profits limit* (£5,715 for 2009-10).

(d) If trading income exceeds the lower profits limit, Class 4 NICs are payable at 8% on profits between the lower profits limit and the upper profits limit. The upper profits limit for 2009-10 is £43,875. Any profits beyond the upper profits limit are charged to Class 4 NICs at 1%.

EXAMPLE 7

Calculate the Class 4 NICs payable for 2009-10 in each of the following cases:

(a) Shawn has trading income for 2009-10 of £14,500.

(b) Catherine has trading income for 2009-10 of £50,000.

(c) Paul has trading income for 2009-10 of £5,120.

Solution

(a) 8% x (£14,500 – £5,715) = £702.80.

(b) 8% x (£43,875 – £5,715) + 1% x (£50,000 – £43,875) = £3,114.05.

(c) Paul's profits are less than the lower profits limit so Class 4 NICs for the year are nil.

Annual maximum contributions

An individual who has more than one employment will normally be required to make Class 1 contributions in respect of each employment. Similarly, an individual who is both employed and self-employed will normally be required to make Class 1 contributions in respect of the employment and Class 2 and Class 4 contributions in respect of the self-employment. In these circumstances, the total NICs payable could become onerous but relief is available in the form of limits on the amount of NICs payable by any one person in any one year. In practice, the calculation of these limits can be very complex but a brief summary of the rules is as follows:

(a) **Maximum Class 1 and 2 contributions**. In any one tax year, the total of the Class 1 contributions payable by an individual *at the main rate* (currently 11%) plus any Class 2 contributions is limited to the amount of the Class 1 contributions which would be payable by a weekly-paid employee who had 53 weeks of earnings equal to the UEL. For 2009-10, this gives a maximum contribution of £4,279.22 (53 × 11% × (£844 − £110)). A refund is made if this limit is exceeded, but the refund calculation takes into account the fact that earnings above the primary threshold which do not attract 11% contributions should attract 1% contributions instead.

(b) **Maximum Class 1, 2 and 4 contributions**. A refund of *Class 4 contributions only* is made if the total main rate (11%) Class 1 contributions, Class 2 contributions and main rate (8%) Class 4 contributions paid by an individual in any one tax year exceed the amount obtained by adding 53 Class 2 contributions to the maximum main rate Class 4 contribution for the year. For 2009-10 this limit is equal to £3,180.00 (53 @ £2.40 + 8% × (£43,875 − £5,715)). The refund calculation takes into account the fact that profits above the lower profits limit which do not attract Class 4 contributions at 8% should attract Class 4 contributions at 1% instead.

If an employee is contracted out, Class 1 contributions paid in the year are recalculated at the not-contracted-out rate before comparison is made with the above limits.

EXAMPLE 8

(a) Sabrina has two employments throughout 2009-10. Calculate the refund of NICs due for the year if she is not contracted out and her regular monthly earnings from the two employments are as follows:

    (i) £850 and £1,250   (ii) £2,000 and £3,000   (iii) £4,000 and £4,500.

(b) Stephanie is employed at a monthly salary of £3,700. She is not contracted out. She also has a small business and pays 53 weekly Class 2 NICs in 2009-10. She pays no Class 4 NICs. Calculate the refund of NICs due for the year.

(c) Stewart is self-employed and pays 53 weekly Class 2 NICs in 2009-10. His trading income for 2009-10 is £33,850. He also receives directors' fees of £13,680 in the year. He is not contracted out. Calculate the refund of NICs due for the year.

Solution

(a) Sabrina will have paid *main rate* Class 1 NICs as follows:

	(i) £	(ii) £	(iii) £
First employment:			
12 x 11% x (£850 – £476)	493.68		
12 x 11% x (£2,000 – £476)		2,011.68	
12 x 11% x (£3,656 – £476)			4,197.60
Second employment:			
12 x 11% x (£1,250 – £476)	1,021.68		
12 x 11% x (£3,000 – £476)		3,331.68	
12 x 11% x (£3,656 – £476)			4,197.60
	1,515.36	5,343.36	8,395.20

In case (i), total contributions do not exceed the maximum, so no refund is due.

In case (ii), contributions exceed the maximum by £1,064.14 (£5,343.36 – £4,279.22) so Sabrina is entitled to a refund. However, the earnings which have given rise to the excess contributions are still subject to 1% contributions, so the refund is reduced by one-eleventh to £967.40.

In case (iii), Sabrina's contributions exceed the maximum by £4,115.98 (£8,395.20 – £4,279.22) so she is entitled to a refund of 10/11 x £4,115.98 = £3,741.80.

(b) Stephanie will have paid *main rate* Class 1 NICs and Class 2 NICs as follows:

	£
Class 1 (12 x 11% x (£3,656 – £476))	4,197.60
Class 2 (53 @ £2.40)	127.20
	4,324.80

This exceeds the maximum by £45.58 (£4,324.80 – £4,279.22). The refund can be made entirely out of Class 2 contributions so there will be no need to collect further 1% contributions on refunded main rate Class 1 contributions. The refund is £45.58.

(c) Stewart will have paid NICs as follows:

	£
Class 1 (11% x (£13,680 – £5,715))	876.15
Class 2 (53 @ £2.40)	127.20
Class 4 (8% x (£33,850 – £5,715))	2,250.80
	3,254.15

The total main rate Class 1 and Class 2 contributions are well within the maximum of £4,279.2. But the total of the main rate Class 1 contributions, Class 2 contributions and main rate Class 4 contributions exceeds the maximum of £3,180.00 by £74.15. Therefore Stewart is entitled to a refund of Class 4 contributions. However, the profits which have given rise to the excess contributions are still subject to 1% contributions, so the refund is reduced by one-eighth to £64.88.

Summary

▸ Primary Class 1 NICs are payable by employees. Secondary Class 1 NICs are payable by their employers. Both primary and secondary contributions are reduced if the employee is contracted out.

▸ Class 1 NICs are calculated with respect to earnings in a contribution period and each contribution period is considered independently.

▸ In 2009-10, primary Class 1 NICs are generally payable at 11% on earnings between the primary threshold and the upper earnings limit. But earnings between the primary threshold and the upper accruals point are charged at 9.4% (rather than 11%) if the employee is contracted out. Earnings which lie beyond the upper earnings limit attract primary Class 1 NICs at 1%.

▸ In 2009-10, secondary Class 1 NICs are generally payable at 12.8% on earnings above the secondary threshold. But earnings between the secondary threshold and the upper accruals point are charged at either 9.1% or 11.4% (rather than 12.8%) if the employee is contracted out.

▸ The Class 1 NICs of company directors are assessed on an annual basis and are unaffected by the distribution of the director's earnings over the year.

▸ Class 1A NICs are payable by employers in relation to benefits in kind which are not convertible into cash. Class 1B NICs are payable by employers in relation to PAYE Settlement Agreements.

▸ Class 2 NICs are payable at a flat rate by self-employed people whose profits exceed the small earnings exception.

▸ Class 4 NICs are paid by self-employed people and are earnings-related. In 2009-10, Class 4 NICs are payable at 8% on profits between the lower and upper profit limits and at 1% on profits beyond the upper limit.

▸ Class 3 NICs are paid voluntarily in order to maintain a full contributions record.

▸ There are annual maximum limits on the amount of NICs payable by an individual.

Exercises

15.1 Compute the primary and secondary Class 1 NICs payable in relation to the following employees (none of whom are contracted out):

(a)   A earns £120 for the week ending 19 June 2009.

(b)   B earns £780 for the week ending 19 June 2009.

(c)   C earns £930 for the week ending 19 June 2009.

(d)   D earns £450 for the month of September 2009.

(e)   E earns £3,300 for the month of September 2009.

(f)   F earns £6,000 for the month of September 2009.

15.2 Rework your answer to Exercise 15.1, assuming now that each of the employees is a member of a COSR scheme.

15.3 Mark is self-employed and makes up his accounts annually to 30 November. His accounts for the year ended 30 November 2009 show a net profit of £7,270 and his accounts for the year ended 30 November 2010 show a net profit of £3,490. His 2009-10 trading income is £8,900. Calculate the NICs payable by Mark for 2009-10.

*15.4 Brenda is a company director and earns a regular monthly salary of £6,000. In December 2009 she received a £20,000 bonus. She is provided with a diesel-engined company car which has an emission rating of 232g/km and which had a list price when new of £16,000. The company pays all the running costs of the car, including fuel. Her BUPA subscription of £750 per year is paid by the company.

Calculate the NICs payable in respect of Brenda for 2009-10. She is a member of a COSR scheme.

*15.5 Leonard is employed and receives a salary of £2,798 per month. He is not contracted out. He also has a small business and pays 53 weekly Class 2 NICs for 2009-10. His trading income for 2009-10 is £10,500. Calculate the refund of NICs due to Leonard for the year.

Review questions (Set A)

A1   Tom Tulliver has been appointed as sales director of Pembridge plc, a company in the building industry. In addition to a basic salary of £83,000, he has been offered a comprehensive benefits package. The proposed deal is:

(i)   The company will provide him with a new car which, together with accessories, will cost £19,500. The car has an emission rating of 235g/km. Petrol for private use will be provided but Mr Tulliver must make a contribution of £400 per year towards its cost.

(ii)   An interest-free loan of £5,250 will be made to him on appointment and need only be repaid on his leaving the company. The loan will be used to purchase various household items.

(iii) He has a choice of meals in the company canteen, which is open to all staff free of charge, or luncheon vouchers worth £5 per day, an amount equivalent to the normal cost of the meals. He has decided to accept the luncheon vouchers. The normal working year is 200 working days.

(iv)   His son, aged three, is presently attending a nursery (which does not have approved childminder status) at a cost of £3,405 per year. Pembridge plc has offered to give his son a free place in their own nursery but Mr Tulliver would like to continue the existing arrangement and for Pembridge to pay the fees to the existing nursery.

Mr Tulliver's wife earns £15,000 per annum. She contributes 6% of her salary to her employer's occupational pension scheme (which operates the net pay arrangement).

Both Mr and Mrs Tulliver have building society accounts which will yield net interest of £6,400 and £2,208 respectively in 2009-10. Mr Tulliver receives UK preference dividends of £4,680 annually.

Mr Tulliver's appointment will begin on 1 April 2009 and he wishes to examine his and his wife's tax position before the start of fiscal year 2009-10.

Required:

(a)   Advise Mr Tulliver on the taxation implications of his employment package.

(b)   Advise him of any changes you consider that he should make to maximise the tax efficiency of the proposed package.

(c)   Using your answer in (a) as to the amount of Mr Tulliver's income, advise him of the likely income tax borne by him and his wife for 2009-10 and, again, suggest how the tax position might be improved. (*Note*: Assume that the official rate of interest is 4.75%).   (*Amended from AAT*)

A2   Jeremy, who has been married for many years, is 77 years old and receives a retirement pension of £17,760 per annum. He also receives dividend income of £6,750 per annum. In 2003 he purchased a life annuity from which a monthly income of £325 (gross) is paid. The capital element of each payment was agreed with HM Revenue and Customs at £300. Income tax is being deducted from the income element.

Jeremy owns a furnished cottage which he rents to holidaymakers. In tax year 2009-10 it was let for 20 weeks at a weekly rental of £300.

The following expenditure was incurred:

	£
Insurance (see note)	400
Water rates	500
Council tax	1,000

Note: The insurance of £400 was paid on 1 January 2010. The insurance paid on 1 January 2009 was £360.

You are required:

To calculate the income tax payable by Jeremy for the year 2009-10, assuming that no elections have been made with respect to the married couple's allowance.   *(ACCA)*

A3   The system of Self Assessment for individuals was introduced in tax year 1996/97 and is now well established. Before 1996/97, the assessment of an individual's tax liability was entirely the responsibility of the Inland Revenue and it was quite possible for taxpayers to delay the assessment and payment of tax by withholding information from the Inland Revenue for as long as they could. The introduction of Self Assessment shifted responsibility from the tax authorities to the taxpayer and made it much more likely that tax is assessed and paid on time.

Required:

Outline the main features of the system of Self Assessment for individuals.   *(CIPFA)*

A4   In May 2009 Bernard, a self-employed plumber, and his son Gerald, a self-employed electrician, purchased 1,000 empty barrels from a Scottish whisky distillery. The barrels were over 100 years old and of no further use to the distillery. Bernard and Gerald sawed the barrels into halves and sold them to several local garden centres for use as ornamental flower tubs. Bernard and Gerald paid £10 per barrel to the distillery and sold a half-barrel for £8. Three-quarters of the barrels were sold by Bernard and Gerald in the summer of 2009 and the remainder in the summer of 2010.

You are required:

To prepare a list of points for consideration prior to writing a report to Bernard and Gerald on the liability to income tax on the profit generated by the venture.   *(ACCA)*

A5   In each of the following situations, show the tax position assuming that the maximum potential reliefs are claimed as soon as possible. Then advise your client of any alternatives that might be available.

(i)   Mr de Praet began trading on 1 January 2004, preparing accounts to 31 December annually. Recent results are:

	£	
Year to 31 December 2008	20,000	Profit
Year to 31 December 2009	(40,000)	Loss

He receives rents of £10,000 annually. It is estimated that the trading profits for the year to 31 December 2010 are likely to be £75,000.

(ii)   Henry Percy started a business on 1 July 2005 and makes up accounts to 30 June annually. His adjusted trading results (before capital allowances) for the last two years have been:

	£	
Year to 30 June 2008	18,000	Profit
Year to 30 June 2009	(10,000)	Loss

Up to 31 December 2008 he always hired his plant and machinery but on 1 January 2009 he purchased a new machine for £7,360. He has no income other than his business profits.   *(Amended from AAT)*

*A6   Your directors are considering paying substantial cash bonuses to a number of senior employees, including some directors.

You are required:

To draft a report to the board setting out the regulations for taxing these bonuses, indicating when the tax and National Insurance contributions on them would be payable.

(CIMA)

*A7 Claud Chapperon is a self-employed wholesale clothing distributor who began trading on 1 July 2002. His summarised accounts for the year to 30 June 2009 are shown below (figures in brackets refer to notes).

	£	£
Sales (1)		400,000
Opening inventory (2)	40,000	
Purchases	224,000	
	264,000	
Closing inventory (2)	32,000	232,000
Gross profit		168,000
Wages and national insurance (3)	52,600	
Rent and rates	29,100	
Repairs and renewals (4)	3,490	
Miscellaneous expenses (5)	665	
Taxation (Claud's own income tax)	17,549	
Bad debts (6)	820	
Legal expenses (7)	1,060	
Depreciation	570	
Lease rental on Claud's car (8)	8,400	
Loss on sale of office furniture	60	
Gift Aid donations (9)	200	
Transport costs	4,141	
Interest (10)	990	
Running expenses of Claud's car (11)	2,000	
Premium on lease (12)	6,000	
Lighting and heating	1,250	
Sundry expenses (all allowable)	710	
Relocation expenditure (13)	2,395	132,000
Net profit		36,000

Notes:

1. Sales include £500 reimbursed by Claud's family for clothing taken from stock. The reimbursement represented cost price.

2. The basis of both the opening and closing inventory valuations was "lower of cost or market value" less a general reserve of 50%.

3. Included in wages are Claud's drawings of £50 per week, his NICs of £121 for the year and his wife's wages and NICs totalling £14,750. His wife works full-time in the business as a secretary.

4. The charge for repairs and renewals includes £3,111 for fitting protective covers over the factory windows and doors to prevent burglary.

5. Miscellaneous expenses comprise:

	£
Theft of money by employee	65
Political donation to Green Party	100
Gifts of 100 "Chapperon" calendars	500
	665

6. Bad debts comprise:

	£
Trade debt written off	720
Loan to former employee written off (not made for trade purposes)	250
Reduction in general allowance	(150)
	820

7. Legal expenses comprise:

	£
Defending action re alleged faulty goods	330
Costs re lease of new larger premises	250
Unsuccessful appeal against previous year's income tax assessment	200
Defending Claud in connection with speeding offence	190
Debt collection	90
	1,060

8. Claud's leased car had a retail price of £20,000 and was leased from 1 July 2008 to 30 June 2009. The car is petrol-driven and is not a low-emission car.

9. Gift Aid donations consist of £120 paid to the local children's hospital and £80 paid to Oxfam. Both payments were made on 30 April 2009.

10. Interest is as follows:

	£
Bank overdraft interest (business account)	1,020
Interest on overdue tax	130
Interest credited on NSB investment a/c (see note 14)	(160)
	990

11. HM Revenue and Customs has agreed that one-third of Claud's mileage is private. Included in the charge for motor running expenses is £65 for a speeding fine incurred by Claud whilst delivering goods to a customer.

12. The premium was for a lease of six years. The lease began on 1 July 2008.

13. The relocation expenditure was incurred in transferring the business to new and larger premises.

14. Interest recently credited to the NSB investment account is as follows:

	£
31 December 2008	160
31 December 2009	70

The following information is also provided:

(i)   Capital allowances for the year to 30 June 2009 are £480.

(ii) Claud was born in 1953. He made net contributions of £9,880 to a registered pension scheme during 2009-10. His wife was also born in 1953.

You are required:

(a)   To prepare a profit adjustment statement in respect of the period of account to 30 June 2009, showing the trading income for 2009-10.

(b)   To calculate the Class 4 NICs payable by Claud for 2009-10.

(c)   To prepare an estimate of Claud's income tax borne for 2009-10.   *(ACCA)*

*A8   When submitting a business's annual accounts to HM Revenue and Customs, it is usual to send schedules under the following expenditure headings:

(i)   Gifts and entertainment

(ii) Major repairs

(iii) Redundancy payments to employees.

You are required:

To state the information which should be included under each of the above headings, explaining why such information will be required.   *(CIMA)*

*A9   Joseph Kent started business on 1 October 2008 as a joiner making conservatories. His tax-adjusted profits (before deduction of capital allowances) were as follows:

	£
Period to 31 December 2009	37,000
Year ended 31 December 2010	24,000
Year ended 31 December 2011	42,000

Capital additions and disposals were as follows:

Additions

		£
1 October 2008	Plant and machinery	3,500
1 October 2008	Car (at valuation)	12,200
1 May 2009	Trailer	2,500
1 December 2010	Car (emissions 184g/km)	13,000
1 December 2011	Plant and machinery	2,400

			£
Disposals			
1 December 2010	Car acquired 1/10/08		7,000
1 January 2011	Plant and machinery (at less than cost)		2,000

Private use of both cars has been agreed with HM Revenue and Customs at 20%. No claim is made to treat any of the assets as short-life assets.

Joseph manufactured the conservatories in rented premises until 1 January 2011, when he purchased a new factory unit on an industrial estate for £20,000 (not in an enterprise zone). All assets were brought into use immediately upon acquisition.

Joseph's wife Sephora is a solicitor employed by a practising firm at a salary of £46,720 per annum. The following additional information is provided for 2009-10:

(i) A new petrol-engined car was provided for Sephora's use in August 2008. The list price at that time was £25,000. Of this amount, £4,000 was contributed by Sephora so that a better car could be provided. She was required to pay £25 per month towards the private use of the car but not towards the private fuel, all of which was provided by her employers. The car's emission rating is 187g/km.

(ii) Sephora has received a loan of £90,000 on the matrimonial home from her employers on which she pays interest at 1.75%.

(iii) Sephora made a qualifying donation to the Oxfam charity on 1 July 2009 of £400 under the Gift Aid scheme.

(iv) Both Joseph and Sephora are under 65 years old.

You are required:

(a) To calculate Joseph's trading income for 2008-09 to 2011-12 inclusive.

(b) To calculate Sephora's income tax liability for 2009-10 (assuming an official rate of interest of 4.75% per annum). *(ACCA)*

Part 2

CAPITAL GAINS TAX

Chapter 16

Introduction to capital gains tax

Introduction

The next six chapters of this book are concerned with capital gains tax (CGT), which was introduced in 1965 with the aim of taxing any gains arising on the disposal of capital assets. Capital gains tax has undergone many changes since its inception and the changes that were made between 1965 and 1992 were consolidated into the Taxation of Chargeable Gains Act 1992. This Act has since been amended by subsequent Finance Acts.

Chargeable persons

A CGT liability may arise when a "chargeable person" makes a "chargeable disposal" of a "chargeable asset". The main categories of chargeable person are as follows:

(a) individuals who are resident or ordinarily resident in the UK

(b) business partners, who are each responsible for their share of the CGT due on the capital gains of a partnership

(c) the trustees of a trust or settlement

(d) the personal representatives of a deceased person.

Husbands and wives are assessed independently for CGT purposes, as are same-sex civil partners. The following are *not* chargeable persons for CGT purposes:

(a) companies and other corporate bodies, which pay corporation tax on their capital gains (not CGT) and therefore cannot incur a CGT liability

(b) registered charities and friendly societies, community amateur sports clubs, local authorities and local authority associations, registered pension schemes, unit trusts, investment trusts and approved scientific research associations, all of which are generally exempt from CGT (subject to certain restrictions).

Chargeable assets

All assets are regarded as chargeable assets except for those which are specifically exempted from CGT. The main exemptions are as follows:

(a) a taxpayer's principal private residence (see Chapter 20)

(b) motor cars, including vintage and veteran cars, but not including personalised car number plates; vehicles not covered by this exemption, such as vans, lorries and motor cycles, will generally fall within the scope of (d) below

(c) items of tangible, movable property (referred to as "chattels") which are disposed of for £6,000 or less (see Chapter 18)

(d) chattels with a predictable useful life of 50 years or less ("wasting chattels") unless used in business and eligible for capital allowances (see Chapter 18)

(e) gilt-edged securities and qualifying corporate bonds (see Chapter 19)

(f) National Savings Certificates and Premium Bonds

(g) foreign currency (if acquired for private use)

(h) winnings from pools, lotteries, betting etc.

(i) decorations for valour (unless acquired by purchase)

(j) damages or compensation received for personal or professional injury and compensation received for mis-sold personal pension schemes

(k) life assurance policies (unless purchased from a third party)

(l) shares in a Venture Capital Trust (see Chapter 6)

(m) investments held in either an Individual Savings Account (ISA) or a Child Trust Fund (see Chapter 6).

It is important to realise that neither a chargeable gain nor an allowable loss can arise on the disposal of an asset that is not a chargeable asset. This means that any gains made on the disposal of such assets are not taxable but it also means that any losses which arise will not attract tax relief.

Chargeable disposals

The main and most obvious instance of a chargeable disposal occurs when a chargeable asset is sold. However, the sale of an asset in the course of trade (i.e. the sale of trading stock or inventory) does *not* constitute a chargeable disposal since any gain arising on such a sale is taxed as a trading profit (see Chapter 8).

Before CGT was introduced in 1965 there was a great incentive for taxpayers to show that the gain arising on the sale of an asset was a capital gain (not taxable) rather than a trading profit (taxable). This incentive diminished with the introduction of CGT, but it is still important to distinguish between capital gains and trading profits since the rules of computation for capital gains and trading profits are different.

As well as the sale of a chargeable asset, the following are also chargeable disposals:

(a) the sale of *part* of a chargeable asset

(b) the gift of all or part of a chargeable asset

(c) the loss or destruction of a chargeable asset

(d) the receipt of a capital sum derived from a chargeable asset (e.g. compensation received from an insurance company if an asset is damaged).

With regard to gifts, it is important to realise that CGT is basically a tax on the increase in value of an asset whilst owned by the taxpayer. This increase in value is chargeable to tax even if the taxpayer gives the asset away and receives nothing in return.

In general, the date on which a chargeable disposal is deemed to occur is the date on which ownership of the asset changes hands, regardless of the date on which any payment is made.

Non-chargeable disposals

The following types of disposal are *not* chargeable disposals and therefore any gains or losses arising on such disposals are exempt from CGT:

(a) gifts to charities, art galleries, museums etc.

(b) disposals caused by the death of the taxpayer.

Disposals between a husband and wife who live together at any time during the tax year in which the disposal occurs *are* chargeable disposals. However, such disposals are deemed to occur at a disposal value such that neither a chargeable gain nor an allowable loss arises on the disposal (see Chapter 17). This rule also applies to same-sex civil partners who have entered into a legally-recognised civil partnership.

A similar treatment may be accorded to gifts of national heritage property, subject to certain undertakings being received (e.g. with regard to reasonable public access).

Basis of assessment

A person's CGT liability for a tax year is based upon the chargeable disposals made by that person during the tax year. For example, the 2009-10 CGT assessment is based upon chargeable disposals made between 6 April 2009 and 5 April 2010 inclusive. No liability to CGT arises until an asset is disposed of, so the mere fact that an asset has appreciated in value will not of itself trigger a CGT assessment. The amount of the CGT assessment for a tax year is calculated as follows:

(a) The chargeable gain or allowable loss arising on each disposal made during the tax year is calculated separately (the method of calculation is described in great detail in subsequent chapters of this book).

(b) If total gains exceed total losses, the losses are subtracted from the gains to give the taxpayer's "net gains" for the year. If total losses exceed total gains, the gains are subtracted from the losses to give the "net losses" for the year.

(c) If there are net gains for the year, these are reduced first by any unrelieved losses brought forward from previous tax years or by any losses carried back on the death of the taxpayer (see later in this chapter).

(d) Net gains are then further reduced by the amount of the "annual exemption" for the year (£10,100 for 2009-10). The amount remaining after deduction of the annual exemption is the CGT assessment for the year. If net gains are too low to allow the whole of the annual exemption to be deducted, the CGT assessment for the year is £nil and the balance of the annual exemption is lost.

(e) If there are net losses for the year, the CGT assessment for that year is £nil and the whole of the annual exemption is lost. The net losses may then be carried forward for relief in future years, as described later in this chapter.

Husbands, wives and civil partners are each entitled to the full annual exemption. This exemption is also available to the trustees of a trust or settlement established for a mentally disabled person or for certain other infirm or disabled persons. For trustees of other settlements the annual exemption is lower (£5,050 for 2009-10). The personal representatives of a deceased person are entitled to the full annual exemption for the year of death and for the following two years.

EXAMPLE 1

Four taxpayers each make three chargeable disposals during 2009-10. Compute their CGT assessments for the year (assuming that there are no unrelieved losses brought forward or carried back) if these disposals give rise to the following gains and losses:

(a) Taxpayer A has gains of £2,900, £3,500 and £5,950.

(b) Taxpayer B has gains of £5,500, £5,840 and a loss of £350.

(c) Taxpayer C has gains of £950, £8,330 and a loss of £2,050.

(d) Taxpayer D has a gain of £8,950 and losses of £9,500 and £800.

Solution

(a) Total gains are £12,350 and there are no losses. Net gains are £12,350. Subtracting the annual exemption of £10,100 gives a CGT assessment for the year of £2,250.

(b) Total gains are £11,340 and total losses are £350. Therefore net gains are £10,990. Subtracting the annual exemption of £10,100 gives a CGT assessment for the year of £890.

(c) Total gains are £9,280 and total losses are £2,050. Net gains are £7,230. This is less than the annual exemption of £10,100, so the CGT assessment for the year is £nil. The unused part of the annual exemption (£2,870) is lost.

(d) Total gains are £8,950 and total losses are £10,300. Net losses are £1,350. The CGT assessment for the year is £nil and the whole of the annual exemption is lost.

Rate of CGT

For tax year 2009-10, there is a single rate of capital gains tax (18%). This rate is the same as in 2008-09 and applies to individuals, trustees and personal representatives.

EXAMPLE 2

Calculate the amount of CGT payable for 2009-10 by an individual whose net gains for the year are:

(a) £6,100   (b) £10,100   (c) £36,200   (d) £100,000.

Assume that there are no unrelieved losses brought forward from previous years and no losses carried back on the death of the taxpayer.

Solution

(a) Net gains are less than the annual exemption. The CGT liability for the year is £nil and £4,000 of the annual exemption is unused.

(b) Net gains are exactly equal to the annual exemption, which is used in full. The CGT liability for the year is £nil.

(c) The CGT liability is (£36,200 − £10,100) x 18% = £4,698.00.

(d) The CGT liability is (£100,000 − £10,100) x 18% = £16,182.00.

Relief for capital losses

If a taxpayer has net losses for a year, the CGT assessment for that year is £nil and the annual exemption is lost. The amount of the net losses may then be carried forward without time limit and set against the net gains of future years.

Losses carried forward must be offset against the first available net gains, but are offset only to the extent that those net gains exceed the annual exemption for the year in which they arise, so preventing the annual exemption from being wasted. Any losses remaining unrelieved are carried forward again to subsequent years. This method of preserving the annual exemption applies *only* to losses brought forward from a previous year. It is *not* possible to preserve the annual exemption by restricting the set-off of current year losses. Since married couples and same-sex civil partners are taxed independently, the losses of one spouse (or partner) cannot be offset against the gains of the other spouse (or partner).

EXAMPLE 3

Four taxpayers each have £3,000 of capital losses brought forward from previous tax years. Calculate their 2009-10 CGT assessments if their total gains and losses in 2009-10 are as follows:

(a) Taxpayer A has gains of £7,500 and losses of £1,300.

(b) Taxpayer B has gains of £10,300 and losses of £200.

(c) Taxpayer C has gains of £12,300 and losses of £500.

(d) Taxpayer D has gains of £16,200 and losses of £1,200.

Solution

(a) Taxpayer A's net gains for the year are £6,200. This is less than the annual exemption of £10,100 so the CGT assessment for the year is £nil and the balance of the annual exemption is lost. There is no scope for relieving losses brought forward, so the entire £3,000 is carried forward to 2010-11.

(b) Taxpayer B's net gains for the year are £10,100. This is exactly equal to the annual exemption so the CGT assessment for the year is £nil. There is no scope for relieving losses brought forward, so the entire £3,000 is carried forward to 2010-11.

(c) Taxpayer C's net gains for the year are £11,800. This exceeds the annual exemption by £1,700 so £1,700 of the losses brought forward are relieved in 2009-10, giving a CGT assessment for the year of £nil. The remaining £1,300 of the losses are unrelieved and are therefore carried forward to 2010-11.

(d) Taxpayer D's net gains for the year are £15,000. This exceeds the annual exemption by £4,900 so the entire £3,000 of losses brought forward are relieved in 2009-10, giving a CGT assessment for the year of £1,900. There are no unrelieved losses to carry forward.

Anti-avoidance rules relating to capital losses

TCGA 1992 contains the following anti-avoidance rules designed to prevent taxpayers from taking unfair advantage of the reliefs available in relation to capital losses:

(a)   Capital losses incurred on a disposal to a connected person can be offset only against gains made on disposals to the *same person*, in the same or subsequent tax years. A taxpayer is deemed to be connected with a number of persons for CGT purposes, mainly relatives and business associates (see Chapter 17).

(b)   A capital loss is not an allowable loss if it arises as a result of arrangements made by the taxpayer and a main purpose of those arrangements is to gain a tax advantage by creating an artificial capital loss. This "targeted anti-avoidance rule" (TAAR) is intended to ensure that allowable capital losses are restricted to those which arise from genuine commercial transactions.

Losses in the year of death

As stated above, disposals caused by the death of a taxpayer are exempt from CGT, though such disposals may give rise to an inheritance tax liability. But disposals made in the year of death (i.e. from 6 April up to the date of death) are *not* exempt from CGT and are taxed in the usual way, with a full annual exemption given for the year.

If a taxpayer suffers net losses in the year of death, such losses cannot (for obvious reasons) be carried forward. However, net losses incurred in the year of death may instead be carried back and set off against the net gains of the previous three years (most recent years first). As is the case with losses carried forward, losses carried back are set against a year's net gains only to the extent that those net gains exceed the annual exemption for the year in which they arise.

EXAMPLE 4

Sarah dies on 16 December 2009, having made net capital losses of £7,300 between 6 April 2009 and the date of her death. Her net gains in the previous three years (and the annual exemption for each of those years) were as follows:

	Net gains	Annual exemption
	£	£
2006-07	9,950	8,800
2007-08	2,400	9,200
2008-09	13,950	9,600

Calculate her CGT assessments for 2006-07 to 2009-10 inclusive.

Note:

Strictly speaking, the CGT assessments for 2006-07 and 2007-08 may have been affected by a relief known as "taper relief" which was available in those tax years but has since been abolished. Taper relief should be ignored in this example.

Solution

Since losses in the year of death are carried back to the most recent year first, it is easier to begin with the year of death and then work backwards.

(a) In 2009-10, Sarah has net losses. Her CGT assessment for the year is therefore £nil and the annual exemption (available in full) is lost. The net losses of £7,300 may be carried back to 2008-09, 2007-08 and 2006-07, in that order.

(b) In 2008-09, Sarah's net gains of £13,950 exceed the annual exemption by £4,350 so £4,350 of the losses carried back are relieved in 2008-09, giving a CGT assessment for the year of £nil. The remaining £2,950 of the losses are carried back to 2007-08.

(c) In 2007-08, Sarah's net gains of £2,400 are less than the annual exemption of £9,200. Therefore the CGT assessment for the year is £nil and the balance of the annual exemption is lost. There is no scope for relieving losses carried back, so the £2,950 is now carried back to 2006-07.

(d) In 2006-07, Sarah's net gains of £9,950 exceed the annual exemption by £1,150 so £1,150 of the losses carried back are relieved in 2006-07, giving a CGT assessment for the year of £nil. The remaining £1,800 of the losses incurred in the year of death cannot be carried back any further and therefore cannot be relieved in any way.

Assuming that CGT assessments have already been made for 2006-07 and 2008-09, it will be necessary to revise these assessments to take into account the relief for losses carried back and to refund any CGT already paid for those years.

Relief for trading losses

If a taxpayer has claimed that a trading loss should be set against his or her total income for a tax year (or if no such claim can be made because total income for that year is zero) the taxpayer may further claim that any unrelieved part of the trading loss should be set against the capital gains of that year (see Chapter 11). If such a claim is made, the amount of the claim must be for the *lower* of the following two amounts:

(a)   the amount of the unrelieved trading loss which is available for relief

(b)   the "maximum amount", which is the amount of the CGT assessment, *disregarding the annual exemption*, that would have been raised for the year if the claim had not been made.

It is important to realise that the "maximum amount" is calculated as if the annual exemption simply did not exist. Not only is the annual exemption itself ignored in this calculation but so is the fact that capital losses brought forward might be restricted so as to preserve the exemption.

A trading loss which is set against capital gains is treated as a capital loss incurred in the year of the claim and is therefore relieved *before* giving relief for capital losses brought forward.

EXAMPLE 5

(a)   Richard has net gains for 2009-10 of £16,300 and capital losses brought forward of £3,300. Calculate his CGT assessment for 2009-10.

(b)   Richard has unrelieved trading losses (eligible for relief against his capital gains in 2009-10) of £27,500. Re-calculate his CGT assessment for 2009-10 if he claims that these losses should (as far as possible) be set against his capital gains.

(c)   Now calculate the CGT assessment for 2009-10 if Richard's capital losses brought forward are £8,300 instead of £3,300.

Solution

(a)   Without a trading losses claim for 2009-10, the CGT assessment for the year will be:

	£
Net gains	16,300
Less: Capital losses b/f	3,300
	13,000
Less: Annual exemption	10,100
CGT assessment	2,900

There will be no unrelieved capital losses to carry forward.

(b) A trading losses claim would have to be for the lower of:

    (i)   the unrelieved trading loss (£27,500)

    (ii)   the CGT assessment (disregarding the annual exemption) that would be raised if a trading losses claim were not made (£13,000).

Therefore the claim would be £13,000. This would be relieved in priority to capital losses brought forward. The CGT assessment would be:

	£
Net gains	16,300
Less: Trading losses	13,000
	3,300
Less: Annual exemption (restricted)	3,300
CGT assessment	nil

The remainder of the annual exemption (£6,800) would be lost. There would be no scope for relieving any of the capital losses brought forward, so the entire £3,300 would be carried forward to 2010-11. This claim would seem to be wasteful, since trading losses of £13,000 are sacrificed in order to reduce the CGT assessment by £2,900 and preserve capital losses of £3,300 (a total of £6,200).

(c) Without a trading losses claim, the CGT assessment would be calculated as follows:

	£
Net gains	16,300
Less: Capital losses b/f (restricted)	6,200
	10,100
Less: Annual exemption	10,100
CGT assessment	nil

There would be unrelieved capital losses of £2,100 carried forward. The maximum amount of a trading loss claim is £8,000 (£16,300 − £8,300) so the claim would have to be for £8,000 and the CGT assessment would be:

	£
Net gains	16,300
Less: Trading losses	8,000
	8,300
Less: Annual exemption (restricted)	8,300
CGT assessment	nil

The remainder of the annual exemption (£1,800) would be lost and the capital losses of £8,300 would be carried forward to 2010-11 in their entirety. The effect of the claim would be to preserve capital losses of £6,200 at the expense of sacrificing trading losses of £8,000. This might be worthwhile if Richard believes that he will have more chance of relieving capital losses than trading losses in future years.

Administration of CGT

The tax administration system which was described in Chapter 1 applies to CGT as well as to income tax. Note that:

(a) Taxpayers are normally not required to fill in the capital gains tax pages of their tax returns if both of the following conditions are satisfied:

  (i) total disposal proceeds for the year do not exceed four times the amount of the annual exemption (£40,400 for 2009-10)

  (ii) total chargeable gains for the year do not exceed the amount of the annual exemption (£10,100 for 2009-10).

  For this purpose, the term "total chargeable gains" means the total chargeable gains for the year *before* deduction of either current year losses or losses brought forward from previous years.

(b) A capital loss is not an allowable loss unless its amount is quantified and notified to HMRC. If the taxpayer receives a tax return for the year in which a loss is incurred, then notification must be made in that return. Otherwise, notification may be made in a later year's tax return or by sending a separate notice to HMRC. Losses are not allowed unless notified to HMRC by 31 January in the sixth tax year following the tax year in which the losses are incurred. As from April 2010, capital losses will have to be notified to HMRC within four years of the end of the tax year concerned.

(c) Acquisitions of chargeable assets do not need to be entered on the tax return.

Payment of CGT

CGT is normally payable on 31 January following the end of the tax year to which the tax relates. For instance, the date on which the 2009-10 CGT liability is normally payable is 31 January 2011. An important difference between the payment of CGT and the payment of income tax is that payments on account of the CGT liability are *not* required.

If the proceeds of a disposal are received by the taxpayer in instalments over a period of more than 18 months, the taxpayer may make a claim for the CGT due in relation to the disposal to be payable over the period of the instalments or over an eight-year period, whichever is the shorter.

Interest, surcharges and penalties

The regime of interest, surcharges and penalties which was described in Chapter 14 applies to both CGT and income tax.

Summary

▸ A liability to CGT may arise when a chargeable person makes a chargeable disposal of a chargeable asset. Individuals resident or ordinarily resident in the UK are chargeable persons. Companies are not chargeable persons.

▸ All assets are chargeable assets unless specifically exempted.

▸ A chargeable disposal occurs when all or part of a chargeable asset is sold other than in the course of trade, given away, lost or destroyed.

▸ An individual's CGT liability for a tax year is based upon the chargeable disposals made by that individual during the year. For 2009-10, the first £10,100 of net gains are exempt from CGT.

▸ Capital gains tax for 2009-10 is payable at the rate of 18%.

▸ Net capital losses may be carried forward and set against the net gains of subsequent years. Net losses incurred in the year of death of a taxpayer may be carried back for up to three years. Losses incurred on a disposal to a connected person may be offset only against gains made on disposals to the same connected person.

▸ In certain circumstances, trading losses may be set against capital gains.

▸ CGT is normally payable on 31 January following the end of the tax year.

Exercises

16.1   Which of the following disposals might give rise to a CGT liability?

(a)   the sale of freehold property by a UK company

(b)   the gift of shares from husband to wife (assuming that the couple live together)

(c)   the gift of an oil painting to a charity

(d)   the sale of an oil painting by a charity

(e)   the sale of an oil painting by an art dealer

(f)   the sale of freehold property by a partnership.

16.2   Which of the following are chargeable assets for CGT purposes?

(a)   shares in British Telecom plc   (b)   gilt-edged securities

(c)   an antique table worth £20,000   (d)   an antique chair worth £5,000

(e)   a taxpayer's home   (f)   a vintage Bentley.

16.3 A taxpayer has capital losses of £2,500 in 2009-10. Compute the CGT assessment for 2009-10 if capital gains for the year are as follows (assuming that there are no unrelieved losses brought forward):

either (a) £nil

or (b) £1,500

or (c) £7,750

or (d) £14,050.

16.4 In 2009-10, a taxpayer has capital gains of £62,600 and allowable losses of £11,400. He has unrelieved capital losses brought forward from previous years of £12,800. Calculate his CGT liability for the year.

16.5 A taxpayer has capital losses brought forward from previous years amounting to £4,800. Compute the CGT assessment for 2009-10 if total gains and losses for the year are as follows:

either (a) gains £9,700, losses £1,500

or (b) gains £11,500, losses £800

or (c) gains £16,100, losses £nil.

16.6 John dies on 3 March 2010. Between 6 April 2009 and 3 March 2010, he has total gains of £1,200 and total losses of £15,400. His net gains in recent tax years (and the annual exemption for each year) have been as follows:

	Net gains	Annual exemption
	£	£
2005-06	52,400	8,500
2006-07	15,300	8,800
2007-08	12,000	9,200
2008-09	2,150	9,600

Calculate John's CGT assessments for 2005-06 to 2009-10 inclusive.

Ignore any "taper relief" that may have been available in tax years 2005-06 to 2007-08, prior to the abolition of this relief in 2008-09.

16.7 On what date is CGT for 2009-10 normally due for payment?

*16.8   Rosemary's capital gains and losses in recent years (and the annual exemption for each year) have been as follows:

	Gains £	Losses £	Annual exemption £
2006-07	6,500	12,700	8,800
2007-08	8,600	2,350	9,200
2008-09	12,400	nil	9,600
2009-10	19,200	7,500	10,100

There were no unrelieved losses to bring forward from 2005-06 or earlier. Compute her CGT assessments for tax years 2006-07 to 2009-10 inclusive.

Ignore any "taper relief" that may have been available in tax years 2006-07 or 2007-08, prior to the abolition of this relief in 2008-09.

*16.9   In 2008-09, Ahmed incurred a capital loss of £3,750 on the disposal of an asset to his father. He also had capital gains in that year of £12,300. In 2009-10, Ahmed has capital gains of £38,700 and no losses. His capital gains in 2009-10 include gains of £2,000 on a disposal to his father and £3,500 on a disposal to his mother.

Compute Ahmed's CGT assessments for the years 2008-09 and 2009-10 given that the annual exemption was £9,600 in 2008-09.

*16.10   Melissa is a sole trader. Her capital gains and capital losses for 2009-10 are £25,900 and £1,000 respectively. She also has capital losses brought forward from 2008-09 of £13,700 and unrelieved trading losses of £18,500 which are eligible for relief against capital gains in 2009-10.

Show Melissa's CGT assessment for 2009-10, assuming that:

(a)   a claim to relieve trading losses against capital gains is not made

(b)   a claim to relieve trading losses against capital gains is made.

Chapter 17

Computation of gains and losses

Introduction

The computation of the gain arising on the disposal of a chargeable asset is basically a matter of subtracting the acquisition cost of the asset from its disposal value. However, it may be necessary to adjust the gain to take account of a number of other costs incurred by the taxpayer and the calculation becomes more complex if only part of the asset has been disposed of. Also, a different method of computation applies if the asset was acquired on or before 31 March 1982.

The purpose of this chapter is to explain the basic method of computation and to show how this method is modified for disposals of older assets.

Layout of a CGT computation

The computation of the chargeable gain or allowable loss arising on a chargeable disposal occurring during tax year 2009-10 is laid out as follows:

	£	£
Disposal value		xxx
Less: Incidental costs of disposal		xxx
		xxx
Less: *Allowable expenditure*:		
Acquisition cost of asset	xxx	
Incidental costs of acquisition	xxx	
Enhancement expenditure	xxx	
Cost of defending the owner's title to the asset	xxx	
Valuation fees	xxx	xxx
Chargeable gain or allowable loss		xxx

Each of the terms used in this layout is explained below.

Disposal value

If a disposal consists of the sale of an asset, disposal value is generally taken to be the proceeds of the sale. But if a sale does not constitute a bargain made at arm's length, the sale proceeds are ignored and disposal value is taken to be the market value of the asset on the date of the sale. This rule applies particularly to transactions between "connected persons". For CGT purposes, a taxpayer is connected to his or her:

(a)   spouse (husband or wife)

(b)   relatives (brothers, sisters, ancestors, direct descendants) and their spouses

(c)   spouse's relatives and their spouses

(d)   business partners and their spouses and relatives.

All references to "spouse" in the above list should be taken to include same-sex civil partners who have entered into a legally-recognised civil partnership.

Market value is also used as disposal value if a disposal takes the form of a gift. But disposals between spouses or civil partners who live together are deemed to occur at a disposal value such that neither a gain nor a loss arises (see Chapter 16). This rule takes precedence over the usual rules concerning sales to connected persons and gifts.

In general, the market value of an asset is the amount which the asset would fetch if sold on the open market. Shares and securities which are listed on a recognised stock exchange ("listed" or "quoted" shares or securities) are valued for CGT purposes in the same way as they are valued for inheritance tax purposes (see Chapter 31).

The incidental costs of disposal which may be deducted when calculating a gain or loss include legal fees, estate agents' and auctioneers' fees, advertising costs etc.

Allowable expenditure

The following expenditure may be set against disposal value when calculating the gain or loss arising on a disposal:

(a)   the acquisition cost of the asset (or its market value on the date of acquisition if it was acquired by gift or otherwise than by way of a bargain made at arm's length)

(b)   incidental costs of acquisition (e.g. legal fees)

(c)   "enhancement expenditure", which is expenditure on making improvements to the asset, so long as that expenditure is still reflected in the state of the asset at the time of disposal (but the costs of mere repairs and maintenance are disallowed)

(d)   costs incurred in defending the owner's title to the asset (generally legal costs)

(e)   valuation fees necessarily incurred for CGT purposes.

If an asset is acquired as the result of a disposal between spouses or civil partners who live together, the deemed acquisition cost for the spouse or partner receiving the asset is equal to the deemed disposal value for the spouse or partner who makes the disposal (see above).

EXAMPLE 1

(a) A chargeable asset was bought in June 2006 for £1,200 and was sold in August 2009 for £3,350. Compute the chargeable gain.

(b) A chargeable asset was bought for £15,000 in August 2001. Legal costs of £500 were incurred when the asset was acquired. The owner of the asset incurred enhancement expenditure of £2,000 in May 2002 and £3,000 in June 2007. The asset was sold in July 2009 for £28,000. Legal costs of £700 were incurred on the sale. Compute the chargeable gain.

(c) A taxpayer bought a chargeable asset for £40,000 in February 2003. The asset was sold for £30,000 in October 2009. Compute the chargeable gain or allowable loss if:

  (i) the asset was sold in an arm's length transaction

  (ii) the asset was sold to the taxpayer's brother and had a market value of £45,000 on the date of the sale

  (iii) the asset was sold to the taxpayer's wife and had a market value of £45,000 on the date of the sale.

Solution

(a)

	£
Sale proceeds	3,350
Less: Acquisition cost	1,200
Chargeable gain	2,150

(b)

	£	£
Sale proceeds		28,000
Less: Incidental costs of disposal		700
		27,300
Less: Acquisition cost	15,000	
Incidental costs of acquisition	500	
Enhancement expenditure (£2,000 + £3,000)	5,000	20,500
Chargeable gain		6,800

(c)

	(i)	(ii)	(iii)
	£	£	£
Disposal value	30,000	45,000	40,000
Less: Acquisition cost	40,000	40,000	40,000
Chargeable gain/(allowable loss)	(10,000)	5,000	-

In case (iii), disposal value is set to £40,000 so as to ensure that neither a gain nor a loss occurs on this disposal to the taxpayer's spouse.

Part disposals

If only *part* of a chargeable asset is disposed of, only part of its cost can be allowed when computing the gain or loss. The allowable part cost is the full cost of the asset multiplied by the following fraction:

$$\frac{A}{A+B}$$

where: A is the value of the part disposed of (i.e. the disposal value), and

B is the value of the part remaining in the taxpayer's ownership.

This part disposal fraction applies not only to the acquisition cost of the asset but also to any other items of allowable expenditure which relate to the whole asset. But any item of expenditure which relates only to the part of the asset which has been disposed of should be allowed in full.

EXAMPLE 2

Peter buys a chargeable asset for £26,000 in May 2000. He sells a one-quarter interest in the asset for £12,000 in August 2009, incurring incidental costs of disposal of £500. The value of the other three-quarters interest in the asset in August 2009 is £40,000. Calculate the chargeable gain.

Solution

	£
Sale proceeds	12,000
Less: Incidental costs of disposal	500
	11,500
Less: Part cost:	
$\dfrac{£12,000}{£12,000 + £40,000}$ x £26,000	6,000
Chargeable gain	5,500

Notes:

(i)   The fact that Peter has sold a one-quarter interest in the asset is irrelevant. What is relevant is that he has sold £12,000 worth out of an asset currently worth £52,000, as indicated by the part disposal fraction.

(ii) If Peter disposes of the remaining three-quarters of the asset at some future time, the remaining £20,000 of the cost (£26,000 – £6,000) will then be allowable.

Small part disposals of land

An exception to the usual part disposal rules occurs when a taxpayer makes a small part disposal of land. A part disposal of land is "small" if the land is freehold, or held on a lease with more than 50 years left to run, and the following conditions are met:

(a) If the disposal is caused by a compulsory purchase order, the disposal proceeds must not exceed 5% of the value of the whole piece of land. However, it is the practice of HM Revenue and Customs to treat disposal proceeds of £3,000 or less as small for this purpose, regardless of whether or not the 5% test is satisfied.

(b) If the disposal is not caused by a compulsory purchase order, the disposal proceeds must not exceed 20% of the value of the whole piece of land and the total proceeds of all disposals of land in the year of assessment (excluding small disposals caused by compulsory purchases) must not exceed £20,000.

In these circumstances, the taxpayer may claim that the transfer of land should not be treated as a disposal but that the disposal proceeds should instead be subtracted from the original cost of the land for CGT purposes. This has the effect of increasing the chargeable gain arising on a subsequent disposal of the remainder of the land and therefore, in effect, the gain arising on the small part disposal is deferred. Obviously, the taxpayer will not make such a claim if the gain arising on the small part disposal is covered by the annual exemption for the year.

It is very important to appreciate that these small part disposal rules apply to land only, whereas the more general part disposal rules explained earlier in this chapter apply to all types of chargeable asset.

EXAMPLE 3

In July 2000, Malcolm bought a piece of land for £40,000. In June 2005 he sold part of the land for £11,000. This was his only land disposal in 2005-06. The value of the remainder of the land at the time of the part disposal was £50,000. Malcolm had substantial capital gains in 2005-06, sufficient to absorb his annual exemption for the year, and therefore decided to make a small part disposal claim.

Calculate the chargeable gain arising in January 2010 when Malcolm sells the remainder of the land for £60,000.

Solution

The small part disposal claim in 2005-06 was valid since the total value of the land immediately prior to the disposal was £61,000 (£11,000 + £50,000) and the disposal raised £11,000 which is less than 20% of £61,000. Furthermore, the disposal proceeds of all land disposals in the year did not exceed £20,000. The gain on the January 2010 disposal is as follows:

	£
Sale proceeds	60,000
Less: Reduced cost (£40,000 – £11,000)	29,000
Chargeable gain	31,000

Assets with negligible value

If the value of a chargeable asset has become negligible, the owner of the asset may make a "negligible value" claim. If this claim is accepted, the asset is treated as if it had been disposed of at its current, negligible value (giving rise to an allowable loss) and then immediately re-acquired at that value.

EXAMPLE 4

In May 2004, Gloria acquired 1,000 shares in ABC plc for £7,000. Trading in the company's shares was suspended in December 2009 and Gloria claimed that the shares then had a negligible value of only 10p per share. This claim was accepted by HMRC. Compute the allowable loss.

Solution

	£
Deemed disposal value (1,000 x 10p)	100
Less: Cost	7,000
Allowable loss	(6,900)

If Gloria succeeds in selling the shares at some time in the future, their deemed acquisition cost for CGT purposes will be £100.

Assets held on 31 March 1982

CGT was originally introduced in 1965 and applied to disposals made on or after 6 April 1965 (the "base date" for CGT). Gains which accrued before 6 April 1965 were not taxable. Therefore, if an asset was acquired before 6 April 1965 and disposed of after that date, only the part of the gain accruing after 6 April 1965 was taxable.

Finance Act 1988 changed the CGT base date to 31 March 1982. Therefore, if an asset is now disposed of which was acquired before 31 March 1982, only the part of the gain accruing since 31 March 1982 is taxable. The calculation of the taxable part of the gain is achieved by means of a technique known as "rebasing" whereby the market value of the asset at 31 March 1982 is substituted for its acquisition cost in the CGT calculation.

Rebasing

Finance Act 2008 has simplified the rules relating to the disposal of assets acquired before 31 March 1982 ("pre-31 March 1982" assets). The situation for disposals taking place on or after 6 April 2008 is as follows:

(a) The gain or loss arising on the disposal of a pre-31 March 1982 asset is calculated by comparing the asset's disposal value with its market value at 31 March 1982. Any enhancement expenditure incurred after 31 March 1982 is taken into account in the usual way when computing the gain or loss.

(b) The original acquisition cost of the asset is entirely irrelevant for CGT purposes and is ignored.

In fact, all costs incurred on or before 31 March 1982 (including any enhancement expenditure incurred on or before that date) are ignored and are replaced in the CGT computation by the asset's market value at 31 March 1982. Effectively, the owner of the asset is treated as if he or she had bought it on 31 March 1982 for its market value on that date.

Finance Act 2008 introduced a number of CGT reforms, including simplification of the rebasing rules. However, none of these reforms apply to companies. The rules which apply when a company makes a disposal of a pre-31 March 1982 asset are explained later in this book (see Chapter 23).

EXAMPLE 5

Alan bought a chargeable asset for £2,000 in April 1980. The asset was sold for £9,500 in January 2010. Compute the chargeable gain if the asset's market value on 31 March 1982 was:

(a) £4,200   (b) £1,500   (c) £12,000

Solution

(a) The original cost of this pre-31 March 1982 asset is irrelevant and the gain or loss is calculated by means of rebasing. The chargeable gain is £5,300 (£9,500 – £4,200). Rebasing has worked in Alan's favour, since he is being taxed on only £5,300 out of a total gain of £7,500 during his period of ownership of the asset.

(b) The chargeable gain is £8,000 (£9,500 – £1,500). This time, rebasing has not worked in Alan's favour, since he is being taxed on £8,000 even though his total gain since 1980 is only £7,500. However, rebasing is mandatory and there is nothing that can be done about this.

(c) There is an allowable loss of £2,500 (£9,500 – £12,000). Rebasing has benefited Alan, since he has enjoyed a total gain of £7,500 during his period of ownership of the asset but is now being granted an allowable loss of £2,500.

Part disposals of pre-31 March 1982 assets

When a part disposal is made of an asset which was held on 31 March 1982, the part disposal fraction which would normally be applied to the cost of the asset when computing the chargeable gain arising on the disposal (see earlier in this chapter) is applied instead to the asset's market value at 31 March 1982.

The gain or loss arising on such a part disposal is calculated by comparing disposal value with the appropriate part of the asset's market value at 31 March 1982. If there has been enhancement expenditure since 31 March 1982, the appropriate part of that expenditure is also taken into account when computing the gain or loss.

EXAMPLE 6

Hilary bought a chargeable asset in November 1978 for £3,000. The asset had a market value on 31 March 1982 of £5,000. She sold part of the asset for £8,000 in November 2009, at which time the remainder of the asset was valued at £12,000. Compute the chargeable gain arising on this disposal.

Solution

	£
Sale proceeds	8,000
Less: Part market value at 31 March 1982:	
$\dfrac{£8,000}{£8,000 + £12,000}$ x £5,000	2,000
Chargeable gain	6,000

Summary

▶ The disposal value of an asset is normally equal to sale proceeds, but if an asset is given away or is sold other than by way of a bargain at arm's length, the disposal value is deemed to be the market value of the asset on the date of disposal.

▶ Allowable costs include an asset's acquisition cost, incidental costs, enhancement expenditure, costs of defending the owner's title and valuation fees.

▶ On a part disposal, the allowable part cost is calculated by multiplying the full cost by the part disposal fraction. Special rules apply to small part disposals of land.

▶ A taxpayer may claim that an asset has negligible value, so triggering a disposal which gives rise to an allowable loss.

▶ Rebasing applies on the disposal of an asset which was held at 31 March 1982. The gain or loss on disposal is calculated by comparing disposal value with the market value of the asset at 31 March 1982.

▶ Finance Act 2008 made a number of reforms to the capital gains tax system. These include a simplification of the rebasing rules. None of these reforms apply to disposals made by companies.

▶ The gain or loss arising on the part disposal of a pre-31 March 1982 asset is calculated by comparing disposal value with the appropriate part of the asset's market value at 31 March 1982.

Exercises

17.1 Carol purchased a holiday flat in December 2000 for £100,000. She spent £5,000 on installing central heating in February 2001 and a further £750 on repainting the interior of the flat in March 2001. The flat was never Carol's main residence.

She sold the flat at auction in February 2010 for £172,000, paying a 5% fee to the auctioneer. Legal costs were £400 in December 2000 and £500 in February 2010. Compute Carol's chargeable gain on the disposal of the flat.

17.2 David was given a chargeable asset in November 2002 at which time the asset had a market value of £4,500. He sold the asset in January 2010. Compute the chargeable gain or the allowable loss if his sale proceeds were:

(a) £4,950

(b) £4,350

(c) £5,780.

17.3   Edwina bought a chargeable asset in August 2000 for £240,000, paying acquisition costs of £12,000. In June 2003 she sold a one-quarter interest in the asset for £100,000, incurring disposal costs of £5,000. The remaining three-quarter interest in the asset was valued at £500,000 in June 2003. Compute the chargeable gain.

Ignore any "taper relief" that may have been available in tax year 2003-04, prior to the abolition of this relief in 2008-09.

In January 2010, Edwina sold her remaining three-quarter interest in the asset for £520,000. Compute the chargeable gain.

17.4   Francis acquired an oil painting for £12,500 in March 1979. He sold the painting for £37,500 in March 2010. Compute the chargeable gain or allowable loss arising on this disposal if the painting's market value on 31 March 1982 was:

(a)   £10,000   (b)   £15,000   (c)   £50,000.

17.5   In June 2000, Gillian was given a chargeable asset with a market value at that time of £6,000. In November 2008 she made a successful claim to the effect that the asset now had a negligible value of only £80.

(a)   Compute the allowable loss.
(b)   Compute the chargeable gain arising in March 2010, when Gillian sold the asset for £120.

*17.6   Jon bought a chargeable asset for £23,000 in May 1979. He incurred enhancement expenditure of £10,000 in June 1981 and a further £14,000 in July 1995. The asset was valued at £58,500 on 31 March 1982 and was sold for £185,000 in February 2010.

(a)   Compute the chargeable gain.
(b)   Now re-compute the gain, assuming that the person who bought the asset from Jon in February 2010 was his wife (who lives with him).

*17.7   Karen bought a house in 1980 for £36,000. The house was valued at £42,000 on 31 March 1982. In November 1987 she spent £18,000 on dividing the house into two self-contained flats and in September 2008 she sold one of the flats for £95,000, at which time the other flat was valued at £105,000. In January 2010 she sold the second flat for £110,000. Karen never lived in either of the flats.

Compute the chargeable gains arising on Karen's two disposals.

Chapter 18

Chattels and wasting assets

Introduction

A "chattel" is an item of tangible, movable property. A "wasting asset" is an asset with a predictable useful life not exceeding 50 years. If an asset is both a chattel and a wasting asset (e.g. a TV set) it is referred to as a "wasting chattel". Special capital gains tax rules apply to disposals of chattels, wasting assets and wasting chattels. The purpose of this chapter is to explain these rules.

The chattels exemption

The disposal of a chattel for £6,000 or less is exempt from capital gains tax. This rule removes from charge a great many trivial disposals and ensures that CGT is levied only if the disposal is material. The following points relate to the chattels exemption:

(a)   This exemption applies only to chattels, not to assets in general.

(b)   The exemption means that gains arising on the disposal of a chattel for £6,000 or less are not chargeable to CGT. It also means that losses arising on such disposals are not generally allowable. However, special rules apply to chattels acquired for more than £6,000 and disposed of for £6,000 or less (see later in this chapter).

(c)   The £6,000 figure relates to the *gross* disposal proceeds. These are the proceeds before deducting incidental costs of disposal.

(d)   If the gross disposal proceeds of a chattel exceed £6,000, the chargeable gain cannot exceed five-thirds of the amount by which the disposal proceeds exceed £6,000. This "marginal relief" ensures that taxpayers who dispose of chattels for slightly more than £6,000 are not unduly penalised by the tax system.

EXAMPLE 1

In 2009-10, a taxpayer makes a number of disposals, as listed below. Which of these disposals would be exempt from CGT?

(a) An antique table sold for £5,000.

(b) A watercolour painting sold at auction. The auctioneer deducted his 10% commission from the selling price and sent the taxpayer a cheque for the remaining £5,670.

(c) A holding of shares sold for £4,500.

Solution

(a) The antique table is a chattel disposed of for £6,000 or less. Therefore the disposal is exempt from CGT.

(b) A watercolour painting is a chattel. The gross disposal proceeds must have been £6,300, since £6,300 less 10% = £5,670. The chattels exemption will not apply but the chargeable gain cannot exceed five-thirds of £300 (i.e. £500).

(c) A shareholding is not a chattel. Therefore the £6,000 exemption does not apply and the disposal will be chargeable to CGT.

EXAMPLE 2

In December 2009, Michael sells a piece of antique furniture for £6,360, paying incidental disposal costs of £320. He had acquired the furniture in January 2002 as a gift from his mother. Compute Michael's chargeable gain if the market value of the furniture in January 2002 was:

(a) £5,500   (b) £4,900

Solution

	(a)	(b)
	£	£
Sale proceeds	6,360	6,360
Less: Incidental costs of disposal	320	320
	6,040	6,040
Less: Deemed acquisition cost	5,500	4,900
Chargeable gain	540	1,140 (restricted to £600)

Notes:

(a) The maximum gain is £360 x 5/3 = £600. The gain of £540 in case (a) is less than £600, so the chargeable gain is £540.

(b) In case (b), £1,140 exceeds £600, so the gain is restricted to £600.

Chattels disposed of at a loss

If a chattel is disposed of at a loss, there are two possibilities. Either:

(a) the disposal proceeds exceed £6,000, in which case the allowable loss is calculated in the usual way, or

(b) the disposal proceeds are £6,000 or less, in which case the chattels exemption applies and it appears that no allowable loss could arise.

However, if a chattel is acquired for more than £6,000 and then disposed of for less than £6,000, the chattels exemption is overruled and an allowable loss is available. But the amount of this loss is restricted to the amount that would arise if the disposal proceeds were exactly £6,000.

EXAMPLE 3

In March 2010, Naomi sells an oil painting which she had acquired many years previously for £10,000. Compute the allowable loss if she sells the painting for:

(a) £7,200   (b) £5,700

Solution

(a) Naomi has disposed of a chattel for more than £6,000, so the disposal is not exempt from capital gains tax. The allowable loss is calculated in the usual way as £10,000 − £7,200 = £2,800.

(b) Naomi has disposed of a chattel for less than £6,000 and normally this disposal would be exempt from capital gains tax. However, since the asset was acquired for more than £6,000, a loss is allowed. This is calculated by substituting £6,000 for the disposal proceeds. The allowable loss is £10,000 − £6,000 = £4,000.

Part disposals of chattels

A part disposal of a chattel may be made in one of two ways. Either:

(a) a part interest in a chattel may be disposed of, or

(b) for chattels forming a set, one or more of the items in the set may be disposed of.

Each of these forms of part disposal is considered below.

Disposal of a part interest in a chattel

If a disposal is made of a part interest in a chattel, this part disposal will be exempt from capital gains tax only if the value of the *whole* chattel immediately prior to the part disposal is £6,000 or less.

If the value of the whole chattel exceeds £6,000 the disposal is not exempt from CGT and the usual part disposal calculation is performed. However, the chargeable gain on the part disposal is limited to five-thirds of the amount by which the value of the whole chattel exceeds £6,000, multiplied by the usual part disposal fraction.

EXAMPLE 4

In October 2003 Jackie bought a statuette for £3,500. In October 2009 she sells a one-third interest in the statuette for £2,000. Compute the chargeable gain if the value of the remaining two-thirds interest in October 2009 is:

(a) £4,000   (b) £5,000.

Solution

(a) The value of the whole chattel on the date of the part disposal is £6,000. Since this value does not exceed £6,000 the part disposal is exempt from CGT.

(b) The value of the whole chattel on the date of the part disposal is £7,000. Since this value exceeds £6,000 the part disposal is not exempt from CGT. The computation of the chargeable gain is as follows:

	£
Sale proceeds	2,000
Less: Part cost:	
$\dfrac{£2,000}{£2,000 + £5,000}$ x £3,500	1,000
Chargeable gain	1,000 (restricted to £476)

The part disposal fraction cancels down to 2/7ths, so the gain is restricted to (£7,000 − £6,000) x 5/3 x 2/7 = £476.

Disposal of part of a set

If a taxpayer acquires a set of chattels (e.g. a set of dining chairs) and then disposes of them individually, each disposal is regarded as a part disposal and will in general be chargeable to CGT only if the disposal proceeds of an individual item exceed £6,000.

However, a taxpayer who wished to dispose of a set of chattels with a total value exceeding £6,000 could use this rule to avoid capital gains tax by disposing of the items one by one (with each disposal raising less than £6,000). In order to prevent such tax avoidance, a series of disposals of chattels which form part of a set *to the same person or to persons connected with each other or acting together* are treated as a single transaction for capital gains tax purposes. If the individual disposals occur in different tax years, any gain which results from this treatment is apportioned between tax years in proportion to the sale proceeds of each disposal.

EXAMPLE 5

Andrew acquired a set of six dining chairs in January 2003 for £1,300. In June 2009 he sold three of the chairs to a friend for £3,500 (the other three chairs also being valued at £3,500 at that time). In August 2009 he sold the remaining chairs to the friend's brother for £3,700. Compute the chargeable gain arising on these disposals.

Solution

If it were not for the rule introduced above, neither of these disposals would be chargeable to CGT since neither of them raises more than £6,000. However, the two disposals are made to connected persons and are therefore to be regarded as a single transaction for CGT purposes. The total disposal proceeds are £7,200 (£3,500 + £3,700). This exceeds £6,000 so the disposals are chargeable. The computation is as follows:

	£
Sale proceeds	7,200
Less: Cost	1,300
Chargeable gain	5,900 (restricted to £2,000)

The maximum gain is (£7,200 − £6,000) x 5/3 = £2,000. £5,900 is greater than this, so the chargeable gain is restricted to £2,000.

Wasting chattels

Chattels which have a predictable useful life not exceeding 50 years in length are referred to as "wasting chattels" and are generally exempt from CGT. Therefore the disposal of a wasting chattel will usually give rise to neither a chargeable gain nor an allowable loss.

An exception to this rule occurs in the case of movable plant and machinery used in business and eligible for capital allowances. Plant and machinery is always regarded as having a predictable useful life not exceeding 50 years and therefore movable plant and machinery is a wasting chattel. Unless disposal proceeds are £6,000 or less (in which case the general chattels exemption applies) disposals of movable plant and machinery used in business and eligible for capital allowances are *not* exempt from CGT. One of two situations may arise on such a disposal:

(a) Disposal proceeds may be less than original cost. In this (the most likely) case, the allowable loss is reduced by the total capital allowances which have been available on the asset. This will reduce the loss to zero.

(b) Disposal proceeds may be greater than original cost. In this case, the total of the available capital allowances on the asset is zero and therefore capital allowances have no effect on the computation, which will proceed in the usual way.

In fact, these rules (other than the £6,000 exemption) also apply to fixed plant and machinery used in business and eligible for capital allowances.

It is worth noting that certain collectors' items such as antique clocks and watches and vintage motor cycles are regarded as plant and machinery. Consequently, these items are treated as wasting chattels, even though their useful lives may in fact considerably exceed 50 years. By virtue of this treatment, such items are exempt from CGT unless used in business and eligible for capital allowances.

EXAMPLE 6

An item of movable plant and machinery is bought in February 2007 for £8,000 and used solely for trade purposes. Capital allowances are available in relation to this item. Compute the chargeable gain arising if the item is sold in July 2009 and the sale proceeds are:

(a) £4,500   (b) £6,500   (c) £8,500   (d) £10,500.

Solution

In case (a), sale proceeds do not exceed £6,000 so the disposal is exempt from CGT. In cases (b), (c) and (d), the sale proceeds exceed £6,000 so there is no exemption. The computations are as follows:

	(b)	(c)	(d)
	£	£	£
Sale proceeds	6,500	8,500	10,500
Less: Acquisition cost	8,000	8,000	8,000
	(1,500)	500	2,500
Less: Available capital allowances	1,500	0	0
Chargeable gain	nil	500	2,500

Notes:

(i)   In case (c), the maximum gain is £4,167 (£2,500 x 5/3). £500 is less than this, so the chargeable gain is £500.

(ii) In case (d), the maximum gain is £7,500 (£4,500 x 5/3). £2,500 is less than this, so the chargeable gain is £2,500.

Wasting assets

A wasting asset which is not a chattel is *not* exempt from CGT. Typical examples of such wasting assets include:

(a)   intangible assets such as copyrights, patents and options with lives not exceeding 50 years in length

(b)   short leases

(c)   fixed plant and machinery (but see earlier in this chapter for the CGT treatment if plant and machinery is used in business and is eligible for capital allowances).

In general, the original cost of a wasting asset is deemed to waste away on a straight line basis over the asset's predictable life. The computation of the gain or loss arising on the disposal of such an asset is achieved by comparing the disposal value with the unexpired portion of the asset's cost at the time of disposal. However, special rules apply to the disposal of a lease (see later in this chapter).

EXAMPLE 7

In January 2000, Fiona acquired a 25-year copyright at a cost of £30,000. In January 2010 she sold the copyright for £35,500. Compute the chargeable gain.

Solution

When the copyright was bought it had a 25-year life. When it was sold there were 15 years remaining. Therefore the computation is as follows:

	£
Sale proceeds	35,500
Less: Unexpired portion of cost	
$\dfrac{15}{25}$ x £30,000	18,000
Chargeable gain	17,500

EXAMPLE 8

On 31 March 1977, Philip acquired a 45-year copyright at a cost of £90,000. The copyright was valued at £88,000 on 31 March 1982. On 31 March 2010, Philip sold the copyright for £47,000. Compute the chargeable gain.

Solution

Rebasing applies since the copyright was acquired before 31 March 1982. The copyright is treated as if it had been bought for £88,000 on 31 March 1982 (with 40 years of its life remaining). The original cost of £90,000 is ignored.

When the copyright was sold there were 12 years of its life remaining. Therefore the CGT computation is as follows:

	£
Sale proceeds	47,000
Less: Unexpired portion of market value at 31 March 1982:	
$\dfrac{12}{40}$ x £88,000	26,400
Chargeable gain	20,600

Leases

For capital gains tax purposes, leases are classified into long leases (those of more than 50 years) and short leases (those of 50 years or less). A chargeable disposal may occur in connection with a lease in any of the following ways:

(a) A taxpayer who has a long lease on a property assigns that lease to someone else.

(b) A taxpayer who has a short lease on a property assigns that lease to someone else.

(c) A taxpayer who owns the freehold of a property (or has a long head-lease) grants a long lease (or long sub-lease) to someone else, the property eventually reverting to the taxpayer concerned.

(d) A taxpayer who owns the freehold of a property (or has a long head-lease) grants a short lease (or short sub-lease) to someone else, the property eventually reverting to the taxpayer concerned.

(e) A taxpayer who has a short head-lease on a property grants a shorter sub-lease to someone else, the property eventually reverting to the taxpayer concerned.

Each of these cases is considered below. If a property is (or has been) the taxpayer's main residence, the gain arising on the disposal of a lease on the property may be subject to the principal private residence exemption described in Chapter 20.

Assignment of a long lease

The assignment of a long lease is treated as a disposal of the whole asset and therefore causes no CGT difficulties at all. The computation proceeds in precisely the same way as the computation on the disposal of any other whole asset.

EXAMPLE 9

In June 2004, Jim acquired a 99-year lease on a flat for £70,000. In January 2010, he assigned the lease to a third party for £92,000. The flat was never Jim's residence. Compute the chargeable gain.

Solution

The chargeable gain is simply £22,000 (£92,000 − £70,000). If the flat had been Jim's main residence for all or part of the period of ownership, the gain may have been reduced or eliminated by the principal private residence exemption.

Assignment of a short lease

A short lease is, by definition, a wasting asset. Therefore the computation of the gain arising on the disposal of a short lease should be achieved by comparing disposal proceeds with the unexpired portion of the lease's cost at the time of disposal.

However, unlike other wasting assets, the cost of a short lease is not deemed to waste away on a straight line basis. Instead, the cost of a short lease is deemed to waste away according to a table of percentages which is given in Schedule 8 of TCGA 1992 and is reproduced at the end of this chapter. The effect of this table is to write off the cost of a short lease slowly in the early years and more quickly in the closing years. The proportion of the cost of a short lease which is allowed in the CGT computation on its disposal is:

$$\frac{\% \text{ relating to number of years lease has left to run on disposal}}{\% \text{ relating to original length of lease}}$$

If the lease was originally a long lease but the taxpayer has owned it for some years so that the lease now being assigned is a short lease, the denominator in the above fraction is taken as 100%, corresponding to "50 or more" in the Schedule 8 table.

Schedule 8 gives percentages for whole numbers of years only. If the duration of a lease is not a whole number of years, then the appropriate percentage is calculated from the table on a pro rata basis.

EXAMPLE 10

Jean acquired a 30-year lease on a property in July 1999 for £32,000. In July 2009 she assigned the lease to a third party for £45,000. The property was never Jean's residence. Compute the chargeable gain.

Solution

When the lease was acquired it had a 30-year life (Sch 8 percentage 87.330%). When it was assigned there were 20 years remaining (Sch 8 percentage 72.770%). Therefore the computation is as follows:

	£
Sale proceeds	45,000
<u>Less</u>: Unexpired portion of cost	
$\dfrac{72.770}{87.330}$ x £32,000	26,665
Chargeable gain	18,335

EXAMPLE 11

A taxpayer assigns a lease of duration 12 years and 5 months. Calculate the appropriate percentage for use in the CGT computation on the disposal.

Solution

The percentage for 12 years is 53.191%. The percentage for 13 years is 56.167%. The difference between these percentages is 2.976%. Therefore the appropriate percentage for a lease of duration 12 years and 5 months is 53.191 + (2.976 x 5/12) = 54.431%.

EXAMPLE 12

Joan acquired a 40-year lease on a property on 31 May 1981 for £38,000. The market value of the lease on 31 March 1982 was £35,000. On 30 November 2009 she assigned the lease to a third party for £65,000. The property was never Joan's residence. Compute the chargeable gain.

Solution

Rebasing applies since the lease was acquired before 31 March 1982. On 31 March 1982 there were 39 years and 2 months of the lease term remaining (Sch 8 percentage 94.842 + 0.615 x 2/12 = 94.945%). When the lease was assigned there were 11 years and 6 months remaining (Sch 8 percentage = 50.038 + (3.153 x 6/12) = 51.615%). Therefore the computation is as follows:

	£
Sale proceeds	65,000
Less: Unexpired portion of market value at 31 March 1982	
$\dfrac{51.615}{94.945}$ x £35,000	19,027
Chargeable gain	45,973

Note:

The original cost of £38,000 is ignored since rebasing applies.

Grant of a long lease

The grant of a long lease (or long sub-lease) out of a freehold (or a long head-lease) is treated as a part disposal for CGT purposes and the normal part disposal rules apply. The value of the part disposed of is usually equal to the proceeds of the disposal. The value of the part remaining takes into account both:

(a) the right of the taxpayer making the disposal to receive rents from the tenant, and

(b) the taxpayer's "reversionary interest", which is the right to take back the property when the lease (or sub-lease) finishes.

Grant of a short lease

The grant of a short lease (or short sub-lease) out of a freehold (or a long head-lease) is also treated as a part disposal for CGT purposes and therefore the part disposal rules apply again. However, part of the premium received on the grant of a short lease is assessable to income tax as property income (see Chapter 5) and therefore, in order to avoid double taxation, the disposal proceeds in the part-disposal computation are reduced by the amount of the premium which is assessable as property income.

EXAMPLE 13

Jeffrey acquired a freehold property in October 2001 for £117,000. In July 2009 he granted Jill a lease on the property for £80,000. The market value of the freehold after the lease had been granted was £100,000. The property was never Jeffrey's residence. Compute the chargeable gain, given that the lease granted to Jill was of duration:

(a) 99 years   (b) 40 years.

Solution

(a) This is a part disposal with A = £80,000 and B = £100,000. The computation is as follows:

	£
Sale proceeds	80,000
Less: Part cost:	
$\dfrac{£80,000}{£80,000+£100,000}$ x £117,000	52,000
Chargeable gain	28,000

(b) This is also a part disposal but £17,600 (£80,000 – (2% x £80,000 x 39)) of Jeffrey's disposal proceeds will be assessable as property income and this must be taken into account in the CGT computation. The computation is as follows:

	£
Sale proceeds (£80,000 – £17,600)	62,400
Less: Part cost:	
$\dfrac{£62,400}{£80,000 + £100,000}$ x £117,000	40,560
Chargeable gain	21,840

Note that the numerator of the part disposal fraction is taken as the disposal proceeds *after* deducting the property income assessment, whilst the denominator takes into account the disposal proceeds *before* deducting the property income assessment.

Grant of a short sub-lease out of a short head-lease

In essence, the grant of a short sub-lease out of a short head-lease is treated in a similar fashion to the assignment of a short lease, as discussed earlier in this chapter. As before, the TCGA 1992 Schedule 8 table of percentages is called into use to determine the part cost that should be deducted in the capital gains tax computation. But since the property will be returning to the original tenant when the sub-lease finishes, the proportion of the cost of the short head-lease which is allowed in the CGT computation on the granting of the sub-lease is equal to:

$$\frac{P1 - P2}{P3}$$

where:

P1 = % relating to the number of years left of the short head-lease when the sub-lease begins

P2 = % relating to the number of years left of the short head-lease when the sub-lease ends

P3 = % relating to original length of the short head-lease.

Since part of the premium received by the taxpayer on the grant of a short sub-lease will be assessable to income tax as property income, the capital gain arising is reduced by the amount of the property income assessment. However, this reduction cannot be used to convert a gain into a loss or to increase a loss.

EXAMPLE 14

Joanna acquired a 15-year lease on a property in September 2003 for £45,000. In September 2009 she granted a 4-year sub-lease to a third party for £20,000. The property was never Joanna's residence. Compute the chargeable gain.

Solution

The computation of the chargeable gain is as follows:

	£
Sale proceeds	20,000
Less: Proportion of cost	
$\dfrac{43.154 - 26.722}{61.617}$ x £45,000	12,001
	7,999
Less: Property income assessment (£10,160)	7,999
Chargeable gain	nil

Notes:

(i) P1 = 43.154 (9 years), P2 = 26.722 (5 years) and P3 = 61.617 (15 years)

(ii) The property income assessment (see Chapter 5) is:

	£
Premium received	20,000
Less: £20,000 x (4 – 1) x 2%	1,200
	18,800
Less: Relief for premium paid:	
$\dfrac{4}{15}$ x (£45,000 – (£45,000 x (15 – 1) x 2%))	8,640
	10,160

(iii) The relief given for the property income assessment is restricted to £7,999 so as not to turn a gain into a loss.

Summary

▸ A chattel is an item of tangible, movable property. A wasting asset is an asset with a predictable useful life of 50 years or less. A wasting asset that is also a chattel is a wasting chattel.

▸ Chattels disposed of for £6,000 or less are exempt from CGT.

▸ The allowable loss on chattels acquired for more than £6,000 and disposed of for less than £6,000 is restricted by substituting £6,000 for the disposal proceeds.

▸ Disposals of a part interest in a chattel are exempt from CGT if the value of the whole chattel is £6,000 or less.

▸ A series of disposals of chattels forming a set will be treated as a single transaction for CGT purposes if the disposals are to connected persons.

▸ Wasting chattels are exempt from CGT apart from movable plant and machinery used in business on which capital allowances are available.

▸ Wasting assets are not exempt from CGT. In general, the original cost of a wasting asset is written off over its predictable life using the straight line method. However, special rules apply to leases.

▸ An assignment of a long lease is regarded as the disposal of a whole asset.

▸ An assignment of a short lease is a disposal of a wasting asset. The original cost of a short lease is written off over its predictable life, using a table of percentages contained in Schedule 8, TCGA 1992.

▸ The grant of a long lease is treated as a part disposal.

▸ The grant of a short lease (or sub-lease) out of a freehold (or long head-lease) is treated as a part disposal. The part of the premium received which is taxable as property income is deducted from disposal proceeds in the CGT computation.

▸ The grant of a short sub-lease out of a short head-lease is a part disposal of a wasting asset. The Schedule 8 table is used to determine the allowable cost used in the CGT computation. The part of the premium received which is taxable as property income is deducted from the gain arising but cannot be used to convert a gain into a loss or to increase a loss.

Short lease amortisation table

(Schedule 8 of TCGA 1992)

Years	Percentage	Years	Percentage	Years	Percentage
50 or more	100	33	90.280	16	64.116
49	99.657	32	89.354	15	61.617
48	99.289	31	88.371	14	58.971
47	98.902	30	87.330	13	56.167
46	98.490	29	86.226	12	53.191
45	98.059	28	85.053	11	50.038
44	97.595	27	83.816	10	46.695
43	97.107	26	82.496	9	43.154
42	96.593	25	81.100	8	39.399
41	96.041	24	79.622	7	35.414
40	95.457	23	78.055	6	31.195
39	94.842	22	76.399	5	26.722
38	94.189	21	74.635	4	21.983
37	93.497	20	72.770	3	16.959
36	92.761	19	70.791	2	11.629
35	91.981	18	68.697	1	5.983
34	91.156	17	66.470	0	0

Exercises

18.1   Classify each of the following assets as either chattels, wasting assets or wasting chattels:

(a)   A domestic washing machine.

(b)   A gold ring.

(c)   A personal computer.

(d)   A 20-year lease on a building.

(e)   A suit of clothes.

(f)   An antique vase.

18.2   In October 2009 Keith sells an antique cabinet for £7,200. He incurs incidental costs of disposal amounting to £200. The cabinet cost Keith £2,000 in July 2001. Compute the chargeable gain.

18.3   In September 2009 Kevin sells a drawing for £2,000. He bought the drawing in February 2003 for £50,000 when it was thought (incorrectly) to be by a famous artist. Compute the allowable loss.

18.4   In January 2010 Karl sells a one-quarter interest in a painting for £25,000. The remaining three-quarter interest is valued at £85,000. The painting had cost Karl £38,500 in January 2001. Compute the chargeable gain.

18.5   In January 2007 Katrina buys an item of movable plant and machinery for use in her business. The plant costs her £50,000 and capital allowances are claimed. Compute the chargeable gain arising in March 2010 when she sells the plant, assuming that sale proceeds are:

(a) £65,000

(b) £35,000.

18.6   In June 2007 Katie acquired a 5-year option to buy a piece of land. The option cost her £10,000. In June 2009 she sold the option for £8,000. Compute the chargeable gain.

18.7   Katherine acquired a 40-year lease on a property on 31 August 1991 for £25,000. On 31 August 2009 she assigned the lease to a third party for £32,500. The property was never Katherine's residence. Compute the chargeable gain.

*18.8**   In March 2002, Sean acquired a pair of matching antique silver candlesticks at a cost of £4,000. In August 2009 he sold one of the candlesticks to James for £6,750. At that time the other candlestick was valued at £5,750. In September 2009 he sold the other candlestick to Julia for £5,800. Calculate the chargeable gain arising on these two disposals if:

(a) James and Julia are unconnected.

(b) James and Julia are a married couple.

*18.9**   On 31 March 1980, Estelle acquired a patent with a 35-year life at a cost of £21,000. The patent was valued at £20,000 on 31 March 1982 and Estelle sold the patent on 31 March 2010 for £13,000. Compute the chargeable gain.

*18.10**   Edward bought a 20-year lease on a flat in May 2001 at a cost of £35,000. In November 2009 he granted a 5-year sub-lease to a third party for £15,000. The flat was never Edward's principal private residence. Compute the chargeable gain.

Chapter 19

Shares and securities

Introduction

A disposal of shares or securities causes no CGT problems unless a taxpayer disposes of part of a shareholding which was built up over a period of time in a number of separate acquisitions. If this happens, it is impossible to identify the shares that have been disposed of, because shares of the same class in the same company are "fungible assets" (i.e. assets that cannot be individually distinguished). But the calculation of the gain or loss arising on the disposal cannot proceed until the cost of the shares has been established. Therefore TCGA 1992 specifies a set of *share identification* or *share matching* rules which are used to match disposals against acquisitions in these circumstances. The main purpose of this chapter is to explain these rules and to show how they are applied when calculating the gain or loss arising on a disposal of shares.

This chapter also explains the CGT rules relating to bonus issues, rights issues and capital distributions and outlines the CGT treatment of the share disposals which occur when one company is taken over by another company.

The share matching rules

For CGT purposes, disposals of shares or securities are matched against acquisitions of *the same class of shares in the same company* in the following order:

(a) First, against any acquisitions made on the same day as the day of the disposal.

(b) Next, against any acquisitions made during the following 30 days, matching with shares acquired earlier rather than later within that 30-day period. This rule is intended to counter the practice known as "bed and breakfasting", whereby shares are sold and then almost immediately re-acquired so as to trigger gains or losses for tax avoidance purposes.

(c) Finally, against shares forming the "Section 104 holding". This consists of a pool of all the shares of that class in that company that were acquired before the date of the disposal and which have not been matched against previous disposals.

The share matching rules used to be much more complex than this, but the rules were simplified by Finance Act 2008. The old share matching rules are not relevant to disposals occurring on or after 6 April 2008 and are not considered in this book.

It is important to note that the share matching rules which apply when a *company* makes a disposal of shares are different from those which apply for CGT purposes. The rules which have effect for corporation tax purposes are explained in Chapter 23.

EXAMPLE 1

Paul made the following acquisitions and disposals of ordinary shares in Crimson plc:

Date		Number of shares
5 June 2008	acquisition	1,000
17 May 2009	acquisition	500
17 May 2009	disposal	800
9 June 2009	acquisition	200
13 March 2010	disposal	2,000
28 March 2010	acquisition	1,750

Against which acquisitions will each disposal be matched?

Solution

(a) The 800 shares which were disposed of on 17 May 2009 are matched as follows:

    (i)   first, against the 500 shares acquired on the same day

    (ii)   next, against the 200 shares acquired in the next 30 days (on 9 June 2009)

    (iii) finally, against 100 of the shares that form the s104 holding; these are the 1,000 shares acquired on 5 June 2008 and there are 900 shares left in this holding after the 17 May 2009 disposal has been matched.

(b) The 2,000 shares disposed of on 13 March 2010 are matched as follows:

    (i)   first, against the 1,750 shares acquired in the next 30 days (on 28 March 2010)

    (ii)   finally, against 250 of the 900 shares that remain in the s104 holding.

The Section 104 holding

A taxpayer's "Section 104 holding" of shares of a certain class in a certain company is a pool containing any shares that were acquired before the date of the current disposal but which have not been matched against previous disposals. The name of this pool is derived from Section 104 of TCGA 1992, which provides the legal basis for its existence.

If it were not for the provisions of Section 104, it would be necessary to maintain detailed records of the date and cost of each individual share acquisition. However, the pooling arrangement provided by Section 104 eliminates the need to keep such detailed records. Instead, all that is required is a record of:

(a)   the total number of shares in the s104 holding, and

(b)   the total allowable expenditure in relation to those shares.

The allowable expenditure is normally equal to the cost (or CGT acquisition value) of the shares concerned. But if any of the shares in the s104 holding were acquired before 31 March 1982, their cost is replaced by their market value at that date. This is because rebasing applies to the disposal of pre-31 March 1982 assets and the cost of such assets is not relevant for CGT purposes.

Note that share acquisitions which are matched against same-day disposals or against disposals occurring within the previous 30 days (by virtue of the first two matching rules explained above) do not enter the s104 holding.

EXAMPLE 2

Pauline makes the following purchases of preference shares in Violet plc:

Date	Number of shares	Cost
		£
23 June 1980	1,000	1,000
14 May 1994	2,000	5,800
8 July 2009	3,000	8,700

The shares had a market value of £2 per share on 31 March 1982. There were no disposals on or before 8 July 2009. Show Pauline's s104 holding of preference shares in Violet plc at 8 July 2009.

Solution

	Number of shares	Allowable expenditure
		£
Acquired 23 June 1980	1,000	2,000
Acquired 14 May 1994	2,000	5,800
Acquired 8 July 2009	3,000	8,700
s104 holding c/f at 8 July 2009	6,000	16,500

Notes:

(i) The shares acquired before 31 March 1982 have been added into the s104 holding at their 31 March 1982 market value.

(ii) The three acquisitions forming the s104 holding have been combined into a single pool of 6,000 shares with total allowable expenditure of £16,500. It is now necessary to carry forward only these two "bottom line" figures, rather than the details of each individual acquisition.

(iii) On average, the allowable expenditure per share is £2.75 (£16,500 ÷ 6,000). When there is a disposal from the pool, this is the expenditure that will be allowed for each share that is disposed of (see below).

Disposals from the s104 holding

When there is a disposal of shares from the s104 holding, the number of shares that have been disposed of is deducted from the number of shares in the pool. It is then necessary to deduct a proportion of the allowable expenditure in the pool.

Strictly speaking, this proportion should be calculated using the part disposal fraction (see Chapter 17) which takes into account the value of the shares disposed of and the value of the remaining shares. In most cases, however, the value per share of the shares disposed of will be the same as the value per share of the shares that remain, so that the proportion of the allowable expenditure which should be deducted from the pool can be based upon the *number* of shares disposed of.

The gain or loss arising on a disposal from the s104 holding is calculated simply as the difference between the disposal value of those shares and the amount which has been subtracted from the allowable expenditure in the pool as a consequence of the disposal.

EXAMPLE 3

Paula makes the following acquisitions of ordinary shares in Indigo plc:

Date	Number of shares	Cost £
1 July 2004	5,000	6,300
2 August 2005	2,000	2,500
3 February 2008	1,200	2,300
4 January 2010	1,800	3,400

She sells 500 shares on 28 March 2010. No shares are acquired within the next 30 days.

(a) Show the s104 holding on 28 March 2010, just prior to and just after the disposal on that date.

(b) Compute the chargeable gain or allowable loss on the disposal if sale proceeds are:

    (i) £1,300   (ii) £1,000   (iii) £700

Solution

(a)   The s104 holding is as follows:

	Number of shares	Allowable expenditure £
Acquired 1 July 2004	5,000	6,300
Acquired 2 August 2005	2,000	2,500
Acquired 3 February 2008	1,200	2,300
Acquired 4 January 2010	1,800	3,400
	10,000	14,500
Sold 28 March 2010 (500/10,000ths)	(500)	(725)
s104 holding c/f	9,500	13,775

Notes:

1.   The disposal in March 2010 must have come from the s104 holding since it cannot be matched against shares acquired on the same day or within the next 30 days.

2.   The disposal is 500 shares out of a pool of 10,000 shares. Therefore 500 shares are deducted from the pool, along with 500/10,000ths of the allowable expenditure.

3.   On average, the allowable expenditure in the pool is £1.45 per share and so the allowable expenditure deducted on the disposal (£725) is equal to 500 shares at £1.45 per share.

(b)

	(i) £	(ii) £	(iii) £
Sale proceeds	1,300	1,000	700
Less: Allowable expenditure	725	725	725
Chargeable gain/(allowable loss)	575	275	(25)

Bonus issues

A bonus issue occurs when a company issues free extra shares to its shareholders. The number of bonus shares received by a shareholder is generally in proportion to his or her existing shareholding. For instance, a "1 for 5" bonus issue would give each shareholder one free extra share for every five shares previously held.

For CGT purposes, a bonus issue is treated as a reorganisation of share capital, rather than as an issue of new shares. Accordingly, when a taxpayer receives bonus shares, the required CGT treatment is to uplift the number of shares in each of the taxpayer's previous acquisitions so as to reflect the bonus issue. Since all of these previous acquisitions are held together in the s104 holding, the desired effect can be achieved by simply adding the bonus shares into the "number of shares" column of the s104 holding. The allowable expenditure associated with this holding is not affected, since bonus shares are issued free of charge.

EXAMPLE 4

Sherjeel made the following acquisitions of ordinary shares in Triangle plc:

Date	Number of shares	Cost
		£
27 September 1981	1,200	2,400
28 July 1999	800	2,800
3 February 2003	500	2,000
5 July 2007	300	1,500

The market value of the company's shares on 31 March 1982 was £3 per share. On 1 September 2009, the company made a 1 for 10 bonus issue. Calculate the chargeable gain arising on 1 March 2010 when Sherjeel sold 1,400 shares for £6 each, assuming that he made no further acquisitions within the next 30 days.

Solution

The disposal cannot be matched against acquisitions on the same day or within the next 30 days, so it must come from the s104 holding. The s104 holding is as follows:

	Number of shares	Allowable expenditure
		£
Acquired 27 September 1981	1,200	3,600
Acquired 28 July 1999	800	2,800
Acquired 3 February 2003	500	2,000
Acquired 5 July 2007	300	1,500
s104 holding c/f	2,800	9,900

	Number of shares	Allowable expenditure £
s104 holding b/f	2,800	9,900
Bonus issue 1 September 2009	280	-
	3,080	9,900
Sold 1 March 2010 (1,400/3,080ths)	(1,400)	(4,500)
s104 holding c/f at 1 March 2010	1,680	5,400

The disposal proceeds are £8,400 (1,400 x £6). Therefore the chargeable gain is £3,900 (£8,400 – £4,500).

Notes:

(i)   The shares acquired before 31 March 1982 are incorporated into the s104 holding at their market value at that date (£3 per share) and not at their cost.

(ii) The 280 bonus shares increase the number of shares in the s104 holding but do not increase the allowable expenditure in that holding.

Rights issues

A rights issue occurs when a company offers its shareholders the right to buy extra shares. Rights issues are similar to bonus issues in that the number of shares offered to each shareholder is generally in proportion to his or her existing shareholding. But rights shares are not issued free of charge. Shareholders who are offered rights shares may either:

(a)   ignore the rights issue (in which case there is no CGT impact)

(b)   sell their "rights" (see later in this chapter)

(c)   buy the shares which they are offered.

For CGT purposes, a rights issue is treated in a very similar way to a bonus issue. If a taxpayer buys rights shares, the number of shares in each of the taxpayer's previous acquisitions is uplifted to reflect the rights issue. But since rights shares are not free, it is also necessary to increase the allowable expenditure for each of these acquisitions. This is achieved by adding the number of rights shares acquired into the s104 holding and increasing the allowable expenditure of this holding by the acquisition cost of these rights shares.

EXAMPLE 5

Tina made the following acquisitions of ordinary shares in Rhombus plc:

Date	Number of shares	Cost £
15 August 1980	500	1,000
23 January 2000	700	2,800

The market value of the company's shares on 31 March 1982 was £2.50 per share. On 1 June 2009, the company made a 1 for 20 rights issue at £8 per share and Tina decided to buy the shares to which she was entitled. Calculate the chargeable gain arising on 12 November 2009 when Tine sold 840 shares for £7 each, assuming that she made no further acquisitions within the next 30 days.

Solution

The disposal cannot be matched against acquisitions on the same day or within the next 30 days, so it must come from the s104 holding. The s104 holding is as follows:

	Number of shares	Allowable expenditure £
Acquired 15 August 1980	500	1,250
Acquired 23 January 2000	700	2,800
	1,200	4,050
Rights issue 1 June 2009	60	480
	1,260	4,530
Sold 12 November 2009 (840/1,260ths)	(840)	(3,020)
s104 holding c/f	420	1,510

The disposal proceeds are £5,880 (840 x £7). Therefore the chargeable gain is £2,860 (£5,880 − £3,020).

Notes:

(i) The shares acquired before 31 March 1982 are incorporated into the s104 holding at their market value at that date (£2.50 per share) and not at their cost.

(ii) The 60 rights shares increase the number of shares in the s104 holding and also increase the allowable expenditure in that holding.

Capital distributions

A capital distribution occurs when shareholders are repaid part of their share capital, usually when a company goes into liquidation. Unless the amount of the distribution is small (see later in this chapter) a capital distribution is regarded as a part disposal for CGT purposes.

EXAMPLE 6

In March 2004, Vincent bought 10,000 ordinary shares in Trapezium plc for £44,000. In June 2009, the company went into liquidation and Vincent received a first distribution of £0.50 per share. The market value of an ordinary share in Trapezium plc just after this distribution was £0.75. Compute the allowable loss arising in June 2009.

Solution

The value of the part disposed of is £5,000 (10,000 @ £0.50) and the value of the part remaining is £7,500 (10,000 @ £0.75). The part disposal fraction is 5,000/12,500 which is equivalent to 2/5ths. The s104 holding is as follows:

	Number of shares	Allowable expenditure £
Acquired March 2004	10,000	44,000
Distribution June 2009 (2/5ths)	-	(17,600)
s104 holding c/f	10,000	26,400

The computation of the allowable loss is as follows:

	£
Disposal proceeds	5,000
Less: Allowable expenditure	(17,600)
Allowable loss	(12,600)

Sale of rights nil paid

Another example of a capital distribution occurs when a company makes a rights issue and a shareholder decides not to buy the shares concerned but instead to sell his or her rights to someone else (a "sale of rights nil paid"). When shareholders sell their rights they are *not* selling shares. What they are selling is the right to buy shares, often at an attractive price. The proceeds of such a sale are treated as a capital distribution. If the amount of money involved is small (see below) the amount received will be treated as a small capital distribution.

Small capital distributions

If the amount of a capital distribution is small when compared with the value of the shares concerned, the distribution is not treated as a disposal. Instead, the proceeds of the distribution are subtracted from the allowable expenditure relating to those shares. The effect of this is that the gain which would have been chargeable on the distribution is deferred until a subsequent disposal takes place. This is very similar to the treatment of small part disposals of land (see Chapter 17). Note that:

(a) A capital distribution is generally regarded as small if it consists of no more than 5% of the value of the company's shares just before the distribution. It is also HMRC practice to regard an amount of £3,000 or less as small for this purpose, even if the 5% test is not satisfied.

(b) HMRC will usually allow a small capital distribution to be treated as a disposal if this is to the taxpayer's advantage (e.g. if any gain is covered by the annual exemption).

EXAMPLE 7

In April 2007, Vanessa bought 100 shares in Pentagon plc at a cost of £5 per share. The company went into liquidation and Vanessa received a first distribution of 40p per share in July 2009. The shares had a market value of £9.75 immediately after the distribution.

(a) Show how the distribution will be dealt with for CGT purposes.

(b) Calculate the chargeable gain arising in March 2010, when Vanessa received a second and final distribution of £9.82 per share.

Solution

(a) The value of the shares immediately prior to the distribution must have been £10.15 (£9.75 + £0.40). 40p is approximately 3.9% of £10.15 so the distribution ranks as a small capital distribution. The £40 received by Vanessa may be deducted from the £500 that she paid for her shares. This reduces the allowable cost on a subsequent disposal to £460.

(b) Assuming that the small capital distribution is not treated as a disposal, the s104 holding is as follows:

	Number of shares	Allowable expenditure £
Acquired April 2007	100	500
Distribution July 2009	-	(40)
	100	460
Disposal March 2010	(100)	(460)
s104 holding c/f	nil	nil

The gain arising on the disposal is:

	£
Disposal proceeds (100 @ £9.82)	982
Less: Allowable expenditure	460
Chargeable gain	522

Takeovers

A takeover occurs when one company acquires the shares of another company. Shareholders of the "target" company exchange their shares in return for cash, or shares of the acquiring company, or a combination of both cash and shares. The CGT treatment of such disposals is as follows:

(a) If a takeover is entirely for cash, the shareholders of the target company have sold their shares and have made chargeable disposals. The fact that shares have been sold as a consequence of a takeover is irrelevant and the gain or loss is computed in the usual way.

(b) If a takeover is entirely for shares (a "paper for paper" takeover), no chargeable disposals have taken place. A shareholder's newly-acquired shares in the acquiring company replace the shares originally held in the target company and are deemed for all CGT purposes to have been acquired on the same date and at the same cost as the original holding.

(c) If a takeover is partly for cash and partly for shares, a part disposal has taken place and a part disposal calculation is usually required. The value of the part disposed of is the amount of cash received and the value of the part remaining is the value of the shares received. However, if the amount of cash received by a taxpayer is no more than 5% of the total consideration (or no more than £3,000) the cash received may be treated as a small capital distribution.

EXAMPLE 8

In October 2003, Winston bought 8,000 shares in Hexagon plc at a cost of £3 per share. In October 2009 Circle plc made a takeover bid for Hexagon plc, offering the Hexagon shareholders three Circle shares plus £1 in cash for every two Hexagon shares. The offer was accepted on 29 October 2009 when the market value of shares in Circle plc was £5 per share. Compute Winston's chargeable gain.

Solution

Winston received 12,000 shares in Circle plc, worth £60,000, plus £4,000 in cash, a total of £64,000. The amount received in cash is 6.25% of the total and exceeds £3,000, so this cannot be treated as a small capital distribution. The s104 holding is as follows:

	Number of shares	Allowable expenditure £
Acquired October 2003	8,000	24,000
Distribution October 2009 (6.25%)	-	(1,500)
s104 holding after distribution	8,000	22,500
s104 holding (Circle plc) c/f	12,000	22,500

The gain arising on the disposal is:

	£
Disposal proceeds	4,000
Less: Allowable expenditure	1,500
Chargeable gain	2,500

EXAMPLE 9

In June 2006, Darren bought 1,000 ordinary shares in Cube plc for £8,400. In November 2009, Sphere plc made a takeover bid for Cube plc, offering two ordinary shares and one preference share in Sphere for each ordinary share in Cube. This offer was accepted on 21 November 2009 when the market value of ordinary shares in Sphere was £4 per share and the market value of preference shares in Sphere was £2 per share.

Show how Darren's cost of £8,400 should be allocated between the shares which he received by virtue of the takeover.

Solution

Darren received 2,000 ordinary shares worth £8,000 and 1,000 preference shares worth £2,000, giving a total consideration of £10,000. Since 80% of this total took the form of ordinary shares in Sphere, these ordinary shares are deemed to have cost him 80% of £8,400 = £6,720. Similarly, the preference shares in Sphere are deemed to have cost him 20% of £8,400 = £1,680. All of these shares are treated as if acquired in June 2006.

Gilts and qualifying corporate bonds

Gilt-edged securities and "qualifying corporate bonds" are not chargeable assets for CGT purposes. Therefore neither a chargeable gain nor an allowable loss can arise on their disposal. Note that:

(a) Gilt-edged securities ("gilts") are UK government securities such as Treasury Stock, Exchequer Stock etc.

(b) Qualifying corporate bonds consist of company debentures and other fixed-interest securities which are expressed in sterling and comprise a normal commercial loan.

(c) Gains and losses arising on the disposal of gilt-edged securities or corporate bonds by a *company* are assessed under the loan relationships rules for corporation tax purposes (see Chapter 22).

Summary

▸ Special matching rules are used to match disposals of shares and securities against acquisitions.

▸ Disposals made on or after 6 April 2008 are matched first against shares acquired on the same day as the disposal, then against shares acquired in the next 30 days and then against shares comprising the s104 holding.

▸ The s104 holding is a pool of shares of the same class in the same company that were acquired before the date of the current disposal but have not been matched against previous disposals. It is necessary to keep a record of the total number of shares in this pool and their total allowable expenditure.

▸ The CGT effect of a bonus issue is to increase the number of shares in the s104 holding. Allowable expenditure is not affected. The CGT effect of a rights issue which is taken up by the shareholder is to increase both the number of shares and the allowable expenditure in the s104 holding.

▸ A sale of rights nil paid is treated as a capital distribution.

▸ A capital distribution is treated for CGT purposes as a part disposal unless it ranks as a small capital distribution, in which case the amount of the distribution is deducted from the acquisition cost of the shares concerned.

▸ If a takeover is entirely for cash, the shareholders of the target company have made chargeable disposals. If a takeover is entirely for shares, no chargeable disposals have taken place. If a takeover is partly for cash and partly for shares, a part disposal has occurred unless the amount of cash can be treated as a small capital distribution.

▸ Gilt-edged securities and qualifying corporate bonds are not chargeable assets for CGT purposes.

Exercises

19.1   A taxpayer makes the following acquisitions of preference shares in Mauve Ltd:

Date	No of shares purchased
10 August 2009	1,000
20 October 2009	200
1 December 2009	150

No further shares are acquired during 2009 or 2010. How will the following disposals be matched against these acquisitions?

(a)   250 shares sold on 20 October 2009

(b)   420 shares sold on 12 November 2009

(c)   300 shares sold on 1 April 2010.

19.2   Sandra acquired the following ordinary shares in Pink plc:

Date	No of shares	Cost
		£
29 January 1982	1,000	3,000
13 August 1996	1,000	9,500
4 October 2007	2,000	22,500

The market value of the shares on 31 March 1982 was £4 per share. On 26 June 2009, Sandra sold 700 of her shares in Pink plc. Assuming that she acquired no further shares in the company during 2009, calculate the chargeable gain or allowable loss if her sale proceeds in June 2009 were:

(a)   £8,400

(b)   £6,300

(c)   £5,200.

19.3   Jeremy acquired the following ordinary shares in Scarlet plc:

Date	No of shares	Cost
		£
19 September 2003	4,000	16,000
20 October 2005	2,000	12,000
21 November 2007	1,000	7,000
22 December 2009	3,000	24,000
13 January 2010	5,000	55,000

He made no further acquisitions during 2010. On 22 December 2009, he sold 10,000 shares in the company for £10 per share. Calculate the chargeable gain or allowable loss arising on this disposal.

19.4   William made the following acquisitions of preference shares in Heptagon plc:

Date	No of shares	Cost
		£
17 February 2001	600	900
13 November 2005	200	400
9 October 2009	100	300

In January 2010, the company made a 1 for 4 bonus issue. In February 2010, William sold 450 shares for £4 per share. Calculate the chargeable gain, assuming that he made no acquisitions in the following 30 days.

19.5   Yvonne made the following acquisitions of ordinary shares in Rectangle plc:

Date	No of shares	Cost
		£
30 September 1999	2,000	1,200
1 December 2003	3,000	3,600

In January 2010, the company made a 1 for 5 rights issue at £1 per share and Yvonne decided to buy the shares which she was offered. In March 2010, she sold one-half of her shares in the company for £1.80 per share. Calculate the chargeable gain arising in March 2010, given that no further shares were acquired within the following 30 days.

19.6   (a)   In November 1999, Yorick bought 6,000 ordinary shares in Octagon plc for £30,000. In March 2010, the company went into liquidation and Yorick received a first distribution of £1 per share. The market value of an ordinary share in Octagon plc just after this distribution was £2. Compute the allowable loss.

(b)   In January 2003, Yolande bought 300 ordinary shares in Ellipse plc at a cost of £1.20 per share. In May 2009, when shares in Ellipse plc had a market value of £2 each, the company made a rights issue. Yolande sold her rights, realising £25. Compute the chargeable gain arising in November 2009 when Yolande sold all of her shares for £780, assuming that no further shares were acquired within the following 30 days.

19.7   In June 2009, Walter bought 10,000 shares in Oval plc at a cost of £7 per share. In September 2009, Round plc made a takeover bid for Oval plc, offering the Oval shareholders eight Round shares plus £4 in cash for every five Oval shares. The offer was accepted on 2 September 2009 when the market value of shares in Round plc was £4.50 per share. Compute Walter's chargeable gain.

*19.8   Suzanne acquired the following ordinary shares in Aquamarine plc:

Date	No of shares	Cost
		£
2 October 1979	200	600
10 January 1981	150	500
5 December 1999	200	680
8 November 2004	250	1,160
24 July 2009	300	1,400
10 August 2009	400	2,500
20 August 2009	350	2,600
31 August 2009	500	2,400

She made no further acquisitions. The shares were valued at £3.20 each on 31 March 1982. On 24 July 2009, Suzanne sold 1,200 shares for £7 per share. Compute the chargeable gain or allowable loss arising on this disposal.

*19.9   Saeed made the following purchases of ordinary shares in Hyperbola plc:

Date	No of shares	Cost
		£
24 August 1975	800	800
25 November 1980	1,200	1,350
26 February 1995	1,600	2,400
11 October 2004	400	800

The company's shares had a market value of £1.20 each on 31 March 1982. In June 2009, the company made a 1 for 20 rights issue at £1.50 per share and Saeed took up the shares which he was offered.

Calculate the chargeable gain arising in November 2009, when Saeed sold 1,260 shares at £3 each. Assume that no further shares were acquired within the following 30 days.

*19.10   Susan made the following purchases of ordinary shares in Semicircle plc:

Date	No of shares	Cost
		£
11 January 2002	1,500	4,800
20 January 2007	1,140	5,700

In January 2010, the company went into liquidation and Susan received a first distribution of £2 per share. The market value of an ordinary share in Semicircle plc just after this distribution was £1. Compute the allowable loss arising in January 2010.

*19.11   Steven made the following purchases of ordinary shares in Convex plc:

Date	No of shares	Cost
		£
9 May 2002	2,000	8,000
28 November 2005	500	2,500

In February 2010, Concave plc made a takeover bid for Convex plc, offering the Convex shareholders two Concave shares plus £2 in cash for every Convex share. The offer was accepted on 21 February 2010 when the market value of shares in Concave plc was £4 per share. Compute Steven's chargeable gain or allowable loss.

Chapter 20

Principal private residences

Introduction

This chapter examines the CGT consequences of the disposal of a taxpayer's principal private residence. Although a principal private residence is not a chargeable asset for CGT purposes, a CGT liability may arise when a property is disposed of which has been used as a residence for only part of the period of ownership or which has been used partly as a residence and partly for other purposes.

Principal private residence

A dwelling which is a taxpayer's only or main residence is known as that taxpayer's principal private residence (PPR). A taxpayer's PPR is not a chargeable asset for CGT purposes. Therefore any gain which arises on the disposal of a PPR is not chargeable to tax and any loss which arises is not allowable. For a property to be regarded as a PPR, the taxpayer must actually occupy the property as a residence. Mere ownership is not sufficient. Furthermore, the term "residence" implies a degree of permanency and it is unlikely that the PPR exemption will apply to a property which has been used only as temporary accommodation. In *Goodwin* v *Curtis* (1998) a property which had been occupied by the taxpayer for only 32 days did not qualify as a residence.

The large majority of taxpayers own (at most) a single property and reside in that property, so that it is obvious that the property is the taxpayer's PPR. However, the following points may be relevant in more complex cases:

(a) A taxpayer may have only one PPR at any given time.

(b) A taxpayer who owns and lives in two (or more) properties may make an election to determine which property is to be regarded as the PPR. Such an election must be made within two years of the date from which it is to take effect.

(c) A married couple who live together may have only one PPR between them. This rule also applies to same-sex civil partners who live together and who have entered into a legally-recognised civil partnership.

(d)   The PPR exemption covers the residence itself together with grounds or gardens of up to half a hectare (5,000 square metres) in area. Larger areas may be included in the exemption if they are warranted by the size of the residence.

(e)   The requirement that there must be actual residence in the property is relaxed if the taxpayer is required to live in job-related accommodation (see Chapter 7). In these circumstances, the PPR exemption is extended to any property which the taxpayer owns so long as he or she intends to occupy the property in the future.

Partial exemption

If a property has been occupied as a PPR for only a part of the period of ownership, only a part of the gain realised on disposal will be exempt from CGT. The exempt part of the gain is equal to:

$$\frac{\text{length of period of residence}}{\text{length of period of ownership}} \times \text{whole gain}$$

The lengths of the periods of residence and ownership are usually calculated to the nearest month. Note the following important points:

(a)   If the property was acquired before 31 March 1982, the period of ownership prior to that date and any period of residence prior to that date are ignored. This is because the base date for CGT is now 31 March 1982 (see Chapter 17).

(b)   If a property has been the taxpayer's PPR at some time, the last 36 months of ownership always count as a period of residence, whether or not the taxpayer was actually resident then (so helping taxpayers who move house and have difficulty in selling their previous residence). This rule applies even if the taxpayer claims another property to be his or her PPR during the 36 months.

EXAMPLE 1

Allan bought a house in January 1979 for £20,000. The market value of the house on 31 March 1982 was £29,000. Allan lived in the house until 1 May 2006 on which date he bought another house and made this his principal private residence. The house he had bought in January 1979 was sold on 31 January 2010 for £145,000. Compute the chargeable gain.

Solution

In examples of this type it is necessary first to calculate the gain arising (ignoring any PPR exemption) and then to consider the PPR exemption as a second stage. The house was acquired before 31 March 1982, so rebasing applies. The gain arising is as follows:

	£
Sale proceeds	145,000
Less: Market value at 31 March 1982	29,000
Chargeable gain (before PPR exemption)	116,000

After 31 March 1982, Allan owned the house for 27 years and 10 months (334 months). He was actually resident for 24 years and 1 month (289 months) and the last 36 months of ownership also count as a period of residence, making a total of 325 months during which the PPR exemption applies. The chargeable gain is therefore as follows:

	£
Total gain (as above)	116,000
Less: $\dfrac{325}{334}$ x £116,000	112,874
Chargeable gain	3,126

Deemed residence

The period of residence in a property is deemed to include certain periods when the taxpayer was not actually resident, so long as:

(a) there is a period of actual residence both at some time before the period of absence and at some time after the period of absence, and

(b) the taxpayer claims no other property to be a PPR during the period of absence.

These periods of "deemed residence" are as follows:

(a) any periods of absence during which the taxpayer is working abroad

(b) a total of up to four years of absence during which the taxpayer is working elsewhere in the UK

(c) a total of up to three years of absence for any reason.

The requirement that the taxpayer must reside in the property at some time after the period of absence is waived if the absence is work-related and the terms of the taxpayer's employment prevent him or her from returning to the residence.

EXAMPLE 2

On 1 June 1987, Alice bought a house in Derby for £35,000.

- She occupied the house as her PPR until 1 May 1989 when she left to work in Exeter, living in rented accommodation.
- She returned to the house in Derby on 1 November 1990 and stayed until 1 July 1993 when she left to take up a post in the USA, again living in rented accommodation.
- She returned to Derby on 1 February 1996 and stayed until 1 December 2005 when she bought a house in Nottingham and made this her principal private residence.
- On 1 February 2010 she sold the house in Derby for £154,000.

Compute the chargeable gain.

Solution

	£
Sale proceeds	154,000
<u>Less</u>: Acquisition cost	35,000
Chargeable gain (before PPR exemption)	119,000

Alice's period of ownership of the house in Derby (a total of 272 months) can be broken down into the following periods:

(i)	1 June 1987 to 30 April 1989	23 months	Actual residence
(ii)	1 May 1989 to 31 October 1990	18 months	Working in UK
(iii)	1 November 1990 to 30 June 1993	32 months	Actual residence
(iv)	1 July 1993 to 31 January 1996	31 months	Working abroad
(v)	1 February 1996 to 30 November 2005	118 months	Actual residence
(vi)	1 December 2005 to 31 January 2010	50 months	Living in new PPR

Periods (i), (iii) and (v) are exempt since Alice was actually resident in the property during those periods. Period (ii) is exempt since Alice was working elsewhere in the UK, the four-year time limit has not been exceeded and she was resident in the property both before and after the absence. Similarly, period (iv) is exempt. The last 36 months of ownership are always exempt, which leaves the first 14 months of period (vi) to consider. During these 14 months Alice was claiming another property to be her PPR, so the period cannot count as a period of deemed residence and the gain arising during these 14 months is chargeable. The remaining 258 months benefit from the PPR exemption. The chargeable gain is therefore as follows:

	£
Total gain (as above)	119,000
<u>Less</u>: $\dfrac{258}{272}$ x £119,000	112,875
Chargeable gain	6,125

Letting relief

An extension to the PPR exemption, known as "letting relief", applies if a PPR has been let to tenants as residential accommodation. There are two situations to consider:

(a) A property might have been used entirely as a residence for part of the period of ownership but let to tenants during periods of absence by the owner. A chargeable gain will arise if the periods of absence are not entirely covered by the exemptions described above, but letting relief will then be available in relation to this gain.

(b) Part of a property might have been used as a residence whilst the other part has been let. In this case, the PPR exemption will cover:

(i) the gain arising on the whole property in the last 36 months of ownership, and

(ii) the remainder of the gain, to the extent that this is attributable to the part of the property which was occupied by the owner.

The balance of the gain will be chargeable to CGT, but letting relief may then be available. In general, letting relief will *not* be granted if the part that has been let forms a dwelling which is entirely separate from the accommodation which forms the owner's residence (e.g. a self-contained flat with its own access from the road). Relief *will* normally be granted if the let accommodation forms part of the owner's dwelling and the owner previously resided in the entire premises.

Letting relief is calculated as the *lowest* of:

(a) the gain which relates to the let part of the property or to the letting period

(b) the gain which is exempt because of the PPR exemptions

(c) £40,000.

EXAMPLE 3

In relation to the previous example in this chapter, assume now that Alice always let her Derby house when she was not resident there. Compute the chargeable gain.

Solution

The only chargeable period was a period of 14 months during which a gain of £6,125 arose and during which the property was let. Letting relief is available as the lowest of:

(a) The part of the gain which relates to the letting period (£6,125)

(b) The part of the gain which is exempt because of the PPR exemptions (£112,875)

(c) £40,000.

Therefore letting relief is £6,125 and the chargeable gain is reduced to £nil.

EXAMPLE 4

Alistair bought a house on 1 April 1989 for £125,000 and occupied the entire house until 1 May 1996 when he rented the top floor (comprising one-half of the house) to tenants. He retained the ground floor as his own residence. This arrangement continued until 1 October 2009 when he sold the house for £615,000. Compute the chargeable gain.

Solution

	£
Sale proceeds	615,000
Less: Original cost	125,000
Chargeable gain (before PPR exemption)	490,000

Alistair owned the house for a total of 20 years and 6 months (246 months). Exemption is available for the 85 months during which he occupied the whole property and for the last 36 months (a total of 121 months). He was resident in half of the property for the remaining 125 months, so 50% of the gain arising during these 125 months is also exempt. The other 50% is chargeable but letting relief is available. The chargeable gain is as follows:

	£	£
Total gain (as above)		490,000
Less: PPR exemption:		
£490,000 x 121/246	241,016	
£490,000 x 125/246 x 1/2	124,492	365,508
		124,492
Less: Letting relief, lowest of:		
(a) £124,492		
(b) £365,508		
(c) £40,000		40,000
Chargeable gain		84,492

Business use

If a property is used partly as a residence and partly for business purposes, the gain which is attributable to the part used for business purposes is chargeable to CGT. No reliefs are available in relation to this gain. The usual exemption for the last 36 months of ownership does not apply to the part of the property which has been used for business purposes.

EXAMPLE 5

Ava bought a house on 1 July 1989 for £32,000. She occupied the entire property as her PPR until 1 August 1996 when she began using one-quarter of the house for business purposes. This continued until 1 November 2009 when she sold the house for £177,000. Compute the chargeable gain.

Solution

	£
Sale proceeds	177,000
Less: Acquisition cost	32,000
Chargeable gain (before PPR exemption)	145,000

Ava owned the house for 20 years and 4 months (244 months). For the first 7 years and 1 month (85 months) she occupied the entire house as her PPR. For the remaining 159 months she occupied three-quarters of the house. The chargeable gain is as follows:

	£	£
Total gain (as above)		145,000
Less: PPR exemption:		
£145,000 x 85/244	50,512	
£145,000 x 159/244 x 3/4	70,866	121,378
Chargeable gain		23,622

Summary

▶ A taxpayer's principal private residence (PPR) is exempt from CGT.

▶ A taxpayer with two or more residences may elect which property is to be regarded as his or her PPR.

▶ A married couple who live together may have only one PPR between them. This rule also applies to civil partners who live together.

▶ If a property has been occupied as a PPR for only a part of the period of ownership, only a part of the gain realised on disposal will be exempt from CGT.

▶ The last 36 months of ownership of a PPR always count as a period of residence.

▶ Certain periods of absence are deemed to be periods of residence.

▶ Letting relief may be available if a residence has been let to tenants as residential accommodation.

▶ If a residence is used partly for business purposes, the gain relating to the part used for business purposes is chargeable to CGT.

Exercises

20.1 Mohammed owns two properties - a flat in Central London and a country cottage in Sussex. In general he lives in his London flat during the week and spends the weekends in his Sussex cottage. Which of his two properties will be regarded as his principal private residence?

20.2 Melanie bought a house in November 1979 for £18,000. The house had a market value of £21,000 on 31 March 1982 and was sold on 31 October 2009 for £163,000. Compute the chargeable gain arising in each of the following cases:

(a) Melanie occupied the house as her principal private residence throughout the period of ownership.

(b) Melanie occupied the house throughout her period of ownership with the exception of the period between 1 June 1987 and 31 May 1991 when she lived with a friend. During this time the house stood empty.

(c) As (b) except that the house was let as residential accommodation during Melanie's absence.

20.3 Rupert bought a house in Manchester on 1 November 1987 for £55,000. He occupied the house until 1 November 1991 when he left to work abroad for a year, moving back into the house on 1 November 1992. He stayed until 1 February 1995 when he left again, this time to work in Aberdeen, where he stayed until his return on 1 May 1999. This time he stayed for only a month, leaving on 1 June 1999 to go to live with a friend. He never returned to the house and it was sold on 1 March 2010 for £232,000. During his absences, Rupert always let his house and he claimed no other property to be his principal private residence. Compute the chargeable gain arising on the disposal.

20.4 Samantha bought a house for £37,500 on 1 August 1988 and occupied the house as her principal private residence. On 1 June 1990 she began to use one-fifth of the house for business purposes. Unfortunately her business eventually failed and on 1 June 1997 she ceased trading. From that date onwards she resided in the entire house until it was sold on 1 August 2009 for £155,000. Compute the chargeable gain.

*20.5 Terry bought a house for £65,000 on 1 June 1989 and occupied the house as his principal private residence. He lived in the house until 1 June 1994 when he went to stay with relatives in Australia, letting the house in his absence. He did not return until 1 June 1998, when he began using one-quarter of the house for business purposes and the other three-quarters as his residence. This arrangement continued until 1 June 2009 when he sold the house for £190,000. Compute the chargeable gain.

Chapter 21

CGT reliefs

Introduction

A taxpayer's capital gains tax liability may sometimes be reduced or deferred by taking advantage of various CGT reliefs. The main reliefs available are concerned with:

(a) damaged or destroyed assets

(b) replacement of business assets

(c) gift of business assets

(d) transfer of a business to a limited company

(e) disposal of a business ("entrepreneurs' relief")

(f) reinvestment into EIS shares

(g) loans to traders.

The purpose of this chapter is to explain, for each of these reliefs, the circumstances in which the relief is available and the way in which the amount of relief is calculated.

Damaged assets

If an asset has been damaged and insurance money or other compensation is received in consequence, the situation is usually treated as a part disposal. The value of the part disposed of (A) is the amount of money received and the value of the part remaining (B) is the value of the asset on the date that the money is received. Any money spent on restoration is treated as enhancement expenditure.

However, in certain circumstances, the taxpayer may elect that the situation should *not* be treated as a part disposal and that the amount of money received should instead be deducted from the allowable expenditure relating to the asset. This has the effect of increasing the gain arising on a subsequent disposal and is very similar to the CGT treatment of small capital distributions (see Chapter 19). The circumstances in which a part disposal may be avoided are as follows:

(a) All of the money received is applied to restoring the asset, or

(b) The asset is not a wasting asset and all the money received is applied to restoring the asset except for an amount which is small in comparison with the amount received and which is not reasonably required for restoration purposes, or

(c) The asset is not a wasting asset and the amount of money received is small in comparison with the value of the asset.

For this purpose, a sum is regarded as "small" if it does not exceed £3,000 or 5% of the amount with which it is being compared, whichever is the higher.

A part disposal calculation is unavoidable if only part of the money received is spent on restoring the asset and neither of the "small" tests is satisfied. However, the taxpayer may elect that the calculation should relate only to the amount which is received but not spent on restoration. If this election is made, the remainder of the money received is deducted from the allowable expenditure relating to the asset.

EXAMPLE 1

In July 2003, Laura bought an oil painting for £120,000. In October 2009, the painting was damaged by fire. In February 2010, Laura received compensation from her insurance company of £30,000. Compute the chargeable gain or allowable loss arising in each of the following circumstances:

(a) Laura spent none of the insurance money on restoration and the damaged painting was valued at £170,000 in February 2010.

(b) Laura spent £30,000 on restoring the painting in November 2009 and elected that the situation should not be treated as a part disposal.

(c) Laura spent £29,000 on restoring the painting in November 2009 and elected that the situation should not be treated as a part disposal.

(d) Laura spent £20,000 on restoring the painting in November 2009 and elected that the part disposal should relate only to the retained £10,000. The restored painting was valued at £200,000 in February 2010.

Solution

(a) This is a part disposal, with A = £30,000 and B = £170,000. The computation is:

	£
Disposal proceeds	30,000
Less: Part cost: $\dfrac{£30,000}{£30,000 + £170,000}$ x £120,000	18,000
Chargeable gain	12,000

The balance of allowable expenditure carried forward and used in the calculation of the gain arising on a subsequent disposal is £102,000 (£120,000 – £18,000).

(b) The entire amount received is spent on restoration so the election to avoid a part disposal is valid. The balance of allowable expenditure carried forward is:

	£
Incurred July 2003	120,000
Incurred November 2009	30,000
	150,000
Less: Received February 2010 (and not treated as a disposal)	30,000
	120,000

(c) The £1,000 retained is small in comparison with the amount received and therefore the election to avoid a part disposal is valid (so long as the £1,000 is not required for restoration purposes). The balance of allowable expenditure carried forward is:

	£
Incurred July 2003	120,000
Incurred November 2009	29,000
	149,000
Less: Received February 2010 (and not treated as a disposal)	30,000
	119,000

(d) The amount retained is not small in comparison with the amount received and so a part disposal is unavoidable. However, by virtue of Laura's election, this will relate only to the retained £10,000, not to the entire £30,000 received. The computation is:

		£	£
Disposal proceeds			10,000
Less: Part original expenditure:			
$\dfrac{£10,000}{£10,000 + £200,000} \times £120,000$		5,714	
Part restoration expenditure:			
$\dfrac{£10,000}{£10,000 + £200,000} \times £20,000$		952	6,666
Chargeable gain			3,334

The balance of allowable expenditure carried forward in this case is:

	£
Incurred July 2003 (£120,000 – £5,714)	114,286
Incurred November 2009 (£20,000 – £952)	19,048
	133,334
Less: Received February 2010 (and not treated as a disposal)	20,000
	113,334

Destroyed assets

The loss or destruction of an asset is a chargeable disposal and usually results in a CGT computation in which disposal value is equal to the amount of any insurance money or other compensation received. However, if *all* of the money received is spent (within 12 months) on the purchase of a replacement asset, the taxpayer may claim that the disposal of the original asset should give rise to neither a gain nor a loss. The cost of the replacement asset is then reduced by the gain which would have been chargeable on the disposal of the original asset if this claim had not been made.

If only *part* of the money received is spent on the purchase of a replacement asset, the taxpayer may claim that the chargeable gain on the disposal of the original asset should be restricted to the amount of money retained (so long as this is less than the gain). The cost of the replacement asset is then reduced by the balance of the gain that would have been chargeable if the claim had not been made.

EXAMPLE 2

Maurice bought an item of jewellery in November 2004 for £125,000. In 2009 the jewellery was stolen. As a result, Maurice's insurance company paid him £141,500 in May 2009. In June 2009 he spent £150,000 on the purchase of replacement jewellery and claimed that neither a gain nor a loss should arise on the disposal of the original jewellery.

(a) Compute the chargeable gain arising in March 2012 when the replacement jewellery is sold for £180,000.

(b) How would this computation differ if the jewellery bought in June 2009 had cost only £140,000 and Maurice had made an appropriate claim?

Solution

(a) Without a claim, the gain arising on the loss of the original jewellery would be £16,500 (£141,500 − £125,000). The entire proceeds were spent on a replacement asset within 12 months so Maurice is entitled to make the claim. This reduces the deemed acquisition cost of the new jewellery to £133,500 (£150,000 − £16,500). The gain arising on the subsequent sale of the new jewellery is as follows:

	£
Disposal proceeds	180,000
Less: Deemed acquisition cost	133,500
Chargeable gain	46,500

(b) £1,500 of the insurance money was retained and so £1,500 of the gain arising on the stolen jewellery is immediately chargeable. The remaining £15,000 of the gain may be deducted from the acquisition cost of the new jewellery, reducing this cost to £125,000 (£140,000 − £15,000). The chargeable gain arising on the March 2012 disposal becomes £55,000 (£180,000 − £125,000).

Replacement of business assets

Subject to certain conditions, a taxpayer may claim that the gain arising on the disposal of a business asset (the "old asset") may be "rolled-over" against the cost of acquiring a replacement business asset (the "new asset"). The main effects of a claim for roll-over relief are as follows:

(a)   The disposal of the old asset is deemed to give rise to neither a gain nor a loss.

(b)   The cost of the new asset is reduced by the gain which would have been chargeable on the disposal of the old asset if the claim for roll-over relief had not been made.

Full relief is available only if the disposal proceeds of the old asset are *wholly* applied in acquiring the new asset. If only *part* of the disposal proceeds are used to acquire the new asset, the effect of a claim for roll-over relief is that the chargeable gain on the disposal of the old asset is restricted to the amount of money retained (so long as this is less than the gain). The cost of the new asset is then reduced by the balance of the gain that would have been chargeable if the claim had not been made. The conditions which must be satisfied if a roll-over claim is to be accepted are:

(a)   Both the old asset and the new asset must be drawn from the following list (though they need not both be the same type of asset):

  (i)   land, buildings and fixed plant and machinery

  (ii)   goodwill

  (iii) ships, aircraft, hovercraft, satellites, space stations and spacecraft

  (iv)   milk, potato and fish quotas and certain EU agricultural quotas

  (v)   Lloyd's syndicate rights.

(b)   The old asset must have been used only for trade purposes throughout the period of ownership and the new asset must be used only for trade purposes.

(c)   The new asset must be acquired during the period beginning one year before and ending three years after the date of disposal of the old asset.

(d)   The taxpayer must claim the relief by 31 January in the sixth tax year following the *later* of the year in which the old asset is disposed of and the year in which the new asset is acquired. As from April 2010, such claims will have to be made within four years of the end of the later of these two tax years.

Note that a similar relief is available to companies (which pay corporation tax on their chargeable gains) when a business asset is disposed of and a replacement business asset is acquired. For companies, however, the list of assets which are eligible for this relief excludes goodwill and quotas. These assets fall instead within the scope of the corporation tax intangible assets regime (see Chapter 22).

EXAMPLE 3

In May 2002, Janine bought a building for £187,525 for use in her business. In July 2009 she sold the building for £260,000 and, in the same month, bought another building for use in her business. Assuming that Janine claims roll-over relief, calculate the chargeable gain arising on the July 2009 disposal if the replacement building has a cost of:

(a) £270,000   (b) £240,000   (c) £185,000.

Solution

The gain on the disposal of the original building is computed as follows:

	£
Sale proceeds	260,000
Less: Acquisition cost	187,525
Chargeable gain	72,475

(a) The entire sale proceeds have been spent on a replacement building. None of the gain is immediately chargeable and the entire gain is rolled-over against the cost of the new building, reducing its allowable cost to £197,525 (£270,000 – £72,475).

(b) £20,000 of the sale proceeds have been retained. Therefore £20,000 of the gain is immediately chargeable. The remaining £52,475 may be rolled-over against the cost of the new building, reducing its allowable cost to £187,525 (£240,000 – £52,475).

(c) £75,000 of the sale proceeds have been retained. This exceeds the amount of the gain. Therefore the whole gain is immediately chargeable and no part of the gain may be rolled-over. The allowable cost of the new building is the full £185,000.

Replacement with a depreciating asset

If the new asset is a "depreciating asset" (an asset with an expected life of 60 years or less at the time of acquisition) the gain arising on the disposal of the old asset cannot be rolled-over and is *not* deducted from the cost of the new asset. Instead, the gain is temporarily deferred or "held-over" until it crystallises (becomes chargeable) on the *earliest* of the following three dates:

(a) the date on which the new asset is disposed of

(b) the date on which the new asset ceases to be used for trade purposes

(c) the 10th anniversary of the acquisition of the new asset.

Clearly, a gain which is held-over in these circumstances will become chargeable no more than ten years after the date of acquisition of the depreciating asset. However, if a suitable non-depreciating asset is acquired at any time before the earliest of the above three dates, the held-over gain may be transferred to this new asset, so converting a temporarily held-over gain into a permanently rolled-over gain.

EXAMPLE 4

In June 2009, Ian sold a freehold building for £200,000, realising a chargeable gain of £25,000. The building had been acquired in May 2004 and used only for trade purposes. In July 2009, he acquired fixed plant and machinery costing £220,000 and elected that the gain on the building should be held-over against the plant and machinery. Explain the way in which the held-over gain would be treated if:

(a) Ian sells the plant and machinery in October 2013.

(b) Ian sells the plant and machinery in March 2021.

Solution

(a) The replacement asset is sold before the 10th anniversary of its acquisition and so the deferred gain becomes chargeable in 2013-14.

(b) The replacement asset is still in Ian's possession ten years after its acquisition, so the held-over gain of £25,000 crystallises in July 2019 and forms part of Ian's chargeable gains in 2019-20.

EXAMPLE 5

Imagine now that Ian (in the above example) buys another freehold building for business use in November 2012 and elects to transfer the held-over gain on the plant and machinery to the new freehold building. Explain the treatment of the held-over gain if the new building costs:

(a) £250,000   (b) £190,000.

Solution

(a) The entire proceeds of the sale of the original building have been invested in a new building so the whole held-over gain of £25,000 can be converted into a rolled-over gain, reducing the allowable cost of the new building to £225,000.

(b) £10,000 out of the sale proceeds of the original building have not been invested in the new building and therefore cannot be rolled-over against its cost. This £10,000 will continue to be held-over against the plant and machinery and will become chargeable no later than July 2019. However, the remaining £15,000 is converted into a rolled-over gain, reducing the allowable cost of the new building to £175,000.

Gift of business assets

The gift of an asset is a chargeable disposal and this is the case whether or not the asset is used in business. However, subject to certain conditions, a claim may be made for the gain arising on a gift of business assets to be held-over until the transferee disposes of the assets concerned. If such a claim is made, the transferor's gain on the disposal is reduced to zero and the transferee's deemed acquisition cost is reduced by the amount of the gain that would have been chargeable on the transferor if the claim had not been made. The conditions which must be satisfied are as follows:

(a)   Both the transferor and the transferee must elect for the gain arising on the gift to be held-over. This election must be made by 31 January in the sixth tax year following the year in which the gift is made. As from April 2010, such an election will have to be made within four years of the end of the tax year in which the gift is made.

(b)   The gifted assets must consist of either:

(i)   assets used in a business carried on by the transferor or by the transferor's *personal trading company* (a trading company in which the transferor has at least 5% of the voting rights), or

(ii)   shares or securities of an unlisted trading company or of the transferor's personal trading company (so long as the transferee is not a company).

If the gift is of shares, rather than of individual business assets, the gain arising on the disposal is apportioned between the amount which relates to chargeable business assets owned by the company on the date of the gift and the amount which relates to other chargeable assets (e.g. investments). Only the part of the gain relating to chargeable business assets is eligible for hold-over relief.

Sale for less than market value

Gift relief is also available if a business asset is sold for less than market value (typically to a connected person). But if the actual consideration received by the transferor exceeds the original cost of the asset (so that part of the gain has been realised) the amount of the gain which may be held-over is reduced by the excess of the actual consideration over the asset's cost.

EXAMPLE 6

In March 2010, Jonathan gives the goodwill of his business to his daughter. Jonathan acquired the goodwill for £25,000 in May 2004 and its market value on the date of the gift is £60,000. Both Jonathan and his daughter elect that the gain arising should be held-over.

(a)   Compute the gain arising on the gift and the amount which may be held-over.

(b)   How would the computation differ if Jonathan's daughter paid him £32,000 for the goodwill?

Solution

(a) The chargeable gain is £35,000 (£60,000 – £25,000). The whole of this gain may be held-over, reducing Jonathan's daughter's deemed acquisition cost to £25,000 (£60,000 – £35,000).

(b) The chargeable gain is still £35,000, since this is not a bargain made at arm's length and therefore disposal value is taken to be the market value of the asset on the date of disposal. However, £7,000 of the gain (£32,000 – £25,000) has been realised in cash, so the amount of the gain which may be held-over is reduced to £28,000. The remaining £7,000 of the gain is immediately chargeable. The daughter's deemed acquisition cost is £32,000 (£60,000 – £28,000).

EXAMPLE 7

Kathy is the managing director of Kathy Ltd (an unlisted trading company). She bought 90% of the voting share capital of the company for £60,000 in July 1999. In May 2009, she gave all her shares to her son and both Kathy and her son elected that the gain arising on this gift should (as far as possible) be held-over. The net assets of the company on the date of the gift (at market value) were as follows:

	£
Goodwill	100,000
Freehold building (used only for business purposes)	150,000
Listed investments	50,000
Net current assets (none of which are chargeable)	40,000
Total net assets	340,000

(a) Compute the gain arising on the gift and the amount which may be held-over.

(b) Compute the gain arising in March 2010 when Kathy's son sells all the shares for £350,000.

Solution

(a) Presumably, the value of the shares on the date of the gift was 90% of £340,000 = £306,000. So the gain arising on the gift was £246,000 (£306,000 – £60,000).

The company's chargeable assets on the date of the gift were £300,000 of which £250,000 were chargeable business assets. So £246,000 x 250,000/300,000 = £205,000 of the gain was held-over whilst the remaining £41,000 was chargeable.

(b) The gain arising in March 2010 is as follows:

	£
Sale proceeds	350,000
Less: Deemed acquisition cost (£306,000 – £205,000)	101,000
Chargeable gain	249,000

Transfer of a business to a limited company

Subject to certain conditions, the gain arising on the transfer of a business to a limited company in return for shares in that company is held-over until the transferor disposes of the shares. If this relief applies, the gain arising on the disposal of the business is deducted from the deemed acquisition cost of the shares. The required conditions are:

(a) The business is transferred as a going concern.

(b) All of the assets of the business (other than cash) are transferred to the company.

(c) The consideration received by the transferor consists wholly or partly of shares in the company.

This relief (known as "incorporation relief") applies automatically, so there is no need for the transferor to make a claim. However, the transferor may elect that incorporation relief should *not* apply. If incorporation relief applies and the consideration for a transfer consists only partly of shares, then only part of the chargeable gain is held-over. The held-over gain is calculated as follows:

$$\frac{\text{value of the shares received}}{\text{total consideration received}} \times \text{whole gain}$$

EXAMPLE 8

In July 2009, Leroy transferred his business to a limited company in exchange for £5,000 in cash and shares valued at £60,000. The gain arising on the transfer was £26,000. Leroy does not elect that incorporation relief should disapply. Calculate the amount of the gain which is immediately chargeable and the amount which is held-over.

Solution

The held-over gain is £26,000 x 60,000/65,000 = £24,000. The remaining £2,000 of the gain is immediately chargeable. The acquisition cost of the shares is reduced to £36,000 (£60,000 – £24,000).

Entrepreneurs' relief

If certain conditions are satisfied, a relief known as "entrepreneurs' relief" (ER) may be available in respect of gains of up to £1 million made by an individual on the disposal of:

(a)   the whole or part of a business carried on by the individual alone or in partnership

(b)   assets of the individual's or the partnership's business after a cessation of trade

(c)   shares and securities of the individual's personal trading company.

In case (a) above, it is important to realise that the disposal must be the disposal of either a whole business or a significant part of a business. Merely disposing of a business asset, without there being a disposal of all or part of the business, does not qualify for ER.

  Gains which qualify for ER are taxed at an effective CGT rate of 10%. Since the rate of CGT is currently 18%, this effect is achieved by reducing qualifying gains by 4/9ths. If the disposal of a business gives rise to both gains and losses, the losses are deducted from the gains before calculating entrepreneurs' relief.

  It is important to note that the £1 million limit is a *lifetime* limit. An individual is able to claim ER on more than one occasion but a total of only £1 million of gains is eligible for relief during the individual's lifetime. Disposals made before the introduction of ER (on 6 April 2008) do not count towards this £1 million limit.

EXAMPLE 9

Wendy disposed of her trading business in December 2009. Calculate the amount of CGT payable in respect of her gain, assuming that entrepreneurs' relief is claimed and that the amount of the gain is:

(a)   £720,000   (b)   £1,000,000   (c)   £2,000,000

Assume that Wendy has made no previous ER claims and that her annual exemption for 2009-10 is fully utilised against other gains.

Solution

(a)   £720,000 does not exceed £1 million, so the whole of the gain qualifies for ER. The amount of relief is 4/9ths of £720,000 = £320,000, leaving £400,000. This is charged to CGT at 18%, giving tax payable of £72,000 (an effective tax rate of 10%).

(b)   The gain does not exceed £1 million, so the whole gain qualifies for ER. The amount of relief is 4/9ths of £1,000,000 = £444,444, leaving £555,556. This is charged to CGT at 18%, giving tax payable of £100,000 (an effective tax rate of 10%).

(c)   The first £1 million of the gain qualifies for ER. The amount of relief is 4/9ths of £1,000,000 = £444,444, leaving £1,555,556. This is charged to CGT at 18%, giving tax payable of £280,000 (an effective tax rate of 14%).

Conditions for entrepreneurs' relief claims

For entrepreneurs' relief to be available, an individual must make a "material disposal" of business assets. In order for this to be the case, the individual must either:

(a) dispose of the whole or part of a business (including a share in a partnership) which the individual has owned throughout the period of one year ending on the date of the disposal, or

(b) dispose of assets used by a business at the time at which it ceases trading, as long as the business was owned by the individual (or by a partnership in which the individual was a member) throughout the year ending on the date of cessation and the assets are disposed of within three years of that date, or

(c) dispose of shares or securities in a company which, throughout the period of one year ending on the date of the disposal, has been the individual's personal trading company and of which the individual has been an officer or employee.

In cases (a) and (b) above, ER is given only in respect of disposals of "relevant business assets". These include goodwill but exclude assets held as investments.

A business qualifies for ER purposes if it is a trade, profession or vocation conducted on a commercial basis with a view to the realisation of profits. At present, this includes the commercial letting of furnished holiday accommodation, but the furnished holiday accommodation rules are to be repealed as from 6 April 2010 (see Chapter 5).

A trading company qualifies as the individual's *personal trading company* if the individual holds at least 5% of the company's ordinary shares and has at least 5% of the company's voting rights.

Entrepreneurs' relief is given only if the individual makes a claim. Claims must be made by the first anniversary of the 31 January following the tax year in which the qualifying disposal is made. For example, if a disposal occurs during tax year 2009-10, an ER claim must be made by 31 January 2012.

Note that a disposal which qualifies for entrepreneurs' relief may also qualify for gift relief (see earlier in this chapter). If this occurs, the held-over gain will be reduced by the amount of ER available on the disposal.

Associated disposals

If an individual qualifies for ER on a disposal of shares or securities or on a disposal of a share in a partnership, relief may also be available in relation to "associated disposals". An associated disposal is the disposal of an asset which is owned by the individual but has been used in the business of the company or partnership concerned.

EXAMPLE 10

Calculate the amount of ER available in respect of the following disposals, assuming in each case that there have been no previous ER claims.

(a) Tom sells his trading business during 2009-10. He realises a gain of £300,000 on the disposal of his business premises but incurs a loss of £120,000 on the disposal of his goodwill. He has owned the business for 15 years.

(b) During 2009-10, Henry sells a property which he has been letting unfurnished to the same tenant since 2004. The gain on this disposal is £150,000.

(c) Brenda sells her trading business during 2009-10, realising gains of £450,000. She has owned the business for many years. In March 2010, she becomes a director of a trading company in which she owns 20% of the ordinary shares. She sells her shares in the company in May 2014 and realises a gain of £800,000.

Solution

(a) Losses must be deducted from gains before computing ER. Tom's net gains are £180,000 (£300,000 – £120,000) so ER is 4/9ths of £180,000 = £80,000.

(b) Henry's use of this property does not qualify as a trade and therefore ER is not available. ER would have been available if the letting of the property had qualified as the commercial letting of furnished holiday accommodation (see Chapter 5).

(c) ER on the first disposal is 4/9ths of £450,000 = £200,000. The second disposal also qualifies for ER but only £550,000 of the gain is eligible (£1,000,000 – £450,000). So ER on the second disposal is 4/9ths of £550,000 = £244,444.

Reinvestment into EIS shares

The gain arising on the disposal of *any* asset may be deferred if an amount of money equal to the gain is used to subscribe for shares which are eligible under the rules of the Enterprise Investment Scheme (see Chapter 6). Note the following points:

(a) The shares must be subscribed for during the period starting one year before and finishing three years after the disposal concerned.

(b) A gain may be deferred if an amount equal to that gain is invested in eligible shares. It is *not* necessary to invest the entire disposal proceeds.

(c) There is no requirement that income tax relief should be available in relation to the investment. It follows that the taxpayer does not have to be unconnected with the company concerned and that the amount of a deferred gain can exceed the maximum amount on which income tax relief is granted.

(d) A taxpayer claiming this relief may restrict the amount of relief claimed so as to avoid wasting the annual exemption.

(e) The deferred gain usually becomes chargeable on the disposal of the EIS shares, but further deferral is possible if further EIS shares are then subscribed for.

Loans to traders

If a taxpayer lends money to a trader and then finds that all or part of the loan is irrecoverable, the loss incurred may be treated as a capital loss and set against the taxpayer's capital gains. This relief is subject to the following conditions:

(a) the trader who has borrowed the money must be resident in the UK

(b) the money must have been borrowed for trade purposes (but not for the trade of money-lending)

(c) the debt must be unsecured.

Subject to these conditions, the amount lost is treated as a capital loss of the year in which the taxpayer makes the claim for relief, though a claim may be backdated for up to two years if it can be shown that the debt was irrecoverable then. If relief is given and then all or part of the loan is recovered, the amount recovered is treated as a capital gain of the year in which recovery takes place.

Summary

▸ If the compensation received on the loss or destruction of an asset is spent on the purchase of a replacement, the taxpayer may claim that the disposal should give rise to neither a gain nor a loss. The gain which would have been chargeable is then subtracted from the cost of the replacement asset.

▸ The gain arising on the disposal of a business asset may be rolled-over against the cost of acquiring a replacement.

▸ If a business asset is replaced by a depreciating asset, the gain arising cannot be permanently rolled-over but may be temporarily held-over instead. This gain will become chargeable no later than 10 years after the replacement asset was acquired (unless the gain is transferred to a non-depreciating asset in the meantime).

▸ The gain arising on the gift of a business asset may be held-over until the transferee disposes of the asset.

▸ The gain arising on the transfer of a business to a limited company is held-over until the transferor disposes of the shares which were received in exchange for the assets of the business. The transferor may elect that this relief should not apply.

▸ Subject to certain conditions, entrepreneurs' relief is available in respect of gains of up to £1 million arising on the disposal of the whole or part of a business. The relief is calculated as 4/9ths of the qualifying gain, so reducing the effective rate of tax from 18% to 10%.

▸ The gain arising on the disposal of any asset may be deferred if the amount of the gain is used to subscribe for shares eligible under the rules of the EIS.

Exercises

21.1   In October 2000, Matthew bought a piece of rare porcelain for £10,000. The porcelain was damaged in early 2006 and in March of that year Matthew spent £3,850 on restoration work. In July 2006, Matthew's insurance company paid him £4,000 and Matthew successfully claimed that this should not be treated as a part disposal. He sold the porcelain in March 2010 for £23,500. Compute the chargeable gain.

21.2   In February 2002, Maria bought a diamond necklace for £13,500. In 2004 the necklace was stolen and, as a result, an insurance payment of £14,000 was received in February 2005. In the same month, Maria spent £14,750 on the purchase of a replacement necklace and claimed that the disposal of the original necklace should give rise to neither a gain nor a loss. Compute the chargeable gain arising in January 2010 when the replacement necklace was sold for £20,000.

21.3   In September 1999, Pamela bought a building for business use at a cost of £150,000. In September 2009 she sold the building for £261,400 and immediately bought another building, again for business use. Assuming that Pamela claims roll-over relief, calculate the chargeable gain arising in September 2009 if the cost of the new building is:

(a)   £258,900

(b)   £149,800

(c)   £276,800.

21.4   In July 2009, Phillip (a sole trader) gave his entire business to his grandson. Both Phillip and his grandson elected that the gains arising on this gift should be held-over. The chargeable gains arising were as follows:

	£
Freehold buildings	23,500
Goodwill	40,000
Listed investments	10,600

State the amount of the gains which could be held-over.

21.5   In August 2009, Susannah (a sole trader) gave her business premises to her son. The premises had been bought by Susannah for £91,500 in July 2000 and extended in May 2001 at a cost of £34,500. Their market value in August 2009 was £215,000. Both Susannah and her son elected that the gain arising should be held-over.

Compute the amount of the held-over gain and explain how the situation would differ if Susannah's son had paid her £150,000 for the premises.

*21.6   In January 1981, Norman bought a freehold building for use in his business at a cost of £120,000. The building had a market value on 31 March 1982 of £125,000. In June 2009 he sold the building for £875,000 and in August 2009 he spent £720,000 on buying another building for use in his business. This building was sold in December 2011 for £730,000. Compute the gains arising on the disposal of each building (assuming that Norman claims roll-over relief).

*21.7   In May 2004, Ruth sold a freehold building which she had used exclusively for business purposes. The building was sold for £220,000, realising a chargeable gain of £42,500. In the following month, Ruth acquired fixed plant for £220,000 and elected to hold-over the gain on the freehold property against this plant and machinery. In August 2009, she acquired another freehold building for £205,000 and elected to transfer the held-over gain to this new building. Explain the treatment of the £42,500 gain.

*21.8   Calculate the 2009-10 CGT liability of the following individuals, assuming in each case that there are no disposals in the year other than those mentioned, there are no allowable losses brought forward and entrepreneurs' relief is claimed whenever possible. None of the individuals has made any previous claims for entrepreneurs' relief.

(a)   In October 2009, Roger sold all of his shares in a trading company, realising a gain of £351,000. He has owned 25% of the company's ordinary share capital since March 2004 and has been a director of the company since June 2005.

(b)   In June 2009, Dennis sold his business (which he has owned since May 1994) and realised gains of £1,250,000.

(c)   In December 2009, Denise sold her interest in a trading partnership and realised a gain of £140,000. She had been a member of the partnership for five years. Also in December 2009, she sold a building which was owned by her personally but had been used by the partnership for business purposes since 2006. She realised a gain of £31,000 in relation to this building.

*21.9   In 2002, Shaun bought 20% of the ordinary shares of a trading company. The shares cost £140,000. He owned the shares (and was a director of the company) until January 2010 when he gave all the shares to a friend. On the date of the gift, the shares had a market value of £500,000 and the company's assets were valued as follows:

	£
Freehold land and buildings	1,700,000
Goodwill	500,000
Investments	100,000
Motor cars	40,000
Net current assets	160,000

Calculate the chargeable gain, assuming that entrepreneurs' relief is claimed and that both Shaun and his friend elect that the gain arising should (as far as possible) be held-over. Assume also that Shaun has made no previous claims for entrepreneurs' relief.

Review questions (Set B)

B1 In March 2010, Vasco sold at auction an antique dressing-table. He received £11,960 after auctioneer's commission of 8%. He had purchased the table in January 2000 for £1,000.

Columbus sold one of his factories on 30 April 2009 for £900,000. The factory had been purchased in September 2001 for £566,700. In March 2010, Columbus purchased another factory for £700,000 and claimed roll-over relief in relation to the gain arising on the factory sold in April 2009.

You are required to:

(i) Calculate Vasco's chargeable gain.

(ii) Calculate the chargeable gain arising on the disposal made by Columbus in April 2009. Also calculate the base cost of the factory acquired in March 2010.

(ACCA)

B2 Yvonne had the following transactions in the shares of Scotia plc:

			£
18 August 1997	Bought	3,000 shares	6,000
19 September 2004	Bought	2,000 shares	5,000
13 March 2010	Sold	5,000 shares	23,000
28 March 2010	Bought	1,000 shares	4,400

Sally's capital gains tax position in 2009-10 was as follows:

	£
Capital gains arising in the year	30,000
Capital losses arising in the year	6,000
Capital losses brought forward	12,000

You are required to:

(i) Calculate Yvonne's chargeable gain.

(ii) Calculate Sally's CGT liability for 2009-10. *(ACCA)*

B3   Ranek sold a factory in November 2009 for £250,000 and moved his business into rented premises. The factory was purchased in April 2001 for £112,800. Ranek purchased fixed plant in December 2008 costing £240,000 and elected to "hold-over" any gain on the sale of the building against the cost of the plant.

You are required to:

(i)   Calculate the chargeable gain on the sale of the factory and the effect of the "hold-over" claim on that gain.

(ii)   State the earliest time that the "hold-over" would cease to be effective.   *(ACCA)*

B4   Consider each of the following situations:

(a)   Marlene has chargeable gains for the year 2009-10 of £12,000 and capital losses for the year 2009-10 of £8,000.

(b)   Moira has chargeable gains for the year 2009-10 of £12,000 and capital losses brought forward of £8,000.

(c)   Marina has chargeable gains for the year 2009-10 of £3,000 and capital losses brought forward of £8,000.

(d)   Melissa has chargeable gains for the year 2009-10 of £12,000, capital losses for the year 2009-10 of £8,000 and capital losses brought forward of £4,000.

You are required to:

For each situation, calculate the capital gains assessable for 2009-10 and state the amount of any losses carried forward.   *(ACCA)*

B5   In the year to 5 April 2010, Thomas More made the following disposals:

(i)   A flat in a house that he had purchased on 1 December 1999 for £80,000. It had never been occupied as the main residence and had been consistently let during his period of ownership. The property had been converted into two flats in September 2000 at a cost of £32,000. The flat was sold for £142,000 on 1 December 2009 and out of this legal fees of £4,000 were paid. It was agreed that the value of the other flat was £130,000 in December 2009.

(ii)   20,000 shares in ICI plc which cost £112,300 in December 2000 and which were sold for £150,000 in December 2009. (No shares were acquired within the next 30 days).

Required:

(a)   Calculate the capital gains tax payable on the sale of the flat and the shares in ICI plc. There were no other chargeable disposals in the year and no capital losses brought forward from previous years.

(b)   If you were told at the start of 2009-10 that Mr More intended making the above disposals and that his wife had capital losses of £30,000 brought forward (and that she did not intend to make any disposals in 2009-10) would there be any advice that you would consider giving to Thomas?   *(Amended from AAT)*

*B6 Mrs Laura Stapleton, a widow, has decided to dispose of her residence and retire to Canada, where she will live with her son, Danny.

She acquired her house on 1 June 1990 and lived there until 31 March 1991 when she left the UK in order to care for Danny and his wife who had been injured in a serious car accident in Canada. Liking it there, she extended her stay and on 1 November 1991 she took a job at a local hospital until 31 December 1992 when she returned to the UK and resumed residence in her property.

She remained living in her house until 31 December 2004, when she left it permanently in order to live in a flat. Contracts were exchanged for the sale of the house on 31 May 2009.

The house originally cost £50,000 and an extension was completed in December 1993 at a cost of £20,000. The agreed sale proceeds are £300,000 and the expenses of sale are £5,200. Throughout the periods of Mrs Stapleton's absence, the property was let at a market rent.

Required:

Calculate the chargeable gain arising on the disposal of Mrs Stapleton's residence.

(Amended from AAT)

*B7 You have been consulted by Mr Christopher Rodrigues on two matters relating to capital gains tax. Extracts from his letter to you are:

"On 31 January 2010, I sold my shares in Fledgeby plc, a listed company. I had acquired them as follows:

1 January 2000	1,000	shares cost £4,200
19 June 2001	700	shares cost £2,950
31 December 2007	1,200	shares cost £5,620
11 August 2009	400	shares cost £2,100

I also took up a 1 for 4 rights issue at £3.50 per share on 31 May 2008. The shares were all sold for £38,000 on 31 January 2010 and I do not intend to buy any shares in the company in the future.

Also on 31 January 2010, I sold for £200,000 a plot of land that I acquired in January 1980 for £10,000. A friend has told me that the gain might be either a capital gain or a trading gain but, as capital gains and trading gains are both taxed, it doesn't really matter which way it is dealt with."

Required:

(a) Calculate the chargeable gain arising on the sale of the shares in Fledgeby plc.

(b) Do you agree with the statement of the other taxation practitioner? Draft brief notes that will form the basis of the letter that you will write to Mr Rodrigues.

(Amended from AAT)

*B8   On 1 May 1995, Nigel acquired a 30-year lease for £20,000. He assigned the lease on 1 November 2009 for £75,000.

Kay purchased a plot of land in February 2001 for £20,000. She sold part of the land for £18,000 in March 2010 when the value of the remainder of the land was £60,000.

Shirley had the following dealings in the shares of Wingfield plc, a listed company:

			£
January 1981	Bought	4,000 shares	18,000
March 1993	1 for 4 rights issue	1,000 shares	7,000
November 1995	Bought	3,000 shares	24,000
January 2001	1 for 2 bonus issue	4,000 shares	-
March 2010	Sold	7,000 shares	56,000

The shares had a market value of £8 per share on 31 March 1982. No further shares were acquired during 2010.

You are required to:

(i)   Calculate Nigel's chargeable gain.

(ii)   Calculate Kay's chargeable gain.

(iii)   Calculate Shirley's chargeable gain.   (ACCA)

*B9   Gillian purchased 10,000 ordinary shares in Downtown plc in January 2004 for £20,000. In October 2009, Upmarket plc acquired the whole of the share capital of Downtown plc following a take-over bid. The terms of the take-over offer were:

> One ordinary share in Upmarket plc, and
>
> Two preference shares in Upmarket plc, and
>
> £3 cash

for every five shares held in Downtown plc. The share prices of Upmarket plc immediately after the take-over were:

> Ordinary shares £10 each, and
>
> Preference shares £3 each.

You are required to:

Calculate the chargeable gain arising in 2009-10.   *(ACCA)*

*B10   Joan has been a full-time director of Sunnybank Pursuits Ltd (a trading company) since 1990 and has owned 10% of the company's ordinary shares since 1992. She retired in February 2010 and gave all of her shares in the company to her daughter, Sylvia. The capital gain on the gift was £720,000 before deducting any reliefs.

Joan claims entrepreneurs' relief in relation to the disposal. Also, Joan and Sylvia have jointly elected that the capital gain arising on the disposal should be held-over.

The market values of the assets in the company's balance sheet at the time that the shares were gifted were:

	£
Land and buildings	4,000,000
Plant and machinery	2,000,000
Goodwill	1,000,000
Listed shares	1,000,000

All items of plant and machinery cost more than £6,000 each and are valued at more than £6,000 each in February 2010.

You are required to:

Calculate Joan's assessable capital gain in 2009-10.   *(ACCA)*

Part 3

CORPORATION TAX

Chapter 23

Corporate chargeable gains

Introduction

A company's chargeable profits for an accounting period include any chargeable gains which arise from disposals made during that period. The chargeable gains of a company are computed in a similar way to the capital gains of an individual, but there are some important differences between the rules which apply to companies and the rules which apply to individuals. The purpose of this chapter is to explain how the chargeable gains of a company are determined for corporation tax purposes. The relevant legislation is in the Taxation of Chargeable Gains Act 1992, as amended by subsequent Finance Acts.

Chargeable disposals and chargeable assets

A chargeable gain or allowable loss may arise if a company makes a chargeable disposal of a chargeable asset. A company's chargeable assets will usually consist of non-current assets (fixed assets) such as land and buildings, plant and machinery or investments, but certain assets are entirely exempt from the chargeable gains legislation. The main exemptions for a company are:

(a) motor cars

(b) items of tangible. movable property ("chattels") worth £6,000 or less

(c) chattels with a predictable useful life of up to 50 years ("wasting chattels") unless used in business and eligible for capital allowances

(d) gilt-edged securities and qualifying corporate bonds, which are dealt with by the loan relationships regime (see Chapter 22).

A chargeable disposal generally occurs when the whole or part of a chargeable asset is sold or given away. However, the gift of a chargeable asset to a charity is exempt.

Basis of assessment

The chargeable gains figure which is included in a company's chargeable profits for an accounting period is based upon the disposals made during that period. This figure is calculated as follows:

(a) The chargeable gain or allowable loss arising on each disposal is calculated.

(b) If total gains exceed total losses, the losses are subtracted from the gains to give net chargeable gains for the accounting period.

(c) If total losses exceed total gains, the chargeable gains figure for the accounting period is nil. The net losses are then carried forward for relief in subsequent accounting periods (see Chapter 26).

Companies are *not* entitled to the annual exemption which is available to individuals who pay capital gains tax (CGT).

Computation of gains and losses

The chargeable gains and allowable losses of a company are computed in a similar way to those of an individual (see Chapters 17-21) but the following important distinctions should be noted:

(a) (i) The gain arising on the disposal of a chargeable asset by a company is reduced by "indexation allowance", which adjusts the gain to take account of inflation. Indexation allowance used to be available when calculating the capital gains of individuals for CGT purposes, but this ceased to be the case in April 2008.

(ii) Rebasing does not always apply when a company disposes of an asset acquired before 31 March 1982.

The way in which indexation allowance is calculated and the corporation tax treatment of assets acquired before 31 March 1982 are both explained below.

(b) The share matching rules that are used when a company makes a disposal of shares or securities are different from the equivalent rules that apply when such a disposal is made by an individual. The share matching rules which are used for corporation tax purposes are explained later in this chapter.

(c) The principal private residence exemption does not apply to companies.

(d) With the introduction of the intangible fixed assets regime (see Chapter 22), goodwill and quotas acquired by a company are removed from the list of assets which qualify for chargeable gains rollover relief.

(e) Gift relief, incorporation relief, entrepreneurs' relief and EIS deferral relief do not apply to companies.

Indexation allowance

Indexation allowance was introduced in 1982 with the intention of ensuring that capital gains caused by inflation should not be charged to tax.

Indexation allowance is calculated separately for each item of allowable expenditure shown in a computation. The indexation allowance available on an item of expenditure is equal to the amount of that expenditure multiplied by an *indexation factor*, which is computed according to the following formula and is rounded to three decimal places:

$$\frac{RD - RI}{RI}$$

where: RD is the Retail Prices Index (RPI) for the month of disposal, and

RI is the RPI for the month in which the expenditure was incurred.

A table of RPIs is given at the end of this chapter.

EXAMPLE 1

A company bought a chargeable asset in June 2001 (RPI 174.4) for £1,200 and sold the asset in August 2009 (RPI 214.0) for £3,350. Compute the chargeable gain.

Solution

	£
Sale proceeds	3,350
<u>Less</u>: Acquisition cost	1,200
Unindexed gain	2,150
<u>Less</u>: Indexation allowance	
$\dfrac{214.0 - 174.4}{174.4}$ = 0.227 x £1,200	272
Chargeable gain	1,878

EXAMPLE 2

A company bought a chargeable asset in November 1999 for £15,000. Enhancement expenditure was £2,000 in January 2001 and £3,000 in June 2005. The asset was sold in February 2010 for £28,000. RPIs are as follows:

November 1999	166.7
January 2001	171.1
June 2005	192.2
February 2010	216.4

Compute the chargeable gain.

Solution

	£	£
Sale proceeds		28,000
Less: Acquisition cost	15,000	
Enhancement expenditure (£2,000 + £3,000)	5,000	20,000
Unindexed gain		8,000

Less: Indexation allowance:

(i) on acquisition cost

$$\frac{216.4 - 166.7}{166.7} = 0.298 \times £15,000 \qquad 4,470$$

(ii) on enhancement January 2001

$$\frac{216.4 - 171.1}{171.1} = 0.265 \times £2,000 \qquad 530$$

(iii) on enhancement June 2005

$$\frac{216.4 - 192.2}{192.2} = 0.126 \times £3,000 \qquad 378 \qquad 5,378$$

Chargeable gain		2,622

Restrictions on indexation allowance

Note the following points about the indexation allowance:

(a) If RPI goes *down* between the month in which expenditure is incurred and the month of disposal, the indexation allowance available in relation to that expenditure is nil.

(b) No indexation allowance is available in respect of the incidental costs of disposal, even if they were incurred prior to the month of disposal.

(c) Indexation allowance cannot be used to convert a gain into a loss. Therefore, if the available indexation allowance (calculated in the normal way) exceeds the unindexed gain, the indexation allowance is restricted so as to give neither a gain nor a loss.

(d) Indexation allowance cannot be used to increase an unindexed loss. If there is an unindexed loss on a disposal then the indexation allowance is nil.

EXAMPLE 3

A company acquired a chargeable asset for £5,000 in February 2002 (RPI 173.8). The asset was sold in January 2010 (RPI 216.0). Compute the chargeable gain or allowable loss if the sale proceeds were:

(a) £9,000   (b) £5,500   (c) £4,800

Solution

	(a) £	(b) £	(c) £
Sale proceeds	9,000	5,500	4,800
Less: Acquisition cost	5,000	5,000	5,000
Unindexed gain or loss	4,000	500	(200)
Less: Indexation allowance			
$\dfrac{216.0-173.8}{173.8} = 0.243 \times £5,000 = £1,215$	1,215	500	nil
Chargeable gain or allowable loss	2,785	nil	(200)

Notes:

(i) In case (a), the indexation allowance can be given in full.

(ii) In case (b), the full indexation allowance would convert an unindexed gain of £500 into a loss of £715. Indexation allowance is restricted to £500 to prevent this.

(iii) In case (c) there is an unindexed loss, so indexation allowance is restricted to £nil.

Assets held on 31 March 1982

If an asset is disposed of which was acquired before 31 March 1982, only the part of the gain accruing since 31 March 1982 is charged to tax (see Chapter 17). The taxable gain is usually calculated by means of the "rebasing" technique, whereby the market value of the asset at 31 March 1982 is substituted for its acquisition cost.

However, although rebasing now always applies for individuals, this is not the case for companies. Under corporation tax rules, rebasing does *not* apply if the rebasing calculation results in a greater gain than the calculation based on original cost.

EXAMPLE 4

A company acquired a chargeable asset for £2,000 in April 1980 and sold the asset for £12,500 in May 2009. Compute the unindexed gain arising on this disposal if the market value of the asset at 31 March 1982 was:

(a)   £4,200   (b)   £500

Solution

(a)   The unindexed gain over the entire period of ownership, based on the original cost of the asset, is £10,500 (£12,500 – £2,000). But the rebasing calculation gives a gain of only £8,300 (£12,500 – £4,200). This is less than the gain based on original cost so rebasing applies and the unindexed gain is £8,300.

(b)   The rebasing calculation gives an unindexed gain of £12,000 (£12,500 – £500). This is more than the gain based on original cost so rebasing does not apply and the unindexed gain is £10,500.

Indexation allowance for pre-31 March 1982 assets

The rules for calculating the indexation allowance available to a company on the disposal of an asset held on 31 March 1982 are as follows:

(a)   Indexation allowance is based on the change in RPI between March 1982 and the month of disposal. No further indexation allowance is available to compensate for the effects of pre-March 1982 inflation (which is why the table of RPIs at the end of this chapter begins with the RPI for March 1982).

(b)   In *both* the rebasing calculation and the calculation based on original cost, indexation allowance is calculated with reference to the *greater* of original cost and market value at 31 March 1982 i.e. the same indexation allowance is given in both calculations.

EXAMPLE 5

Calculate the chargeable gain arising on the disposal described in the above example. RPIs are 79.44 for March 1982 and 212.8 for May 2009.

Solution

(a)

	Original cost £	Rebasing £
Sale proceeds	12,500	12,500
Less: Original cost	2,000	
Market value 31/3/82		4,200
Unindexed gain	10,500	8,300
Less: Indexation allowance		
$\dfrac{212.8 - 79.44}{79.44} = 1.679 \times £4,200$	7,052	7,052
Chargeable gain	3,448	1,248

The rebasing calculation gives the lower gain, so rebasing applies and the chargeable gain is £1,248.

(b)

	Original cost £	Rebasing £
Sale proceeds	12,500	12,500
Less: Original cost	2,000	
Market value 31/3/82		500
Unindexed gain	10,500	12,000
Less: Indexation allowance		
$\dfrac{212.8 - 79.44}{79.44} = 1.679 \times £2,000$	3,358	3,358
Chargeable gain	7,142	8,642

The rebasing calculation gives the higher gain, so rebasing does not apply and the chargeable gain is £7,142.

Losses on disposal of pre-31 March 1982 assets

As shown above, if the rebasing calculation gives a gain and the original cost calculation also gives a gain, the chargeable gain is the *smaller* of these two gains. Similarly, if the rebasing calculation gives a loss and the original cost calculation also gives a loss, the allowable loss is the *smaller* of these two losses. Finally, if the rebasing calculation gives a loss and the original cost calculation gives a gain (or vice versa), or if either of the calculations gives a nil result, the situation is "no gain, no loss". In these circumstances there is no chargeable gain and no allowable loss.

EXAMPLE 6

A company acquired a chargeable asset in 1979. The asset was sold in December 2009 (RPI 215.6) for £2,800. Compute the chargeable gain or allowable loss if the original cost of the asset and its market value on 31 March 1982 (RPI 79.44) were respectively:

(a)   £3,500 and £4,000   (b)   £750 and £850   (c)   £10 and £1,050.

Solution

(a)

	Original cost £	Rebasing £
Sale proceeds	2,800	2,800
Less: Original cost	3,500	
Market value 31/3/82		4,000
Allowable loss	(700)	(1,200)

The rebasing calculation gives the higher loss, so rebasing does not apply and the allowable loss is £700. Indexation allowance was £nil in both calculations, since indexation allowance cannot be used to increase an unindexed loss.

(b)

	Original cost £	Rebasing £
Sale proceeds	2,800	2,800
Less: Original cost	750	
Market value 31/3/82		850
Unindexed gain	2,050	1,950
Less: Indexation allowance		
$\dfrac{215.6-79.44}{79.44}$ = 1.714 x £850	1,457	1,457
Chargeable gain	593	493

The rebasing calculation gives the lower gain. Therefore rebasing applies and the chargeable gain is £493.

(c)

	Original cost £	Rebasing £
Sale proceeds	2,800	2,800
Less: Original cost	10	
Market value 31/3/82		1,050
Unindexed gain	2,790	1,750
Less: Indexation allowance		
$\dfrac{215.6-79.44}{79.44}$ = 1.714 x £1,050 = £1,800	1,800	1,750
Chargeable gain	990	nil

The rebasing calculation gives a nil result, whilst the calculation based on original cost gives a gain. Therefore the situation is "no gain, no loss". Indexation allowance was restricted to £1,750 in the rebasing calculation so as to avoid converting a gain into a loss.

The rebasing election

A company may make an *irrevocable* election to the effect that gains and losses arising on all future disposals of assets held on 31 March 1982 should be calculated by the rebasing method, with no reference whatsoever to the costs incurred before 31 March 1982.

If this election is made, costs incurred before 31 March 1982 are completely ignored for all purposes, including calculation of the indexation allowance. Therefore indexation allowance will always be based upon market value at 31 March 1982, even if this is lower than the costs incurred before 31 March 1982.

Assets acquired before 6 April 1965

When the tax on chargeable gains was introduced, special rules applied to the disposal of an asset acquired before 6 April 1965. These rules no longer apply to individuals and are now rarely used for companies, as it becomes increasingly uncommon for a disposal to involve an asset acquired before 6 April 1965. Also, from the perspective of disposals made in the 21st century, the disposal of an asset acquired before 6 April 1965 must also be the disposal of an asset held on 31 March 1982. Therefore rebasing is available in relation to such disposals and rebasing will generally give a lower gain than the gain calculated according to the special rules mentioned above. However, these rules are still used for companies if they give the lower gain.

A summary of the treatment of assets acquired before 6 April 1965, together with a number of worked examples, can be found on the website which accompanies this book. The website address is *www.pearsoned.co.uk/melville*.

Disposals of shares or securities

The share matching rules which apply on a disposal of shares or securities by an individual were explained in Chapter 19 of this book. The main principle is that shares of the same class in the same company are pooled into the "Section 104 holding" and that disposals are generally matched against shares taken from this holding. Special rules apply if shares are bought and sold on the same day or if shares are sold and re-acquired within 30 days.

However, the share matching rules which are used when a *company* makes a disposal of shares or securities are not the same as the rules for individuals. A disposal of shares or securities by a company is matched against acquisitions in the following order:

(a) first, against acquisitions made on the same day

(b) next, against acquisitions made in the previous nine days (on a FIFO basis)

(c) next, against shares taken from the Section 104 holding, which (for companies) is the pool of shares acquired on or after 1 April 1982

(d) next, against the "1982 holding", which is a pool of shares acquired between 6 April 1965 and 31 March 1982 inclusive

(e) finally, against shares acquired before 6 April 1965 (on a LIFO basis).

These rules have to be more complex than their CGT equivalents because companies are entitled to indexation allowance and because rebasing does not always apply when a company disposes of a pre-31 March 1982 asset.

The Section 104 holding

A company's s104 holding of shares of a certain class in a certain company consists of the pool of shares which were acquired on or after 1 April 1982. Share acquisitions which are matched against disposals made on the same day or during the following nine days do not join the s104 holding.

The distinguishing characteristic of shares acquired on or after 1 April 1982 is that the indexation factor used on their disposal will differ according to the date of acquisition. If it were not for Section 104, it would be necessary to keep detailed records of the date and cost of each share acquisition made on or after 1 April 1982, so that indexation allowance could be calculated correctly on a disposal. However, the pooling system provided by Section 104 eliminates the need to keep these records. All that is required is a record of:

(a) the total number of shares in the pool

(b) their total cost

(c) their total *indexed cost*, which consists of total cost plus all indexation allowance due up to the date of the most recent "operative event". An operative event occurs whenever shares enter or leave the pool.

The indexed cost of the s104 holding is calculated as follows:

(a) The number of shares in the pool at 1 April 1985 (if any) is totalled and the cost of these shares is also totalled. The indexed cost of the pool at 1 April 1985 is calculated as total cost, plus an indexation allowance for each acquisition forming part of the pool, based on the change in RPI between the date of the acquisition and April 1985.

(b) On the occurrence of a subsequent operative event, the indexed cost of the pool is increased by reference to the change in RPI since the previous operative event (if any) or since April 1985 (if the previous event was before April 1985). TCGA 1992 does not require the indexation factor used in this calculation to be rounded to 3 decimal places. The pool is then adjusted as follows:

    (i) If the event is an acquisition, the number of shares acquired is added to the number of shares in the pool and their cost is added to the cost and to the indexed cost of the pool.

    (ii) If the event is a disposal, the number of shares disposed of is subtracted from the number of shares in the pool. It is then necessary to deduct a proportion of the cost and indexed cost of the pool. Strictly speaking, this proportion should be calculated using the part disposal fraction (see Chapter 17) which takes into account the value of the shares disposed of and the value of the shares remaining. In most cases, however, the value per share of the shares disposed of will be the same as the value per share of the shares remaining, so that the proportion to be deducted from the cost and indexed cost of the pool can be based upon the *number* of shares disposed of.

The unindexed gain (or loss) arising on a disposal from the pool is calculated as the difference between the disposal proceeds and the amount which has been subtracted from the cost of the pool as a consequence of the disposal. The indexation allowance due on the disposal is the difference between the amount subtracted from the cost of the pool and the amount subtracted from the indexed cost of the pool. As usual, indexation allowance cannot be used to create a loss or to increase a loss.

EXAMPLE 7

A company makes the following acquisitions of ordinary shares in JK plc:

Date	No of shares	Cost £	RPI
1 July 1983	5,000	6,300	85.30
2 August 1984	2,000	2,500	89.94
3 February 1997	1,200	2,300	155.0
4 June 2003	1,800	3,400	181.3

The company sells 500 shares on 8 July 2009 (RPI 213.6).

(a) Calculate the cost and indexed cost of the s104 holding on 8 July 2009, just prior to and just after the above disposal (RPI for April 1985 is 94.78).

(b) Compute the chargeable gain or allowable loss on the disposal if sale proceeds are:

  (i)   £1,800   (ii)   £1,000   (iii)   £700

Solution

(a) The cost and indexed cost of the s104 holding on 8 July 2009 are calculated as follows:

	No of shares	Cost £	Indexed cost £
Bought 1 July 1983	5,000	6,300	6,300
Bought 2 August 1984	2,000	2,500	2,500
Add: Indexation to April 1985			
(a) $\dfrac{94.78-85.30}{85.30}=0.111$			
0.111 x £6,300			699
(b) $\dfrac{94.78-89.94}{89.94}=0.054$			
0.054 x £2,500			135
s104 holding at 5 April 1985	7,000	8,800	9,634
Add: Indexation to February 1997			
$\dfrac{155.0-94.78}{94.78}$ x £9,634			6,121
			15,755
Bought 3 February 1997	1,200	2,300	2,300
s104 holding at 3 February 1997	8,200	11,100	18,055

	No of shares	Cost	Indexed cost
		£	£
s104 holding at 3 February 1997	8,200	11,100	18,055
Add: Indexation to June 2003			
$\dfrac{181.3 - 155.0}{155.0}$ x £18,055			3,064
			21,119
Bought 4 June 2003	1,800	3,400	3,400
s104 holding at 4 June 2003	10,000	14,500	24,519
Add: Indexation to July 2009			
$\dfrac{213.6 - 181.3}{181.3}$ x £24,519			4,368
			28,887
Sold 8 July 2009 (500/10,000ths)	(500)	(725)	(1,444)
s104 holding c/f at 8 July 2009	9,500	13,775	27,443

Notes:

1. The indexation allowance calculated on operative events occurring after 5 April 1985 has not been rounded off to 3 decimal places.

2. The disposal in July 2009 must have come from the s104 holding since it cannot be matched against shares acquired on the same day or in the previous nine days.

3. The disposal is 500 shares out of a holding of 10,000. Therefore 500/10,000ths or 1/20th of the pool has been sold and so 1/20th of the cost and indexed cost are subtracted from the pool.

4. The cost of the shares disposed of is £725. Since the equivalent indexed cost is £1,444, the indexation allowance due on the disposal is £719 (£1,444 - £725).

(b)

	(i)	(ii)	(iii)
	£	£	£
Sale proceeds	1,800	1,000	700
Less: Cost	725	725	725
Unindexed gain or loss	1,075	275	(25)
Less: Indexation allowance (£719)	719	275	nil
Chargeable gain/(allowable loss)	356	nil	(25)

The 1982 holding

For a company, the 1982 holding is a pool of shares acquired between 6 April 1965 and 31 March 1982 inclusive. All of the shares in this pool attract the same rate of indexation allowance, based on the change in RPI between March 1982 and the date of disposal. This means that the calculation of this pool's value is much simpler than the calculation of the value of the s104 holding. All that is needed is a record of:

(a)   the number of shares in the pool

(b)   the total cost of these shares

(c)   their market value at 31 March 1982.

When a disposal occurs, the number of shares in the pool is reduced and proportionate amounts are deducted from the pool's cost and from its market value at 31 March 1982. The gain or loss arising on the disposal is then calculated in the usual way, as for any disposal of a pre-31 March 1982 asset.

EXAMPLE 8

A company made the following acquisitions of ordinary shares in CDE plc:

Date	No of shares	Cost £
1 June 1970	1,000	3,000
30 October 1975	800	2,500
15 August 1981	900	3,100

The shares had a market value of £1.80 per share on 31 March 1982 (RPI 79.44). The company made no further acquisitions and sold 750 of the shares on 18 January 2010 (RPI 216.0) for £8,500. Compute the chargeable gain.

Solution

The sale of 750 shares on 18 January 2010 cannot be matched against any acquisitions made on the same day or during the previous nine days and there is no s104 holding. The next step is to match against the 1982 holding, as follows:

	No of shares	Cost £	MV 31/3/82 £
Acquired 1 June 1970	1,000	3,000	1,800
Acquired 30 October 1975	800	2,500	1,440
Acquired 15 August 1981	900	3,100	1,620
	2,700	8,600	4,860
Sold 18 January 2010 (750/2,700ths)	(750)	(2,389)	(1,350)
1982 holding c/f	1,950	6,211	3,510

The sold shares are deemed to have cost £2,389 and their market value at 31 March 1982 was £1,350. The calculation of the gain arising on the disposal is:

	Original cost £	Rebasing £
Sale proceeds	8,500	8,500
Less: Original cost	2,389	
Market value 31/3/82		1,350
Unindexed gain	6,111	7,150
Less: Indexation allowance		
$\dfrac{216.0 - 79.44}{79.44} = 1.719 \times £2,389$	4,107	4,107
Chargeable gain	2,004	3,043

The rebasing calculation gives the higher gain, so rebasing does not apply and the chargeable gain is £2,004.

Bonus issues and rights issues

As explained in Chapter 19, bonus issues and rights issues are regarded as reorganisations of share capital and shares acquired as a consequence of such issues are not treated as acquisitions in the normal way. Instead, the required treatment of bonus shares and rights shares is to uplift the number of shares in each of the taxpayer's existing holdings. In the case of rights issues, it is also necessary to increase the cost of those holdings, since rights shares (unlike bonus shares) are not acquired free of charge.

This treatment applies to companies as well as to individuals, but one complication that may arise in the case of a company is that rights shares acquired after 31 March 1982 might join the 1982 holding. If this occurs, the cost of the rights shares is treated as enhancement expenditure and it is necessary (for indexation purposes) to keep a separate record of the cost and acquisition date of those rights shares. The required procedure is illustrated in the following example.

EXAMPLE 9

A company made the following acquisitions of ordinary shares in RST plc:

Date	No of shares	Cost £	RPI
15 August 1980	500	1,000	
23 January 1997	600	2,500	154.4

The market value of the shares on 31 March 1982 (RPI 79.44) was £2.50 per share. In June 2004 (RPI 186.8), RST plc made a 1 for 20 rights issue at £8 per share and the company decided to buy the shares it was offered. Calculate the chargeable gain arising in November 2009 (RPI 215.2) when the company sold 840 shares for £10 each.

Solution

<u>The s104 holding:</u>

	No of shares	Cost £	Indexed cost £
Bought 23 January 1997	600	2,500	2,500
Add: Indexation to June 2004			
$\dfrac{186.8 - 154.4}{154.4}$ x £2,500			525
			3,025
Rights issue June 2004 (1 for 20)	30	240	240
	630	2,740	3,265
Add: Indexation to November 2009			
$\dfrac{215.2 - 186.8}{186.8}$ x £3,265			496
			3,761
Sold November 2009	(630)	(2,740)	(3,761)
s104 holding c/f	nil	nil	nil

The gain arising on the disposal of the s104 holding is:

	£
Sale proceeds (630 @ £10)	6,300
Less: Cost	2,740
Unindexed gain	3,560
Less: Indexation allowance	
(£3,761 - £2,740)	1,021
Chargeable gain	2,539

<u>The 1982 holding:</u>

	No of shares	Cost (original) £	Cost (rights) £	MV 31/3/82 £
Acquired 15 August 1980	500	1,000		1,250
Rights issue June 2004 (1 for 20)	25		200	
	525	1,000	200	1,250
Sold November 2009 (210/525ths)	(210)	(400)	(80)	(500)
1982 holding c/f	315	600	120	750

The gain arising on the disposal from the 1982 holding is calculated on the basis that the company has sold an asset with a cost of £400 and a market value at 31 March 1982 of £500. The calculation also takes into account enhancement expenditure of £80 incurred in June 2004. The calculation of the gain is as follows:

	Original cost £	Rebasing £
Sale proceeds (210 @ £10)	2,100	2,100
Less: Cost up to 31 March 1982	(400)	
Market value 31/3/82		(500)
Cost June 2004	(80)	(80)
Unindexed gain	1,620	1,520
Less: Indexation allowance		
$\dfrac{215.2 - 79.44}{79.44} = 1.709 \times £500$	(855)	(855)
$\dfrac{215.2 - 186.8}{186.8} = 0.152 \times £80$	(12)	(12)
Chargeable gain	753	653

The rebasing calculation gives the lower gain, so rebasing applies and the gain is £653. The total gain on the entire disposal of 840 shares is therefore £3,192 (£2,539 + £653).

Shares acquired before 6 April 1965

Special rules apply if a company disposes of shares which were originally acquired before 6 April 1965. However, these rules are now falling into disuse as it becomes increasingly uncommon for a disposal to involve shares acquired before that date.

A summary of the treatment of shares acquired before 6 April 1965, together with a number of worked examples, can be found on the website which accompanies this book. The website address is *www.pearsoned.co.uk/melville*.

Disposal of a substantial shareholding

A gain arising on the disposal of all or part of a "substantial shareholding" by a trading company or a member of a trading group is exempt from corporation tax so long as certain conditions are satisfied. Similarly, any loss arising on such a disposal is not an allowable loss. The main conditions which must be satisfied are:

(a) The company making the disposal must have held a substantial shareholding in the investee company throughout a 12-month period beginning not more than two years before the disposal takes place.

(b) The investee company must be a trading company or the holding company of a trading group.

For this purpose, a company holds a substantial shareholding in another company if it holds at least 10% of that company's ordinary share capital and is entitled to at least 10% of that company's profits and assets.

Summary

▸ A company's chargeable assets usually consist of non-current assets such as land and buildings, plant and investments. Non-chargeable assets include motor cars, chattels worth up to £6,000, wasting chattels, gilts and qualifying corporate bonds.

▸ A chargeable disposal occurs when the whole or part of a chargeable asset is sold or given away (unless given to a charity).

▸ If allowable losses for an accounting period exceed chargeable gains, the net losses are carried forward and relieved against chargeable gains in subsequent periods.

▸ Companies may claim indexation allowance but indexation allowance cannot be used to create or increase an allowable loss.

▸ Rebasing does not always apply when a company disposes of an asset acquired before 31 March 1982. It is necessary to perform a calculation based on original cost as well as the rebasing calculation. The chargeable gain (allowable loss) is the lower of the two gains (losses) given by these calculations.

▸ When a company makes a disposal of shares or securities, the disposal is matched first against shares acquired on the same day, then against shares acquired in the previous nine days, then against the s104 holding and then against the 1982 holding.

▸ The s104 holding consists of a pool of shares acquired on or after 1 April 1982. It is necessary to keep a record of the number of shares in this pool, their total cost and their total indexed cost.

▸ The 1982 holding is a pool of shares acquired between 6 April 1965 and 31 March 1982 inclusive. It is necessary to keep a record of the number of shares in this pool, their total cost and their market value at 31 March 1982.

▸ A gain arising on the disposal of a substantial shareholding by a trading company is exempt from corporation tax, subject to certain conditions.

Retail Prices Index (RPI)

(*Source*: Office for National Statistics)

	Jan	Feb	Mar	Apr	May	Jun	Jul	Aug	Sep	Oct	Nov	Dec
1982			79.44	81.04	81.62	81.85	81.88	81.90	81.85	82.26	82.66	82.51
1983	82.61	82.97	83.12	84.28	84.64	84.84	85.30	85.68	86.06	86.36	86.67	86.89
1984	86.84	87.20	87.48	88.64	88.97	89.20	89.10	89.94	90.11	90.67	90.95	90.87
1985	91.20	91.94	92.80	94.78	95.21	95.41	95.23	95.49	95.44	95.59	95.92	96.05
1986	96.25	96.60	96.73	97.67	97.85	97.79	97.52	97.82	98.30	98.45	99.29	99.62
1987	100.0	100.4	100.6	101.8	101.9	101.9	101.8	102.1	102.4	102.9	103.4	103.3
1988	103.3	103.7	104.1	105.8	106.2	106.6	106.7	107.9	108.4	109.5	110.0	110.3
1989	111.0	111.8	112.3	114.3	115.0	115.4	115.5	115.8	116.6	117.5	118.5	118.8
1990	119.5	120.2	121.4	125.1	126.2	126.7	126.8	128.1	129.3	130.3	130.0	129.9
1991	130.2	130.9	131.4	133.1	133.5	134.1	133.8	134.1	134.6	135.1	135.6	135.7
1992	135.6	136.3	136.7	138.8	139.3	139.3	138.8	138.9	139.4	139.9	139.7	139.2
1993	137.9	138.8	139.3	140.6	141.1	141.0	140.7	141.3	141.9	141.8	141.6	141.9
1994	141.3	142.1	142.5	144.2	144.7	144.7	144.0	144.7	145.0	145.2	145.3	146.0
1995	146.0	146.9	147.5	149.0	149.6	149.8	149.1	149.9	150.6	149.8	149.8	150.7
1996	150.2	150.9	151.5	152.6	152.9	153.0	152.4	153.1	153.8	153.8	153.9	154.4
1997	154.4	155.0	155.4	156.3	156.9	157.5	157.5	158.5	159.3	159.5	159.6	160.0
1998	159.5	160.3	160.8	162.6	163.5	163.4	163.0	163.7	164.4	164.5	164.4	164.4
1999	163.4	163.7	164.1	165.2	165.6	165.6	165.1	165.5	166.2	166.5	166.7	167.3
2000	166.6	167.5	168.4	170.1	170.7	171.1	170.5	170.5	171.7	171.6	172.1	172.2
2001	171.1	172.0	172.2	173.1	174.2	174.4	173.3	174.0	174.6	174.3	173.6	173.4
2002	173.3	173.8	174.5	175.7	176.2	176.2	175.9	176.4	177.6	177.9	178.2	178.5
2003	178.4	179.3	179.9	181.2	181.5	181.3	181.3	181.6	182.5	182.6	182.7	183.5
2004	183.1	183.8	184.6	185.7	186.5	186.8	186.8	187.4	188.1	188.6	189.0	189.9
2005	188.9	189.6	190.5	191.6	192.0	192.2	192.2	192.6	193.1	193.3	193.6	194.1
2006	193.4	194.2	195.0	196.5	197.7	198.5	198.5	199.2	200.1	200.4	201.1	202.7
2007	201.6	203.1	204.4	205.4	206.2	207.3	206.1	207.3	208.0	208.9	209.7	210.9
2008	209.8	211.4	212.1	214.0	215.1	216.8	216.5	217.2	218.4	217.7	216.0	212.9
2009	210.1	211.4	211.3	211.5	212.8	*213.2*	*213.6*	*214.0*	*214.4*	*214.8*	*215.2*	*215.6*
2010	*216.0*	*216.4*	*216.8*									

Note:

RPIs for June 2009 and later months have been estimated by the author.

Exercises

23.1   A company made the following disposals during the year to 31 March 2010:

(a)   A factory building was sold for £500,000 on 13 June 2009 (RPI 213.2). This building had cost £300,000 in August 2000 (RPI 170.5) and was extended in July 2002 (RPI 175.9) at a cost of £50,000.

(b)   An office building was sold for £1,000,000 on 15 August 2009 (RPI 214.0) and was immediately replaced by another office building costing £925,000. The building sold in August 2009 had cost £650,000 in February 2002 (RPI 173.8). Rollover relief was claimed on the disposal of this building.

(c)   A computer system was given to a charity on 14 July 2009 (RPI 213.6). This computer system had cost £5,000 in September 2005 (RPI 193.1) and had a market value of £500 in July 2009. Capital allowances had been claimed in relation to the computer system.

(d)   A motor car was sold for £80,000 on 12 May 2009 (RPI 212.8). The car had cost £100,000 in June 2007 (RPI 207.3). Capital allowances had been claimed.

(e)   An item of movable plant and machinery was sold for £30,000 on 16 September 2009 (RPI 214.4). This item had cost £70,000 in January 2004 (RPI 183.1) and capital allowances had been claimed in relation to the item.

(f)   8,000 ordinary shares in XYZ plc were sold for £80,000 on 18 November 2009 (RPI 215.2). Shares in XYZ plc had been bought as follows:

Date	No. of shares	Cost £	RPI
22 November 2002	4,000	16,000	178.2
14 December 2006	6,000	30,000	202.7
12 November 2009	3,000	36,000	215.2

(g)   Government securities were sold for £40,000 on 17 October 2009 (RPI 214.8). These securities had cost £45,000 in October 2008 (RPI 217.7).

Compute the chargeable gain or allowable loss arising on each of the above disposals and outline any other corporation tax consequences of each disposal. Also compute the net chargeable gains figure which should be included in the company's chargeable profits for the year to 31 March 2010.

Chapter 25

Income tax and advance corporation tax

Introduction

Companies are liable to corporation tax, not income tax. Therefore, companies which suffer income tax by deduction at source from any of their income are entitled to a repayment of the income tax suffered. Similarly, companies which deduct income tax at source from any of their payments must account for this income tax to HMRC. The first purpose of this chapter is to explain how the necessary repayments and payments of income tax are made.

Until 6 April 1999, companies were obliged to pay Advance Corporation Tax (ACT) when paying dividends. Subject to certain conditions, the ACT paid for an accounting period was then treated as an advance payment of the corporation tax liability for that period, so reducing the amount of tax payable on the normal due date. ACT was abolished with effect from 6 April 1999 but some aspects of the ACT system will linger on for years to come. The second purpose of this chapter is to provide a brief description of the way in which the ACT system operated before abolition and then to explain the present situation with regard to ACT.

Income received net of income tax

A company which receives any of its income net of income tax is able to reclaim the income tax deducted at source but must then pay corporation tax on the grossed-up amount of the income. Such "taxed income" was fairly common at one time, but companies now receive very little income with tax deducted in this way. The main sources of taxed income are as follows:

Type of income	Rate of income tax deducted at source
Patent royalties (*if received from an individual*)	basic rate (20%)
Interest on Government securities (*if net interest opted for*)	basic rate (20%)

Patent royalties and interest on Government securities (or "gilts") are generally assessed to corporation tax on the accruals basis (see Chapter 22). But the income tax which may be reclaimed for an accounting period is the amount of income tax suffered on the income actually *received* in that period. Note that:

(a) Patent royalties received from another UK company are received gross. Patent royalties received from an individual are subject to deduction of tax at source.

(b) As stated in Chapter 22, companies (unlike individuals) receive their bank deposit interest and building society interest gross.

(c) The holders of gilt-edged securities may usually choose whether to receive their interest gross or net. Most companies would opt to receive such interest gross.

Payments made net of income tax

Certain types of payment made by companies are made net of income tax. A company which makes such a payment must account to HMRC for the income tax deducted at source but the gross amount of the payment then attracts tax relief in the company's corporation tax computation. The main types of payment which companies make net of income tax are as follows:

Type of income		Rate of income tax deducted at source
Patent royalties }	*unless paid to other*	basic rate (20%)
Loan interest }	*UK companies*	basic rate (20%)

Patent royalties and loan interest are generally relieved on the accruals basis in the paying company's corporation tax computation (see Chapter 22). But the income tax which must be accounted for to HMRC in an accounting period is the income tax which was deducted from amounts actually *paid* in that period. Note that:

(a) Patent royalties and loan interest are paid gross if paid by one UK company to another. Patent royalties and loan interest paid to an individual are subject to deduction of income tax at source.

(b) Royalties and interest paid by a UK company to an EU company are paid gross if the two companies are "associated". For this purpose, two companies are associated if one holds at least 25% of the other's share capital or if a third company holds at least 25% of the share capital of each of them.

(c) A company which has become a UK-REIT must deduct basic rate income tax when paying certain dividends (see Chapter 22). The tax deducted from such dividends is then accounted for to HMRC on form CT61(Z). The same form is also used to make returns of income tax deducted from patent royalties and loan interest (see below).

The quarterly accounting system

Companies are required to make periodic (usually quarterly) returns to HM Revenue and Customs of the income tax deducted from payments and the income tax suffered on taxed income. A return, on form CT61(Z), is required for:

(a) each of the four quarters ending on 31 March, 30 June, 30 September and 31 December which fall completely into an accounting period, and

(b) each part of an accounting period which does not comprise a complete quarter.

A company with an annual accounting date which coincides with one of the above four dates will make four returns each year but companies with any other accounting date will need to submit a fifth return each year. Each return must be submitted (and any tax due must be paid) within 14 days of the end of the period to which the return relates. Nil returns are not required.

EXAMPLE 1

(a) A company prepares accounts to 30 June each year. Identify the income tax return periods for the year to 30 June 2009.

(b) A company prepares accounts to 31 January each year. Identify the income tax return periods for the year to 31 January 2010.

Solution

(a) The company's accounting date coincides with one of the four standard dates, so there will be four return periods each year. The return periods for the year to 30 June 2009 are 1 July 2008 to 30 September 2008, 1 October 2008 to 31 December 2008, 1 January 2009 to 31 March 2009 and 1 April 2009 to 30 June 2009.

(b) The company's accounting date does not coincide with one of the four standard dates, so there will be five return periods each year. The return periods for the year to 31 January 2010 are 1 February 2009 to 31 March 2009, 1 April 2009 to 30 June 2009, 1 July 2009 to 30 September 2009, 1 October 2009 to 31 December 2009 and 1 January 2010 to 31 January 2010.

The quarterly procedure

The procedure adopted for each return period is as follows:

(a) The income tax suffered on taxed income received during the return period is subtracted from the income tax deducted from payments made during the return period. The result of this calculation is the excess of income tax deducted over income tax suffered (or vice versa).

(b) The cumulative excess of income tax deducted over income tax suffered (or vice versa) for the accounting period to date is then calculated.

(c) If there is a cumulative excess of income tax deducted over income tax suffered, this excess is compared with the total of the income tax payments made to HMRC in previous return periods during the same accounting period (if any) and the difference is payable by the company or repayable to the company.

(d) If there is a cumulative excess of income tax suffered over income tax deducted, then no income tax payment is required for the current return period and any payments made to HMRC in previous return periods during the same accounting period may be reclaimed. However, the excess itself is *not* repayable to the company but is carried forward to the next return period.

EXAMPLE 2

A company has the following payments made net of income tax and income received net of income tax for the year to 31 March 2010 (amounts are stated net):

		Payments £	Income £
1 May 2009	Debenture interest paid	4,000	
5 July 2009	Patent royalties paid	800	
1 September 2009	Patent royalties received		5,600
1 November 2009	Debenture interest paid	4,000	
12 January 2010	Patent royalties paid	9,600	
31 March 2010	Patent royalties received		1,600

Compute the amounts of income tax payable or repayable in each return period.

Solution

Return period	Tax deducted £	Tax suffered £	Tax deducted less tax suffered £	Cumulative £	Income tax payable (repayable) £
1/4/09 - 30/6/09	1,000		1,000	1,000	1,000
1/7/09 - 30/9/09	200	1,400	(1,200)	(200)	(1,000)
1/10/09 - 31/12/09	1,000		1,000	800	800
1/1/10 - 31/3/10	2,400	400	2,000	2,800	2,000
	4,600	1,800	2,800		2,800

Notes:

(i) The net payments and the net income in each return period are grossed up at the appropriate rate to give the amounts of income tax deducted and suffered, as shown in the first two columns of the table. For each return period, the excess of tax deducted over tax suffered is shown in the third column. If tax suffered exceeds tax deducted, the figure is shown in parentheses. The cumulative total of tax deducted less tax suffered is shown in the fourth column.

(ii) At the end of the first return period, tax deducted exceeds tax suffered by £1,000, so £1,000 is due for payment on 14 July 2009.

(iii) At the end of the second return period, there is a cumulative excess of tax suffered over tax deducted of £200. The company now has no income tax liability for the accounting period to date and may reclaim the £1,000 paid in the previous return period. The excess tax suffered of £200 is *not* repayable to the company but the cumulative nature of the system ensures that this excess will automatically be taken into account in future return periods.

(iv) At the end of the third return period, there is a cumulative excess of tax deducted over tax suffered of £800. Since the tax paid in previous return periods is £nil (£1,000 paid less £1,000 reclaimed), income tax of £800 is due for payment on 14 January 2010.

(v) At the end of the fourth return period, there is a cumulative excess of tax deducted over tax suffered of £2,800. Since the tax paid in previous return periods is £800, income tax of £2,000 is due for payment on 14 April 2010.

Tax suffered in excess of tax deducted

At the end of an accounting period, one of two possible situations will apply:

(a) The income tax deducted from payments made in the accounting period exceeds the income tax suffered on income received during that period. In this case, the excess will have been paid over to HMRC by virtue of the system described above and no further action is required.

(b) The income tax suffered on income received during the accounting period exceeds the income tax deducted from payments made in that period. In this case the quarterly system will not have provided the necessary income tax repayment.

EXAMPLE 3

A company has the following payments made net of income tax and income received net of income tax for the year to 31 March 2010 (amounts are stated net):

		Payments £	Income £
1 May 2009	Debenture interest paid	8,000	
1 August 2009	Patent royalties received		11,200
1 November 2009	Debenture interest paid	8,000	
1 February 2010	Patent royalties received		11,200

Compute the amounts of income tax payable or repayable in each return period.

Solution

Return period	Tax deducted	Tax suffered	Tax deducted less tax suffered	Cumulative	Income tax payable (repayable)
	£	£	£	£	£
1/4/09 - 30/6/09	2,000		2,000	2,000	2,000
1/7/09 - 30/9/09		2,800	(2,800)	(800)	(2,000)
1/10/09 - 31/12/09	2,000		2,000	1,200	1,200
1/1/10 - 31/3/10		2,800	(2,800)	(1,600)	(1,200)
	4,000	5,600	(1,600)		0

Note:

The income tax suffered exceeds the income tax deducted by £1,600 but the operation of the quarterly accounting system has not resulted in repayment of this income tax.

Set-off against corporation tax liability

If the amount of income tax suffered during an accounting period exceeds the amount of income tax deducted from payments, the required repayment of income tax is made by means of a reduction in the company's corporation tax liability for the accounting period in which the surplus arises. If this liability is less than the required repayment, the balance is repaid in cash.

EXAMPLE 4

In the year to 30 June 2010, a company receives net patent royalties of £40,000 and makes no payments net of tax. Calculate the required income tax repayment and show how this repayment will be made if the company's corporation tax liability for the year is:

(a)   £100,000

(b)   £7,000.

The company is not a large company for the purposes of payment by instalments.

Solution

(a)   The required repayment is £40,000 x 20/80 = £10,000. This will be offset against the company's corporation tax liability payable on 1 April 2011, reducing this liability from £100,000 to £90,000.

(b)   If the company's corporation tax liability for the year is only £7,000, this liability will be reduced to £nil and the remaining £3,000 will be repaid to the company in cash.

ACT before 6 April 1999

A company which made a "qualifying distribution" before 6 April 1999 was required to make a payment of Advance Corporation Tax (ACT). By far the most common example of a qualifying distribution was the payment of a dividend.

The ACT payable in relation to a dividend was calculated as a specified fraction of the amount of that dividend. The *ACT fraction* was most recently set at 20/80, so that the ACT payable in relation to a dividend was equal to one-quarter of the dividend payment. Note the following points:

(a) The sum of a dividend and its related ACT was known as a "franked payment". The franked payment was equal to the dividend paid multiplied by 100/80.

(b) The ACT attributable to a dividend could be expressed as 20% of the franked payment. Thus the *rate of ACT* was 20%.

EXAMPLE 5

On 3 April 1999, a company with an issued share capital of ten million £1 ordinary shares paid a dividend of 40p per share.

(a) Compute the amount of ACT payable in relation to this dividend.

(b) Compute the amount of the franked payment.

Solution

(a) The amount of the dividend was £4,000,000. The ACT fraction was 20/80. Therefore the ACT payable in relation to the dividend was £4,000,000 x 20/80 = £1,000,000.

(b) The franked payment was £5,000,000 (i.e. the dividend plus the attributable ACT). The ACT payable could be expressed as 20% of £5,000,000 = £1,000,000.

Franked investment income

As explained in Chapter 22, the term "franked investment income" (FII) refers to the UK dividends (and exempt foreign dividends) received by a company, plus the attached tax credits. These tax credits cannot be paid to the company but, before 6 April 1999, they *could* be used to reduce the amount of ACT payable by the company. In essence, the FII for an accounting period was set against the franked payments made in that period and ACT was then payable only on the excess. Note the following points:

(a) The tax credit attached to a dividend received before 6 April 1999 was *not* equal to one-ninth of the amount of the dividend (as is now the case) but was instead equal to *one-quarter* of the amount of the dividend.

(b) If there was an excess of FII over franked payments for an accounting period then the company had "surplus FII". There was no ACT liability in such an accounting period. Surplus FII was carried forward to the next accounting period and treated as if it were FII received on the first day of that period.

EXAMPLE 6

In the year to 31 March 1999, a company paid dividends totalling £6,000 and received UK dividends totalling £5,300. Compute the amount of ACT payable for the year.

Solution

(i)   Dividends paid were £6,000, so franked payments were £7,500 (£6,000 x 100/80).

(ii)   Dividends received were £5,300, so FII was £6,625 (£5,300 + £1,325).

(iii) The excess of franked payments over FII was £875. Therefore the amount of ACT payable for the year was £175 (20% x £875).

EXAMPLE 7

In the year to 31 March 1998, a company paid dividends of £5,000 and received UK dividends of £9,000. In the year to 31 March 1999, the company paid dividends of £4,800 and received none. Compute the amounts of ACT payable for each year.

Solution

In the year to 31 March 1998, franked payments were £6,250 (£5,000 x 100/80) and FII was £11,250 (£9,000 + £2,250). Therefore there was surplus FII of £5,000. There was no ACT liability for the year and surplus FII of £5,000 was carried forward to the following year.

In the year to 31 March 1999, the surplus FII brought forward was treated as if received on the first day of the year. Therefore FII for the year was £5,000. Franked payments were £6,000 (£4,800 x 100/80). The excess of franked payments over FII was £1,000, so ACT of £200 (20% x £1,000) was payable for the year.

Set-off of ACT

In general, the ACT paid for an accounting period ending before 6 April 1999 was treated as a payment on account of the company's tax liability for the period. However, there was an upper limit on the amount of ACT which could be set against the company's corporation tax liability. The *maximum ACT set-off* was equal to the amount of ACT which would be attributable to a franked payment equal in size to the company's entire chargeable profits. If the amount of ACT paid by a company in relation to an accounting period exceeded the maximum set-off allowed, the company had "surplus ACT" equal to the excess.

EXAMPLE 8

A company had chargeable profits of £100,000 for the year to 31 March 1999 and paid a dividend of £28,000 on 1 January 1999. No other dividends were paid or received during the year.

(a) Calculate the ACT payable for the year and the amount of any surplus ACT.

(b) Repeat the calculation, now assuming that the amount of the dividend was £88,000 rather than £28,000.

Solution

(a) ACT payable for the year was £7,000 (£28,000 x 20/80). This is within the maximum ACT set-off of £20,000 (20% of £100,000) so there was no surplus ACT. The whole of the £7,000 could be set against the corporation tax liability for the year.

(b) ACT payable for the year was £22,000 (£88,000 x 20/80), exceeding the maximum ACT set-off. Only £20,000 of the £22,000 could be set against the corporation tax liability for the year and there was surplus ACT of £2,000.

Relief of surplus ACT

Prior to 6 April 1999, surplus ACT could be carried forward and relieved against the company's corporation tax liability for the next accounting period. To the extent that it could not be relieved in that accounting period it could be carried forward again, without time limit, until it could eventually be relieved.

It is important to note that the total amount of ACT relieved in any accounting period (including surplus ACT brought forward) could not exceed the maximum ACT set-off for that accounting period, calculated as described above.

Surplus ACT on a change of ownership

A company which incurred losses (or made fairly low profits) over a number of years prior to 6 April 1999 and yet managed to maintain dividend payments during those years may have accumulated a substantial amount of surplus ACT. Such a company could be a desirable acquisition, since a new owner could use the company to operate a profitable business and then set the pre-acquisition surplus ACT against the tax payable on the post-acquisition profits, so avoiding liability to corporation tax.

Before 6 April 1999, this manoeuvre was prevented from succeeding by anti-avoidance legislation. If there was a change in the ownership of a company and certain conditions were satisfied, surplus ACT arising before the change in ownership could not be set against a corporation tax liability arising after the change.

Abolition of ACT

As stated at the beginning of this chapter, ACT was abolished with effect from 6 April 1999. The main consequences of this abolition are as follows:

(a) No ACT is payable on a dividend (or other qualifying distribution) which is paid after 5 April 1999 and therefore no ACT liability can arise in connection with accounting periods which begin after that date.

(b) If a company has unrelieved surplus ACT at 6 April 1999, the extent to which the surplus may be relieved against future corporation tax liabilities is determined by the "shadow ACT" regulations (see below).

Shadow ACT

The legislation which allowed surplus ACT to be carried forward was repealed with effect from 6 April 1999. However, unrelieved surplus ACT existing on that date is dealt with by the "shadow ACT" system, which substantially preserves previous rights with regard to the carry-forward of surplus ACT. The main features of this system are as follows:

(a) The previous limit on the set-off of ACT is retained, so that a company may use ACT of up to 20% of chargeable profits to satisfy its corporation tax liability for an accounting period.

(b) The capacity for relieving ACT in an accounting period must first be filled by "shadow ACT", which is calculated in the way that real ACT would have been calculated on the dividends paid in the period if ACT had not been abolished but had continued at the rate of 20%. However, *shadow ACT does not result in any reduction in the corporation tax liability* for the period. All that it does is to reduce the scope for set-off of surplus ACT brought forward.

(c) When calculating the shadow ACT arising in an accounting period, the FII for that period must be multiplied by nine-eighths before being used in the computation. This is because the rate of tax credits on dividends was reduced from one-quarter to one-ninth as from 6 April 1999. For example, a UK dividend of £720 received before 6 April 1999 was equivalent to FII of £900. The same dividend received on or after that date is equivalent to FII of only £800. Therefore it is necessary to multiply the post-6 April 1999 FII by nine-eighths to convert the FII figure to a pre-6 April 1999 equivalent ($£800 \times 9/8 = £900$).

(d) If there is still capacity for relieving ACT in an accounting period after shadow ACT has been deducted, this capacity may be used to relieve surplus ACT brought forward from before 6 April 1999. Subtracting surplus ACT results in an actual reduction in the corporation tax liability for the period.

(e) If the amount of shadow ACT for an accounting period exceeds the maximum ACT set-off for that period, then the company has "surplus shadow ACT". The consequences of this are as follows:

(i)   There is no scope for relieving real surplus ACT in such a period.

(ii) The surplus shadow ACT is first carried back to any accounting periods beginning in the previous six years (but not before 6 April 1999) in which shadow ACT has not filled the capacity available for relieving it. The carry-back is to more recent years in priority to earlier years.

(iii) Carried-back surplus shadow ACT displaces any real surplus ACT relieved in periods beginning in the 24 months before the end of the period in which the surplus shadow ACT arose. Any real surplus ACT which is displaced by surplus shadow ACT in this way is payable to HMRC.

(iv) Any remaining surplus shadow ACT is carried forward and regarded as shadow ACT of the next accounting period.

(f) The process continues (for as many accounting periods as required) until all of the surplus ACT brought forward from before 6 April 1999 is relieved. However, companies may opt out of the shadow ACT system if they wish (so avoiding all of the computations involved) and simply write off their surplus ACT instead.

(g) The shadow ACT regulations contain certain anti-avoidance provisions. These are very similar to the surplus ACT anti-avoidance legislation which was repealed as from 6 April 1999 (see above).

EXAMPLE 9

A company has unrelieved surplus ACT of £70,000 brought forward from before 6 April 1999. In the year to 31 March 2010, the company has chargeable profits of £200,000, pays dividends of £80,000 and receives UK dividends of £36,000. Calculate the amount of surplus ACT which will be relieved in the year.

Solution

The maximum ACT set-off for the year is £40,000 (20% x £200,000). If ACT had not been abolished on 6 April 1999, franked payments for the year would have been £100,000 (£80,000 x 100/80). The company has FII of £40,000 (£36,000 + £4,000) so the amount of FII taken into account in ACT calculations is £45,000 (£40,000 x 9/8).

The excess of franked payments over uplifted FII is £55,000 so there is shadow ACT of £11,000 (20% x £55,000). This reduces the scope for relieving surplus ACT brought forward to £29,000 (£40,000 − £11,000). Therefore the company's corporation tax liability for the year is reduced by £29,000 and the remaining £41,000 of surplus ACT is carried forward.

Summary

▸ Companies receive certain types of income net of income tax at the basic rate.

▸ Companies make certain types of payment net of income tax at the basic rate.

▸ Companies must submit quarterly returns of the income tax suffered on taxed income and deducted from relevant payments. From the information given in these returns, the amount of income tax payable/repayable for each return period can be calculated.

▸ If the income tax suffered in an accounting period exceeds the income tax deducted from payments made in that period, the excess is deducted from the company's corporation tax liability.

▸ Until 6 April 1999 (when ACT was abolished) ACT was payable when a company made a qualifying distribution. The most common example of a qualifying distribution was the payment of a dividend.

▸ The amount of a dividend paid, plus its associated ACT, was known as a franked payment. The ACT liability for an accounting period was based upon the excess of franked payments over franked investment income for the period.

▸ Surplus FII could be carried forward to subsequent accounting periods and used to reduce the company's ACT liability in those accounting periods.

▸ The maximum ACT set-off for an accounting period was the ACT which would be attributable to a franked payment equal to the entire chargeable profits for that accounting period.

▸ Unrelieved surplus ACT on 6 April 1999 is dealt with by the shadow ACT system.

Exercises

25.1   Classify each of the following as paid/received by companies net of income tax or paid/received by companies gross:

(a)   debenture interest paid to an individual

(b)   debenture interest received from another UK company

(c)   patent royalties received from an individual

(d)   Gift Aid donations

(e)   interest received from a UK bank.

25.2   A company has the following payments made net of income tax and income received net of income tax for the year to 31 March 2010 (amounts are stated net):

		Payments £	Income £
1 May 2009	Debenture interest paid	16,000	
30 June 2009	Patent royalties received		8,000
1 November 2009	Debenture interest paid	16,000	
1 January 2010	Patent royalties received		5,600

Compute the amounts of income tax payable or repayable in each return period.

25.3   A company has chargeable profits of £240,000 for the year to 31 March 2010. Payments made net of income tax and income received net of income tax during the year were as follows (amounts are stated net):

		Payments £	Income £
30 June 2009	Patent royalties received		28,800
17 August 2009	Debenture interest paid	36,000	
1 January 2010	Patent royalties received		28,800

Compute the corporation tax payable on 1 January 2011, assuming FII of £nil.

25.4   (a)   Outline the main features of the ACT system as it operated until 6 April 1999.

(b)   Outline the main features of the shadow ACT system as it now operates.

*25.5   A company's income statement for the year to 31 March 2010 is as follows:

	£	£
Sales		254,628
Less: Cost of sales		112,876
Gross profit		141,752
Add: Profit on sale of tangible fixed asset	542	
Other income	15,000	15,542
		157,294
Less: Distribution costs	32,189	
Administrative expenses	42,974	
Interest payable	22,876	98,039
Net profit		59,255

Notes:

(i)   The sale of the fixed asset gave rise to a chargeable gain of £212.

(ii)   Other income consists of:

	£
UK dividends received	9,000
Patent royalties received (gross amount)	4,000
Patent royalties accrued (gross amount)	2,000
	15,000

The patent royalties are all received from individuals with 20% income tax deducted at source. The patents were not acquired for trade purposes.

(iii)   Administrative expenses include:

	£
Directors' fees	20,000
Depreciation of tangible fixed assets	5,764
Audit fee	1,000

(iv)   Interest payable consists of:

	£
Debenture interest paid (gross amount)	2,000
Debenture interest accrued (gross amount)	1,000
Bank overdraft interest	19,876
	22,876

The debenture interest is all paid to individuals with 20% income tax deducted at source. The debentures were issued for trade purposes.

(v)   Capital allowances of £5,318 are claimed for the year.

Calculate the corporation tax payable on 1 January 2011.

*25.6   On 1 October 2008, a company had surplus ACT brought forward of £2,000. The company's chargeable profits for the year to 30 September 2009 were £32,000. In that year, the company paid dividends and received dividends (all from UK companies) as follows:

	Paid	*Received*
	£	£
31 July 2009		9,000
30 September 2009	30,000	

Calculate the amount of ACT set against the company's corporation tax liability for the year and state the amount of any surplus ACT carried forward at the end of the year.

Chapter 26

Corporation tax losses

Introduction

The loss reliefs which are available to a company incurring a trading loss are similar to those available to individuals (see Chapter 11) and generally involve either carrying the loss forward against future trading profits or setting the loss against the company's total profits for a specified period. The main purpose of this chapter is to describe these loss reliefs and to explain the factors which might influence a company when choosing between them. The tax treatment of a company's non-trading losses is also considered in this chapter.

Relief for trading losses

A company's trading losses may be relieved in any of the following ways:

(a) Under Section 393(1) of ICTA 1988, trading losses may be carried forward and relieved against future trading profits.

(b) Under Section 393A(1)(a) of ICTA 1988, trading losses may be relieved against the total profits of the accounting period in which the loss arises.

(c) Under Section 393A(1)(b) of ICTA 1988, trading losses may be relieved against the total profits of the 12 months prior to the accounting period in which the loss arises.

Each of these loss reliefs is described below. The loss reliefs are usually referred to by their section numbers in the Income and Corporation Taxes Act 1988 and this practice is followed for the remainder of this chapter.

Section 393(1) relief

Unless a company claims any other form of loss relief, trading losses are carried forward under s393(1) and relieved against the company's future trading profits. It is important to note the following points:

(a) Relief under s393(1) is given only against future *trading* profits, not against any other form of profits.

(b) Furthermore, relief is given only against future trading profits arising from *the same trade* as that in which the loss was incurred. If a company ceases one trade and commences another, the losses of the old trade cannot be carried forward and relieved against the future profits of the new trade. Similarly, if a company carries on two trades simultaneously, a loss incurred in one of the trades cannot be carried forward and relieved against the future profits of the other trade.

(c) Relief must be given against the *first available* future trading profits.

(d) There are restrictions on the carry-forward of trading losses when there is a change in the ownership of a company (see later in this chapter).

EXAMPLE 1

In the year to 31 March 2008, a company incurred a trading loss of £140,000 which was carried forward under s393(1). The company's results for the next two years were:

	y/e 31 March 2009 £	y/e 31 March 2010 £
Trading profits	110,000	1,850,000
Bank interest receivable	50,000	60,000
Chargeable gains	125,000	572,000
Franked investment income	nil	nil

Compute the company's chargeable profits for the years to 31 March 2009 and 2010 and identify the tax rate(s) at which the trading loss is relieved. How would the situation differ if the company's trading profits for the year to 31 March 2010 were lower by £1 million?

Solution

	y/e 31 March 2009 £	y/e 31 March 2010 £
Trading profits	110,000	1,850,000
Less: s393(1) relief	110,000	30,000
Trading income	0	1,820,000
Income from non-trading loans	50,000	60,000
Chargeable gains	125,000	572,000
Chargeable profits	175,000	2,452,000

Notes:

(i) In the year to 31 March 2009, trading losses brought forward are relieved to the fullest possible extent against the trading profits of the year. The losses of £30,000 which remain unrelieved cannot be offset against the bank interest or chargeable gains but must be carried forward and relieved against the trading profits of the following year.

(ii) In the year to 31 March 2009, trading losses reduce the company's chargeable profits from £285,000 to £175,000, saving tax at 21% (the SCR for FY2008).

In the year to 31 March 2010, losses reduce chargeable profits from £2,482,000 to £2,452,000, saving tax at 28% (the main rate for FY2009).

Total tax saved is £31,500 (£110,000 x 21% + £30,000 x 28%). If the company could defer the whole £140,000 of loss relief until the year to 31 March 2010, the total tax saved would be £39,200 (£140,000 x 28%), but s393(1) relief must be given against the first available future trading profits.

If trading profits were £1 million lower in the year to 31 March 2010, total profits would be under £1,500,000 and the company would pay tax for that year at 28% less marginal relief. Marginal rate would be 29.75% (see Chapter 24) and therefore £30,000 of the loss would be relieved at 29.75%.

Unrelieved charges on income

As stated in Chapter 22, the only items which now rank as charges on income when computing the corporation tax liability of a company are:

(a) qualifying donations under the Gift Aid scheme

(b) gifts of listed shares or securities to a charity

(c) gifts of land and buildings to a charity.

All of these are "non-trade charges" (i.e. charges not incurred for trade purposes). The list of payments which are treated as charges on income used to include certain "trade charges", but the payments concerned have now been reclassified for corporation tax purposes and therefore trade charges no longer exist.

In general, charges on income are deducted when computing a company's chargeable profits and so serve to reduce the company's tax liability. But if a company incurs a trading loss, its total income and gains for the period concerned may be insufficient to cover its charges, in which case some or all of those charges will be unrelieved.

In these circumstances, the tax saving that the unrelieved charges would normally have provided is permanently lost. Non-trade charges are eligible for relief only in the accounting period in which they are paid and cannot be carried forwards for relief in subsequent periods or backwards for relief in previous periods.

EXAMPLE 2

A company has the following results for the three years to 31 March 2010:

	y/e 31/3/2008	y/e 31/3/2009	y/e 31/3/2010
	£	£	£
Trading profits/(losses)	(78,900)	36,300	64,900
Bank interest receivable	21,500	-	-
Gift Aid donations	1,000	1,000	1,000

Assuming that the trading loss of £78,900 is to be carried forward under s393(1), calculate the company's chargeable profits for each of the three years.

Solution

	y/e 31/3/2008	y/e 31/3/2009	y/e 31/3/2010
	£	£	£
Trading profits	-	36,300	64,900
Less: s393(1) relief	-	36,300	42,600
Trading income	-	0	22,300
Income from non-trading loans	21,500	-	-
	21,500	0	22,300
Less: Charges	1,000	-	1,000
Chargeable profits	20,500	0	21,300
Trading losses c/f	78,900	42,600	-
Unrelieved charges	-	1,000	-

Notes:

(i) In the year to 31 March 2008, the charges of £1,000 are relieved against the bank interest receivable. The £78,900 of trading losses are carried forward.

(ii) In the year to 31 March 2009, the trading income of £36,300 is used to relieve part of the losses brought forward, leaving £42,600 to carry forward. The charges for the year are completely unrelieved.

(iii) In the year to 31 March 2010, the losses brought forward are fully relieved. The remaining profits of £22,300 are then reduced by the charges of £1,000, leaving chargeable profits of £21,300 for the year.

Section 393A(1) relief

Section 393A(1) relief allows trading losses to be relieved against total profits. The relief is available in two parts:

(a) Under s393A(1)(a), a company may claim that a trading loss incurred during an accounting period should be relieved against the total profits of that accounting period (*before* deducting charges on income).

(b) Under s393A(1)(b), the company may further claim that any part of the trading loss which remains unrelieved after a claim has been made under s393A(1)(a) should be relieved against the total profits of accounting periods falling wholly or partly within the 12 months prior to the loss-making period. Note the following points:

   (i) Relief under s393A(1)(b) is also given *before* deducting charges on income.

   (ii) If more than one accounting period falls wholly or partly into the 12 months preceding a loss-making period, s393A(1)(b) relief is given in later accounting periods in priority to earlier accounting periods.

   (iii) If an accounting period falls only partly into the 12 months preceding a loss-making period, the profits of that period are time-apportioned and relief is available against only the profits which fall into the specified 12 months.

Section 393A(1) relief is voluntary. A company wishing to relieve a trading loss in this way must make a claim within two years of the end of the accounting period in which the trading loss arises. A claim may be made under s393A(1)(a) without a further claim under s393A(1)(b), but a s393A(1)(b) claim cannot be made without a prior s393A(1)(a) claim.

A company may not specify how much of its trading loss should be relieved under s393A(1). The effect of a claim is to relieve trading losses to the fullest possible extent in each affected accounting period. Any part of the loss which remains unrelieved after a s393A(1) claim has been made is automatically carried forward under s393(1). If no claim at all is made under s393A(1) then the entire loss is carried forward under s393(1).

Temporary extension of carry-back relief

As explained above, a company's trading losses can normally be carried back for only 12 months. However, Finance Act 2009 has introduced a temporary extension to the carry-back period. The details of this extension are as follows:

(a) For trading losses incurred in accounting periods ending between 24 November 2008 and 23 November 2010, a claim under s393A(1)(b) relieves a trading loss against the company's total profits of the *previous three years* (instead of 12 months).

(b) As usual, relief is given in later accounting periods in priority to earlier accounting periods. The profits of an accounting period falling only partly into the three years preceding a loss-making period are time-apportioned and relief is available against only the profits which fall into the specified three years.

(c) If a s393A(1)(b) claim is made in relation to a trading loss, the amount of the loss which is carried back to the previous 12 months remains unlimited. But the amount of the loss which is then carried back a further two years is capped at £50,000.

There is one £50,000 limit for trading losses incurred in accounting periods ending between 24 November 2008 and 23 November 2009. There is a second £50,000 limit for trading losses incurred in accounting periods ending between 24 November 2009 and 23 November 2010.

(d) If a loss-making accounting period which ends between 24 November 2008 and 23 November 2010 is of less than 12 months in duration, the £50,000 cap referred to above is reduced proportionately.

EXAMPLE 3

A company has the following results for the year to 31 December 2009:

	£
Trading loss	(92,500)
Building society interest receivable	14,000
Chargeable gains	103,000
Gift Aid donations	28,700

Assuming that a claim is made for the trading loss to be relieved under s393A(1)(a), compute the company's chargeable profits for the year.

Solution

Total profits (before loss relief or charges) are £117,000 (£14,000 + £103,000). Deducting loss relief of £92,500 under s393A(1)(a) leaves £24,500 against which to set charges on income (the Gift Aid donations). Deducting charges of £24,500 leaves chargeable profits of zero. The remaining £4,200 of charges cannot be relieved and are lost.

EXAMPLE 4

A company has the following results for the three years to 31 March 2010:

	y/e 31/3/2008	y/e 31/3/2009	y/e 31/3/2010
	£	£	£
Trading profits/(losses)	112,500	110,700	(186,500)
Income from property	3,300	8,400	8,800
Gift Aid donations	2,000	2,000	2,000

Assuming that a claim is made under both s393A(1)(a) and s393A(1)(b) in relation to the trading loss incurred in the year to 31 March 2010, calculate the company's chargeable profits for each of the three years.

Solution

	y/e 31/3/2008 £	y/e 31/3/2009 £	y/e 31/3/2010 £
Trading income	112,500	110,700	-
Income from property	3,300	8,400	8,800
	115,800	119,100	8,800
Less: s393A(1)(a) relief	-	-	8,800
	115,800	119,100	0
Less: s393A(1)(b) relief	50,000	119,100	-
	65,800	0	0
Less: Charges	2,000	-	-
Chargeable profits	63,800	0	0
Trading loss c/f	-	-	8,600
Unrelieved charges	-	2,000	2,000

Notes:

(i) In the year to 31 March 2010, the claim under s393A(1)(a) must be for the maximum possible amount of £8,800. This leaves nothing against which to relieve the charges and therefore they are lost.

(ii) The remaining £177,700 of the trading loss is eligible for s393A(1)(b) relief in the year to 31 March 2009. The claim must be for the maximum possible amount of £119,100. This leaves nothing against which to relieve the charges, which are lost.

(iii) The unrelieved loss is now £58,600. Since the loss-making period ended between 24 November 2008 and 23 November 2010, £50,000 of this loss is carried back for a further two years. The full £50,000 is relieved in the year to 31 March 2008, leaving nothing to carry back to the year to 31 March 2007.

(iv) A total of £177,900 (£8,800 + £119,100 + £50,000) of the trading loss has been relieved under s393A(1)(a) and s393A(1)(b). The remaining £8,600 is carried forward under s393(1).

EXAMPLE 5

A company has the following results for the three accounting periods to 31 March 2011:

	y/e 30/6/2009 £	9 months to 31/3/2010 £	y/e 31/3/2011 £
Trading profits/(losses)	13,400	69,900	(122,800)
Chargeable gains	1,200	3,500	38,600

Assuming that a claim is made under both s393A(1)(a) and s393A(1)(b) in relation to the trading loss incurred in the year to 31 March 2011, calculate the company's chargeable profits for each of the three accounting periods.

Solution

		y/e 30/6/2009	9 months to 31/3/2010	y/e 31/3/2011
		£	£	£
Trading income		13,400	69,900	-
Chargeable gains		1,200	3,500	38,600
		14,600	73,400	38,600
Less: s393A(1)(a) relief		-	-	38,600
		14,600	73,400	0
Less: s393A(1)(b) relief	(1)		73,400	
	(2)	3,650		
Chargeable profits		10,950	0	0
Trading losses c/f		-	-	7,150

Notes:

(i) £38,600 of the trading losses incurred in the year to 31 March 2011 are relieved under s393A(1)(a). This leaves losses of £84,200 which are eligible for s393A(1)(b) relief. The loss-making period did not end between 24 November 2008 and 23 November 2010, so the carry-back is for 12 months only.

(ii) The 9-month accounting period to 31 March 2010 is entirely contained within the specified 12 months and so losses of £73,400 are relieved under s393A(1)(b). Losses relieved so far now total £112,000, leaving £10,800 still to be relieved.

(iii) Only 3 months of the year to 30 June 2009 fall into the specified 12-month period. The maximum s393A(1)(b) relief available is therefore £3,650 (£14,600 x 3/12). The remaining £7,150 of the trading loss is carried forward under s393(1).

Further points relating to s393A(1) relief

(a) A trading loss can be carried back under s393A(1)(b) only to accounting periods in which the loss-making trade was being carried on.

(b) If more than one loss is eligible for relief against the profits of a given accounting period, earlier losses are relieved before later losses.

(c) Trading losses incurred by a company in the 12 months before the loss-making trade ceases may be carried back and set against the profits of the preceding three years.

(d) Relief under s393A(1) is available only if the loss-making trade is being carried on "on a commercial basis" with a view to profit.

(e) In the case of *farming companies*, a loss is usually not eligible for relief under s393A(1) if losses have also been incurred for the previous five years.

(f) There are restrictions on the carry-back of trading losses under s393A(1)(b) when there is a change in the ownership of a company (see below).

(g) If a trading loss is set against the profits of an accounting period under s393A(1)(a) or s393A(1)(b), the chargeable profits of that period are reduced and therefore the scope for relieving surplus ACT brought forward from before 6 April 1999 is also reduced (see Chapter 25).

Repayments of corporation tax

If a claim under s393A(1)(b) results in a repayment of corporation tax for an earlier accounting period, this repayment will attract interest. The interest is calculated in the usual way (see Chapter 24) unless the accounting period for which repayment is being made began more than 12 months before the loss-making accounting period. In these circumstances, the interest is calculated as if the repayment were a repayment of tax for the loss-making accounting period itself.

EXAMPLE 6

A company which began trading on 1 April 2008 has the following results for its first three accounting periods:

	y/e 31/3/2009	6 months to 30/9/2009	y/e 30/9/2010
	£	£	£
Chargeable profits	180,000	120,000	nil
Franked investment income	nil	nil	nil

A claim is made under s393A(1)(b) in relation to trading losses of £290,000 incurred in the year to 30 September 2010. All corporation tax was originally paid on the due date and the necessary repayment of corporation tax is made on 1 August 2011. Calculate the amount of the repayment and the interest which will accompany this repayment, assuming an interest rate of 1% per annum.

Solution

A s393A(1)(b) claim will relieve the trading loss first against the £120,000 profit of the six months to 30 September 2009 and then against the £90,000 profit of the six months to 31 March 2009. Since the loss-making period ended between 24 November 2008 and 23 November 2010, a further £50,000 of the loss is then relieved against the profit of the six months to 30 September 2008, making a total of £140,000 of loss relief in the year to 31 March 2009. The remaining loss of £30,000 will be carried forward under s393(1). The s393A(1)(b) claim will generate the following repayment:

		£
6 months to 30 September 2009	120,000 @ 21%	25,200
y/e 31 March 2009	140,000 @ 21%	29,400
Total repayment		54,600

Notes:

(i)   The six months to 30 September 2009 did not begin more than 12 months before the loss-making period so interest on the £25,200 will run from 1 July 2010 (the due date of payment for the six months to 30 September 2009).

(ii) The year to 31 March 2009 began more than 12 months before the loss-making period so interest on the £29,400 will run from 1 July 2011 (the due date of payment for the loss-making period itself).

(iii) The repayment takes place on 1 August 2011, which is 396 days after 1 July 2010 and 31 days after 1 July 2011. Therefore the interest due is:

$$(£25,200 \times 1\% \times \frac{396}{365}) + (£29,400 \times 1\% \times \frac{31}{365}) = £298.37.$$

Anti-avoidance legislation

Specific anti-avoidance legislation exists to prevent the following manoeuvre, which would otherwise be very tax-efficient:

(a)   Acquire a company with substantial amounts of unrelieved trading losses.

(b)   Revive the loss-making trade.

(c)   Use s393(1) relief to set the company's pre-acquisition trading losses against its post-acquisition trading profits, so avoiding liability to corporation tax.

The legislation referred to above provides that if there is a change in the ownership of a company and certain conditions are satisfied, trading losses arising before the change cannot be set against trading profits arising after the change. Nor can trading losses arising after the change be set (by virtue of s393A) against profits arising before the change. The required conditions are that:

(a)   a change in ownership has occurred at a time when the company's business has become negligible and then (at any time after the change) there has been a revival of the company's business, or

(b)   a change in ownership and a major change in the nature or conduct of the company's business have both occurred within the same three-year period.

For this purpose, a change in ownership is deemed to occur if over half of the company's ordinary share capital is acquired either by one person or by a group of people, each acquiring at least a 5% shareholding.

Choice of loss relief

A company which incurs a trading loss must choose between carrying the loss forward against future trading profits or relieving the loss against the total profits of the current period and (possibly) the total profits of the previous 12 months (or three years). Some of the main criteria which will influence this choice are as follows:

(a) the likelihood and expected amount of future profits arising from the same trade as that in which the loss was incurred

(b) the company's cash flow situation (a cash shortage may dictate that loss relief should be obtained as soon as possible)

(c) the rates of corporation tax in earlier accounting periods and the expected rates in future periods

(d) the possibility that relief for trading losses may reduce the chargeable profits of an accounting period to such an extent that the rate of corporation tax payable for that period is reduced

(e) the possibility that charges may be unrelieved

(f) the possibility of reducing the scope for relieving surplus ACT brought forward from before 6 April 1999

(g) in general, the desire to maximise the tax saved as a result of loss relief claims.

Non-trading losses

A company may incur non-trading losses in a number of ways. The main classes of non-trading loss and the reliefs available for each are as follows:

(a) **Property business losses**. A loss incurred by a company on its property business is set against the company's total profits for the accounting period in which the loss occurs. To the extent that the loss cannot be relieved in this way, it is either:

(i) carried forward and set against the company's total profits in succeeding accounting periods (as long as the property business is still being carried on in those accounting periods), or

(ii) relieved by means of group relief (see Chapter 28).

These reliefs are more generous than their income tax equivalents (see Chapter 5). Note that there are restrictions on the carry-forward of property losses when there is a change in the ownership of a company. These restrictions are similar to those relating to trading losses (see earlier in this chapter).

(b) **Net debits on non-trading loan relationships**. If a company incurs a deficit on its non-trading loan relationships (see Chapter 22), a claim may be made for the deficit to be relieved in any of the following ways:

(i) by set-off against the company's total profits for the accounting period in which the deficit occurs (*after* deducting any trading losses brought forward and relieved under s393(1) but *before* deducting any trading losses relieved under s393A(1) and *before* deducting charges)

(ii) by group relief (see Chapter 28)

(iii) by set-off against the company's income from non-trading loan relationships in the previous 12 months.

Part of the deficit may be relieved in one way and part in another, if the company so wishes. Claims must be made within two years of the end of the accounting period in which the deficit occurs. Any part of the deficit which is not subject to such a claim is carried forward automatically and set against non-trading profits of subsequent accounting periods.

(c) **Non-trading losses on intangible fixed assets**. A company which incurs a non-trading loss on intangible fixed assets in an accounting period (see Chapter 22) may claim that all or part of the loss should be set against the company's total profits for that period. Any part of the loss which is not subject to such a claim and which is not relieved by means of group relief (see Chapter 28) is carried forward and treated as non-trading expenditure of the next accounting period.

(d) **Capital losses**. A company's capital losses are treated in a similar way to those of an individual (see Chapter 16). Capital losses are relieved first against capital gains of the same accounting period and then against the capital gains of subsequent accounting periods. Since companies are not entitled to the annual exemption, there is no need to restrict capital losses brought forward so as to conserve the exemption. Capital losses cannot be relieved against any other form of income.

Summary

▸ A company's trading losses are carried forward under s393(1) and relieved against the first available profits of the same trade, unless the company makes a claim under s393A(1).

▸ Charges on income which cannot be relieved in the accounting period in which they are paid are lost and cannot be carried forwards or backwards for relief in subsequent or previous accounting periods.

▸ Under s393A(1)(a), a trading loss may be relieved against the total profits of the loss-making accounting period.

▶ Under s393A(1)(b), a trading loss may be further relieved against the total profits of the previous 12 months. The carry-back period is extended from 12 months to three years for trading losses incurred in accounting periods ending between 24 November 2008 and 23 November 2010, but only £50,000 per annum of such losses may be carried back further than 12 months.

▶ If a claim under s393A(1)(b) results in a repayment of corporation tax for an earlier accounting period, this repayment will attract interest.

▶ Loss reliefs are also available in relation to property business losses, net debits on non-trading loan relationships, non-trading losses on intangible fixed assets and capital losses.

Exercises

26.1   A Ltd has the following results for the three years to 31 May 2009:

	y/e 31/5/07 £	y/e 31/5/08 £	y/e 31/5/09 £
Trading profits/(losses)	(32,200)	23,800	40,300
Gift Aid donations	400	500	600

Assuming that the trading loss is to be carried forward under s393(1), calculate the company's chargeable profits for each of the three years, showing the amount of the losses carried forward at the end of each year.

26.2   B Ltd has the following results for the year to 31 October 2009:

	£
Trading loss	(232,300)
Income from property	190,200
Chargeable gains	45,540
Gift Aid donations	24,000

Assuming that a loss relief claim is made under s393A(1)(a), calculate the chargeable profits for the year.

26.3   Which of the following statements is true?

(a)   Capital losses may be carried forward and relieved against future trading profits.

(b)   Trading losses may be carried forward and relieved against future capital gains.

(c)   Trading losses may be relieved against capital gains of the same period.

(d)   Capital losses may be relieved against trading profits of the same period.

26.4   C Ltd has the following results for the four years to 31 January 2010:

	y/e 31/1/07	y/e 31/1/08	y/e 31/1/09	y/e 31/1/10
	£	£	£	£
Trading profits/(losses)	62,300	22,700	73,600	(205,700)
Capital gains	-	-	-	48,700
Gift Aid donations	1,000	1,000	1,000	1,000

Assuming that a claim is made under both s393A(1)(a) and s393A(1)(b) in relation to the trading loss incurred in the year to 31 January 2010, calculate the company's chargeable profits for each of the four years.

26.5   In the year to 31 March 2009, D Ltd has chargeable profits of £800,000. In the nine months to 31 December 2009, the company incurs a trading loss of £600,000 and has no other income or gains. There is no franked investment income and there are no charges in either period.

(a)   Describe the corporation tax effects of a claim under s393A(1)(b) in relation to the trading loss (detailed computations are not required).

(b)   Assuming that the company still has a substantial amount of unrelieved surplus ACT brought forward from before 6 April 1999, explain how a s393A(1)(b) claim would affect the scope for relieving this ACT.

*26.6   E Ltd has the following results for the four years to 31 March 2010:

	y/e 31/3/07	y/e 31/3/08	y/e 31/3/09	y/e 31/3/10
	£	£	£	£
Trading profits/(losses)	61,900	77,400	64,200	(172,500)
Capital gains/(losses)	(7,500)	4,300	2,700	5,700
Gift Aid donations	3,400	3,400	3,400	3,400

Calculate the total repayment of corporation tax (with interest) to which the company is entitled, assuming that:

(a)   claims under s393A(1)(a) and s393A(1)(b) are made in relation to the trading loss for the year to 31 March 2010

(b)   any repayment of corporation tax which is generated by these claims is made on 15 January 2011

(c)   corporation tax for the three years to 31 March 2009 was all paid on the due dates

(d)   the company has received no dividends in any of the four years

(e)   the rate of interest paid on repayments of corporation tax is 1%.

The small companies rate of corporation tax is 19% in FY2006, 20% in FY2007, 21% in FY2008 and 21% in FY2009.

Also explain how the situation would differ if the company had ceased trading on 31 March 2010 (computations are not required).

Chapter 27

Close companies and companies with investment business

Introduction

In general terms, a "close company" is one which is controlled by a small number of people and a "company with investment business" is one whose business consists at least partly of making investments. Special corporation tax rules apply to each of these types of company and the main purpose of this chapter is to explain the nature of these rules. The tax implications of incorporation are also considered in this chapter.

Close companies

The essence of a close company is that its affairs can be controlled and manipulated by a small group of people, possibly for tax-avoidance purposes. In fact, most companies in the UK are close companies. Certain anti-avoidance legislation exists in relation to close companies and the main points of this legislation are explained later in this chapter. The first step, however, is to provide a precise definition of the term "close company".

Definition of a close company

A close company is defined as a UK resident company which is under the *control* of:

(a)   five or fewer *participators*, or

(b)   any number of participators who are also *directors* of the company.

The rights of a participator's *associates* are aggregated with that participator's own rights for the purpose of determining whether a company is a close company. Some important terms used in this definition are explained below.

Control

Persons are deemed to have "control" over a company if, taken together, they:

(a) own over 50% of the company's issued share capital, or

(b) have over 50% of the company's voting power, or

(c) would receive over 50% of the company's income, if it were all distributed, or

(d) would receive over 50% of the company's assets, if the company were wound up.

Participators

A "participator" is defined as someone who has a share or interest in the capital or income of the company. In many cases, a company's only participators are its shareholders, but other persons (e.g. option holders, loan creditors) might also rank as participators.

Directors

A "director", for this purpose, is any person:

(a) who occupies the position of director (whether called a director or not), or

(b) whose directions or instructions are normally obeyed by the directors, or

(c) who is a manager of the company and (possibly together with associates) controls at least 20% of the company's ordinary share capital.

Associates

The "associates" of a participator are defined as:

(a) the participator's business partners

(b) the participator's relatives

(c) the trustees of a settlement established by the participator or by his/her relatives.

For this purpose, a participator's relatives comprise his or her spouse (or civil partner), parents and remoter ancestors, children and remoter issue, brothers and sisters.

EXAMPLE 1

A company's issued share capital consists of 1,000 £1 ordinary shares, held as follows:

	No of shares		No of shares
David	200	Helen	50
Emma	50	Ian	30
Frederick	100	Jacqueline	40
George	50	Others (1 share each)	480

None of the shareholders are associated in any way and no shareholder is also a director.

(a) Is the company a close company?

(b) Would the company be a close company:

  (i) if David were Jacqueline's brother, or

  (ii) if Emma married Ian, or

  (iii) if David were Jacqueline's brother and Emma married Ian?

Solution

(a) The five largest shareholders own 45% of the share capital, so the company is not under the control of five or fewer participators. The company is also not under the control of its directors. Therefore the company is not a close company.

(b) (i) If David were Jacqueline's brother, her 4% holding would be aggregated with his and the five largest shareholders would control 49% (45% + 4%) of the share capital. The company would not be a close company.

  (ii) If Emma married Ian, his 3% would be aggregated with hers and the five largest shareholders would control 48% (45% + 3%) of the share capital. The company would still not be a close company.

  (iii) If David were Jacqueline's brother and Emma married Ian, the five largest shareholders would control 52% (45% + 4% + 3%) of the share capital. The company would then be a close company.

EXAMPLE 2

A company's issued share capital consists entirely of ordinary shares, held as follows:

	% holding	Director
Keith	7	Yes
Leonora	7	Yes
Martin	7	Yes
Norma	7	Yes
Oliver	7	Yes
Penny	16	No
Richard	4	No
Others (all non-directors owning under 1%)	45	
Total	100	

None of the shareholders are associated in any way.

(a) Is the company a close company?

(b) Would the company be a close company:

  (i) if Penny were a manager, or

  (ii) if Penny were Richard's daughter, or

  (iii) if Penny were both a manager and Richard's daughter?

Solution

(a) The five largest shareholders own 44% of the share capital, so the company is not under the control of five or fewer participators. The company is also not under the control of its directors, who own 35% of the share capital. Therefore the company is not a close company.

(b) (i) If Penny were a manager, she would not rank as a director since her shareholding is less than 20%. The situation would be unaltered and the company would not be a close company.

    (ii) If Penny were Richard's daughter, then his 4% holding would be aggregated with hers and the five largest shareholders would control 48% (44% + 4%) of the share capital. The company would still not be a close company.

    (iii) If Penny were both a manager and Richard's daughter, then her deemed 20% holding (16% + 4%) would make her a director. The six directors would control 55% of the share capital and the company would then be a close company.

Exceptions

Certain types of company are statutorily excepted from close company status, even if they are controlled by five or fewer participators or by the participator-directors. The main exception consists of listed companies with a substantial public interest. In order for this exception to apply, a company must satisfy all of the following conditions:

(a) The company's voting shares must have been both dealt in and listed on a recognised stock exchange within the 12 months prior to the date on which the company's status is being determined.

(b) The total voting power possessed by the *principal members* of the company must not exceed 85% of the total voting power.

(c) At least 35% of the company's voting power must be in the hands of the public.

For this purpose, a "principal member" is a shareholder who (possibly with associates) has more than 5% of the voting power of the company and is also one of the top five shareholders. If two or more shareholders, each holding more than 5%, tie for fifth place, there will be more than five principal members.

  The "public" excludes the company's directors, their associates and most principal members. But principal members which are themselves either non-close companies or occupational pension schemes (other than schemes established for the benefit of the company's own employees) are included within the definition of the public.

EXAMPLE 3

The issued share capital of XYZ plc consists entirely of ordinary shares. For many years, these shares have been listed on the London Stock Exchange and there have been frequent dealings in these shares within the last 12 months. The company's shares are owned as follows:

	% holding	Director
ABC Ltd (a non-close company)	13	-
DEF Ltd (a close company)	7	-
Terry	8	Yes
Ursula	10	Yes
Vincent (a manager)	33	No
Wendy	4	No
Others (all non-directors owning under 1%)	25	
Total	100	

None of the shareholders are associated in any way. Is the company a close company?

Solution

At first sight, XYZ plc seems to be a close company. It is under the control of its directors (since Vincent ranks as a director) and it is also under the control of five or fewer participators. However, the company is listed on a recognised stock exchange and its shares have been dealt in within the past 12 months. Furthermore, its principal members (the top five shareholders, each owning more than 5% of the voting shares) hold only 71% of the company's voting power and the public (ABC Ltd, Wendy and the others) hold 42%. Therefore the company is excepted from being a close company.

Consequences of close company status

There are two main tax consequences of being a close company. These are:

(a) Benefits in kind provided by the company to participators or their associates are generally treated as distributions.

(b) Loans made to participators or their associates are assessed to tax.

Each of these consequences is explained below.

Benefits in kind provided to participators

Benefits in kind provided by a close company to its participators (or their associates) are generally regarded as distributions. The taxation effects of this are as follows:

(a)   The cost to the company of providing the benefit is disallowed when computing its corporation tax liability.

(b)   The company is deemed to have made a distribution equal to the amount which would be assessed on a director or employee earning at least £8,500 per annum if the benefit had been received by such a employee (see Chapter 7).

(c)   The person receiving the benefit is taxed as if he or she had received a dividend of the same amount as the deemed distribution.

A benefit in kind provided to a participator is *not* treated as a distribution if it is already assessable as employment income. This will be the case if the participator is a director of the company or an employee earning at least £8,500 p.a. (see Chapter 7).

EXAMPLE 4

On 31 August 2009, a close company which prepares accounts to 31 March each year provides the brother of one of its major shareholders with a free holiday abroad. The cost of the holiday is £3,600 and this amount is charged as an expense in the income statement for the year to 31 March 2010. Explain the tax treatment of this item.

Solution

The £3,600 is disallowed in the company's tax computation for the year to 31 March 2010. The company is deemed to have made a distribution of £3,600 and the shareholder's brother is taxed as if he had received a UK dividend of £3,600 (tax credit £400).

Loans made to participators

If a close company makes a loan to a participator (or associate), the tax consequences are as follows:

(a)   The company is required to pay an amount of tax which is calculated at 25% of the amount of the loan. This tax is payable nine months and one day after the end of the accounting period in which the loan is made. However, no tax is payable in relation to any part of a loan which is repaid to the company before the date on which the tax falls due.

(b)   The tax paid when the loan was made is repaid to the company if the participator repays the loan or if the loan is written off. This tax repayment is made nine months and one day after the end of the accounting period in which the loan is repaid or written off.

(c) If a loan to a participator is wholly or partly written off, the participator is deemed to have received income equal to the amount written off. This income is treated as if received net of income tax at the dividend ordinary rate (currently 10%).

The tax which is deemed to have been deducted at source from this income is not repayable to the participator, even if he or she is a non-taxpayer. However, further tax at the dividend upper rate (currently 32.5%) is payable on any part of the grossed-up income which, when added to the participator's other income, falls beyond the basic rate limit.

In the case of a participator who is also an employee, this tax charge takes priority over the usual rules which apply to employee loans written off (see Chapter 7).

(d) Certain loans are excluded from the treatment described above. These include loans made to a participator in the normal course of the company's business and loans not exceeding £15,000 made to a participator who is a full-time employee or director of the company, so long as that participator (with associates) has no more than a 5% interest in the company.

EXAMPLE 5

On 1 May 2009, a close company which prepares accounts to 30 June each year lends £30,000 to Ravi, who is one of its directors. No interest is charged on this loan. Ravi owns 25% of the company's ordinary share capital. Explain the tax treatment of the loan if:

(a) it is repaid in full on 30 April 2010

(b) £12,000 is repaid on 30 April 2010 and the remainder of the loan is written off on the same day.

Solution

Tax of £7,500 (25% of £30,000) is payable by the company on 1 April 2010. Since the loan is made interest-free, it is treated as a beneficial loan and Ravi is subject to income tax on the related benefit in kind. As regards the eventual repayment or write-off of the loan:

(a) The tax of £7,500 is repaid to the company on 1 April 2011.

(b) The tax of £7,500 is repaid to the company on 1 April 2011. Ravi is taxed as if he had received income in 2010-11 of £18,000 (net) with tax deducted at source of £2,000.

Close investment-holding companies

A close company is also a close investment-holding company (CIC) unless it exists wholly or mainly for one or more of a number of purposes defined by statute. The main purposes which except a company from CIC status are:

(a)   the carrying on of a trade on a commercial basis, or

(b)   the letting of property (other than to connected persons).

A close investment-holding company is subject to the usual close company rules described above, but is also subject to further provisions. The most important of these is that a CIC is not entitled to the small companies rate of corporation tax. Nor can it benefit from marginal relief. A CIC always pays corporation tax at the main rate, no matter how small its chargeable profits.

Companies with investment business

A "company with investment business" is defined by the Corporation Tax Act 2009 as "a company whose business consists wholly or partly of making investments". The investment income of such a company will normally consist of:

(a)   income from property

(b)   net credits on non-trading loan relationships

(c)   chargeable gains.

The company may also receive franked investment income but of course this is not chargeable to corporation tax. The expenses incurred by a company in relation to its investment business fall into two categories:

(a)   expenses which are directly related to one of the company's sources of income and which may be set against that income (e.g. property expenses offset against property income, debits on non-trading loan relationships set against credits)

(b)   management expenses, which are not related to any particular source of income but which may be set against the company's total income.

Note that only genuine management expenses are allowed. For example, in *L G Berry Investments Ltd* v *Attwooll* (1964), excessive directors' remuneration included in management expenses was disallowed.

   To the extent that management expenses cannot be relieved in the accounting period in which they are incurred they may be carried forward (without time limit) to future periods. There are restrictions on the carry-forward of management expenses when there is a change in the ownership of a company. These restrictions are similar to those relating to the carry-forward of trading losses (see Chapter 26).

Unincorporated business vs close company

An individual who starts trading is faced with a choice between two alternatives:

(a) To trade as an unincorporated business, either as a sole trader or in partnership with others. In this case the individual is self-employed and the business profits are assessed to income tax as trading income.

(b) To trade as a limited company (probably a close company) with the individual concerned being a director and/or shareholder of the company. In this case, the company's profits are assessed to corporation tax and the individual's earnings and dividends from the company are assessed to income tax.

The choice between these two alternatives will be determined partly (though not solely) by taxation considerations. A full analysis of these considerations is beyond the scope of this book but some of the main factors which should be taken into account when deciding whether to trade as an unincorporated business or as a company include:

(a) the rates of income tax and corporation tax

(b) the NI contributions which are payable by the self-employed and by employees and employers

(c) the tax effects of distributing profits to the owner of the business

(d) the tax reliefs available on pension contributions

(e) the dates on which tax and NI contributions are due for payment

(f) the tax reliefs available in relation to trading losses

(g) the taxation of chargeable gains

(h) the tax treatment of loans made to the owner of the business.

Each of these factors is discussed below.

Rates of tax

The entire profits of an unincorporated business are charged to income tax, regardless of whether or not the profits are drawn out of the business. The rate of tax in 2009-10 is 20% or 40%, depending upon the owner's taxable income. A marginal rate of 40% applies if the owner's taxable income exceeds £37,400 (a relatively small sum).

By contrast, the profits of a company for FY2009 are charged to corporation tax at 21% or 28% with a marginal rate of 29.75% if profits lie between the small companies rate lower and upper limits. The marginal rate of 29.75% does not apply until profits reach £300,000. The 28% rate does not apply until profits reach £1,500,000. Furthermore, the owners of a company can determine the amount of profits to be paid out as directors' remuneration and can therefore control the extent to which profits are assessed to personal income tax rather than corporation tax.

Note, however, that retaining profits in a company so as to minimise the tax liability in the short term will serve to increase the value of the company's shares. This may result in an increased capital gains tax liability in the longer term when shareholders dispose of their shares, though the gains made on disposal might be eligible for entrepreneurs' relief and/or other CGT reliefs.

National Insurance

In 2009-10, the self-employed pay flat-rate Class 2 NICs of £2.40 per week. Class 4 contributions are also payable, calculated as 8% of profits between £5,715 and £43,875 and 1% of profits beyond £43,875.

The total amount of the Class 1 NICs payable in respect of directors' remuneration can be much higher than this. A director who is not contracted out pays primary contributions at 11% on earnings between £5,715 and £43,875 and at 1% on further earnings. In addition, the company pays 12.8% secondary contributions on all earnings in excess of £5,715. However, these secondary contributions are deductible in the company's corporation tax computation.

Distribution of profits

The amount of income tax payable on the profits of an unincorporated business is entirely unaffected by the level of the owner's drawings. But the distribution of profits by a company (either as directors' remuneration or as dividends) has tax implications:

(a) The payment of directors' remuneration reduces the company's corporation tax liability at the expense of increasing the income tax liability of the directors concerned and creating a liability to both primary and secondary NICs.

(b) The payment of a dividend avoids the NI liability and a dividend has an attached tax credit. But dividends are an appropriation of profit and are not allowed in the company's corporation tax computation.

The decision as to whether to pay out a company's profits as directors' remuneration or dividends (or a mixture of both) is a complex one and should take into account the personal circumstances of the shareholders and directors as well as all of the factors listed above. A constraint which should be borne in mind is the need to pay sufficient directors' remuneration to comply with National Minimum Wage regulations.

EXAMPLE 6

A close company which prepares accounts to 31 March each year is owned and managed by a single shareholder/director who is paid a salary of £5,000 per month. In addition to this salary, the company's owner intends to withdraw £20,000 from the company on 31 March 2010. Two approaches are being considered:

(a) that the company should make an extra salary payment to the owner, such that the total of this payment and the related secondary NICs will equal £20,000

(b) that the company should pay a dividend to the owner, such that the total of this dividend and the company's extra corporation tax liability (when compared with the other approach) will equal £20,000.

Consider the tax-effectiveness of each of these two approaches. For the approach which involves the payment of a dividend, show separately the situation which will apply if the company's marginal rate of corporation tax for the year is 21%, 28% or 29.75%. (Perform all calculations to the nearest £.)

Solution

	Extra salary £	Dividend (21%) £	Dividend (28%) £	Dividend (29.75%) £
Payments made by company:				
Salary	17,730			
Secondary Class 1 NICs @ 12.8%	2,270			
Corporation tax on £20,000		4,200	5,600	5,950
Dividend		15,800	14,400	14,050
Total payments	20,000	20,000	20,000	20,000
Amount received by owner:				
Gross salary	17,730			
Dividend + tax credit (1/9th)		17,556	16,000	15,611
Primary Class 1 NICs @ 1%	(177)			
Income tax @ 40%	(7,092)			
Income tax @ 32.5%		(5,706)	(5,200)	(5,074)
Income remaining after tax	10,461	11,850	10,800	10,537

Notes:

(i)   The owner's regular salary is sufficient to ensure that any further income is subject to primary Class 1 NICs at 1% and income tax at the higher rate or dividend upper rate.

(ii) The payment of a dividend to the owner seems to be more tax-effective than the payment of extra salary. The distinction is particularly noticeable if the company's marginal rate of corporation tax is 21%.

Pension contributions

In 2009-10, a self-employed individual may obtain tax relief on pension contributions of up to £3,600 or 100% of self-employment income (whichever is the greater). Similarly, a company director may obtain tax relief on pension contributions of up to £3,600 or 100% of director's remuneration (whichever is the greater) and the company itself may make unlimited pension contributions on the director's behalf and deduct these contributions when computing chargeable profits. However, this deduction is available only if the contributions are paid wholly and exclusively for trade purposes. If the contributions are made in respect of a controlling director, the "wholly and exclusively" test will not be satisfied unless the contributions are in line with those which would have been paid in respect of an ordinary employee in a similar situation.

Dividends do not rank as earnings and are ignored when computing the maximum pension contributions on which an individual may obtain tax relief. Furthermore, a shareholder is not (per se) an employee and so a company cannot make employer contributions in relation to one of its shareholders unless that shareholder is also a director or other employee.

Dates of payment of tax and NICs

A self-employed person must make payments on account of his or her liability to income tax and Class 4 NICs. These payments are due on 31 January in the tax year and on the following 31 July. The balance of the liability (if any) is payable on the following 31 January. Note that:

(a)   Choosing an accounting date early in the tax year (e.g. 30 April) maximises the delay between earning profits and paying tax on them. For example, the tax on profits for the year to 30 April 2009 (basis period for 2009-10) is payable on 31 January 2010 and 31 July 2010 with a balancing payment on 31 January 2011.

(b)   However, choosing an accounting date early in the tax year has the adverse effect of maximising the amount of overlap profits which are assessed twice on the commencement of trade.

(c)   Class 2 NICs of £2.40 per week are payable throughout the tax year.

In general, close companies will pay their corporation tax nine months and one day after the end of the accounting period. Income tax and Class 1 NICs in relation to directors' remuneration must be accounted for via the PAYE system.

Relief for trading losses

For both individuals and companies, trading losses may be carried forward and set against future profits of the same trade. The main distinctions between trading loss reliefs for individuals and companies are concerned with the opportunities to set such losses against total income:

(a)   The trading losses of a self-employed individual may be set against that person's total income for the year of the loss, the previous year or both of these years.

In the case of a company, a Section 393A(1)(b) claim to set trading losses against total profits of the previous 12 months cannot be made unless a claim has already been made under Section 393A(1)(a) to set trading losses against total profits of the current accounting period.

(b)   In the case of an individual, the temporary extension of carry-back relief for trading losses (see Chapter 11) allows losses of up to £50,000 incurred in each of the years 2008-09 and 2009-10 to be carried back for three years. However, such losses may be relieved only against profits of the same trade.

In the case of a company, the temporary extension relates to losses of up to £50,000 incurred in each of the years to 23 November 2009 and 23 November 2010. The carry-back is again for three years but the losses are set against the company's total profits, not just profits of the same trade (see Chapter 26).

(c)   In certain circumstances, the trading losses of an individual may be set against capital gains (see Chapter 11). A company receives a similar relief by virtue of the fact that a company's capital gains are automatically included in its total profits.

(d)   Trading losses of an individual incurred in the opening years of a business may be relieved against total income of the previous three years. There is no equivalent relief for companies.

Note that a company's losses can be relieved only against the company's own income and gains, not against the income and gains of individual shareholders.

Chargeable gains

If an unincorporated business disposes of a chargeable asset, any gain that arises is assessed to capital gains tax on the owner of the business. The rate of tax for disposals occurring during tax year 2009-10 is 18%. The annual exemption is available.

The computational rules which apply when a company makes a chargeable disposal are somewhat different from those which apply for CGT. In particular, indexation allowance is available to companies but not to individuals. Gains arising in FY2009 are subject to corporation tax at either 21%, 28% or 29.75%. No annual exemption is available. Gains retained in the company increase the value of the company's shares, so resulting in an increased CGT liability when shareholders eventually dispose of their shares. In effect a gain may be taxed twice, first to corporation tax and then to CGT.

Close company loans to participators

As explained earlier in this chapter, close companies must pay tax when making loans to participators. A tax charge of this type can sometimes be triggered accidentally if a director who is also a shareholder overdraws his or her current account with the company. These provisions have no relevance to unincorporated businesses.

Incorporation

If the initial choice is to trade as an unincorporated business, the trader may still consider incorporation at some future time. Some of the main tax consequences of incorporation are as follows:

(a) The transfer of the assets of a business to a company might give rise to a CGT liability. However, subject to certain conditions, the gains arising may be held-over until the shares which were acquired in exchange for the business assets are disposed of (see Chapter 21).

(b) If the company is under the control of the person who was previously the owner of the unincorporated business, assets which are eligible for capital allowances can be transferred at their written down values for capital allowances purposes, so avoiding the need for balancing adjustments (see Chapter 10).

(c) The transfer of assets to the company will not be treated as a supply for VAT purposes so long as the business is transferred as a going concern and the company is a taxable person at the time of the transfer (see Chapter 29).

(d) If the proprietor of the unincorporated business has unrelieved trade losses, these cannot be carried forward and used by the company. However, subject to certain conditions, such unrelieved losses may be relieved against the proprietor's income from the company (see Chapter 11).

Summary

▸ A close company is one which is under the control of five or fewer participators or any number of participator-directors. The rights of the associates of a participator are aggregated with the participator's own rights when determining whether or not a company is a close company.

▸ Certain types of company (mainly listed companies with a substantial public interest) are excepted from close company status.

▸ Benefits in kind provided to the participators of a close company are treated as distributions. Loans to the participators are charged to tax.

▸ A close company is also a close investment-holding company unless it exists wholly or mainly for the purposes of trading or the letting of property. A close investment-holding company always pays corporation tax at the main rate.

▸ A company with investment business is a company whose business consists wholly or partly of making investments. Management expenses incurred by such companies are generally set against total income.

Exercises

27.1   Andrew Pearson is a shareholder of A Pearson (Nottingham) Ltd. Which of the following (if any) are his associates for the purposes of deciding whether the company is a close company?

(a)   his sister   (b)   his brother-in-law

(c)   his nephew   (d)   his father

(e)   his partner in a firm of solicitors.

27.2   The share capital of Romans Ltd consists of 5,000 ordinary shares, held as follows:

	Number of shares
Sejanus (a manager)	900
Claudius (a director)	400
Agrippa (a director)	300
Cleopatra (a director)	300
Tiberius (a director)	200
Gaius (a director)	200
Ptolemy	190
Livia (the grandmother of Claudius)	190
Apicata (the wife of Sejanus)	120
Others (all non-directors owning 10 shares or less)	2,200
Total	5,000

Is the company a close company?

27.3   On 31 October 2009, a close company which prepares accounts to 31 March each year provides one of its full-time working directors with:

(a)   an interest-free loan of £12,000 (the company does not provide loans in the ordinary course of its business)

(b)   a season ticket for the opera, costing the company £1,800.

Explain the tax treatment of these two items, assuming that the director in question owns 10% of the company's ordinary share capital.

*27.4   On 19 April 2008, a close company (which makes up accounts to 31 March annually) lends £100,000 to Siobhan, who is a director of the company and who owns 30% of its ordinary share capital. The company does not provide loans in the ordinary course of its business. Siobhan pays a commercial rate of interest on this loan until 1 October 2009, when she repays £55,000. She then continues to pay a commercial rate of interest on the remainder of the loan until it is written off by the company on 31 March 2010. Explain the tax implications of these transactions.

*27.5   A close company has the following results for the year to 31 March 2010:

	£
Income from letting property	89,000
Chargeable gains	600
Franked investment income	1,200

(a)   Compute the corporation tax payable for the year.

(b)   Would it make any difference if the property income were trading income instead?

(c)   Would it make any difference if the property income were a net credit on non-trading loan relationships instead?

Chapter 28

Groups of companies and reconstructions

Introduction

For corporation tax purposes, groups of companies are divided into a number of categories and each category enjoys certain tax advantages. These advantages may include:

(a) the transfer of trading losses and certain other deficits between group members

(b) the transfer of chargeable assets from one group member to another in such a way that no chargeable gain arises on the transfer.

However, group companies also incur certain tax disadvantages, principally a reduction in the small companies rate upper and lower limits. The main purpose of this chapter is to describe the categories of group which exist and the extent to which these advantages and disadvantages apply to each category. The tax implications of company reconstructions are also briefly considered in this chapter.

Associated companies

For taxation purposes, two companies are associated if one of the companies is under the control of the other or if they are both under the control of a third party, which may be an individual, a partnership or a company. In this context, the word "control" means the same as it does with regard to close companies (see Chapter 27). Control over a company is deemed to accompany:

(a) ownership of over 50% of the company's issued share capital or voting power, or

(b) entitlement to over 50% of the company's income or assets.

The main consequence of two or more companies being associated is that the small companies rate upper and lower limits are divided equally between the companies concerned. This is an anti-avoidance measure, designed to block the practice of breaking large companies into several smaller ones in order to take advantage of the small companies rate. The following points should be noted:

(a) Companies which are associated for only part of an accounting period are deemed to be associated for the entire period. However, if an accounting period straddles two FYs and the SCR limits have changed between those two FYs, the accounting period is treated as two separate "notional accounting periods" for this purpose.

(b) Associated companies which are dormant are ignored.

(c) Associated companies are counted whether or not they are resident in the UK. For instance, if a UK company has nine overseas subsidiaries, the upper and lower limits will be divided between all ten of the companies concerned, even though the overseas subsidiaries are outside the charge to UK corporation tax.

(d) If a company controls a second company which in turn controls a third company, then (for this purpose) the first company also controls the third company, even though it may own (indirectly) less than 50% of the third company's shares.

EXAMPLE 1

A Ltd owns 100% of the issued share capital of B Ltd and 70% of the issued share capital of C Ltd. C Ltd owns 70% of the issued share capital of D Ltd. Which of these companies are associated with one another?

Solution

A Ltd clearly controls B Ltd and C Ltd. Even though A Ltd (indirectly) owns only 49% of the issued share capital of D Ltd (70% x 70%), D Ltd is controlled by C Ltd which is controlled by A Ltd. Therefore A Ltd controls D Ltd as well and all four companies are associated.

EXAMPLE 2

S Ltd has chargeable profits of £120,000 for the six months to 30 September 2009 and no franked investment income. Until 1 July 2009 the company had no associated companies but, on that date, its entire share capital was acquired by H Ltd. H Ltd has five other wholly-owned subsidiaries, two of which are dormant. Compute S Ltd's corporation tax liability for the period.

Solution

S Ltd is deemed to have had four associated companies (H Ltd and its three active subsidiaries) throughout the entire accounting period. Therefore the small companies rate lower and upper limits are reduced to £60,000 and £300,000 respectively (one-fifth of their usual values). These are annual figures, which are multiplied by 6/12 for a six-month accounting period, giving £30,000 and £150,000. Profits of £120,000 fall between these limits, so marginal relief is available. The corporation tax computation is:

FY2009	£
£120,000 @ 28%	33,600.00

Less: Marginal relief:

$$\frac{7}{400} \text{ x } (£150,000 - £120,000) \text{ x } \frac{£120,000}{£120,000}$$

	525.00
Corporation tax liability	33,075.00

Transfer pricing

For many years, the UK tax system has contained "transfer pricing" rules which prevent UK companies from gaining a tax advantage by carrying out transactions at artificial prices with connected companies overseas (see Chapter 32). The transfer pricing rules require companies to compute their profits for corporation tax purposes as if the transactions in question had been carried out at "arm's length" (i.e. at the prices which would have applied between unconnected parties).

The original transfer pricing rules applied only to transactions with connected companies situated overseas, but these rules have now been extended to cover transactions between connected UK companies. Broadly, companies are connected for this purpose if one controls the other or they are under common control. The rules require an adjustment for tax purposes to the profits of the company which gains a potential tax advantage from the transactions and a corresponding adjustment to the profits of the other company.

Small and medium-sized companies are generally exempt from all of the transfer pricing legislation.

51% groups

Company B is said to be a 51% subsidiary of Company A if *all* of the following conditions are satisfied:

(a) Company A owns (directly or indirectly) over 50% of the ordinary share capital of Company B, and

(b) Company A is entitled to more than 50% of the profits available to the ordinary shareholders of Company B, and

(c) Company A would be entitled to more than 50% of the assets available to the ordinary shareholders of Company B if Company B were to be wound-up.

Two companies are members of a 51% group if one company is a 51% subsidiary of the other or they are both 51% subsidiaries of a third company.

By definition, members of a 51% group are also associated companies and so suffer from a reduction in the small companies rate upper and lower limits, as described above. On the other hand, 51% groups used to enjoy certain tax advantages. Most of these have now ceased to exist but there are still some tax provisions which relate specifically to 51% groups. These are as follows:

(a) Franked investment income received from a 51% subsidiary or from a fellow 51% subsidiary is disregarded when computing the profits of the receiving company for the purpose of determining the applicable rate of corporation tax (see Chapter 24).

(b) If at least one of the companies in a 51% group is liable to pay corporation tax by instalments (see Chapter 24) one of the group members may be nominated to pay all of the corporation tax due from all of the group members. In these circumstances, instalments are based upon the estimated tax liability of the group as a whole. When the total liability of each group member is finally determined, the instalments already paid may be allocated between the group members in such a way as to minimise any interest payable on underpaid instalments.

Shadow ACT and 51% groups

As explained in Chapter 25, any surplus ACT existing on 6 April 1999 is dealt with by means of the shadow ACT system. The shadow ACT regulations contain the following rules relating to 51% groups:

(a) If a member of a 51% group has surplus shadow ACT in an accounting period and that surplus cannot be carried back to accounting periods beginning on or after 6 April 1999 and during the previous six years, the surplus *must* be allocated (so far as is possible) to other companies in the group. This reduces the capacity of those other companies to relieve surplus ACT.

(b) The allocation should be performed by the parent company of the group. Failing this, the allocation will be done by HM Revenue and Customs.

(c) If the surplus to be allocated exceeds the total amount which can be utilised by all of the companies in the group, the excess is retained by the company in which the surplus arose and is carried forward to the next accounting period.

(d) Intra-group dividends are not treated as distributions when computing the shadow ACT of the paying company. Similarly, such dividends are not treated as FII when computing the shadow ACT of the receiving company.

(e) If a group company receives FII from outside the group, it may elect to pay an intra-group dividend of an equivalent amount and treat this dividend as a distribution. This election has the effect of transferring FII from one group company to another and allows the company which receives the intra-group dividend to reduce the shadow ACT arising on its own dividends.

75% groups

Company B is said to be a 75% subsidiary of Company A if *all* of the following conditions are satisfied:

(a) Company A owns (directly or indirectly) at least 75% of the ordinary share capital of Company B, and

(b) Company A is entitled to at least 75% of the profits available to the ordinary share-holders of Company B, and

(c) Company A would be entitled to at least 75% of the assets available to the ordinary shareholders of Company B if Company B were to be wound-up.

Two companies are members of a 75% group if one company is a 75% subsidiary of the other or they are both 75% subsidiaries of a third company.

The UK resident members of a 75% group benefit from two main tax reliefs. These are the right to transfer trading losses and certain other items between themselves ("group relief") and the transfer of chargeable assets between themselves in such a way that no chargeable gain arises on the transfer. These reliefs are described below.

EXAMPLE 3

P Ltd is the parent company of a small group. All companies in the group are UK resident and all of the issued shares of each company are ordinary shares. Shareholdings within the group are as follows:

(a) P Ltd owns 80% of Q Ltd, 100% of R Ltd and 60% of S Ltd.

(b) Q Ltd owns 90% of T Ltd.

(c) S Ltd owns 70% of W Ltd.

Identify associated companies, 51% subsidiaries and 75% subsidiaries within this group structure.

Solution

P Ltd controls Q Ltd (which controls T Ltd) , R Ltd and S Ltd (which controls W Ltd), so all six companies are associated.

P Ltd owns (indirectly) 72% of the ordinary share capital of T Ltd (80% x 90%) and 42% of the ordinary share capital of W Ltd (60% x 70%). Therefore:

(i) Q Ltd and R Ltd are 75% subsidiaries (and 51% subsidiaries) of P Ltd.

(ii) S Ltd and T Ltd are 51% subsidiaries of P Ltd.

(iii) T Ltd is a 75% subsidiary (and a 51% subsidiary) of Q Ltd.

(iv) W Ltd is a 51% subsidiary of S Ltd.

Group relief

Group relief consists of the surrender of trading losses and/or certain other items by one member of a 75% group (the "surrendering company") to another member of the same group (the "claimant company"). The main items which may be surrendered are:

(a) trading losses and deficits on non-trading loan relationships

(b) property business losses, non-trading losses on intangible fixed assets and charges on income.

Capital losses cannot be surrendered under the group relief rules, but a capital loss can in effect be transferred from one group company to another by a different means (see later in this chapter). Note the following points with regard to group relief:

(a) The surrender may be in whole or in part as best meets the requirements of the surrendering company and the claimant company. Trading losses and deficits on non-trading loan relationships may be surrendered even if they could instead be set against the profits of the accounting period in which they are incurred. The remaining items are available for surrender only to the extent that (in aggregate) they exceed the surrendering company's gross profits for the period in which they are incurred.

For this purpose, a company's "gross profits" are its profits before deducting amounts which are eligible for group relief and before deducting losses or other amounts carried forward or back from any other period.

(b) A surrender may be made from subsidiary to parent, from parent to subsidiary or from subsidiary to fellow subsidiary.

(c) Only current-period losses (or other items) are eligible for group relief and these must be set against the claimant company's profits for a *corresponding* accounting period. If the accounting periods of the surrendering company and the claimant company do not correspond exactly, group relief is available only in respect of the period of overlap between the two periods. The losses of the surrendering company and the profits of the claimant company are time-apportioned so as to determine the amounts which fall into the overlap period. A similar time-apportionment is required when a company joins or leaves a group part-way through an accounting period.

(d) The amount of losses and other items surrendered to a claimant company cannot exceed that company's profits for the corresponding accounting period, *before* deduction of any reliefs derived from a subsequent period but *after* deduction of:

- trading losses brought forward under Section 393(1)
- current-period trading losses which are relieved (or which could have been relieved) under Section 393A(1)(a)
- property business losses of the current period or previous periods
- deficits on non-trading loan relationships which are set against profits of the current period or brought forward from previous periods

- non-trading losses on intangible fixed assets which are set against profits of the current period or brought forward from previous periods

- charges for the accounting period.

The reference to "reliefs derived from a subsequent accounting period" means that group relief is given before relief for trading losses carried back and before relief for deficits on non-trading loan relationships carried back.

(e) A group relief claim must normally be made within two years of the end of the claimant company's accounting period.

(f) Any amount paid to the surrendering company by the claimant company as consideration for the surrendered items is ignored for tax purposes so long as the payment does not exceed the amount of the surrendered items.

(g) In certain circumstances, group relief may now be claimed in relation to losses incurred by foreign subsidiaries of UK parent companies (see Chapter 32).

EXAMPLE 4

Low Ltd is a wholly-owned subsidiary of High Ltd. Both companies are UK resident and prepare accounts to 31 March each year. Results for the year to 31 March 2010 are:

	High Ltd £	Low Ltd £
Trading profit/(loss)	100,000	(180,000)
Chargeable gains	5,000	75,000
Charges	12,000	-

Show how the trading loss sustained by Low Ltd may be relieved.

Solution

High Ltd has chargeable profits of £93,000 (£100,000 + £5,000 − £12,000). This sets an upper limit on the amount of group relief which may be claimed. The trading loss sustained by Low Ltd may be relieved in a number of ways. For example:

(a) The entire loss could be carried forward under s393(1).

(b) £75,000 of the loss could be relieved against the company's chargeable gains under s393A(1)(a) and the balance of £105,000 carried forward.

(c) The claim under s393A(1)(a) could be supplemented by a further claim under s393A(1)(b) to set the remaining £105,000 of the loss against the profits of Low Ltd for the previous three years (since the loss was incurred in a period ending between 24 November 2008 and 23 November 2010).

(d) Group relief of anything up to £93,000 could be claimed and the balance of the loss then dealt with as above.

EXAMPLE 5

L Ltd prepares accounts annually to 31 March and is a 75% subsidiary of H Ltd, which prepares accounts annually to 31 December. Both companies are UK resident. Recent results are as follows:

	H Ltd £	L Ltd £
Trading loss for year to 31 March 2009		(40,000)
Chargeable profits year to 31 December 2008	35,000	
Chargeable profits year to 31 December 2009	56,000	

Compute the amount of group relief that may be claimed.

Solution

The accounting periods of H Ltd and L Ltd do not correspond, so it is necessary to time-apportion profits and losses, as follows:

	1/4/08 - 31/12/08 (9 months) £	1/1/09 - 31/3/09 (3 months) £
(i) H Ltd profit	26,250	14,000
(ii) L Ltd loss	(30,000)	(10,000)

The group relief available in each period is the lower of (i) and (ii). Therefore, H Ltd may claim that group relief of up to £26,250 should be set against its 2008 profits and that group relief of up to £10,000 should be set against its 2009 profits. The remaining £3,750 of the loss is not eligible for group relief.

Using group relief effectively

Group relief should be used to ensure that trading losses (and other eligible items) are relieved as tax-effectively as possible and that the group's overall tax liability is minimised. Points to bear in mind are:

(a) Losses should be surrendered first to claimant companies which pay corporation tax (in FY2009) at the marginal rate of 29.75%, then to companies paying tax at the main rate of 28% and finally to companies paying tax at the small companies rate of 21%.

(b) Claimant companies should consider claiming less than the full amount of capital allowances available for an accounting period, so maximising the profits available for group relief set-off.

(c) A company which has incurred a trading loss should use the loss itself in a claim under s393A(1)(a) and s393A(1)(b) if this would save more tax than surrendering the loss to another group company.

Transfer of chargeable assets within a group

If a chargeable asset is transferred from one member of a 75% group to another, the transfer is deemed to have occurred at a value giving rise to neither a gain nor a loss. When an asset which has been transferred between group members in this way is finally disposed of outside the group, the chargeable gain arising on the disposal is then (in effect) calculated with reference to the original cost of the asset to the group.

The definition of a 75% group for this purpose is less rigorous than the definition given above in relation to group relief. A *capital gains group* consists of a principal company plus its 75% subsidiaries (as previously defined) plus the subsidiaries' 75% subsidiaries and so forth, subject to the over-riding requirement that the principal company must have more than a 50% interest in each member of the group.

EXAMPLE 6

J Ltd owns 80% of the ordinary share capital of K Ltd, which owns 80% of the share capital of L Ltd, which owns 80% of the share capital of M Ltd, which owns 80% of the share capital of N Ltd. All of these companies are UK resident. Which of the companies belongs to a capital gains group with J Ltd as the principal company?

Solution

At first sight, all five companies seem to belong to the capital gains group which has J Ltd at its head. However, J Ltd must have more than a 50% interest in each member of the group. J Ltd's actual interests in each member are as follows:

K Ltd	80%
L Ltd	80% x 80% = 64%
M Ltd	80% x 80% x 80% = 51.2%
N Ltd	80% x 80% x 80% x 80% = 40.96%

Therefore, N Ltd is not a member of this capital gains group.

Degrouping charge

A chargeable gain may arise in relation to an intra-group transfer if a company has a chargeable asset transferred to it from another group member and then leaves the group within six years of the date of the transfer. The company leaving the group is deemed to have sold the asset on the date of the intra-group transfer for its market value on that date (perhaps giving rise to a chargeable gain) and then immediately to have re-acquired the asset on the same date and for the same amount.

Any chargeable gain arising from this treatment is charged to tax in the accounting period in which the company leaves the group. However, such a gain may be treated as if it had accrued to another company in the group (subject to a joint election) and is also eligible for roll-over relief.

EXAMPLE 7

SubOne Ltd and SubTwo Ltd are members of a capital gains group. In January 2005, SubOne Ltd transferred a chargeable asset to SubTwo Ltd. The asset had originally cost £10,000 and its market value in January 2005 was £25,000. If the asset had been sold outside the group in January 2005, indexation allowance of £1,350 would have been available. In March 2009, SubTwo Ltd (which prepares accounts to 31 December each year) left the group. Calculate the chargeable gain arising on SubTwo Ltd's departure.

Solution

SubTwo Ltd is deemed to have sold the asset for £25,000 in January 2005 and then to have immediately re-acquired it for the same amount. The sale would have given rise to a chargeable gain of £13,650 (£25,000 − £10,000 − £1,350) so a chargeable gain of £13,650 arises in SubTwo Ltd's accounting period for the year to 31 December 2009.

Roll-over relief for capital gains groups

For the purposes of roll-over relief on the replacement of a business asset (see Chapter 21) all of the companies in a capital gains group are treated as a single company. This means that a gain arising on the disposal of a business asset by one member of a group can be rolled-over against the cost of a qualifying business asset acquired by any other member of the same group.

It is important to note that the qualifying business asset against which a gain is rolled-over must be an asset which has been newly acquired *by the group as a whole*. It is not possible to roll-over a gain against an asset which has been acquired by one group member from another.

Capital losses

Capital losses cannot be surrendered to another member of the group. This is in contrast to the treatment of trading losses and certain other items which can be surrendered (see above). At one time, the only way around this problem was to transfer assets between group members in such a way that chargeable gains and capital losses arose in the same company. Imagine that Company L and Company G were both members of a capital gains group, that Company L had capital losses and that Company G was about to dispose of an asset and realise a chargeable gain. Company L's capital losses could be set against this gain in the following way:

(a) Company G could transfer its asset to Company L (on a no gain/no loss basis).

(b) Company L could then dispose of the asset. The gain arising would in this way be realised by Company L rather than Company G, so allowing Company L's losses to be set against it.

However a simpler procedure is now available. Two companies that are members of a 75% group may jointly elect that all or part of the gain (or loss) arising on a disposal by one of the companies should be treated as if it had been realised (or incurred) by the other company. This allows gains and losses to be brought together in the same company without having to actually transfer assets between group members. The election must be made within two years of the end of the accounting period in which the disposal occurs.

Pre-entry capital losses

A group which anticipates making disposals which will give rise to substantial chargeable gains might try to shelter those gains from tax by acquiring a "capital loss company". This is a company which has capital losses brought forward or assets which would realise capital losses on disposal. The intention of the acquisition would be to set these capital losses against the group's chargeable gains (by means of the procedure outlined above) and so reduce the group's overall corporation tax liability.

Anti-avoidance legislation exists which prevents groups from gaining a tax advantage in this way. This legislation applies only if certain conditions are satisfied. These conditions are as follows:

(a) There must be a change of ownership of the company concerned. (This condition is satisfied if the company joins a group).

(b) The change of ownership must occur in connection with "arrangements", of which one of the main purposes is to secure a tax advantage.

If these conditions are satisfied, the anti-avoidance legislation applies and it is not possible to set the acquired capital losses against the group's chargeable gains. However, if the conditions are *not* satisfied (e.g. if the existence of the necessary "arrangements" cannot be demonstrated) there is in any case a restriction on the amount of relief available in relation to *pre-entry capital losses*. A company's pre-entry capital losses (see below) may be set only against gains arising on disposals of the following types of asset:

(a) assets which the company owned before it joined the group ("pre-entry assets")

(b) assets acquired by the company *from outside the group* since joining the group.

The "pre-entry capital losses" of a company are defined as:

(a) any capital losses incurred by the company before joining the group, and

(b) the pre-entry part of any capital losses incurred by the company after joining the group on the disposal of pre-entry assets.

The pre-entry part of a capital loss incurred on the disposal of a pre-entry asset is derived by applying a formula to each item of allowable expenditure in the computation of the loss and then aggregating the results. The formula used is:

$$A \times \frac{B}{C} \times \frac{D}{E}$$

where: A = the total amount of the allowable loss

  B = the amount of the item of allowable expenditure

  C = the sum of the amounts of all the items of allowable expenditure

  D = the length of time between the date of the expenditure (or 1 April 1982, if later) and the date of joining the group

  E = the length of time between the date of the expenditure (or 1 April 1982, if later) and the date of disposal.

EXAMPLE 8

A company acquired a chargeable asset on 1 January 2000 at a cost of £200,000 and incurred enhancement expenditure of £50,000 on 1 January 2004. The company joined a capital gains group on 1 April 2009 and the asset was sold on 1 September 2009 for £130,000. Calculate the total loss arising on this disposal and the amount of the pre-entry loss (working to the nearest whole month).

Solution

	£	£
Sale proceeds		130,000
<u>Less</u>: Cost	200,000	
Enhancement expenditure	50,000	250,000
Allowable loss		(120,000)

Notes:

(i) Indexation allowance is £nil, since indexation allowance cannot be used to increase an unindexed loss.

(ii) The asset was originally acquired 111 months before joining the group and 116 months before disposal. The enhancement expenditure was incurred 63 months before joining the group and 68 months before disposal.

(iii) The pre-entry loss is:

$$(£120,000 \times \frac{£200,000}{£250,000} \times \frac{111}{116}) + (£120,000 \times \frac{£50,000}{£250,000} \times \frac{63}{68}) = £114,097.$$

Consortia

A company is owned by a consortium and is known as a *consortium company* if at least 75% of its ordinary share capital is owned by other companies (who are known as *consortium members*) each of which:

(a) owns at least 5% but less than 75% of the consortium company's ordinary share capital, and

(b) is entitled to at least 5% of the profits available to the consortium company's ordinary shareholders, and

(c) would be entitled to at least 5% of the assets available to the consortium company's ordinary shareholders on a winding-up.

A 90% subsidiary of a consortium company is also a consortium company.

Group relief for a consortium

Group relief is available in either direction between a consortium member and a consortium company, so long as both companies are UK resident and the consortium company is either a trading company or a company whose business consists wholly or mainly of holding shares in trading companies which are its 90% subsidiaries. Note the following points with regard to group relief for a consortium:

(a) The relief is restricted in proportion to the consortium member's shareholding in the consortium company. For instance, if CC Ltd is a consortium company and CM Ltd is a consortium member which owns x% of CC Ltd, CM Ltd may claim up to x% of CC Ltd's losses. Alternatively, CM Ltd may surrender to CC Ltd losses of up to x% of CC Ltd's profits.

(b)   A group relief claim must be agreed by all the consortium members.

(c)   The amount of a consortium company's trading loss which is available for group relief is the amount of that loss less any potential claim for loss relief under s393A(1)(a), whether or not such a claim is actually made.

EXAMPLE 9

The ordinary share capital of W Ltd (a UK trading company) is owned 30% by X Ltd, 25% by Y Ltd and 45% by Z Ltd. All companies are UK resident and prepare accounts to 31 March annually. Results for the year to 31 March 2010 are as follows:

	W Ltd £	X Ltd £	Y Ltd £	Z Ltd £
Trading profit/(loss)	(62,000)	41,000	11,000	38,000
Chargeable gains	10,000	-	-	-

What are the maximum possible group relief claims which may be made?

Solution

The amount of W Ltd's loss which is available for group relief is £52,000 (£62,000 less a potential s393A(1)(a) claim of £10,000, whether or not that claim is actually made). This is shared between the consortium members in proportion to their shares in the consortium, as follows:

	X Ltd £	Y Ltd £	Z Ltd £
Share of W Ltd's available loss	15,600	13,000	23,400
Chargeable profits	41,000	11,000	38,000
Maximum group relief claim	15,600	11,000	23,400

Company reconstructions

If a company transfers a trade to another company, this ranks as a cessation of that trade and unrelieved trading losses incurred before the date of the transfer cannot normally be carried forward under s393(1) and set against the subsequent profits of the transferred trade. But if a trade is transferred between two companies (both within the charge to UK corporation tax in respect of that trade) and at least 75% of the trade is effectively owned by the same persons both:

(a) at some time within the year before the date of the transfer, and

(b) at some time within the two years after the date of the transfer

then any unrelieved trading losses of the transferor company may be carried forward and set against subsequent profits (from the same trade) of the transferee company. For instance, this "succession of trade" relief would be available if a company created a new 75% subsidiary and then transferred a trade to that subsidiary. However, this relief does not extend to non-trading losses or capital losses, neither of which can be carried forward from the transferor company to the transferee company.

Subject to certain conditions, the following provisions also apply to such "company reconstructions":

(a) For capital allowances purposes, assets are transferred at their tax-written down values, with no balancing adjustments.

(b) Chargeable business assets are transferred to the transferee company on a no-gain, no-loss basis, as long as the transferor company receives no consideration for the assets and the assets remain within the scope of UK corporation tax.

Summary

▶ Two companies are associated if one of the companies is under the control of the other, or if they are both under the control of a third party.

▶ The small companies rate upper and lower limits are shared equally between associated companies.

▶ Transfer pricing rules apply to transactions carried out an artificial prices between group companies.

▶ Trading losses and certain other items may be surrendered between members of a 75% group. This is known as "group relief".

▶ Chargeable assets may be transferred between members of a capital gains group without giving rise to a chargeable gain.

▶ Subject to certain conditions, group relief is available between consortium members and consortium companies.

▶ If a trade is transferred between two companies, the unrelieved trading losses of the transferor company may (subject to certain conditions) be carried forward and set against the subsequent trading profits of the transferee company.

Exercises

28.1 Arm Ltd and Foot Ltd are both 100% subsidiaries of Head Ltd, which has no other subsidiaries. They are all UK resident. How will the relationship of the three companies affect the way in which they are taxed?

28.2 Alpha Ltd is a wholly-owned subsidiary of Beta Ltd, which has two other wholly-owned subsidiaries (one of which is dormant). In the year to 31 March 2010, Alpha Ltd has the following results:

	£
Trading profits	220,000
Bank deposit interest	6,000
Income from property	4,000
UK dividend received from non-group company on 1 May 2009	27,000
Charges paid	17,000

Compute the corporation tax liability for the year.

28.3   Base Ltd is a wholly-owned subsidiary of Apex Ltd. Both companies are UK resident and prepare accounts annually to 31 March. The results for the year to 31 March 2010 are as follows:

	Apex Ltd £	Base Ltd £
Trading profit/(loss)	120,000	(90,000)
Trading losses b/f under s393(1)	(42,000)	(19,000)
Income from property	7,000	3,000
Charges paid	12,000	4,000

Calculate the maximum group relief that may be claimed for the year by Apex Ltd.

28.4   A1 Ltd owns 90% of the ordinary share capital of A2 Ltd. A2 Ltd owns 80% of the ordinary share capital of A3 Ltd and 70% of the ordinary share capital of A4 Ltd. Which of these companies (all UK resident) form a capital gains group with A1 Ltd as its principal company?

28.5   The ordinary share capital of PP Ltd (a UK trading company) is owned 32% by QQ Ltd, 35% by RR Ltd, 23% by SS Ltd. The remaining 10% is owned by various individuals, none of whom own more than 1%. All companies are UK resident and prepare accounts to 31 July annually. Results for the year to 31 July 2009 are as follows:

	PP Ltd £	QQ Ltd £	RR Ltd £	SS Ltd £
Trading profit/(loss)	(96,000)	41,000	38,000	11,000
Chargeable gains	-	15,000	-	-
Bank interest receivable	12,000	6,000	11,000	4,000
Charges paid	-	(3,000)	(2,000)	(1,000)

Compute the maximum possible group relief claims.

*__28.6__   T Ltd has owned 90% of the ordinary share capital of B Ltd for many years. Both are UK resident. Recent results for the two companies are as follows:

	T Ltd y/e 31/3/09 £	T Ltd y/e 31/3/10 £	B Ltd y/e 30/11/09 £
Trading profit/(loss)	190,000	130,000	(174,000)
Chargeable gains	25,000	13,000	3,000
Charges paid	5,000	5,000	-

No dividends have been paid or received by either company in any of these accounting periods and maximum group relief is claimed. Calculate the corporation tax which is payable by each company for each accounting period, making and stating any necessary assumptions.

Review questions (Set C)

C1   Tolbooth Ltd is a small manufacturing company. It commenced trading on 1 April 2008 and prepared its first set of accounts for the 18 month period to 30 September 2009. As the accounting technician responsible for preparing the tax computation, you have extracted the following information from the audit file:

		£
(i)	Trading profits (before capital allowances)	390,000

(ii) Rental income:
     £20,000 per year from property rented on 1 April 2008.
     Rent received annually in advance on 1 April.

(iii) Bank deposit interest:

	Received 30 June 2008	2,000
	Received 31 December 2008	2,000
	Accrued to 31 March 2009	1,000
	Received 30 June 2009	12,000
	Accrued to 30 September 2009	4,000

(iv) Plant and machinery was purchased on
     30 June 2008, costing   120,000

(v) Charges paid:

	Paid 31 December 2008	5,000
	Accrued to 31 March 2009	2,500
	Paid 30 June 2009	5,000
	Accrued to 30 September 2009	2,500

(vi) Chargeable gain on disposal 1 August 2009   10,000

Required:

(a) State how the first period of account to 30 September 2009 will be divided into accounting periods.

(b) Calculate the corporation tax liability for each accounting period.

(Amended from AAT)

C2   P Ltd is in receipt of periodic payments in respect of patent royalties and pays debenture interest twice in each accounting period. Income tax is deducted at source from both the royalties and the debenture interest. The following is a list, in date order, of the various transactions of these types during the year to 31 March 2010 (amounts are shown net):

		£
10/5/09	Patent royalties received	28,160
12/7/09	Debenture interest paid	36,000
30/8/09	Patent royalties received	17,600
24/11/09	Debenture interest paid	41,600
15/1/10	Patent royalties received	24,640

The directors wish to have information on the cash inflows and outflows arising from the taxation associated with each transaction.

You are required:

To calculate, by means of quarterly settlement statements for income tax, the amounts which became payable and/or recoverable in each case, stating the date (or approximate date) concerned. *(CIMA)*

C3   Poynton Producers Ltd, who make up annual accounts to 30 September, purchased a new industrial building for £150,000 on 1 April 2001. The building was not in an enterprise zone and was brought into industrial use immediately. On 31 August 2003, production ceased and the building was leased to a national charity as a collection centre. Production in the factory re-commenced on 1 February 2005. On 1 April 2008, the building was sold to Sale Switches Ltd, who make up annual accounts to 31 December, for £140,000. It was brought into industrial use immediately.

You are required to:

(a)   calculate the Industrial Buildings Allowances for all accounting periods when the building was owned by Poynton Producers Ltd

(b)   state the balancing adjustment on the sale of the building in 2008

(c)   calculate the Industrial Buildings Allowances claimable in respect of the building by Sale Switches Ltd in all periods (perform calculations to the nearest month). *(ACCA)*

C4   Unusual Urns Limited is a UK resident company. It has no associated companies. Recent results are as follows:

	Year to *30 September 2008* £	*6 months to* *31 March 2009* £
Trading profit/(loss)	210,000	(150,000)
Gift Aid donations	1,500	750

The company's chargeable profits for the year to 31 March 2010 are expected to be approximately £700,000, derived mostly from trading income. The company receives no dividends.

You are required:

(a)   to state the alternative methods by which the company can obtain relief for the loss of £150,000 sustained in the period to 31 March 2009, and

(b)   to state, with your reasons, which of these alternatives you would choose so as to obtain the maximum tax advantage when claiming relief in respect of the £150,000 loss. You should also state the effect that your proposed treatment will have on the charges on income paid by the company.   *(ACCA)*

C5   Antietam Ltd makes up accounts to 31 March annually. Results for the 12 months to 31 March 2010 are as follows:

	£
Trading profits (before capital allowances)	170,000
Capital allowances	32,000
Rental income	46,000
Capital gains	6,400

The company has capital losses brought forward from previous accounting periods of £1,400 and made a Gift Aid donation of £20,000 on 31 March 2010. It also received a dividend from ICI plc on 16 December 2009 of £14,400.

Required:

(a)   Calculate the corporation tax liability of Antietam Ltd for the year to 31 March 2010.

(b)   Recalculate the liability if you are told that the company has one subsidiary company.   *(Amended from AAT)*

*C6   Undulating Uplands Ltd is a UK resident manufacturing company with no associated companies. It had always made up accounts to 30 November but decided to change the year end from November to February. The company's results for the period from 1 December 2008 to 28 February 2010 are as follows:

	Notes	£
Adjusted trading profit		750,000
Dividends received from UK companies	1	45,000
Bank interest received	2,5	13,500
Building society interest received	3,5	8,400
Gift Aid donations	4	16,000
Capital allowances on plant and machinery	10	65,000

The following additional information is available:

1.   Dividends were received from UK companies as follows:

	£
30 December 2008	7,200
30 March 2009	10,800
30 September 2009	9,000
30 January 2010	18,000

2.   Bank interest was credited by Natland Bank plc as follows:

	£
21 December 2008	4,900
20 June 2009	3,800
21 December 2009	4,800

Accrued interest was £4,500 on 30 November 2008, £4,300 on 30 November 2009 and £4,000 on 28 February 2010.

3.   Building society interest was credited by Northshires Building Society as follows:

	£
31 March 2009	4,000
30 September 2009	4,400

The account was opened on 1 December 2008 and closed on 30 September 2009.

4.   The Gift Aid donations were paid as follows:

	£
15 May 2009	8,000
15 November 2009	8,000

5.   The amounts shown for bank and building society interest received are the actual amounts received.

6.   The company had trading losses brought forward of £400,000 on 1 December 2008.

7.   The company had capital losses brought forward of £15,000 on 1 December 2008.

8.   On 1 March 2009, the company bought a factory which qualifies for Industrial Buildings Allowances (IBAs) from the original owner for £450,000. The factory was first brought into qualifying use by the original owner on 1 March 1990 and had a tax written down value prior to the sale of £250,000.

9.   The company had purchased a new factory, which qualified for IBAs, on 1 January 2004 for £150,000. It was brought into use immediately. The factory was sold on 1 January 2010 for £350,000 and an appropriate claim was made to minimise the chargeable gain. (The RPI was 183.1 in January 2004 and 216.0 in January 2010.)

10.   The capital allowances figure of £65,000 comprised:

	£
12 months to 30 November 2009	39,000
3 months to 28 February 2010	26,000

You are required:

To calculate the corporation tax liability for the period to 28 February 2010 and to state when this is payable (perform all calculations to the nearest month).   *(ACCA)*

*C7   R Ltd is a small company engaged in the manufacture and distribution of plumbing equipment. Following a period of poor trading results, its annual chargeable profit in recent years has been approximately £180,000. Early in 2009 the directors estimated that the chargeable profit for the year to 31 March 2010 would be £220,000.

In March 2009, the directors were considering the possibility of R Ltd acquiring a controlling interest in two other small companies in the same trade - S Ltd and T Ltd. The chargeable profit of each of these companies for the year to 31 March 2010 was estimated at £20,000.

You are required:

To advise the directors of the differing aggregate corporation tax liabilities which will arise for the year to 31 March 2010 if:

(i)   the above plan is adopted

(ii)   R Ltd acquires the businesses of S Ltd and T Ltd - taking over their assets, trades and workforces, but not acquiring a shareholding. S Ltd and T Ltd would then be wound up.   *(CIMA)*

*C8   On 1 August 2006 X Ltd granted a 20-year lease to Y Ltd on the following terms:

- An annual rental of £20,000, payable quarterly in advance on 1 August, 1 November, 1 February and 1 May each year.

- A premium of £80,000 payable by Y Ltd on 1 August 2006.

On 1 April 2009, Y Ltd intends sub-letting the premises to Z Ltd on the following terms:

- A term of five years, at the end of which Y Ltd will resume occupancy.

- An annual rental of £28,000, payable in advance each year on 1 April.

- A premium of £45,000 payable by Z Ltd on 1 April 2009.

You are required:

(a)   To compute, for the year to 31 March 2007, the amount of property income assessed to corporation tax on X Ltd and the amount of the premium which Y Ltd may deduct in arriving at its trading profits chargeable to corporation tax. Assume that both companies make up accounts annually to 31 March.

(b)   To compute the amount of property income assessed to corporation tax on Y Ltd for its year to 31 March 2010.

(c)   To comment briefly on the capital gains implications of the above transactions.

(CIMA)

*C9   Mr B has been production manager in a large engineering firm for several years, earning approximately £50,000 p.a. He has recently decided to start up his own business and seeks your advice on all of the differences, from a taxation point of view, between trading as a sole trader or as a limited company. It is possible that his wife will become involved in the running of the business.

He has estimated that during the first year, while the business is developing, it is unlikely that any profit will result. Indeed, it is possible that a loss will arise. Thereafter he anticipates that profits will rise rapidly to approximately £70,000 p.a. His living expenses amount to about £20,000 per year and initially this will be provided from his savings.

You are required:

To prepare a list of headings which would be contained in a report designed to highlight these differences. Under each heading, you should give a brief description of the difference between trading as a sole trader or as a company. You are not required to write the complete report.
(CIMA)

*C10 HD Ltd owns 80% of the ordinary share capital of SD Ltd. These shares were acquired during 1995. Both companies are UK resident for tax purposes and neither has any other associated companies. Their most recent results have been:

	HD Ltd y/e 31/12/09 £	SD Ltd 9 months to 31/3/10 £
INCOME		
Trading profit	890,000	-
Trading loss	-	(102,000)
Bank interest	6,000	4,000
Property income	2,000	8,000
Capital gains	-	20,000
Capital losses brought forward	(15,000)	-
Dividend from SD Ltd	27,000	
Dividends from UK companies		32,000
CHARGES PAID		
Gift Aid donations	4,000	5,000
DIVIDEND PAID	327,000	33,750

You are required:

(a) To compute the corporation tax payable by each company for the above accounting periods, assuming that maximum group relief is claimed by HD Ltd.

(b) To suggest a more tax-efficient way in which HD Ltd and SD Ltd might have dealt with the capital gains and losses shown above.

(CIMA)

Part 4

MISCELLANEOUS

end of the quarter. A balancing payment is due one month after the end of the quarter. All of these payments must be made electronically (e.g. by means of the Bankers Automated Clearing System (BACS)).

Each of the two payments on account is usually calculated as 1/24th of the person's total VAT liability for the previous year. However, the person concerned may choose to pay the actual VAT liability for each month rather than the set POAs.

The tax point

The date on which a supply is deemed to occur is known as the "tax point" of that supply. The tax point of a supply determines:

(a)   for outputs, the tax period in which the tax on that supply must be accounted for

(b)   for inputs, the tax period in which the tax on that supply may be reclaimed

(c)   the rate of VAT applicable to the supply (if VAT rates change).

For a supply of goods the "basic tax point" is the date on which the goods are removed or made available to the customer. For a supply of services the basic tax point is the date on which the services are performed. However, the actual tax point of a supply will differ from the basic tax point in the following circumstances:

(a)   If the supplier issues a tax invoice or receives payment on a date which is earlier than the basic tax point, then the actual tax point is the date on which the invoice is issued or payment is received, whichever occurs first.

(b)   Otherwise, if the supplier issues a tax invoice within 14 days after the basic tax point, then the invoice date becomes the actual tax point.

HMRC may extend the 14-day rule mentioned above if asked to do so by a registered person who is genuinely unable to issue invoices within 14 days of the basic tax point. This may occur if customer invoice prices cannot be determined until the business has received suppliers' invoices for materials etc.

Tax invoices

If a taxable person makes a taxable supply to another taxable person, a "tax invoice" must be issued. The purpose of this invoice is to provide documentary evidence of the transaction, so allowing the person receiving the supply to reclaim the input tax related to that supply. The required contents of a valid tax invoice (which may be on paper or issued electronically) are:

(a)   the invoice number, date and tax point

(b)   the name, address and VAT registration number of the supplier

(c)   the name and address of the customer

(d)   for each invoice item, a description of the goods or services supplied

(e)   for each description, the quantity of the goods or the extent of the services, the unit price, the amount payable (before VAT) and the rate of VAT applicable.

(f)   the total amount due, before VAT

(g)   the rate of any cash discount available

(h)   the total amount of VAT chargeable.

The issue of a tax invoice is optional if a supply is made to a customer who is not a taxable person. Retailers are not required to issue a tax invoice unless asked for one by the customer and may then issue a less detailed tax invoice if the consideration for the supply does not exceed £250. A less detailed tax invoice need show only:

(a)   the name, address and VAT registration number of the retailer

(b)   the tax point

(c)   a description of the goods or services supplied

(d)   the total amount payable by the customer, including VAT

(e)   for each rate of VAT chargeable, the gross amount payable (including VAT) and the rate of tax which is applicable.

Accounting records

Every taxable person must keep such records as are required by HMRC. The main records which must be kept are as follows:

(a)   business and accounting records (including orders, delivery notes, business correspondence, purchases and sales books, cashbooks and other account books, till rolls, bank statements, paying-in slips and annual accounts)

(b)   a VAT account

(c)   a copy of each tax invoice issued

(d)   all tax invoices received, though tax invoices are not required for payments of £25 or less relating to telephone calls, parking fees or purchases made through coin-operated machines

(e)   documentation relating to imports and exports.

HMRC may also specify additional record-keeping requirements for all businesses of a particular description and (in cases where additional records might assist in identifying supplies on which VAT might otherwise go unpaid) for individual businesses.

All records must be retained for a period of six years or for such lesser period as HMRC may allow. HMRC is empowered to require a taxable person to provide their VAT records for inspection and is also empowered to inspect these records at the business premises.

Special schemes

The VAT system offers a number of special schemes which are intended to simplify the workings of the VAT system, especially for smaller businesses. The main schemes are as follows:

(a)   the cash accounting scheme

(b)   the annual accounting scheme

(c)   the flat-rate scheme for small businesses

(d)   the flat-rate scheme for farmers

(e)   the margin scheme for second-hand goods.

Each of these schemes is explained below. There are also several special schemes for use only by retailers. These "retail schemes" are explained later in this chapter.

Cash accounting scheme

A registered person whose taxable turnover is not expected to exceed £1,350,000 in the next 12 months may opt to join the cash accounting scheme. Those who belong to this scheme account for output tax in the tax period in which *payment is received* from the customer and reclaim input tax in the tax period in which *payment is made* to the supplier. The tax point is ignored when allocating inputs and outputs to tax periods.

Joining this scheme allows a registered person to delay the payment of output tax to HMRC until the tax has actually been received from customers, which is beneficial if customers are given extended credit. The scheme also provides automatic relief for bad debts. On the other hand, input tax cannot be reclaimed until the tax has actually been paid to suppliers. A person may not join the cash accounting scheme unless:

(a)   the person's taxable turnover (excluding sales of capital items) is not expected to exceed £1,350,000 in the next 12 months

(b)   the person's VAT returns are up to date

(c)   all amounts due to be paid to HMRC have in fact been paid, or the person has come to an arrangement for such payments to be made by instalments

(d)   within the previous 12 months, the person has not been convicted of a VAT offence or assessed to a penalty for VAT evasion involving dishonest conduct.

A person who belongs to the cash accounting scheme must withdraw from the scheme at the end of a tax period if taxable turnover for the 12 months to date has exceeded £1,600,000. HMRC will allow such a person to remain in the scheme only if it can be demonstrated that the high turnover is not expected to recur and that taxable turnover for the next 12 months is expected to be no more than £1,350,000.

The cash accounting scheme cannot be used for supplies of goods and services which are invoiced before the supply is made or for supplies where payment is not due for more than six months after the date of the invoice.

Annual accounting scheme

A person with a taxable turnover which is not expected to exceed £1,350,000 in the next 12 months may apply to join the annual accounting scheme and submit only one VAT return per year. The scheme operates as follows:

(a) During the year the person makes nine interim payments to HMRC, each equal to 10% of the VAT liability for the previous year. These payments must be made by direct debit or by other electronic means and begin in the fourth month of the year.

(b) Optionally, the person may choose to make three interim payments in months four, seven and ten rather than the nine payments referred to above. In this case, each payment is equal to 25% of the VAT liability for the previous year.

(c) If a person joins the annual accounting scheme when first registering for VAT (or less than 12 months after registration), the interim payments are based initially upon the person's expected VAT liability for the year.

(d) At the end of the year the annual return is submitted together with a final payment consisting of the balance of the VAT liability. The return and payment must be made within two months of the end of the year.

(e) A person who operates the annual accounting scheme must withdraw from the scheme if taxable turnover exceeds £1,600,000 for the previous year.

The advantages of the scheme include a reduction in the number of VAT returns each year (usually from four to one) and more predictable cash flows. Furthermore, there is an extra month at the end of the year in which to complete the annual return and to pay any VAT which is due.

Flat-rate scheme for small businesses

An eligible business which is registered for VAT may opt to join the flat-rate scheme (FRS) for small businesses. This scheme enables a small business to calculate its VAT liability as a flat-rate percentage of total turnover and so avoids the need to keep detailed records of input tax and output tax. The FRS operates as follows:

(a) Output tax is charged to customers at the normal rate for the supply. Similarly, input tax is paid to suppliers at the normal rate. However, the output tax charged to customers is not paid over to HMRC and (in general) input tax cannot be recovered.

(b) In each tax period, a flat-rate percentage is applied to the VAT-inclusive turnover for the period (including the value of any exempt supplies). The result of this calculation is the amount of VAT payable to HMRC for the period.

(c) The applicable flat-rate percentage depends upon the trade sector in which the business operates. With a standard rate of 17.5%, the flat-rate percentage ranges from 2% to 13.5% (*or 2% to 12% with a standard rate of 15%*).

(d) Input tax on the purchase of capital assets costing at least £2,000 (including VAT) can be reclaimed in the usual way, in which case output tax must be accounted for in the usual way on the eventual disposal of the asset.

(e) The FRS can be used in conjunction with the annual accounting scheme. It *cannot* be used in conjunction with the cash accounting scheme, the retail schemes or the margin scheme for second-hand goods. However, the FRS offers an optional cash-based turnover method and an optional retailer's turnover method.

The FRS is available to businesses with a taxable turnover which is not expected to exceed £150,000 in the next 12 months. A business must leave the FRS if its VAT-inclusive income exceeds £225,000 during any 12-month period ending on an anniversary of the date that it joined the scheme.

Flat-rate scheme for farmers

In general, a farmer making taxable supplies which exceed the registration threshold is liable to register for VAT in the normal way. Similarly, a farmer whose taxable supplies are below the threshold may register voluntarily. Since farmers make mainly zero-rated supplies, a farmer who is registered will usually receive regular repayments of input tax, at the expense of maintaining the necessary VAT records.

An alternative to registration is the flat-rate scheme for farmers. This scheme is available to farmers regardless of the size of their taxable turnover and is intended to reduce administrative costs. The scheme operates as follows:

(a) A farmer who joins the scheme does not register for VAT. This reduces administrative costs but deprives the farmer of the opportunity to reclaim input tax.

(b) In compensation, the farmer is allowed to add a flat-rate 4% to his or her selling prices and to retain this addition. The flat-rate addition may be charged only when selling designated goods or services to VAT-registered persons.

(c) From the point of view of a taxable person buying goods from a flat-rate farmer, the flat-rate addition is treated as input tax and may be reclaimed, subject to the usual rules.

A farmer may not join this scheme if the total of the flat-rate additions which would be charged if the farmer were a member of the scheme exceeds the total amount of input tax which the farmer would otherwise be entitled to reclaim by £3,000 p.a. or more.

Margin scheme for second-hand goods

In general, VAT is charged on the full value of goods sold, regardless of whether those goods are new or second-hand. However, subject to certain conditions, a taxable person selling second-hand goods may choose to sell them through the margin scheme and charge VAT only on his or her profit margin. The scheme operates as follows:

(a) VAT is charged only on the seller's profit margin. This is the difference between the price at which the goods were obtained and their selling price.

(b) The seller's profit margin is deemed to be VAT-inclusive, so that the amount of tax due is calculated by multiplying this margin by the VAT fraction.

(c) Any expenses incurred by the seller (e.g. the costs of restoration, repairs, spare parts and so forth) are ignored when establishing the amount of the profit margin.

(d) The sales invoice must include a declaration to the effect that input tax has not been reclaimed (and will not be reclaimed) by the seller in respect of the goods concerned.

(e) The buyer of the goods cannot reclaim the input tax suffered, even if he or she is a taxable person.

The margin scheme is intended mainly for those who deal in second-hand goods. The main conditions which must be satisfied for the scheme to be used are that the goods concerned are second-hand and that they were acquired either on a supply on which no VAT was chargeable (e.g. the goods were acquired from a member of the public or a non-registered business) or from someone who also sold the goods under the margin scheme.

EXAMPLE 1

An antiques dealer buys a table from a member of the public for £2,000. The dealer spends a further £500 on restoration work and then sells the table for £5,000. Compute the output tax which must be accounted for in relation to this sale, assuming that the table is sold through the margin scheme.

Solution

The dealer's margin is £3,000, ignoring the restoration costs. The output tax due is therefore £3,000 x 7/47 = £446.81.

Bad debts

If a taxable person makes use of the cash accounting scheme, the output tax relating to a supply is not accounted for until the consideration for that supply has been received and so automatic relief is given for bad debts. But persons who do not use the cash accounting scheme might account for the output tax relating to a supply before the consideration for that supply is received and then find that a bad debt has occurred. In these circumstances, a claim may be made for a refund of the VAT lost, so long as:

(a) goods or services have been supplied for a consideration and the related output tax has been accounted for to HMRC

(b) the value of the supply was no more than its open market value

(c) the debt has been written off in the books of account

(d) at least six months have elapsed since both the date of the supply and the date that payment was due

(e) the claim for bad debt relief is made within three years and six months from the later of the date of the supply and the date that payment was due.

Any business that has made a claim to recover the input tax relating to a supply but has not paid the supplier within six months of the date of that supply (or the date on which payment was due, if later) must repay the input tax to HMRC.

Non-deductible input tax

In general, a taxable person can reclaim the input tax relating to a supply so long as the supply is evidenced by a tax invoice and the goods or services involved are for use in the person's business. However, input tax is not reclaimable on certain types of supply, even though the supply is received in the course of business. The main examples of such "non-deductible input tax" are:

(a) VAT on business entertainment provided to clients, although there is now some doubt as to whether this input tax block applies if entertainment is supplied to overseas clients (the situation is under review).

(b) VAT on costs incurred by a company in relation to the provision of domestic accommodation for a director of the company.

(c) VAT on the purchase of motor cars, apart from:

  (i) cars acquired by a car dealer, as stock in trade

  (ii) cars acquired for use by a driving school, car rental business or taxi business

  (iii) cars acquired *wholly* for business use.

  If the input tax on the purchase of a car cannot be reclaimed, the subsequent sale of that car should be treated as an exempt supply.

(d) VAT on second-hand goods that are to be sold under the margin scheme (see earlier in this chapter).

The VAT on goods or services which are not used at all for business purposes cannot be reclaimed. If goods or services are used partly for business purposes and partly for private purposes, then there are two possible treatments. Either:

(a) the input tax on the supply is apportioned and the business element of the tax is then reclaimed, or

(b) the whole of the input tax on the supply is reclaimed, but output tax is then accounted for in relation to the element of private use (the "Lennartz method").

The first treatment may be applied to a supply of either goods or services. The second treatment may be applied to a supply of goods but cannot usually be applied to a supply of services (except in certain limited circumstances).

Fuel for private motoring

If an employee or the owner of a business is provided with fuel for private motoring, all of the input tax relating to purchases of fuel by the business may be reclaimed but output tax must then be accounted for on the supply of fuel for private use. The amount of this output tax depends upon the vehicle's level of carbon dioxide emissions (rounded down to the nearest 5g/km) and is determined by reference to a table of scale charges. As from 1 May 2009, the scale charges for a three-month period are as follows:

Emission rating (g/km)	VAT-inclusive scale charge £	VAT due (17.5%) £	VAT due (15%) £
120 or less	126.00	18.77	16.43
125 to 135	189.00	28.15	24.65
140	201.00	29.94	26.22
145	214.00	31.87	27.91
150	226.00	33.66	29.48
155	239.00	35.60	31.17
160	251.00	37.38	32.74
165	264.00	39.32	34.43
170	276.00	41.11	36.00
175	289.00	43.04	37.70
180	302.00	44.98	39.39
185	314.00	46.77	40.96
190	327.00	48.70	42.65
195	339.00	50.49	44.22
200	352.00	52.43	45.91
205	365.00	54.36	47.61
210	378.00	56.30	49.30
215	390.00	58.09	50.87
220	403.00	60.02	52.57
225	416.00	61.96	54.26
230	428.00	63.74	55.83
235 or more	441.00	65.68	57.52

Note the following points:

(a)   With a standard rate of 17.5% (*or 15%*), VAT due is 7/47ths (*or 3/23rds*) of the scale charge. Scale charges can be avoided only if no input tax is reclaimed in relation to car fuel. Similar tables are also available for one-month and 12-month periods.

(b)   The input tax suffered in relation to car repairs and maintenance is reclaimable in full (with no adjustment for private use) so long as the car is used for business purposes to some extent. However, only 50% of the input tax relating to car leasing charges is reclaimable if there is any private use of the car.

Partial exemption

As explained in the previous chapter, a taxable person making wholly taxable supplies may reclaim all input tax suffered (with the exceptions listed above). A person making wholly exempt supplies is not a taxable person and may reclaim no input tax at all.

A taxable person making partly taxable and partly exempt supplies is "partially exempt" and may reclaim only part of the input tax suffered. The amount of input tax which may be reclaimed for a tax period is the amount which is "attributed to taxable supplies". This amount is usually calculated as follows:

(a) Input tax suffered in the period on goods and services which are used exclusively for the purpose of making taxable supplies is attributed to taxable supplies and is reclaimable in full.

(b) Input tax suffered in the period on goods and services which are used exclusively for the purpose of making exempt supplies is attributed to exempt supplies and cannot be reclaimed at all.

(c) A proportion of any unattributed or "residual" input tax suffered in the period (on goods and services used for making both taxable and exempt supplies) is attributed to taxable supplies and may be reclaimed. This proportion is equal to:

$$\text{Residual input tax} \times \frac{\text{Value of taxable supplies}}{\text{Value of all supplies}}$$

The ratio of taxable supplies to all supplies is generally expressed as a percentage rounded up to the nearest whole number. But the percentage is rounded to two decimal places if residual input tax exceeds £400,000 per month on average. When computing this ratio, certain supplies made by the person are omitted from the calculation, including self-supplies and supplies consisting of capital assets.

A taxable person may now use the previous year's overall percentage to determine the provisional recovery of residual input tax in each tax period (see below) thereby avoiding the need to calculate a separate percentage for each period.

(d) If the total amount of input tax not attributed to taxable supplies for a tax period does not exceed a "de minimis" limit of £625 per month (on average) and is also no more than 50% of all the input tax for the period, then it is treated as being attributed to taxable supplies and is reclaimable in full.

Note that the calculation of reclaimable input tax for a tax period is only provisional. The calculation is performed again at the end of each year, taking into account input tax for the whole year and using a de minimis limit of £7,500 (12 × £625). Any difference between the amount of reclaimable input tax for the year and the amount calculated provisionally is an underpayment or overpayment of VAT and must be accounted for to HMRC.

The procedure described above is known as the "standard method" of computing reclaimable input tax for a partially exempt person. HMRC may approve or direct the use of an alternative method if this gives a more fair and reasonable result.

EXAMPLE 2

During the quarter to 31 March 2010, Nancy makes supplies as follows:

	£
Standard-rated supplies (excluding VAT)	120,000
Zero-rated supplies	80,000
Exempt supplies	50,000

She suffers input tax as follows:

	£
Attributed to taxable supplies	7,500
Attributed to exempt supplies	8,500
Unattributed	12,000

Compute the VAT provisionally payable to HMRC for the quarter.

Solution

	£	£
Output tax		
Standard-rated supplies £120,000 @ 17.5%		21,000
Zero-rated supplies £80,000 @ 0%		0
		21,000
Input tax		
Attributed to taxable supplies	7,500	
Unattributed:		
$\dfrac{£120,000 + £80,000}{£120,000 + £80,000 + £50,000} = 80\% \times £12,000$	9,600	17,100
Payable to HMRC		3,900

The input tax not attributed to taxable supplies for the quarter is £10,900 (£8,500 + 20% x £12,000). This is more than £625 per month on average and so cannot be reclaimed.

Retail schemes

Retailers are those who supply goods and services directly to the public. A retailer's sales will often consist of a very large number of relatively small transactions and in these circumstances it would sometimes be difficult and expensive to keep detailed records of each transaction for VAT purposes. In response to this problem, retail schemes have been devised which enable retailers to calculate their output tax in a fairly straightforward way. The standard retail schemes (*which are available only to retailers with a taxable turnover of up to £130 million a year*) are as follows:

(a) **Point of Sale Scheme**. This scheme is the only standard retail scheme available to retailers who make supplies at just one positive rate of tax (i.e. all standard-rate or all reduced-rate). The scheme is also available to retailers who make supplies at two or more rates, so long as they can distinguish at the point of sale between supplies made at each rate (usually by having a till which can accumulate separate daily totals for supplies at each rate or by having separate tills).

Retailers operating this scheme keep a record of their daily gross takings (DGT) for supplies at each rate. Output tax is then calculated by multiplying DGT by either 7/47 (standard rate 17.5%) or 3/23 (standard rate 15%) or 1/21 (reduced rate).

(b) **Apportionment Scheme 1**. This scheme is available to retailers with an annual taxable turnover of £1 million or less who make supplies at more than one rate of tax. The scheme covers only the supply of goods bought for resale. It cannot be used in relation to supplies of services or supplies of self-made or self-grown goods. For a retailer operating this scheme, the computation of output tax for a tax period involves the following steps (assuming a standard rate of 17.5%):

Step 1   Calculate total DGT for the period.

Step 2   Calculate the VAT-inclusive cost (S) of goods bought in the period for resale at the standard rate.

Step 3   Calculate the VAT-inclusive cost (R) of goods bought in the period for resale at the reduced rate.

Step 4   Calculate the VAT-inclusive cost (A) of all goods bought in the period for resale (at any rate).

Step 5   Output tax on sales at the standard rate = Total DGT × S/A × 7/47.

Step 6   Output tax on sales at the reduced rate = Total DGT × R/A × 1/21.

This computation is performed again at the end of each year, taking into account takings and purchases for the whole year. Any difference between the result of this computation and the total of the amounts which were computed during the year must be accounted for to HMRC.

(c) **Apportionment Scheme 2**. This scheme is available to retailers who make supplies at more than one rate of tax. It can be used for supplies of goods bought for resale and for supplies of self-made or self-grown goods. It cannot be used for supplies of services. The computation of output tax for a tax period for retailers making quarterly returns (assuming a standard rate of 17.5%) normally proceeds as follows:

Step 1   Calculate total DGT for the period.

Step 2   Calculate the total (S) of the expected selling prices, including VAT, of standard-rate goods received, made or grown for retail sale in the current tax period and in the three previous periods.

Step 3   Calculate the total (R) of the expected selling prices, including VAT, of reduced-rate goods received, made or grown for retail sale in the current tax period and in the three previous periods.

Step 4   Calculate the total (A) of the expected selling prices, including VAT, of all goods (standard, reduced and zero-rate) received, made or grown for retail sale in the current tax period and in the three previous periods.

Step 5   Output tax on sales at the standard rate = Total DGT $\times$ S/A $\times$ 7/47.

Step 6   Output tax on sales at the reduced rate = Total DGT $\times$ R/A $\times$ 1/21.

The computation for the first three tax periods in which the scheme is used is slightly more complex, since an adjustment is required for the expected selling prices of opening stock on the date that the retailer started using the scheme.

For a retailer making monthly returns, each monthly computation will involve the expected selling prices of the previous eleven tax periods (rather than the previous three) and the computation for the first eleven tax periods in which the scheme is used will involve a stock adjustment.

(d)   **Direct Calculation Scheme 1**. This scheme is available to retailers with an annual taxable turnover of £1 million or less who make supplies at more than one rate of tax. The scheme works by calculating the expected selling prices of the retailer's "minority goods". These are defined as those goods which are supplied at the rate (or rates) of tax which:

(i)   forms the smaller proportion of retail supplies (where goods are supplied at two rates of VAT) or

(ii)   form the two smaller proportions of retail supplies (where goods are supplied at three rates of VAT).

The scheme can be used for supplies of goods bought for resale and for supplies of self-made or self-grown goods. Supplies of services cannot be included unless they are taxable at a different rate from the minority goods. If a retailer's minority goods are taxed at the zero rate and/or the reduced rate, the computation of output tax for a tax period involves the following steps (assuming a standard rate of 17.5%):

Step 1   Calculate total DGT for the period.

Step 2   Calculate the total (Z) of the expected selling prices of zero-rate goods received, made or grown for retail sale in the period.

Step 3   Calculate the total (R) of the expected selling prices of reduced-rate goods received, made or grown for retail sale in the period.

Step 4   The standard-rate element of takings (S) = Total DGT – Z – R.

Step 5   Output tax on sales at the standard rate = S $\times$ 7/47.

Step 6   Output tax on sales at the reduced rate = R $\times$ 1/21.

However, if a retailer's minority goods are taxed at the standard rate and/or the reduced rate, the computation of output tax for a tax period is as follows:

Step 1   Calculate total DGT for the period. Although this figure is not used in the calculation it must still be calculated and entered on the retailer's VAT return.

Step 2   Calculate the total (S) of the expected selling prices of standard-rate goods received, made or grown for retail sale in the period.

Step 3   Calculate the total (R) of the expected selling prices of reduced-rate goods received, made or grown for retail sale in the period.

Step 4   Output tax on sales at the standard rate = $S \times 7/47$.

Step 5   Output tax on sales at the reduced rate = $R \times 1/21$.

(e) **Direct Calculation Scheme 2**. This scheme works in a very similar way to Direct Calculation Scheme 1 but requires an annual stock adjustment. The £1 million turnover limit does not apply to this scheme.

Retailers with an annual taxable turnover exceeding £130 million cannot use any of the standard schemes listed above. If such retailers wish to use a retail scheme they must negotiate an individual "bespoke retail scheme" with HMRC.

It should be noted that the growing use of information technology by large retailers and by many small retailers means that it is now much easier to record individual sales than it was when VAT was introduced in 1973. This means that the original rationale for the retail schemes has been diminished over the years. Accordingly, retailers may not use any of these schemes unless permitted to do so. HMRC permission will be granted only if a retailer cannot reasonably be expected to account for VAT in the normal way, so that the use of a retail scheme is strictly necessary.

Administration of VAT

Overall responsibility for administration of the VAT system lies with the Commissioners for Revenue and Customs. VAT registration and the collection of VAT are dealt with by the VAT Central Unit. The main functions of this unit are:

(a)   to maintain registration records

(b)   to issue VAT return forms to registered persons (unless returns are made online) and to receive completed returns

(c)   to collect VAT due from registered persons and to make repayments of tax where necessary.

There is also a network of local offices throughout the UK which deal with local VAT administration matters. HMRC officials from these offices may visit the business premises of registered persons in their area to check the accuracy of VAT returns and to ensure that the VAT system is being operated correctly.

VAT assessments

VAT is largely a self-assessed tax and so it is not normally necessary to raise formal VAT assessments. But HMRC may issue such an assessment if a taxable person has failed to make a VAT return or has made a return which is incorrect or incomplete.

VAT assessments cannot usually be raised any later than four years after the end of the tax period to which they relate, but this time limit is extended to twenty years if the taxable person has behaved dishonestly or fraudulently. Any claim for a refund of overpaid VAT must also be made within four years in most cases.

Appeals

A person who disagrees with an "appealable" VAT decision made by HMRC may ask for the decision to be internally reviewed. The person concerned also has the right of appeal to a tribunal. Appeals are permitted in relation to most VAT matters, but certain matters cannot be the subject of an appeal.

The internal review process and the appeals system are very similar to their direct tax counterparts (see Chapter 1). In summary:

(a)   A request that an appealable HMRC decision should be reviewed must normally be made in writing within 30 days of the date of the decision. A request may be accepted later than this if the person concerned has a reasonable excuse for failing to meet the 30-day time limit.

(b)   An internal review is carried out by an HMRC officer who has not previously been involved with the decision in question. The review is normally completed within 45 days. The review officer then writes to the person concerned to inform him or her of the review's conclusions.

(c)   If no internal review is requested, an appeal to a tribunal may be made within 30 days of the date of the original decision. Otherwise, an appeal to a tribunal may be made within 30 days of the date of the review conclusion letter.

(d)   Most VAT appeals are dealt with by the Tax Chamber of the First-tier Tribunal. The Finance and Tax Chamber of the Upper Tribunal hears appeals against decisions made by the First-tier Tribunal.

(e)   If either HMRC or the person concerned is dissatisfied with a decision made by the Upper Tribunal, a dispute on a point of law may be referred to the Court of Appeal.

Avoidance schemes

Businesses with a taxable turnover of £600,000 or more are required to notify HMRC if they make use of certain VAT avoidance schemes which are listed on a statutory register. Similarly, businesses with a taxable turnover exceeding £10 million are required to notify HMRC if they make use of schemes which bear certain hallmarks of VAT avoidance.

Penalties, surcharges and interest

The main penalties which may be imposed in relation to VAT are as follows:

(a) **Criminal fraud**. A person who attempts to evade VAT in such a way that his or her conduct amounts to criminal fraud may, on a summary conviction obtained before a magistrate, be imprisoned for up to six months. The person may also be liable to pay a fine of up to £5,000 (the "statutory maximum") or three times the amount of tax evaded, whichever is the greater. If the conviction is on indictment, the person may be imprisoned for up to seven years and there is no limit to the size of any fine.

(b) **Conduct involving dishonesty**. A person who attempts to evade VAT in such a way that his or her conduct involves dishonesty is liable to a maximum penalty of up to 100% of the amount of tax evaded. This penalty does not apply if the dishonest conduct is within the scope of the penalty regime relating to an incorrect VAT return or a failure to notify HMRC of an under-assessment (see below).

  As from 1 April 2010, the dishonest conduct penalty will not apply if the conduct is dealt with by the new penalties being introduced on that date in relation to a failure to register and VAT "wrongdoing" (see below).

(c) **Late registration**. A taxable person who fails to notify HMRC of his or her liability to register, or makes late notification, is liable to a penalty. The penalty is calculated as a percentage of the amount of tax due between the date on which registration should have occurred and the date on which notification is eventually made. The percentage is 5% for a delay of up to nine months, 10% for a delay of between nine and 18 months and 15% for a longer delay. The minimum penalty is £50.

  However, it is important to note that revised penalties for failing to register are being introduced as from 1 April 2010. These penalties form part of the new penalty regime relating to any failure to notify HMRC of a taxable activity (see Chapter 14).

(d) **Incorrect VAT returns**. As explained in Chapter 14, a new penalty regime has now been introduced in relation to the submission of incorrect tax returns. This regime affects a number of taxes, including VAT, and applies to VAT returns for which the required filing date is on or after 1 April 2009. Under the new regime, a penalty may be charged if an incorrect VAT return leads to an understatement of the amount of tax due and the inaccuracy was either careless or deliberate. A penalty may also be charged if a VAT assessment issued by HMRC understates the amount of tax due and the taxable person has failed to take reasonable steps to notify HMRC of this fact within 30 days.

  The amount of any penalty imposed under the new regime depends upon the person's degree of culpability and will usually vary between 30% and 100% of the additional tax which is payable as a result of correcting the inaccuracy or the under-statement. But these penalties are substantially reduced if the taxable person voluntarily discloses either the inaccuracy or the failure to notify HMRC of an under-assessment (see Chapter 14 for further details).

(e) **Default surcharge**. A "default" occurs if a taxable person submits a late VAT return and/or makes a late payment of VAT. In these circumstances, HMRC will usually issue a surcharge liability notice specifying a surcharge period running for 12 months from the end of the tax period concerned. If a further default is made within this period, then:

- the surcharge period is extended to the first anniversary of the tax period to which the new default relates, and

- if the new default has resulted in any VAT not being paid on time, a default surcharge will be levied, calculated as the greater of £30 and a percentage of the tax paid late. The surcharge percentage is 2% for the first default within the surcharge period, 5% for the second default, 10% for the third default and 15% for the fourth and any subsequent default. However, surcharges are not imposed at the 2% or 5% rate for an amount of less than £400.

A surcharge period comes to an end only when no defaults have occurred for a continuous 12-month period. Automatic late payment penalties do not apply to businesses with a turnover not exceeding £150,000 per year. Such businesses are initially offered help and advice if they are late with their VAT payments.

It is important to note that a new penalty regime is being introduced in relation to late returns and late payment of tax (see Chapter 14). This penalty regime will apply to a number of taxes but will not initially apply to VAT. However, it is expected that the new regime will eventually be extended to VAT.

(f) **VAT "wrongdoing"**. As from 1 April 2010, a penalty will be charged if a person makes an unauthorised issue of a VAT invoice. This situation would arise if VAT invoices were issued by a person who is not registered for VAT.

The amount of the penalty will vary from 30% to 100% of the amount shown as VAT on an unauthorised invoice, with substantial reductions if the person concerned voluntarily discloses the wrongdoing.

(g) **Breaches of regulations**. A taxable person who fails to comply with sundry VAT regulations will initially receive a written warning from HMRC. If non-compliance is continued, the person is liable on a first offence to a penalty of £5 per day until the breach is remedied. The penalty rises to £10 per day on a second offence within a period of two years and again to £15 per day on a third or subsequent offence. The maximum penalty which may be charged is equal to 100 times the daily rate and the minimum penalty is £50.

Certain penalties may be mitigated (i.e. reduced or not charged at all) if the taxable person has a reasonable excuse for his or her conduct. As noted above, some penalties may also be mitigated if the person concerned has voluntarily disclosed any non-compliance and has co-operated fully with HMRC.

Interest

"Default interest" is charged on VAT which has been assessed (see above) or which could have been assessed but for the fact that payment was made before an assessment was raised. Such interest runs from the date on which the tax should have been paid to the date of payment. Conversely, if a taxable person makes an overpayment of VAT and this has been caused by an HMRC error, the person is paid interest on the tax that is refunded.

When a taxable person discovers that an error on a previous VAT return has resulted in an underpayment of VAT, default interest is not charged if the error is corrected in a later return. This is permissible as long as the error does not exceed a "de minimis" limit. As from 1 July 2008, this limit is equal to the greater of £10,000 and 1% of taxable turnover for the return period, subject to a maximum of £50,000.

Repayment supplement

If a taxable person is entitled to a repayment of VAT for a tax period, this repayment is increased by a "repayment supplement" of 5% (or £50, if greater) so long as:

(a) the return for the relevant tax period is submitted on time, and

(b) the amount stated to be repayable in the return is correct or differs from the correct figure by no more than 5% or £250 (whichever is greater), and

(c) HMRC fails to issue written instructions for the repayment to be made within 30 days from the date on which the return was received.

Summary

▸ VAT is normally accounted for to HMRC on a quarterly basis, although a person who is entitled to a VAT repayment in most tax periods may submit monthly returns instead.

▸ The date on which a supply is deemed to occur is known as the "tax point".

▸ A tax invoice must normally be issued if a taxable person makes a taxable supply to another taxable person.

▸ There are several special schemes which simplify the workings of the VAT system. These include the cash accounting scheme, the annual accounting scheme, the flat-rate scheme for small businesses, the flat-rate scheme for farmers and the margin scheme. There are also several special schemes for retailers.

▸ The input tax suffered in relation to certain types of supply (e.g. business entertainment) is not recoverable.

▸ A person making a mixture of taxable supplies and exempt supplies is "partially exempt" and may reclaim only part of the input tax suffered.

▸ The VAT system is administered by HM Revenue and Customs. Penalties are imposed for non-compliance with VAT regulations.

Exercises

30.1 List the required contents of a valid VAT invoice.

30.2 Describe the main features of:

    (a)   the cash accounting scheme

    (b)   the annual accounting scheme.

30.3 Calculate the output tax which must be accounted for or the input tax which may be reclaimed by a taxable person in respect of each of the transactions below. All of the amounts shown exclude any VAT which may be applicable.

    (a)   the purchase of a book for £18.95

    (b)   the sale for £3,000 of a motor car used for both business and private purposes

    (c)   the sale of a used commercial building for £200,000.

30.4 Sebastian is self-employed. He drives a car with an emission rating of 223 g/km and he charges the cost of all the petrol used to his business bank account. In the quarter to 31 March 2010 he drives 3,800 miles on business and 1,400 miles for private purposes. The VAT-inclusive cost of all the petrol bought in the quarter is £799. How should Sebastian deal with petrol in his VAT return for the quarter?

*30.5 During the quarter to 31 March 2010, a taxable person makes the following supplies:

	£
Standard-rated supplies (including VAT)	319,600
Zero-rated supplies	88,000
Exempt supplies	440,000

Input tax for the quarter is £118,000, attributed as follows:

	%
Attributed to taxable supplies	35
Attributed to exempt supplies	40
Unattributed	25

Compute the VAT provisionally payable to or reclaimable from HMRC for the quarter.

*30.6 Tracey is a sole trader. She has the following transactions during the quarter to 31 March 2010 (all amounts shown are VAT-exclusive):

	£
Sales to UK customers:	
Standard-rated	39,400
Zero-rated	12,600
Exports:	
To non-EU members	8,600
To EU members (all customers are VAT registered)	17,300
Purchases:	
Standard-rated	25,800
Zero-rated	6,200
Expenses:	
Wages and salaries	22,450
Car repairs	120
Insurances	260
Entertaining UK customers	420
Other expenses (all standard-rated)	9,700
Capital transactions:	
Purchase of new plant and machinery	8,000
Purchase of motor van	12,000

Tracey drives a car with an emission rating of 194 g/km and charges the cost of all the petrol used by this car, whether for business or private motoring, to her business bank account. Calculate the amount of VAT due for the quarter.

Chapter 31

Inheritance tax

Introduction

This chapter provides a basic introduction to inheritance tax (IHT). An IHT liability can arise in a number of ways but the events which most commonly trigger such a liability are the transfer of assets on the death of their owner and the gift of assets during the lifetime of their owner.

IHT was introduced in 1986 to replace capital transfer tax. Current IHT legislation is to be found in the Inheritance Tax Act 1984 (originally the Capital Transfer Tax Act 1984) as amended by subsequent Finance Acts.

Chargeable transfers of value

The main situation in which a charge to IHT may arise is when a *transfer of value* of *chargeable property* is made by a *chargeable person*.

Transfers of value

A transfer of value occurs when a transferor makes a "disposition" such that his or her estate is lower in value than it was before the disposition occurred. The value of a transfer for IHT purposes is equal to the reduction in the value of the transferor's estate. If the transferor also pays the IHT in relation to the transfer, this further reduces the value of the estate, so that the total value of the transfer is then equal to the amount of the disposition plus the associated IHT.

A disposition is a disposal of property or an interest in property. This includes disposals made during the lifetime of the transferor ("lifetime transfers") as well as disposals caused by the death of the transferor. However, certain dispositions are not regarded as transfers of value for IHT purposes and so cannot give rise to an IHT liability. The most significant of these dispositions are:

(a) dispositions without gratuitous intent (i.e. genuine commercial transactions which give rise to a loss and so cause a reduction in the value of the transferor's estate)

(b) dispositions made during the transferor's lifetime which are allowable expenditure for income tax or corporation tax purposes or which consist of pension contributions made by an employer for the benefit of employees

(c) dispositions made during the transferor's lifetime for the maintenance of his or her family (including spouses, civil partners, children and dependent relatives)

(d) dispositions caused by the fact that the transferor has died whilst on active service.

Chargeable property

For IHT purposes, the word "property" encompasses all types of asset, including legally enforceable rights and interests of any description. All property is chargeable property unless specifically excluded from charge. The main exclusions are:

(a) property situated outside the UK and owned by a person who is domiciled outside the UK (i.e. a person whose permanent home is situated outside the UK)

(b) government securities issued on terms which grant tax exemption under certain conditions and held by a person who satisfies those conditions (e.g. government securities which give tax exemption to persons who are not ordinarily resident in the UK and held by someone who is not ordinarily resident)

(c) "heritage property" designated as such by the Treasury, so long as undertakings are given with regard to maintenance of the property and the provision of public access

(d) a reversionary interest in a trust or settlement, unless acquired by purchase (see later in this chapter for more information on trusts and types of trust).

Chargeable persons

An individual who is domiciled in the UK (i.e. whose permanent home is in the UK) is a chargeable person and is liable to IHT in relation to all of his or her chargeable property situated throughout the world An individual who is not domiciled in the UK is liable to IHT only in relation to property situated in the UK. Note that:

(a) Husbands and wives (and civil partners) are assessed to IHT independently.

(b) A partnership is not a chargeable person. Each partner is individually liable to IHT in relation to his or her share of the partnership assets.

(c) A company is not a chargeable person. But the participators of a close company (see Chapter 27) may incur IHT in relation to transfers made by that company.

(d) The life tenants of an interest in possession trust created before 22 March 2006 are regarded for IHT purposes as owning the assets of the trust, divided between them in proportion to their interests. The trust itself is not a chargeable person. However, most other trusts are chargeable to IHT (see later in this chapter).

Exempt transfers

Certain transfers are wholly exempt from IHT. In other cases, an exemption or relief may reduce the value of a transfer for IHT purposes. The main exemptions and reliefs are:

(a) business and agricultural property reliefs (see later in this chapter)

(b) exemptions for transfers made to certain transferees (see below)

(c) exemptions available to the transferor (see below).

These exemptions and reliefs are applied to a transfer in the order given above.

Exemptions for transfers made to certain transferees

The following transfers are wholly exempt from IHT whether made on death or during the lifetime of the transferor:

(a) transfers to the transferor's spouse (husband or wife) or same-sex civil partner (so long as a legally-recognised civil partnership has been established)

(b) transfers to charities, community amateur sports clubs or political parties

(c) transfers made for national purposes to designated bodies (e.g. museums, libraries, art galleries etc.)

(d) subject to certain conditions, transfers made into a settlement established for the maintenance, repair or preservation of designated heritage property.

In the case of transfers between spouses, there is no requirement that the husband and wife should live together, only that the marriage should be valid under UK law. This exemption ceases when the marriage is dissolved by a decree absolute.

Exemptions available to the transferor

The following exemptions are available in relation to lifetime transfers only:

(a) **Normal expenditure out of income**. Transfers consisting of "normal expenditure out of income" (e.g. birthday and Christmas presents) are wholly exempt from IHT. In order for a transfer to benefit from this exemption, HM Revenue and Customs must believe that the transfer:

   (i) is part of the normal expenditure of the transferor, and

   (ii) is made out of income rather than capital, and

   (iii) leaves the transferor sufficient income to maintain his or her usual standard of living.

(b) **Small gifts**. Gifts to individuals with a value of up to £250 per transferee per tax year (from 6 April to 5 April) are wholly exempt from IHT. This exemption cannot be used to exempt part of a gift which has a value exceeding £250.

(c) **Gifts in consideration of marriage**. Gifts made to a bride or to a bridegroom in consideration of their marriage are exempt from IHT up to the following limits:

    (i) £5,000 if made by a parent of the bride or groom

    (ii) £2,500 if made by the grandparent or remoter ancestor of the bride or groom

    (iii) £2,500 if made by the bride to the groom or vice versa

    (iv) £1,000 in any other case.

The above exemptions are per transferor per marriage and can be used to exempt part of the value of larger gifts. Similar rules now also apply to gifts made on the registration of a civil partnership.

(d) **Annual exemption**. The first £3,000 of lifetime transfers made in any tax year is exempt from IHT. Note that:

    (i) If the total of the lifetime transfers made in a tax year exceeds £3,000, the exemption is set against the year's transfers in chronological order.

    (ii) Any unused part of the annual exemption may be carried forward to the following tax year (but no further) and set against the excess of that year's lifetime transfers over that year's annual exemption.

    (iii) It is HM Revenue and Customs practice to set the annual exemption against potentially exempt transfers (see below) as well as chargeable lifetime transfers, even though potentially exempt transfers may never become chargeable to inheritance tax. There is some doubt as to whether this practice is statutorily correct but it has been followed in this book.

EXAMPLE 1

Tania makes no transfers during 2007-08. Her only transfers during 2008-09 and 2009-10 are as follows:

		£
2008-09		
June 2008	Gift to her son on his marriage	6,000
October 2008	Gift to her granddaughter	4,500
January 2009	Gift to Oxfam	10,000
March 2009	Gift to a friend	100
2009-10		
July 2009	Gift to her nephew	1,000
August 2009	Gift to her cousin	3,500

Calculate the value of each of the above transfers after deduction of all the relevant exemptions. None of the gifts are regarded as normal expenditure out of income.

Solution

(AE = Annual exemption)

	Value before AE £	AE for current year £	AE for previous year £	Value after AE £
2008-09				
Gift to son on marriage (£6,000 – £5,000)	1,000	1,000	-	-
Gift to granddaughter	4,500	2,000	2,500	-
Gift to charity (exempt)	-	-	-	-
Gift to friend (exempt as a small gift)	-	-	-	-
	5,500	3,000	2,500	-
2009-10				
Gift to nephew	1,000	1,000		-
Gift to cousin	3,500	2,000		1,500
	4,500	3,000		1,500

Note:

£500 of the 2007-08 annual exemption remains unused but cannot be carried forward beyond 2008-09. The 2008-09 and 2009-10 annual exemptions are fully utilised.

Potentially exempt transfers (PETs)

If a lifetime transfer is not exempt from IHT as a result of the various exemptions listed above, the transfer will be either a "chargeable lifetime transfer" or a "potentially exempt transfer". Chargeable lifetime transfers are charged to IHT immediately. But potentially exempt transfers (PETs) are charged to IHT only if the transferor dies within seven years of the date of the transfer.

A potentially exempt transfer is a lifetime transfer made by an individual to any of the following:

(a)   another individual

(b)   a trust for the benefit of a disabled person

(c)   a trust for the benefit of a bereaved minor.

Most lifetime transfers are in fact PETs. But lifetime transfers made to trusts other than those mentioned above are chargeable lifetime transfers.

Types of trust

The above definition of a PET makes reference to various types of trust. Trusts were introduced briefly in Chapter 6 but are explained again below:

(a) A trust (or settlement) is an arrangement whereby property is held by persons known as trustees for the benefit of other persons known as beneficiaries.

(b) If one or more persons are entitled to the lifetime use of the trust property or to the income generated by the trust property, those persons are "life tenants" and the trust is a trust with an "interest in possession" (IIP). A person whose interest in the trust property will not take effect until some future event occurs (e.g. the death of a life tenant) is said to have a "reversionary interest".

(c) A trust with no interest in possession is sometimes referred to as a "discretionary trust". The trustees of such a trust have the discretion to distribute as much or as little of the trust income to the beneficiaries as they see fit.

For IHT purposes, most trusts are classified as "relevant property trusts" and are subject to a special IHT regime. This involves a "periodic" tax charge on the trust property every ten years and an "exit" charge whenever property leaves the trust.

However, trusts for the disabled and trusts for bereaved minors are not relevant property trusts. Nor are IIP trusts set up before 22 March 2006 (until the life interest at that date comes to an end). In these cases, the trust is not liable to the periodic or exit charges.

EXAMPLE 2

Consider each of the following lifetime transfers and classify each one as either an exempt transfer, a PET or a chargeable lifetime transfer. Assume in each case that the transfer was made during 2009-10 and that the annual exemption for both the current year and the previous year have been set against earlier transfers.

(a) a gift of £10,000 made by a husband to his wife

(b) a gift of £20,000 made by a mother to her son on his marriage

(c) a gift of £50,000 made to a trust for the benefit of a disabled person

(d) a gift of £100,000 made to a relevant property trust.

Solution

(a) wholly exempt   (b) exempt £5,000; PET £15,000

(c) PET   (d) chargeable lifetime transfer.

IHT payable on chargeable lifetime transfers

The amount of IHT payable on a chargeable lifetime transfer depends upon:

(a) the value of the transfer (less any relevant exemptions), which must be grossed-up if the tax is paid by the transferor

(b) the rates of IHT in force on the date of the transfer

(c) the total (including the current transfer) of the gross chargeable lifetime transfers made during the seven years ending on the date of the current transfer.

Grossing-up

IHT is chargeable on the *gross* value of a transfer. This is the reduction in the value of the transferor's estate which the transfer has caused. If the transferee pays the tax due on a transfer, the gross value of the transfer is simply the amount received by the transferee (less any exemptions). However, if the tax due is paid by the transferor, the amount received by the transferee (less exemptions) is only the net value of the transfer and this must be grossed-up at the appropriate rates to find the gross value.

In general, any capital gains tax payable by the transferor in relation to the transfer is ignored when calculating the reduction in value of the transferor's estate.

Rates of IHT applicable to chargeable lifetime transfers

The rates of IHT applicable to chargeable lifetime transfers made on or after 6 April 2009 are as follows:

Gross chargeable lifetime transfers for the seven years to date	Rate of tax	Grossing-up fraction
first £325,000 ("nil-rate band")	0%	nil
remainder after the first £325,000	20%	100/80

The rates of tax have been 0% and 20% for many years but the threshold beyond which 20% tax is payable is usually increased in each tax year, so increasing the width of the nil-rate band. Recent values of the threshold have been:

Date of transfer	£
6 April 2002 to 5 April 2003	250,000
6 April 2003 to 5 April 2004	255,000
6 April 2004 to 5 April 2005	263,000
6 April 2005 to 5 April 2006	275,000
6 April 2006 to 5 April 2007	285,000
6 April 2007 to 5 April 2008	300,000
6 April 2008 to 5 April 2009	312,000

It has been announced that the IHT threshold will rise to £350,000 in 2010-11.

For each transfer, the calculation of the tax due involves the following steps:

(a) The total gross value of previous chargeable lifetime transfers made during the seven years to date is brought forward.

(b) If the total brought forward has utilised the whole of the nil-rate band, tax is due at 20% on the gross value of the current transfer.

(c) If the total brought forward has not utilised the whole of the nil-rate band, the balance of that band is set against the current transfer. If this does not absorb the whole of the transfer, tax is due at 20% on the gross value of the remainder.

EXAMPLE 3

On 1 July 2009, Violet makes a chargeable lifetime transfer (after deduction of relevant exemptions) of £48,000. Her only previous chargeable lifetime transfer was made in 2005 and had a gross value (after exemptions) of £283,000. Calculate the IHT due if:

(a) the transferee agrees to pay the tax due

(b) the tax due is paid by Violet.

Solution

The total of transfers brought forward is £283,000, leaving £42,000 of the nil-rate band to set against the current transfer.

(a) If the transferee pays the tax, the gross value of the transfer is £48,000 and the IHT due is £42,000 @ 0% + £6,000 @ 20% = £1,200. The total of gross transfers for the seven years to 1 July 2009 is now £331,000.

(b) If Violet pays the tax, the net value of the transfer is £48,000. The gross value and the tax due are calculated as follows:

	Net	Gross	Tax
	£	£	£
£42,000 grossed up @ 0%	42,000	42,000	0
£6,000 grossed up @ 20%	6,000	7,500	1,500
Totals	48,000	49,500	1,500

The gross value of the transfer is £49,500 and the tax due is £1,500. The total of gross transfers for the seven years to 1 July 2009 is now £332,500.

IHT payable on death

The IHT payable on death consists of:

(a) additional tax on any chargeable lifetime transfers made by the deceased person during the seven years ending on the date of death

(b) tax on any PETs made by the deceased person during those seven years

(c) tax on the estate of the deceased person as at the date of death, to the extent that the transfers made on death are not exempt from IHT.

Tax on chargeable lifetime transfers and PETs

The tax payable on death in respect of the chargeable lifetime transfers and PETs made in the seven years ending on the date of death is calculated as follows:

(a) The transfers are considered in chronological order with no distinction made between chargeable lifetime transfers and PETs.

(b) Tax is recalculated on the gross value of each transfer using the IHT bands and rates in force *on the date of death* and taking into account any other chargeable transfers made in the seven years ending on the date of the transfer. For deaths occurring on or after 6 April 2009 the applicable rates are as follows:

Gross chargeable transfers for the seven years to date	Rate of tax
first £325,000 ("nil-rate band")	0%
remainder after the first £325,000	40%

For deaths occurring on or after 9 October 2007, the deceased person's nil-rate band may be increased by a transfer of unused nil-rate band from a previously deceased spouse or civil partner (see later in this chapter).

(c) The tax calculated at (b) for each transfer may then be reduced by *taper relief*, depending upon the number of years which have elapsed between the date of the transfer and the date of death. Taper relief is given as follows:

Period between transfer and death	Percentage tax reduction
3 years or less	0%
Over 3 but not more than 4 years	20%
Over 4 but not more than 5 years	40%
Over 5 but not more than 6 years	60%
Over 6 but not more than 7 years	80%

(d) Finally, for each transfer, any tax paid during the lifetime of the transferor is subtracted, leaving a balance of tax due on that transfer. This tax liability is the responsibility of the transferee. No repayment is given if the lifetime tax paid in relation to a transfer exceeds the liability on death.

EXAMPLE 4

Wilson dies on 20 December 2009, having made only the following transfers during his lifetime:

		£
6 June 1999	Gift to daughter	50,000
4 May 2005	Gift to relevant property trust	476,000
11 June 2006	Gift to son on marriage	50,000

Calculate the IHT payable during Wilson's lifetime (if any) in relation to each of the above transfers, assuming that Wilson paid this tax himself. Also calculate any further IHT payable in relation to these transfers on Wilson's death.

Solution

The value of each gift after deduction of exemptions is as follows:

		Value before AE £	AE for current year £	AE for previous year £	Value after AE £
1999-00	Daughter	50,000	3,000	3,000	44,000
2005-06	Relevant property trust	476,000	3,000	3,000	470,000
2006-07	Son (£50,000 – £5,000)	45,000	3,000	-	42,000

Lifetime tax liability

The gifts to Wilson's son and daughter were PETs and gave rise to no immediate tax liability but the gift to the trust was a chargeable lifetime transfer. There were no other such transfers during the seven years to date so the whole of the nil-rate band (£275,000 at that time) was set against the gift. The tax due was £48,750, calculated as follows:

	Net £	Gross £	Tax £
£275,000 grossed up @ 0%	275,000	275,000	0
£195,000 grossed up @ 20%	195,000	243,750	48,750
Totals	470,000	518,750	48,750

Tax liability on death

The June 1999 PET is more than seven years old at the time of Wilson's death. This PET is exempt from tax and can be completely ignored for IHT purposes. The tax due on the other two transfers is calculated as follows:

(i) *Transfer made on 4 May 2005*

The gross value of this transfer is £518,750 and there were no other chargeable transfers in the seven years to date (5 May 1998 to 4 May 2005). The tax due at the death rates applicable on 20 December 2009 is:

	£
£325,000 @ 0%	0
£193,750 @ 40%	77,500
	77,500
<u>Less</u>: Taper relief (4-5 years) @ 40%	31,000
	46,500
<u>Less</u>: Lifetime tax paid (£48,750)	46,500
IHT payable by transferee	nil

The lifetime tax paid exceeds the tax liability calculated on death. There is no further inheritance tax to pay but the excess of £2,250 is not repayable.

(ii) *Transfer made on 11 June 2006*

The gross value of this transfer is £42,000. Previous gross chargeable transfers in the seven years to date (12 June 1999 to 11 June 2006) were £518,750, completely absorbing the nil-rate band. Therefore the tax due at the death rates applicable on 20 December 2009 is:

	£
£42,000 @ 40%	16,800
<u>Less</u>: Taper relief (3-4 years) @ 20%	3,360
	13,440
<u>Less</u>: Lifetime tax paid	0
IHT payable by transferee	13,440

Tax on the deceased person's estate

IHT on the deceased person's estate (to the extent that the transfers made on death are not exempt from IHT) is calculated using the rates of tax applicable on death. The calculation proceeds as follows:

(a) First, the nil-rate band is reduced by the total of gross chargeable transfers (including any PETs) made in the seven years ending on the date of death.

(b) The remainder of the nil-rate band (if any) is then set against the value of the estate and tax at 40% is calculated on the balance.

(c) The tax due is divided by the value of the estate and the result (expressed as a percentage) is the "estate rate" i.e. the average rate of tax borne by the estate.

As mentioned earlier, the deceased person's nil-rate band may be increased by a transfer of unused nil-rate band from a previously deceased spouse or civil partner (see below).

EXAMPLE 5

Toby dies on 2 March 2010, leaving an estate valued at £400,000. None of the transfers made on death are exempt from IHT. Calculate the IHT due on the estate if the total of the gross chargeable transfers made by Toby in the seven years up to his death was:

(a)   Nil   (b)   £125,000   (c)   £370,000.

Solution

(a)   £325,000 @ 0% + £75,000 @ 40% = £30,000. (Estate rate 7.5%)
(b)   £200,000 @ 0% + £200,000 @ 40% = £80,000. (Estate rate 20%)
(c)   £400,000 @ 40% = £160,000. (Estate rate 40%).

Transfer of unused part of nil-rate band

A transferable nil-rate band arises when one party to a marriage or civil partnership dies and the amount that is chargeable to IHT on his or her death (including any transfers made in the previous seven years) does not use up all of the nil-rate band. In these circumstances, the unused part of the nil-rate band may be transferred to the surviving spouse or civil partner for use on his or her death. Note that:

(a)   This provision applies only if the surviving spouse or civil partner dies on or after 9 October 2007.

(b)   The transferred part of the nil-rate band may be used only when the surviving spouse or civil partner dies and cannot be used to reduce the lifetime tax payable on any chargeable lifetime transfers made by the survivor.

(c)   The amount available for transfer is calculated by determining the proportion of the nil-rate band which was unused when the survivor's spouse or civil partner died. This proportion is then applied to the amount of the nil-rate band which is in force on the date of the survivor's death.

EXAMPLE 6

Harriet died on 21 October 2009. Her husband had died previously and his estate on death (including transfers made in the last seven years of his life) had absorbed £100,000 of the nil-rate band at that time. Calculate the nil-rate band which is available when calculating the IHT due on Harriet's death, assuming that her husband died in:

(a)   February 2003   (b)   July 2007.

Solution

(a) When Harriet's husband died, the nil-rate band was £250,000. His estate absorbed £100,000 of this, leaving £150,000 (i.e. 60% of the nil-rate band) unused. Therefore Harriet's nil-rate band on death is £325,000 + 60% of £325,000 = £520,000.

(b) When Harriet's husband died, the nil-rate band was £300,000. His estate absorbed £100,000 of this, leaving £200,000 (i.e. 2/3rds of the nil-rate band) unused. Therefore Harriet's nil-rate band on death is £325,000 + 2/3rds of £325,000 = £541,667.

Quick succession relief

Quick succession relief (QSR) is available when property which is transferred on death was transferred to the deceased person within the previous five years and was charged to IHT at that time. The tax (if any) payable in relation to the transfer made on death is reduced by an amount which depends upon the value of the earlier transfer and the amount of IHT paid on that transfer. The relief is calculated as:

$$\frac{\text{net value of earlier transfer}}{\text{gross value of earlier transfer}} \times \text{IHT paid on earlier transfer} \times \text{QSR\%}$$

The QSR percentage depends upon the date of the earlier transfer, as follows:

Period between earlier transfer and death	QSR percentage
1 year or less	100%
Over 1 but not more than 2 years	80%
Over 2 but not more than 3 years	60%
Over 3 but not more than 4 years	40%
Over 4 but not more than 5 years	20%

Gifts with reservation

A "gift with reservation" is a gift of any property made in such a way that either:

(a) possession and enjoyment of the property is not bona fide assumed by the donee at or before the start of the "relevant period", or

(b) the property is not enjoyed to the entire exclusion of the donor throughout the whole of the relevant period.

For this purpose, the "relevant period" is the period which ends on the date of the donor's death and which begins seven years before that date or (if later) on the date of the gift.

If there were no special rules relating to gifts with reservation, taxpayers would be able to divest themselves of property (and so reduce the IHT charge arising on death) whilst continuing to receive a benefit from that property. This is prevented by IHT legislation which ensures that:

(a) property which is subject to a reservation at the date of the donor's death is treated as part of the donor's estate, and

(b) if any property ceased to be subject to a reservation before the donor's death, the donor is treated as having made a PET on the date that the reservation ceased to exist.

These rules are supplemented by regulations which deal with the possibility of a double tax charge arising if the gift is also a chargeable transfer.

Valuation

As stated at the beginning of this chapter, the value of a transfer for IHT purposes is equal to the reduction in value of the transferor's estate as a result of that transfer. In general, this is equivalent to the open market value of the transferred assets on the date of the transfer but it should not be assumed that this will always be the case. For instance, if the transferor disposes of:

(a) a single item from a matching set of such items, or

(b) a small number of shares in a company, sufficient to convert a majority shareholding into a minority shareholding

it is likely that the true reduction in value of the transferor's estate (and therefore the value of the transfer for IHT purposes) will exceed the market value of the transferred assets. This caveat aside, determining the market value of the transferred assets may in itself cause difficulty and special valuation rules are sometimes required. The most important of these rules are described below.

Listed shares

Shares which are listed on a recognised stock exchange (referred to as "listed shares" or "quoted shares") are valued at the *lower* of:

(a) the lower of the two prices quoted for those shares on the day of the transfer, plus one-quarter of the difference between these two prices (the "quarter-up" rule)

(b) the average of the highest and lowest prices at which bargains have been marked on that day (if any).

If listed shares are transferred on a non-working day (for which prices are unavailable) the shares are valued as if transferred on the last working day before the date of the transfer or the first working day after it, whichever gives the lower figure.

EXAMPLE 7

On 1 June 2009, Shirley gives 5,000 shares in Listed plc to her daughter. Shares in the company are quoted at 189p - 197p on that date, with bargains marked at 190p, 192p and 196p. Calculate the market value of the shares for IHT purposes.

Solution

The quarter-up rule gives 189p + 1/4 x (197p − 189p) = 191p. The average of the highest and lowest marked bargains is 193p, so the shares are valued at 191p and the transfer has a market value of 5,000 x £1.91 = £9,550.

Related property

When calculating the value of a transfer for IHT purposes, the existence of any "related property" may be taken into account. Related property consists of property which:

(a)   is owned by the transferor's spouse or civil partner, or

(b)   is owned (or has been owned within the previous five years) by a charity, political party etc. as a result of an exempt transfer made either by the transferor or by his or her spouse or civil partner.

Under the related property rules, the property being transferred and the related property are valued together (as a whole) and then part of that value is apportioned to the property being transferred. These rules are intended to prevent taxpayers from avoiding IHT by fragmenting the ownership of an asset and will only be used if the valuation given by the related property rules is greater than the valuation that would be calculated normally.

EXAMPLE 8

Roy owns 3,500 ordinary shares in R Ltd, an unlisted company which has an issued share capital of 10,000 ordinary shares. Roy's wife owns a further 1,600 shares. Shareholdings in R Ltd are valued as follows:

	£		£
500 shares	5,000	4,600 shares	64,400
3,000 shares	33,000	5,100 shares	96,900
3,500 shares	43,750		

Roy now transfers 500 of his shares to a relevant property trust. Calculate the value of this transfer for IHT purposes.

Solution

Ignoring related property, Roy's estate has reduced in value by £10,750 (£43,750 – £33,000) and this would normally be the value of the transfer. But taking related property into account, the value of the transfer is calculated as follows:

	£
Value of Roy's holding before the transfer (£96,900 x 3,500/5,100)	66,500
Value of Roy's holding after the transfer (£64,400 x 3,000/4,600)	42,000
Value of the transfer	24,500

Since £24,500 exceeds £10,750, the value of the transfer is £24,500.

Valuation of overseas property

Property situated outside the UK is valued in the appropriate foreign currency. This value is then converted into sterling, using the exchange rate for the day of the transfer which gives the lowest sterling value.

Business property relief

Business property relief of either 100% or 50% is available in relation to a transfer which meets *all* of the following conditions:

(a) the property transferred consists of "relevant business property"

(b) the business concerned is a "qualifying business" (non-profit making businesses and investment businesses do not qualify)

(c) the property has been owned by the transferor for at least two years, or has replaced other relevant business property, such that the combined period of ownership of both the original and replacement property is at least two years out of the five years preceding the date of the transfer.

The main categories of relevant business property, together with the applicable rates of relief, are as follows:

		Rate of relief
(a)	Property consisting of a business or an interest in a business (e.g. a share in a partnership)	100%
(b)	Securities in an unlisted company which (either by themselves or with other such securities or unlisted shares) gave the transferor control of the company immediately before the transfer	100%
(c)	Shares in an unlisted company	100%
(d)	Shares transferred from a controlling holding in a listed company	50%

	Rate of relief

(e) Land, buildings, plant and machinery which, immediately before   50%
the transfer, were used for business purposes by a partnership in
which the transferor was a partner or by a company of which
he/she had control

(f) Land, buildings, plant and machinery which, immediately before   50%
the transfer, were used in the transferor's business and owned by
a trust of which the transferor was a life tenant.

No relief is given in relation to "excepted assets". These are assets which have not been used for business purposes throughout the two years prior to the transfer (or since they were acquired, if within the last two years) and which are not required for the future use of the business.

Agricultural property relief

Agricultural property relief of either 100% or 50% is available in relation to a transfer of agricultural property so long as that property has been either:

(a) occupied by the transferor and used for agricultural purposes throughout the two years preceding the transfer, or

(b) owned by the transferor throughout the seven years preceding the transfer and occupied by the transferor or someone else for agricultural purposes throughout those seven years.

For this purpose, agricultural property consists mainly of agricultural land and pasture, woodlands and associated buildings. Land managed according to the terms of certain wildlife habitat schemes (together with associated buildings) is also eligible for agricultural property relief. The rates of relief are:

(a) 100% if, immediately before the transfer, the transferor enjoys vacant possession of the property or the right to obtain it within the following 12 months (extended to 24 months in certain cases)

(b) Otherwise, 100% if the property is let on a tenancy starting after 31 August 1995 and 50% if the property is let on a tenancy starting before 1 September 1995.

These rates apply only to the "agricultural value" of the property. This is the value that the property would have if it could only ever be used for agricultural purposes. No relief is available in respect of any extra value that the property might have by virtue of its development potential. If a property qualifies for both business property relief and agricultural property relief, agricultural property relief is given first.

Administration of IHT

Inheritance tax is administered by the Capital Taxes Office (CTO) of HM Revenue and Customs. For chargeable lifetime transfers and transfers caused by the death of the transferor, an "account" must be delivered to this office, giving details of the transfers made and their value. Details of this procedure are as follows:

(a) **Chargeable lifetime transfers**. The transferor must deliver an account to the CTO within 12 months of the end of the month in which the transfer occurred. There is no need to deliver an account if the transfer is exempt or potentially exempt, or if:

   (i)   for chargeable lifetime transfers consisting wholly of cash or quoted stocks and securities, the total of all chargeable transfers made in the seven years to date does not exceed the IHT threshold

   (ii) for chargeable lifetime transfers not consisting wholly of cash or quoted stocks and securities, the total of all chargeable transfers made in the seven years to date does not exceed 80% of the IHT threshold.

(b) **Death**. The personal representatives of a deceased person must deliver an account to the CTO within 12 months of the end of the month in which the death occurred. But there is no need to deliver an account if the person was UK-domiciled and:

   (i)   the gross value of the estate (plus transfers made during the seven years prior to death) does not exceed the IHT threshold, and

   (ii) no more than £100,000 of the estate is situated outside the UK, and

   (iii) any trust assets included in the estate of the deceased person are held in a single trust and do not exceed £150,000 in value, and

   (iv) there have been no chargeable lifetime transfers (or PETs) made within the seven years to date, other than transfers consisting of cash, listed shares, listed securities or land and buildings (and contents) with a total gross value not exceeding £150,000.

   If the deceased person was not UK-domiciled (and never had been) an account is not required so long as the value of UK assets transferred on death does not exceed £150,000 and these assets consist solely of cash, listed shares or listed securities.

When a transfer gives rise to an IHT liability, the CTO issues a notice showing the value of the transfer for IHT purposes and the amount of IHT payable. Appeals may be lodged within 30 days of the date of the notice.

Payment of IHT

The IHT relating to a transfer is usually payable six months after the end of the month in which the transfer (or the death) occurred. However, the tax on chargeable lifetime transfers made in roughly the first half of the tax year (6 April to 30 September) is not payable until 30 April in the following tax year.

It is notable that the tax on a transfer is usually due for payment before the end of the 12-month period within which an account of the transfer must be delivered to the CTO. Since interest is charged on tax paid late, there is an incentive to deliver the account (and pay the tax due) on or before the due date of payment.

Summary

▶ The main occasion on which IHT is charged is when a transfer of value of chargeable property is made by a chargeable person. A transfer may be a lifetime transfer or a transfer made on death.

▶ The value of a transfer is equal to the reduction in value of the transferor's estate as a result of the transfer. The value of a transfer for IHT purposes may be reduced by business property relief and/or agricultural property relief.

▶ Transfers made to certain transferees (e.g. spouses, civil partners, charities and political parties) are exempt from IHT.

▶ Lifetime transfers comprising small gifts, gifts made out of income and gifts made on marriage or civil partnership are wholly or partly exempt from IHT. The first £3,000 of lifetime transfers made in any tax year is exempt from IHT.

▶ A potentially exempt transfer (PET) is not chargeable to IHT unless the transferor dies within seven years. A chargeable lifetime transfer may be charged to IHT when the transfer is made (depending upon the total of the transfers made in the previous seven years) and may attract additional tax when the transferor dies.

▶ The amount of IHT charged on the estate of a deceased person depends upon the size of the estate and the total of any chargeable transfers made in the seven years before the person's death.

▶ The IHT on a transfer is normally payable six months after the end of the month in which the transfer takes place.

Exercises

31.1　Phoebe made the following transfers during 2009-10:

		£
12 April 2009	Gift to grandson	50
17 May 2009	Gift to her nephew on his marriage	3,000
3 August 2009	Gift to her husband	25,000
31 October 2009	Gift to a relevant property trust	10,000
1 January 2010	Gift to the Labour Party	5,000

None of the gifts are regarded as normal expenditure out of income. Phoebe made no transfers at all during 2008-09. Calculate the value of each of her 2009-10 transfers after deduction of all the available exemptions.

31.2 Classify each of the following lifetime transfers as either exempt, potentially exempt, or chargeable:

(a) a gift to the transferor's favourite charity

(b) a gift to a relevant property trust

(c) a gift to the transferor's grandfather.

31.3 On 5 December 2009, Nicholas makes a gift of £80,000 (after deduction of all relevant exemptions) to a relevant property trust. His only previous chargeable lifetime transfers were in June 2000 (gross chargeable value £200,000) and July 2004 (gross chargeable value £281,000). Calculate the lifetime IHT payable in relation to the £80,000 gift and state the due date of payment:

(a) if the trustees pay the tax   (b) if Nicholas pays the tax.

31.4 On 31 August 2004, Martha gave £500,000 to her daughter as a wedding present. On 1 June 2008 she gave £500,000 to a relevant property trust. Martha died on 1 January 2010, having made only these two transfers during her life.

(a) Calculate any lifetime tax due on each of the above transfers and state the due date of payment, assuming that Martha paid this tax herself.

(b) Calculate any further tax due on Martha's death in relation to these transfers and state the due date of payment. (Assume that there is no unused nil-rate band to be transferred from a previously deceased spouse or civil partner).

31.5 On 29 September 2009, Hyacinth makes a transfer consisting of 1,000 shares in a listed company. The shares are quoted at 572p - 588p on that date, with bargains marked at 572p, 577p and 578p. Calculate the market value of the transfer for IHT purposes.

*31.6 On 12 November 1999, Hazel made a gross chargeable transfer to a relevant property trust of £266,000 (after deduction of exemptions). On 1 April 2005 she gave £300,000 to her grandson. These were her only transfers. She died on 17 December 2009.

Calculate the tax payable by her grandson as a result of Hazel's death. (Assume that there is no unused nil-rate band to be transferred from a previously deceased spouse or civil partner).

*31.7 Tony died on 11 July 2009, leaving an estate valued at £500,000. None of the transfers made on his death were exempt from IHT. He had made the following transfers during his lifetime:

		£
3 May 2001	Gift to relevant property trust (tax paid by trustees)	100,000
1 July 2002	Gift to daughter	250,000
1 August 2002	Gift to son	250,000
10 June 2006	Gift to relevant property trust (tax paid by Tony)	450,000

Calculate the tax payable as a result of Tony's death. (Assume that there is no unused nil-rate band to be transferred from a previously deceased spouse or civil partner).

Chapter 32

Overseas aspects of taxation

Introduction

The main purpose of this final chapter is to consider the way in which the UK tax system deals with the overseas income and gains of UK resident individuals and companies. The treatment of non-resident individuals and companies with income or gains arising in the UK is also briefly considered.

The chapter begins by explaining the factors which affect an individual's UK tax status and then continues with a brief review of the overseas aspects of income tax, capital gains tax and inheritance tax. The UK tax status of companies and overseas aspects of corporation tax are dealt with towards the end of the chapter.

Residence, ordinary residence and domicile

The extent to which an individual is chargeable to UK tax depends entirely upon that individual's *residence*, *ordinary residence* and *domicile*. These three key concepts are explained below. It should be noted that an individual's nationality is usually *not* an important factor when determining that individual's UK tax status.

Residence

The term "residence" is not clearly defined in statute law and therefore the meaning of the term has evolved from case law. The main circumstances in which an individual is normally deemed to be UK resident are as follows:

(a) An individual who is physically present in the UK for at least 183 days during a tax year is deemed to be resident in the UK for the whole of that tax year. Any day on which the individual is present in the UK at midnight generally counts as a day of presence. However, there is an exemption for passengers who are in transit between two places outside the UK but find themselves in the UK at midnight. Days spent in transit are not counted as days of presence unless the individual engages in activities on that day that are unrelated to his or her passage through the UK (e.g. attending a business meeting).

(b) An individual who is in the habit of making regular visits to the UK averaging at least 91 days per tax year (excluding days that are spent in the UK because of circumstances beyond the individual's control, such as illness) is usually regarded as UK resident. Two situations are possible:

(i) An ex-resident who has now left the UK but who makes regular visits as described above is deemed to be UK resident for the whole of each tax year during which the visits continue.

(ii) An individual who was not previously a UK resident but who begins making regular visits as described above is normally deemed to be UK resident with effect from the fifth year of the visits. However, if it is clear from the outset that the visits are going to be regular, the individual may be regarded as UK resident with effect from the first year of the visits.

It is important to appreciate that the concept of UK residence normally applies to *whole* tax years. An individual is deemed to be UK resident for the whole of a tax year or for none of it and it is not usually possible to apportion a tax year into periods of residence and non-residence. The significance of this will become clear when the tax implications of residence and non-residence are described (see below). However, such apportionment is permitted in the following cases:

(a) in the year of arrival, if an individual takes up permanent residence in the UK or comes to stay in the UK for at least two years

(b) in the year of departure, if an individual leaves the UK in order to take up permanent residence abroad or to live abroad for at least three years

(c) in the years of departure and return, if an individual leaves the UK in order to take up employment abroad under a contract of employment for at least a whole tax year; in this case the individual concerned is normally regarded as being non-resident throughout the period of the contract, so long as UK visits during that period do not exceed 183 days in any one tax year or 91 days per year on average.

If a tax year is apportioned into periods of residence and non-residence, any personal allowances to which the individual is entitled are available in full for that year.

Ordinary residence

The term "ordinary residence" is also without a statutory definition. In general terms, an individual is ordinarily resident in the UK if he or she is habitually UK resident (i.e. resident year after year). In a given tax year, it is quite possible to be resident but not ordinarily resident, or vice versa.

An individual who is ordinarily resident in the UK but who is temporarily abroad during a particular tax year (i.e. not present for at least 183 days but not absent for the entire tax year either) is deemed to be resident in the UK for the whole of that tax year.

EXAMPLE 1

(a) Pierre, who has lived in France for the whole of his life, arrives in the UK on 1 May 2009 and remains in the UK until 31 March 2010, when he returns permanently to France. What is his UK residence status for 2009-10?

(b) Peter, who has lived in the UK for the whole of his life, leaves the UK on 1 May 2009 and returns permanently on 31 March 2010. What is his UK residence status for 2009-10?

(c) Petra, who has lived in the UK for the whole of her life, leaves the UK on 1 April 2009 and returns permanently on 30 April 2010. She makes no visits to the UK during her time abroad. What is her UK residence status for 2009-10?

Solution

(a) Pierre is *resident* in 2009-10 (spending at least 183 days in the UK during the year) but he is *not ordinarily resident*.

(b) Peter does not spend at least 183 days in the UK during 2009-10. However, he does spend at least some time in the UK during the year and he is *ordinarily resident*. Therefore he is also *resident* for the year.

(c) Petra is *ordinarily resident*. However, she is absent from the UK for the whole of 2009-10 and therefore she is *not resident* for that year.

Domicile

An individual's domicile is the country in which the individual has his or her permanent home. It is not possible to have more than one domicile at a time.

Individuals acquire a "domicile of origin" on birth. This is usually the domicile of the father or other person on whom the individual is dependent and is not necessarily the country of birth. Having reached the age of 16, an individual may then change domicile and acquire a "domicile of choice", but such a domicile can only be acquired by settling in the chosen country.

If an individual acquires a domicile of choice, that domicile is also acquired by anyone under the age of 16 who is dependent on that individual. A domicile acquired in this way is known as a "domicile of dependency".

Income tax - general rules

The general rules governing an individual's liability to UK income tax are as follows:

(a) Individuals who are *resident* in the UK for a tax year are liable to pay UK income tax on all of their income for that year, including any overseas income. Note that:

   (i) Overseas employment income is taxed in accordance with the rules of ITEPA 2003 (see below). Overseas trading income, property income and investment income are taxed by ITTOIA 2005 (see below).

   (ii) ITTOIA 2005 provides that the "relevant foreign income" of a UK resident who is either not domiciled in the UK or not ordinarily resident in the UK (or both) may be taxed only to the extent that the income is remitted to the UK. This is known as the "remittance basis". The term "relevant foreign income" covers most of the forms of overseas income to which ITTOIA 2005 applies.

   In general, an individual who wishes that the remittance basis should apply for a tax year must make a claim to that effect. However, the remittance basis is automatically assumed to apply to an individual whose unremitted income and gains are less than £2,000 in the year concerned (unless the individual notifies HMRC that he/she does not wish the remittance basis to apply).

   (iii) Adults who claim the remittance basis and have been UK resident for more than seven of the past ten tax years (including the current year) cannot continue to use the remittance basis unless they pay an annual tax charge of £30,000 in relation to their unremitted income and gains. Since this rule applies only to those who *claim* the remittance basis, it does not apply to individuals whose unremitted income and gains are less than £2,000 for the tax year.

   (iv) Personal allowances may generally be claimed by UK residents. But individuals who claim the remittance basis are not entitled to personal allowances (or the CGT annual exempt amount). Again, this rule applies only to those who *claim* the remittance basis and so does not apply to individuals whose unremitted income and gains are less than £2,000 for the tax year.

(b) Individuals who are *not resident* in the UK are liable to pay UK income tax on their UK income only. Note that:

   (i) The property income of non-residents is usually payable after deduction of basic rate income tax by the letting agent or tenant.

   (ii) Personal allowances may be claimed by certain non-residents, principally those who are citizens of the European Economic Area (see Chapter 3).

(c) If a tax year is apportioned into periods of residence and non-residence, the above rules apply to the two periods as if they were separate tax years.

These general rules are subject to a number of exceptions, depending upon the type of income involved (see below).

Unremittable income

A UK resident who would normally be liable to income tax on income arising from an overseas source may make a claim to the effect that the income is "unremittable". Such a claim may be made if the income cannot be remitted to the UK because of:

(a)   the laws of the country in which the income arises, or

(b)   the executive actions of the government of that country, or

(c)   the impossibility of obtaining foreign currency in that country which could be transferred to the UK.

The effect of the claim is that the income is not taxed in the year in which it arises but is taxed instead in the year in which it ceases to be unremittable (if that occurs).

Double taxation relief (DTR)

The rules given above are likely to lead to a number of situations in which income is taxed twice. For example, the overseas income of a UK resident will be taxed in the UK and might also be taxed in the country in which the income arises, depending upon that country's tax laws. Similarly, the UK income of a non-resident will be taxed in the UK and might also be taxed overseas. In order to avoid this situation, the UK has made "double taxation treaties" with many overseas countries. Typically, such a treaty might provide that certain forms of income should be exempt from income tax in the country of origin (or charged at a reduced rate) if receivable by a non-resident.

Unilateral double tax relief

Unless over-ridden by a double taxation treaty, the UK tax system provides "unilateral double tax relief" for any foreign tax which has been suffered by a UK resident who receives overseas income. Overseas income received net of foreign tax is grossed-up and charged to UK income tax in the usual way, but the taxpayer is then given tax relief equal to the *lower* of:

(a)   the amount of foreign tax suffered (the "withholding tax") and

(b)   the amount of UK tax due on the overseas income.

The amount of UK tax due on the overseas income is equal to the difference between the tax due on the taxpayer's total income (including overseas income) and the tax which would be due if the overseas income were ignored. If the foreign tax suffered exceeds the UK tax due, part of the foreign tax suffered will be unrelieved.

Unilateral relief is available only if the taxpayer has taken all reasonable steps to minimise the amount of the foreign tax liability.

EXAMPLE 2

Vicky's income for 2009-10 consists of her salary from UK employment of £44,130 and rents from overseas property (net of 30% withholding tax) of £3,500. Vicky is UK resident in 2009-10. Calculate her UK income tax liability for the year.

Solution

	£
Employment income	44,130
Property income (£3,500 x 100/70)	5,000
	49,130
Less: Personal allowance	6,475
Taxable income	42,655

Income tax	
37,400 @ 20%	7,480.00
5,255 @ 40%	2,102.00
42,655	9,582.00

Less: Double tax relief, lower of:	
(a) foreign tax (£1,500)	1,500.00
(b) UK tax on foreign income (40% x £5,000)	
UK tax liability	8,082.00

Income from employment

Income from employment is taxed according to detailed rules contained in the Income Tax (Earnings and Pensions) Act 2003. Broadly, the extent to which an individual's income from employment is taxable depends upon the individual's residence status and whether the duties of the employment are performed in the UK or overseas. The rules are briefly summarised as follows:

(a) **Employee resident in UK**. Unless the remittance basis applies to the individual concerned (see below) the entire employment income of an individual who is UK resident is taxable on the receipts basis, regardless of whether the duties of the employment are performed in the UK or overseas.

(b) **Employee resident in UK (remittance basis)**. As explained earlier in this chapter, the remittance basis may apply to a UK resident individual who is either not domiciled in the UK or not ordinarily resident in the UK (or both). If the remittance basis applies, then the extent to which employment income is taxable depends upon whether the individual is ordinarily resident in the UK. The situation is as follows:

(i)   If the individual is ordinarily resident in the UK, any employment income that is classified as "chargeable overseas earnings" is taxed on the remittance basis. All other employment income is fully taxable (on the receipts basis). Chargeable overseas earnings are those which are derived from a foreign employer in respect of duties performed wholly outside the UK.

(ii) If the individual is *not* ordinarily resident in the UK, employment income that is classified as "foreign earnings" is taxed on the remittance basis. All other employment income is fully taxable (on the receipts basis). Foreign earnings are those which are in respect of duties performed wholly outside the UK.

(c)   **Employee not resident in UK**. The employment income of an individual who is not resident in the UK is taxable (on the receipts basis) only to the extent that the income is in respect of duties performed in the UK.

Note that the income tax on *foreign pensions* received by a UK resident is calculated on only 90% of the amount arising unless the remittance basis applies, in which case the whole of the amount remitted to the UK is taxable.

The 100% deduction for seafarers

Individuals who are resident, ordinarily resident and domiciled in the UK are normally taxed on all of their employment income, whether their duties are performed in the UK or abroad. However, in the case of *seafarers*, if the duties are performed wholly or partly outside the UK throughout a continuous qualifying period of 365 days or more, a 100% deduction is given against all of the earnings for that period (including earnings relating to any work performed in the UK). In effect, the earnings attributable to such a qualifying period are exempt from UK income tax.

A qualifying period begins when an individual leaves the UK to work abroad as a seafarer and the period is treated as continuous even if the individual returns to the UK from time to time, so long as:

(a)   no visit in the UK during the period lasts for more than 183 days, and

(b)   on each day of return to the UK, the total number of days present in the UK since the period began is no more than one-half of the total length of the period so far.

If condition (a) is broken, the qualifying period ends immediately before the start of the offending UK visit. If condition (b) is broken, the qualifying period ends immediately before the start of the most recent UK visit.

Travelling and subsistence expenses

If the duties of an employment are performed abroad, the employee is both resident and ordinarily resident in the UK and the earnings from the employment are not classed as "chargeable overseas earnings" (see above), then the following expenses may be deducted from the employee's earnings for tax purposes:

(a)   where duties are performed wholly abroad:

    (i)   the costs of travelling abroad at the start of the employment and travelling back to the UK at the end of it

    (ii) the costs of overseas board and lodging provided or reimbursed by the employer to enable the employee to perform the duties of the overseas employment

(b)   where duties are performed partly in the UK and partly abroad, travelling and subsistence expenses paid for or reimbursed by the employer (and assessable as earnings) relating to:

    (i)   travel by the employee between the UK and the overseas place of work

    (ii) travel by the employee's spouse and minor children, if the employee is working abroad for a continuous period of 60 days or more, but limited to two return journeys per person per tax year.

Similar deductions to those described at (b) above are available to non-UK domiciled individuals who are working in the UK but these deductions are available for only five years, beginning with the date of arrival in the UK.

Trading income

The extent to which the profits of a trade, profession or vocation are charged to UK income tax depends upon whether or not the owner of the business is UK resident and whether the business is carried on in the UK or overseas. The rules are as follows:

(a)   Trading profits arising to a UK resident are charged to income tax wherever in the world the trade is carried on. Therefore UK residents are taxed on the profits of businesses which are carried on wholly or partly overseas.

(b)   If a business is carried on wholly overseas, then income arising from that business ranks as "relevant foreign income" (see above). Therefore a UK resident who is not domiciled in the UK or who is not ordinarily resident in the UK may claim that the income concerned should be taxed on the remittance basis.

(c)   Trading losses arising from a business carried on wholly overseas may be carried forward in the usual way (see Chapter 11). Such losses are also eligible for terminal loss relief if incurred in the final year of trading. But "sideways relief" against total income is available only against overseas income which is not charged on the remittance basis and which consists of:

    (i)   trading profits arising from a business which is carried on wholly overseas

    (ii) employment income ranking as "chargeable overseas earnings" (see above)

    (iii) overseas pensions.

(d) Trading profits arising to a non-UK resident are charged to income tax only if the trade is carried on wholly or partly in the UK. In the case of a trade which is carried on only partly in the UK, the profits which are charged to income tax are the profits arising from the UK part of the trade.

Travelling and subsistence expenses

If a trade is carried on wholly overseas and the owner of the business is absent from the UK wholly and exclusively for business purposes, then the expenses listed below are allowable deductions when computing trading profits (so long as those profits are not taxed on the remittance basis):

(a) expenses incurred by the trader in travelling between the UK and the location of the overseas business

(b) overseas board and lodging expenses

(c) expenses relating to travel by the proprietor's spouse and minor children, if the proprietor is abroad for a continuous period of 60 days or more, but limited to two return journeys per person per tax year.

Income from property and investments

Income from property and income from savings and investments are charged to UK income tax according to the following rules:

(a) Income from property situated in the UK is taxable whether or not the person to whom the income arises is UK resident. Income from property situated overseas is taxable only if the person to whom the income arises is UK resident.

(b) Savings and investment income from a UK source is generally taxable whether or not the person to whom the income arises is UK resident. However, interest on UK Government securities is exempt from UK income tax if the recipient is *not ordinarily resident* in the UK. Savings and investment income from an overseas source is taxable only if the person to whom the income arises is UK resident.

(c) Overseas property income and overseas savings and investment income generally rank as "relevant foreign income" (see above). Therefore a UK resident who is not domiciled in the UK or who is not ordinarily resident in the UK may claim that these forms of income should be taxed on the remittance basis. However, overseas savings and investment income which is taxed on the remittance basis is taxed as if it were non-savings income (see Chapter 2) and so cannot benefit from the starting rate for savings (10%) or the dividend lower and upper rates (10% and 32.5%).

(d) Dividends received from UK companies by UK resident individuals (and by certain non-residents, mainly nationals of the European Economic Area) carry a one-ninth tax credit. As from 6 April 2008, one-ninth tax credits are also available in relation to dividends received from non-UK companies, as long as the individual who receives the dividend owns less than 10% of the company's shares.

As from 6 April 2009, the one-ninth tax credit is extended to individuals who own 10% or more of a non-UK company's shares, subject to certain conditions. The main condition (broadly) is that the company must be resident in a territory which charges a tax on corporate profits that is similar to corporation tax.

Capital gains tax - general rules

The general rules which govern an individual's liability to UK capital gains tax (CGT) are as follows:

(a) Individuals who are resident or ordinarily resident in the UK for a tax year are liable to CGT in relation to all disposals of chargeable assets which occur in that year, no matter where in the world the assets are situated. Double tax relief may be available.

(b) Individuals who are neither resident nor ordinarily resident in the UK are not liable to CGT at all, even in relation to disposals of assets situated in the UK.

There are three main exceptions to these general rules:

(a) A non-UK domiciled individual who is resident or ordinarily resident in the UK is fully liable to CGT on the disposal of assets situated in the UK. However, gains arising from disposals of assets situated overseas may (in certain circumstances) be taxable only on the remittance basis.

(b) An individual who is neither resident nor ordinarily resident in the UK but who carries on a business in the UK is chargeable to CGT in relation to disposals of business assets situated in the UK.

(c) Individuals who acquire assets before temporarily leaving the UK (for up to five tax years) and then dispose of those assets whilst abroad remain chargeable to CGT in relation to these disposals. Gains arising in the tax year of departure are taxed in that year. Later gains are taxed in the year in which residence resumes.

A claim may be made to defer a CGT assessment relating to a disposal of overseas assets if it can be shown that the gain in question cannot be remitted to the UK. The conditions which must be satisfied in order that such a claim should be successful are the same as the equivalent conditions for income tax (see above). The taxpayer must show that the gain cannot be remitted to the UK because of either:

(a) the laws of the country in which the gain arises, or

(b) the executive actions of the government of that country, or

(c) the impossibility of obtaining foreign currency in that country.

If the conditions preventing remittance of the gain to the UK subsequently cease to exist, the gain is chargeable in the year in which this occurs.

Inheritance tax - general rules

An individual who is domiciled in the UK is liable to inheritance tax (IHT) in relation to all of his or her chargeable property, wherever in the world that property is situated. An individual who is not domiciled in the UK is liable to IHT only in relation to property situated in the UK. The definition of "domicile" for IHT purposes is broader than the general definition given earlier in this chapter. An individual is treated as domiciled in the UK on the date of a transfer if that individual:

(a) was domiciled in the UK at any time within the previous three years, or

(b) was UK resident for at least seventeen of the twenty tax years ending with the year in which the transfer takes place.

In general, transfers between spouses are exempt from IHT (see Chapter 31). However, transfers made by a UK-domiciled spouse to a spouse who is not UK-domiciled are exempt only up to a cumulative total of £55,000. This rule applies equally to same-sex civil partners who have entered into a legally-recognised civil partnership.

Corporation tax - general rules

A company's liability to UK corporation tax depends upon whether or not it is resident in the UK. A company is regarded as resident in the UK if it is incorporated in the UK or if its central management and control is situated in the UK. The general rules which govern a company's liability to UK corporation tax are as follows:

(a) A UK resident company is chargeable to UK corporation tax on all of its profits, no matter where in the world those profits are earned. Note the following points:

    (i) The profits of a trade conducted through a permanent establishment situated overseas (e.g. an overseas branch) are treated as trading income. Trading losses may be relieved as usual and group relief is generally available. However, the losses of an overseas establishment may be surrendered to another UK resident company in the same group only to the extent that those losses are not relievable in the overseas country.

    (ii) As from 1 July 2009, most foreign dividends received by UK companies are exempt from corporation tax (subject to certain exceptions and anti-avoidance provisions) and are treated as if they were dividends received from other UK companies An exempt foreign dividend received on or after 1 July 2009 is therefore deemed to have an attached one-ninth tax credit and the amount of the dividend (plus the tax credit) is treated as FII.

    (iii) Gains arising on the disposal of overseas assets are chargeable gains and form part of the company's chargeable profits.

(b) A non-UK resident company is chargeable to UK corporation tax only if it carries on a trade through a permanent establishment situated in the UK. If so, the company is taxed on:

(i) the trading profits of the UK establishment

(ii) income from property in the possession of the UK establishment

(iii) gains arising from the disposal of assets used by the UK establishment.

The trading losses of a UK permanent establishment of a non-UK resident company may generally be set against any other profits of the establishment or may be carried forward against the establishment's future trading profits. The establishment may also surrender its losses to UK resident companies in the same group, so long as those losses are not relievable in the overseas country. Similarly, the establishment may claim losses surrendered by other UK resident group companies. Also, assets transferred between such an establishment and a UK resident group company are transferred on a no-gain, no-loss basis, so long as the assets concerned remain within the charge to UK corporation tax.

A non-UK resident company is not generally entitled to the small companies rate of corporation tax or to marginal relief. But this rule will not apply if it is over-ridden by a double taxation treaty between the UK and the country in which the non-UK company is resident.

Overseas subsidiaries

The profits of a non-UK resident subsidiary of a UK resident parent company may be subject to overseas tax but are not generally subject to UK tax unless the subsidiary is treated as a controlled foreign company (see later in this chapter). The UK resident parent company is of course liable to corporation tax on any non-exempt income received from the overseas subsidiary (e.g. interest) and the subsidiary will count as an associated company for small company relief purposes.

As explained in Chapter 28, groups of companies enjoy a number of corporation tax reliefs, including (subject to certain conditions):

(a) transfer of trading losses and certain other items between group members

(b) transfer of chargeable assets between group members on a no-gain, no-loss basis.

These reliefs are generally available only to UK resident companies and do not usually apply to an overseas subsidiary. However, the losses of a subsidiary which is resident in the European Economic Area (EEA) may be surrendered to a UK company, but only after all possibilities of relief in any other country have been exhausted. In order to obtain relief against UK profits, the foreign losses must be re-computed under UK tax rules.

Company migration

A UK resident company may wish to "migrate" overseas in order to escape paying UK corporation tax on its worldwide profits. This is only possible for companies which are incorporated outside the UK and involves moving the central management and control of the company from the UK to an overseas location. A company wishing to take this step must:

(a) notify HMRC of its intentions, specifying the date on which it intends to become non-resident, and

(b) provide HMRC with a statement of all the tax payable up to that date, specifying the arrangements which will be made to ensure that this tax is paid.

On the date that a company becomes non-resident it is deemed to make a disposal of all its assets at their market value on that date. This deemed disposal is likely to result in a sizeable chargeable gain, which is sometimes referred to as the "exit charge". However, this charge is not made in full in the following circumstances:

(a) If the company retains a permanent establishment in the UK, the deemed disposal does not include assets which are situated in the UK and which are used for trade purposes by that establishment.

(b) If the company is a 75% subsidiary of a UK resident company (termed the "principal company") the gains arising in connection with the deemed disposal of the company's *foreign* assets may be postponed, so long as both companies make an election in writing to that effect. The postponed gains will crystallise if:

(i) within the following six years, any of the foreign assets are disposed of, or

(ii) at any time, the company which is migrating ceases to be a 75% subsidiary of the principal company, or

(iii) at any time, the principal company ceases to be UK resident.

Any gains which crystallise are chargeable on the principal company.

Transfer pricing

A UK resident company might try to reduce its corporation tax liability by transferring goods at an artificially low price to an overseas subsidiary. This would have the effect of lowering the UK company's profits (which are liable to UK tax) and increasing the subsidiary's profits (which are not liable to UK tax).

However, this tax avoidance manoeuvre is blocked by "transfer pricing" legislation which requires that a true market price should be substituted for the transfer price in these circumstances and that the UK company should make the necessary adjustment when completing its self-assessment tax return (see Chapter 28). Small and medium-sized companies are generally exempt from the transfer pricing legislation.

Controlled foreign companies (CFCs)

A UK resident company which wishes to operate overseas may operate through an overseas permanent establishment (e.g. an overseas branch) or through a separate non-UK resident company which is under its control (an overseas subsidiary).

Since the profits of a non-UK resident company are not generally chargeable to UK corporation tax, it would seem to be beneficial for a UK company to adopt the second of these alternatives, especially if the operation is carried on in a country with low tax rates. The overseas profits would not be subject to UK tax at all and (as from 1 July 2009) any dividends paid to the UK company by the overseas subsidiary would be exempt from corporation tax (subject to certain exceptions).

As an anti-avoidance measure, the profits of a *controlled foreign company* (CFC) are apportioned between its shareholders for tax purposes and CFC profits apportioned to a UK resident company are charged to corporation tax. This tax is calculated at the average rate payable by the UK company for the accounting period in which the CFC's accounting period ends. Double taxation relief (see below) is available. However, no assessment is raised on a UK company to which less than 25% of a CFC's profits are apportioned. A CFC is a company which:

(a) is resident overseas but is under UK control, and

(b) is subject to a level of taxation in the country in which it is resident which is less than 75% of the corresponding UK tax, or

(c) is resident in one of a number of countries which (in effect) allow companies to choose their own "designer rate" of tax as a means of side-stepping the CFC rules.

The definition of "control" for this purpose normally means that the overseas company must be more than 50% controlled from the UK. However, an overseas company will also be treated as a CFC if it is at least 40% controlled by a UK company and at least 40% (but not more than 55%) controlled by a foreign company. The profits of a CFC for an accounting period are usually *not* apportioned between its shareholders if any of the following conditions are satisfied for that period:

(a) The profits of the CFC for the period do not exceed £50,000 per annum.

(b) The CFC is engaged in certain exempt activities.

(c) The CFC was not set up mainly to achieve a reduction in UK tax.

The CFC rules do not apply to profits which arise from "genuine economic activities" conducted from a business establishment located in the European Economic Area (EEA). This comprises all EU states plus Norway, Iceland and Liechtenstein.

Double taxation relief for companies

A UK resident company which receives income from overseas is generally entitled to unilateral double taxation relief (unless this is over-ridden by the terms of a double taxation treaty). Unilateral relief takes the form of a tax credit equal to the *lower* of the amount of foreign tax suffered and the amount of UK tax which is payable on the foreign income. Any excess foreign tax is unrelieved, but it may be possible to carry the excess back or forward to other accounting periods (see below).

EXAMPLE 3

In the year to 31 March 2010, a UK resident company had UK trading profits of £5,200,000 and overseas property income (net of 35% withholding tax) of £130,000. Compute the corporation tax liability for the year.

Solution

	UK	Overseas	Total
	£	£	£
Trading income	5,200,000		5,200,000
Property income £130,000 x 100/65		200,000	200,000
Chargeable profits	5,200,000	200,000	5,400,000
Corporation tax @ 28%	1,456,000	56,000	1,512,000
Less: Unilateral DTR		(56,000)	(56,000)
Corporation tax due	1,456,000	-	1,456,000

Note:

The unilateral relief given is restricted to the UK tax due on the overseas income. The remaining £14,000 (£70,000 – £56,000) of foreign tax paid is unrelieved.

Unrelieved foreign tax

Unrelieved foreign tax arising in connection with certain types of overseas income is known as eligible unrelieved foreign tax (EUFT). EUFT may be carried back to accounting periods beginning not more than three years before the period in which the EUFT arises or may be carried forward without time limit. Note that:

(a) When EUFT arising in respect of a source of income is carried back or forward, it is treated as if it were foreign tax paid in respect of that same source of income in the accounting period to which it is carried back or forward.

(b) The carry-back and carry-forward provisions relate only to foreign tax on the profits of an overseas establishment and foreign tax on non-exempt dividends. In the case of dividends, the rules extend to underlying tax (see below) as well as to direct tax.

Underlying DTR

If a UK resident company owns at least 10% of the voting power of an overseas company from which it receives a non-exempt dividend, then an additional form of unilateral double taxation relief, known as "underlying relief", is available. The idea of underlying DTR is to give relief for the foreign tax suffered on the profits out of which the dividend has been paid. Underlying relief is calculated by the formula:

$$\frac{D}{P} \times T$$

where: D = the gross dividend received

P = the profit available for distribution as shown in the accounts for the accounting period to which the dividend relates

T = the overseas tax actually paid on the profits of that period.

However, since most foreign dividends received by UK companies on or after 1 July 2009 are exempt from corporation tax, it would seem that underlying double tax relief will now be claimed only infrequently.

EXAMPLE 4

On 1 May 2009, a UK company receives a dividend from an overseas company (of which it has 15% of the voting power) of £10,500, net of 30% withholding tax. The income statement of the overseas company for the year to which the dividend relates is as follows:

	£
Profit before tax	400,000
Less: Provision for taxation liability	150,000
Profits after tax	250,000
Dividends	100,000
Retained profits c/f	150,000

The actual tax liability of the overseas company is finally agreed at £160,000. Compute the maximum unilateral double tax relief available in respect of the £10,500 dividend.

Solution

The dividend is not exempt from tax, since it was received before 1 July 2009. The DTR calculation is as follows:

(i) D = £10,500 x 100/70 = £15,000. P = £250,000. T = £160,000

(ii) Withholding tax = £4,500

(iii)   Underlying tax $= \dfrac{D}{P} \times T = \dfrac{£15,000}{£250,000} \times £160,000 = £9,600$

(iv)   Maximum unilateral DTR $= £4,500 + £9,600 = £14,100$. Therefore the gross dividend is £24,600 (net £10,500 + tax £14,100).

Unilateral expense relief

A company may waive the right to claim unilateral "credit relief" (where DTR takes the form of a tax credit) and opt for unilateral "expense relief". In this case, the company is assessed on the *net* foreign income, so that the foreign tax is treated as if it were an expense. Unilateral expense relief may be attractive if a company makes a s393A(1)(a) claim to set a trading loss against its total profits, so that it has no corporation tax liability on the foreign income and cannot obtain any credit relief.

EXAMPLE 5

A UK company has a trading loss of £50,000 for the year to 31 March 2010. During the year, the company receives overseas property income of £12,000, net of 40% withholding tax. Show the corporation tax computation for the year if:

(a)   unilateral credit relief is claimed

(b)   unilateral expense relief is claimed.

Note: The company will be claiming loss relief under s393A(1)(a).

Solution

	Credit relief £	Expense relief £
Trading income	0	0
Property income (gross)	20,000	
Property income (net of foreign tax)		12,000
	20,000	12,000
Less: s393A(1)(a) relief	(20,000)	(12,000)
Chargeable profits	0	0
Corporation tax liability	0	0
Unrelieved trading losses	30,000	38,000
Unrelieved foreign tax	8,000	nil

Notes:

(i)   No unilateral credit relief is available since the overseas income is absorbed by the s393A(1)(a) claim, leaving a UK tax liability of £nil.

(ii)   Credit relief gives £8,000 of unrelieved foreign tax. This might be relievable by carry-forward or by carry-back (see earlier in this chapter). But if the overseas income is always received net of 40% tax and UK tax rates are generally much lower than this, it is unlikely that there will be any scope for relieving the £8,000.

(iii) Expense relief increases by £8,000 the trading losses available for carry-back under s393A(1)(b) or carry-forward under s393(1).

Interaction of charges, loss reliefs and DTR

As explained in Chapters 23 and 26, a company's chargeable profits are reduced by the amount of any charges paid in the accounting period and by the amount of any loss relief claimed under s393A(1). Normally, it is sufficient simply to subtract the charges and loss reliefs from total income without allocating these deductions to particular sources of income. However, if unilateral double tax relief is claimed, such an allocation must be made so that the amount of UK tax payable on the foreign income can then be computed.

Clearly, if any charges or losses are deemed to be set against the foreign income, this will have the effect of reducing the UK tax due on that foreign income and so reducing the maximum unilateral DTR available. Therefore charges and losses should be set first against UK income, then against foreign income. If a company has more than one source of foreign income, charges and losses should be set against foreign income which has suffered low rates of foreign tax in preference to foreign income which has suffered high rates of foreign tax.

DTR and relief of surplus ACT

If a company has surplus ACT brought forward from before 6 April 1999, the amount of that ACT which can be relieved in an accounting period is governed by the shadow ACT regulations (see Chapter 25). These regulations stipulate that the maximum ACT set-off for an accounting period is equal to the ACT which would be payable on a franked payment equal to the chargeable profits for that period. If double tax relief is claimed, the maximum offset is further restricted to the amount of corporation tax payable on each source of income after DTR has been deducted.

EXAMPLE 6

In the year to 31 March 2010, a UK company has UK trading profits of £4,800,000 and receives overseas property income (net of 45% withholding tax) of £2,750,000. Charges of £1,000,000 are paid in the year.

(a) Compute the corporation tax liability for the year.

(b) Compute the maximum ACT set-off for the year.

Solution

	UK £	Overseas £	Total £
Trading income	4,800,000		4,800,000
Income from property:			
£2,750,000 x 100/55		5,000,000	5,000,000
	4,800,000	5,000,000	9,800,000
Less: Charges	1,000,000	-	1,000,000
Chargeable profits	3,800,000	5,000,000	8,800,000
Corporation tax @ 28%	1,064,000	1,400,000	2,464,000
Less: Unilateral DTR		(1,400,000)	(1,400,000)
Corporation tax liability	1,064,000	-	1,064,000
Maximum ACT set-off	760,000	-	760,000

Notes:

(i) The charges are set against the UK income so as to maximise double tax relief on the overseas income.

(ii) DTR is limited to the UK tax due on the overseas income. Foreign tax paid is £2,250,000, of which £850,000 is unrelieved.

(iii) ACT set-off is restricted in the usual way but is also restricted to the corporation tax liability on each source of income after deduction of DTR. For the UK income, the first of these restrictions gives a maximum set-off of £760,000 (20% of £3,800,000). For the overseas income, the second restriction gives a maximum set-off of £nil.

(iv) As usual, the shadow ACT arising on any dividends paid in the year will use up some or all of the maximum ACT set-off and so reduce the scope for relieving surplus ACT brought forward from before 6 April 1999.

Summary

▶ An individual's liability to UK tax depends upon that individual's residence, ordinary residence and domicile.

▶ Individuals who are resident in the UK for a tax year are liable to UK income tax on their worldwide income for that year. Non-residents are liable to tax on their UK income only.

▶ Double taxation relief may be available if income is subject to both UK tax and overseas tax.

▶ The extent to which an individual's income from employment is taxable depends upon the individual's residence status and whether the duties of the employment are performed in the UK or overseas.

▶ Trading profits arising to a UK resident are charged to income tax wherever in the world the trade is carried on. Trading profits arising to a non-resident are charged to income tax only if the trade is carried on wholly or partly in the UK.

▶ Income from UK property and investments is generally taxable whether or not the person to whom the income arises is UK resident. Income from overseas property and investments is taxable only if the person to whom the income arises is UK resident.

▶ Individuals who are resident or ordinarily resident in the UK for a tax year are liable to UK CGT on their disposals throughout the world in that year.

▶ Individuals who are domiciled in the UK are liable to UK IHT. The definition of "domicile" for IHT purposes is broader than the general definition.

▶ UK resident companies are liable to UK corporation tax on their worldwide profits. A non-UK resident company is liable to UK corporation tax only if it carries on a trade through a permanent establishment situated in the UK.

▶ As from 1 July 2009, most foreign dividends received by UK companies are exempt from corporation tax.

▶ The profits of a controlled foreign company may be apportioned between the controlling UK companies and assessed to UK corporation tax.

▶ Double tax relief for companies may take the form of credit relief, underlying tax relief or expense relief.

Exercises

32.1   Jean-Paul is a Canadian citizen. He owns a house in Canada and regards Canada as his home but he lives in London for nearly all of tax year 2009-10. His income for the year is derived from the following sources:

(a)   a part-time employment with a UK company (the duties of which are performed entirely in London)

(b)   a second part-time employment with a Belgian company (the duties of which are performed entirely in Brussels, which he visits on one day each month)

(c)   dividends from stocks and shares held in Canada

(d)   interest on UK Government securities.

To what extent is any of his income chargeable to UK income tax?

32.2   Amy is domiciled in the UK and has lived in the UK all her life. On 1 January 2008 she leaves to work in Australia for three years. Explain her UK income tax status for tax years 2007-08 to 2010-11 inclusive.

32.3   Cara is a UK resident. She receives a pension of £10,000 per annum from the Italian company for whom she used to work when she lived in Italy. Explain how the UK income tax system will treat this pension if Cara is:

(a)   domiciled in the UK

(b)   domiciled in Italy.

32.4   How would a UK resident company proceed if it wished to "migrate" overseas? Why might this be a desirable step?

32.5   Explain the term "controlled foreign company" (CFC). In what circumstances are the profits of a CFC chargeable to UK corporation tax?

32.6   Brits Ltd is a UK resident company and has a trading profit of £2,120,000 for the year ended 31 March 2010. On 3 May 2009, the company received a dividend from a wholly-owned overseas subsidiary of £57,400 (net of 18% withholding tax).

The overseas company is liable to 50% overseas tax on all of its profits and has provided for this correctly in its financial statements. Compute the corporation tax liability of Brits Ltd for the year.

*32.7   Donald is domiciled, resident and ordinarily resident in the UK. He has the following income in 2009-10:

	£
UK trading profits	38,175
UK bank interest (net amount)	1,600
Income from foreign property (net of 45% withholding tax)	2,200

Donald claims only the personal allowance. Compute the amount of income tax payable for 2009-10.

*32.8   X Ltd is a UK resident company with nineteen subsidiaries, one of which is situated abroad. In the year to 31 March 2010, X Ltd had the following results:

	£
UK trading profits	720,000
UK dividends received	40,000
UK chargeable gains	120,000
Dividend from overseas subsidiary received April 2009 (net of 30% withholding tax)	8,400
Charges paid (gross amount)	80,000

X Ltd owns 60% of the ordinary share capital of the overseas subsidiary (which is not a controlled foreign company). The summarised income statement of this subsidiary for the year to which the April 2009 dividend relates is as follows:

	£
Profit before tax	75,000
Less: Provision for taxation liability	25,000
Profits after tax	50,000
Dividends	20,000
Retained profits c/f	30,000

The subsidiary's actual tax liability for the year was £25,000.

(a)   Calculate the corporation tax liability of X Ltd for the year to 31 March 2010.

(b)   Calculate the maximum ACT set-off for the year.

Review questions (Set D)

D1   You have received a letter from the managing director of Wakem & Co. Ltd, a company making wholly standard rated supplies. Extracts from the letter are as follows:

"During the course of the last quarter, sales have been very good. In particular, we sold £30,000 worth of goods to St. Oggs Inc, an American company, and we also sold £20,000 worth of goods to Rappit Ltd in Scotland. Mr Jakin, the managing director of Rappit Ltd, drove a hard bargain and to secure the order we had to allow a 5% discount for prompt settlement. As we closed down the box manufacturing line, we sold off the machinery and made a useful £15,000. The electrical equipment remaining has been hired to Mudport Ltd for £1,000 per month. One piece of bad news is that Garum Furs plc has gone into liquidation owing us £14,000, though there is a possibility of recovering part of that amount in the liquidation."

Required:

Explain the significance for VAT purposes of the events described in this letter.

(Amended from AAT)

D2   A Ltd is the holding company for a group of five companies. The relationships between the companies in the group are shown in the diagram below:

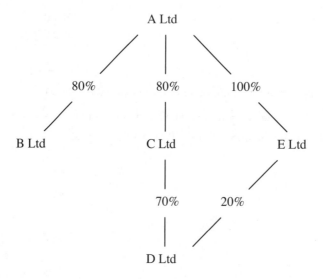

All of the companies are UK resident except for E Ltd which is resident in a non-EEA country where the rate of tax is 5%. For the purposes of this question, E Ltd can be regarded as a Controlled Foreign Company. All of the companies have an accounting year ended 31 March 2010 and their incomes/(losses) for the year were as follows:

	Trading income £	Bank interest £
A Ltd	90,000	-
B Ltd	100,000	15,000
C Ltd	(90,000)	12,000
D Ltd	(5,000)	-
E Ltd	15,000	-

You are required:

(a) To identify the companies which are treated as associated companies.

(b) To identify the companies which form a group (or groups) for group relief purposes.

(c) To compute the corporation tax liability of each company, assuming that the most efficient use is made by the group of any trading losses. Assume also that none of the companies paid or received any dividends during the year.   *(CIMA)*

D3   Your company has a number of branches and subsidiaries trading outside the UK. The board is about to offer contracts to employees working in UK locations which will allow them to transfer to foreign locations on a temporary basis, with all of their duties being performed outside the UK. There are two contracts being offered - one lasting nine months and one lasting eighteen months. The employees concerned are all currently resident, ordinarily resident and domiciled in the UK.

You are required:

To draft a report to the board on the taxation implications, for the employees, of each of the possible contracts.   *(CIMA)*

D4   M Ltd, a UK resident trading company, owns 6% of the share capital of Z Inc and 8% of the share capital of X S.A. Neither of these companies is resident in the UK for tax purposes. In addition, M Ltd has a controlling interest in two UK resident companies - N Ltd and O Ltd. The following information relates to M Ltd's 12-month accounting period ended 31 March 2010:

	£
INCOME	
Trading income	500,000
Dividend received from Z Inc on 1 April 2009 (after 30% withholding tax)	35,000
Dividend received from X S.A. on 1 May 2009 (after 5% withholding tax)	38,000
CHARGE PAID (gross amount)	10,000

M Ltd also has a substantial amount of unrelieved surplus ACT brought forward from before 6 April 1999.

You are required:

To compute the corporation tax liability of M Ltd for the above period, showing clearly the relief for double taxation. Also calculate the maximum ACT set-off for the period.

(CIMA)

*D5   David Deans started trading as a painter and decorator on 1 July 2009. He has notified you of his turnover each month which, up to November 2009, has been as follows:

	£
July 2009	6,000
August 2009	7,000
September 2009	8,000
October 2009	9,200
November 2009	10,000

In anticipation of a meeting with Mr Deans, you have received a letter from him, of which the following is an extract:

"In preparation for our meeting, I have some further information for you and some questions which I hope you will be able to answer for me. I anticipate that my turnover is likely to be £13,000 in December 2009 and £15,500 in January 2010. It must be reaching the time at which I need to be registered for VAT. Could you give me some idea of when this might be and whether I could delay it in order to improve my cash flow?

Since starting business I have purchased substantial quantities of stock. Will I be able to recover any of the VAT I have paid?

In June next year, I intend to buy a new van and a new car for the business. Their cost, including VAT, will be £14,000 and £8,000 respectively. I assume that I will be able to recover the VAT on both items. The van will be used wholly for business and the car for both business and private use. The firm will pay for all the petrol used by both vehicles.

As yet, I have not suffered any bad debts but as the business expands there is always the risk that they might arise. Are there any special VAT arrangements to deal with them?"

Required:

Draft notes in preparation for the meeting with Mr Deans, responding to the queries which he has raised.   *(Amended from AAT)*

*D6   Mrs Lammle, who is registered for VAT, has traded as a manufacturer of standard-rated items since 1 January 1992. She has decided to retire on 31 May 2009, her 65th birthday, and you are asked to finalise her tax position up to that date. You are provided with the following information:

(i) Mrs Lammle's first accounts covered the period to 31 May 1993. Since then, she has prepared accounts annually to 31 May. Adjusted profits for the year to 31 May 1997 were £45,000.

(ii) The last accounts will be for the year to 31 May 2009. Interim accounts have been prepared to 28 February 2009, revealing the following:

	£
Sales	100,200
Cost of sales	24,700
Gross profit	75,500
Expenses	29,000
Net profit	46,500

All of the above figures are net of VAT and contain no disallowable items.

(iii) For the last three months to 31 May 2009 (which is also the last VAT quarter), you have extracted the following figures from the accounting records:

	£
Sales:	
To UK customers	29,900
To overseas customers	8,000
Materials purchased:	
Standard-rated	4,025
Zero-rated	2,000
Exempt	800
Expenses:	
General (all standard-rated)	5,934
Wages	7,000
Hire of machinery	621
Business bank charges	500
Entertaining UK clients	400

All of the above include VAT if appropriate. There was no stock at 1 March 2009 and there is no outstanding stock left at 31 May 2009. All of the general expenses are allowable for income tax purposes.

(iv) The tax written down value of the plant and machinery carried forward after capital allowances had been calculated for the year to 31 May 2008 was:

	£
Plant and machinery main pool	12,375
Expensive car (with no private use)	5,250

No plant and machinery was acquired during the year to 31 May 2009.

(v)   The business was sold as a going concern on 31 May 2009. The items sold were:

	£
Freehold shop	200,000
Freehold workshop	130,000
Goodwill	180,000
Plant (no item worth more than £6,000)	25,000
Car	6,000

The shop and workshop were acquired on 1 January 1992 for £30,000 and £21,000 respectively.

Required:

(a)   Calculate the VAT due for the quarter to 31 May 2009.

(b)   Calculate the final adjusted profit for the year to 31 May 2009, after deduction of capital allowances.

(c)   Calculate Mrs Lammle's trading income for 2009-10.

(d)   Calculate the chargeable gain arising on the disposal of the business, assuming that entrepreneurs' relief is claimed and that Mrs Lammle has made no previous claims for this relief.   *(Amended from AAT)*

*D7   The group structure below shows holdings in ordinary shares in other companies. All of the companies are UK resident except for O Inc which is resident in a non-EEA country.

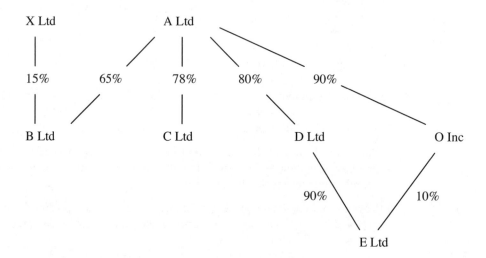

The results for each of the above companies for the accounting year ended 31 March 2010 are as follows (all profits and losses are trading profits and losses):

		£			£
X Ltd	Loss	(40,000)	D Ltd	Profit	35,000
B Ltd	Profit	60,000	O Inc	Loss	(30,000)
A Ltd	Profit	103,000	E Ltd	Loss	(2,000)
C Ltd	Loss	(70,000)			

You are required:

(a) To identify the associated companies for small companies rate purposes and to state the upper and lower thresholds for each of the companies shown.

(b) To identify any groups and consortia in the above structure qualifying for group relief.

(c) To compute the corporation tax liability of each company, assuming that loss relief has been claimed in the most efficient manner.

(d) To advise the directors of A Ltd on the weakness, from a tax point of view, of the existing structure. *(CIMA)*

*D8 You are the chief accountant of Z Ltd, a UK resident company, whose activities to date have been confined wholly to the UK. The company is about to acquire three UK resident subsidiaries and the members of the newly-formed group will engage, for the first time, in import and export activities (all with non-EU countries).

You are required:

To draft a brief report to the board on the VAT implications of the above changes.

(CIMA)

Part 5

ANSWERS

Answers to exercises

Chapter 2

2.1

(a) 1,830 @ 20% = £366.00.

(b) 32,300 @ 20% = £6,460.00.

(c) 37,400 @ 20% + 33,703 @ 40% = £20,961.20.

2.2

(a)

	Total £	Non-savings £	Savings £
Business profits	22,080	22,080	
Bank interest £720 × 100/80	900		900
Total income	22,980	22,080	900
<u>Less</u>: Personal allowance	6,475	6,475	
Taxable income	16,505	15,605	900

Income tax due

Non-savings income	: Basic rate	15,605	@ 20%	3,121.00	
Savings income	: Basic rate	900	@ 20%	180.00	
		16,505			
Tax borne				3,301.00	
<u>Less</u>: Tax deducted at source				180.00	
Tax payable				3,121.00	

(b)

	Total £	Non-savings £	Savings £
Business profits	31,610	31,610	
Building society interest £8,000 × 100/80	10,000		10,000
Bank interest £2,300 × 100/80	2,875		2,875
Total income	44,485	31,610	12,875
<u>Less</u>: Personal allowance	6,475	6,475	
Taxable income	38,010	25,135	12,875

Income tax due

Non-savings income	: Basic rate	25,135	@ 20%	5,027.00
Savings income	: Basic rate	12,265	@ 20%	2,453.00
	: Higher rate	610	@ 40%	244.00
		38,010		

Tax borne	7,724.00
Less: Tax deducted at source	2,575.00
Tax payable	5,149.00

(c)

Total (all savings income)

£

Building society interest £35,784 × 100/80	44,730
Total income	44,730
Less: Personal allowance	6,475
Taxable income	38,255

Income tax due

Savings income	: Starting rate	2,440	@ 10%	244.00
	: Basic rate	34,960	@ 20%	6,992.00
	: Higher rate	855	@ 40%	342.00
		38,255		

Tax borne	7,578.00
Less: Tax deducted at source	8,946.00
Tax refund due	(1,368.00)

2.3

	Total	Non-savings	Savings	Dividends
	£	£	£	£
Employment income	28,755	28,755		
Income from property	14,730	14,730		
Bank interest £144 × 100/80	180		180	
NSB investment a/c interest	20		20	
UK dividends £225 + tax credit £25	250			250
Total income	43,935	43,485	200	250
Less: Personal allowance	6,475	6,475		
Taxable income	37,460	37,010	200	250

Note: NSB investment a/c interest is received gross and so does not need to be grossed-up.

Income tax due

Non-savings income	: Basic rate	37,010	@ 20%	7,402.00
Savings income	: Basic rate	200	@ 20%	40.00
Dividend income	: Ordinary rate	190	@ 10%	19.00
	: Upper rate	60	@ 32.5%	19.50
		37,460		

Tax borne	7,480.50
Less: Tax credits on dividends	25.00
Tax payable	7,455.50
Less: Tax deducted at source	36.00
Tax payable	7,419.50

Note: Stephanie would also be given credit for any PAYE tax paid.

2.4

	Total £	Non-savings £	Savings £
Retirement pension	5,865	5,865	
Bank interest £416 × 100/80	520		520
Total income	6,385	5,865	520
Less: Personal allowance	6,385	5,865	520
Taxable income	0	0	0

£90 of the personal allowance (£6,475 – £6,385) is unused. Tax borne is £nil and Ernest is entitled to repayment of the £104.00 of tax deducted at source. If he received dividends of £468, dividend income of £520 (£468 + £52) would replace the bank interest but he would not be able to claim payment of the £52 tax credit.

Chapter 3

3.1

(a) This taxpayer is in the 65-74 age group and is entitled to a PA of £9,490 for the year.

(b) This taxpayer is over 75 and has an income which exceeds the limit by £1,000, giving a PA of £9,140 (£9,640 – 1/2 × £1,000).

(c) This taxpayer reaches the age of 65 during tax year 2009-10 and has an income which exceeds the limit by £8,600. This would give a PA of £5,190 (£9,490 – 1/2 × £8,600) but the allowance is not reduced to less than the PA for those under 65 so the taxpayer will claim £6,475.

3.2

(a) The husband is over 75 and therefore receives a PA of £9,640. His wife is over 65 but her income exceeds the limit by £300, giving her a PA of £9,340 (£9,490 – 1/2 × £300). MCA is £6,965 (which is not reduced, since the husband's income does not exceed the limit).

(b) The husband is over 75 but his income exceeds the limit by £700, giving him a PA of £9,290 (£9,640 − 1/2 × £700). His wife is over 75 and is entitled to a PA of £9,640 (of which £590 is unused). An MCA of £6,965 is also available. This is not reduced at all since the reduction required because of the husband's income has already been made in full against his PA.

(c) The husband is over 75 but his income exceeds the limit by £6,400. Therefore he must lose a total of £3,200 in allowances. His own PA is first reduced from £9,640 to the minimum of £6,475 (a reduction of £3,165). The remaining £35 is deducted from the MCA of £6,965 giving an MCA of £6,930. His wife is over 65 and is therefore entitled to a PA of £9,490.

3.3

	(a) £	(b) £	(c) £
HUSBAND			
Net income	16,280	9,500	9,975
Less: Personal allowance	9,640	9,500	9,640
Taxable income	6,640	0	335
Income tax			
£6,640 @ 20%	1,328.00		
£0 @ 20%		0.00	
£335 @ 20%			67.00
Less: MCA £6,965 @ 10%	696.50		
MCA £6,965 @ 10% = £696.50			67.00
(£629.50 transferred to wife)			
Tax borne	631.50	0.00	0.00
WIFE			
Net income	17,580	13,515	17,445
Less: Personal allowance	9,640	9,640	9,640
Taxable income	7,940	3,875	7,805
Income tax			
£7,940 @ 20%	1,588.00		
£3,875 @ 20%		775.00	
£7,805 @ 20%			1,561.00
Less: MCA £6,965 × 8/12 @ 10%		464.33	
(higher-income partner)			
MCA transferred from husband			629.50
Tax borne	1,588.00	310.67	931.50

3.4

(a) No MCA is available if both taxpayers were born on or after 6 April 1935.

(b) The MCA is reduced to £6,965 × 2/12 = £1,161.

(c)   The husband has the higher net income and this is £1,600 over the limit. He cannot claim age-related PA so the MCA of £6,965 is reduced by £800 (1/2 × £1,600), giving £6,165. This is further reduced to £6,165 × 4/12 = £2,055.

3.5

	Total	Non-savings	Savings
	£	£	£
Retirement pension	8,620	8,620	
Bank interest £912 × 100/80	1,140		1,140
Total income	9,760	8,620	1,140
Less: Personal allowance	9,640	8,620	1,020
Taxable income	120	0	120

Income tax due

£120 @ 10%	12.00
Less: Tax deducted at source	228.00
Refund due	(216.00)

3.6

(a)   PA £6,475, Blind person's allowance £1,890   (b)   PA £6,475.

(c)   PA £6,475 (which is mostly unused).

3.7

	Richard	Patricia
	£	£
Business profits	22,930	
UK dividends £3,600 + £400		4,000
Less: Personal allowance	6,475	4,000
Taxable income	16,455	0

Income tax

	Richard	Patricia
£16,455 @ 20%	3,291.00	
£0 @ 10%		0.00
Less: MCA £6,950 @ 10%	695.00	
Tax borne	2,596.00	0.00
Less: Tax credits on dividends		0.00
Tax payable	2,596.00	0.00

Note:

Patricia is entitled to a PA of £9,640 but can use only £4,000 of this. She cannot claim payment of the £400 tax credits on dividends. MCA is £6,950 (£6,965 – 1/2 × £30).

Chapter 4

4.1

	£
Total income	21,180
<u>Less</u>: Payment £200 × 100/80	250
Net income	20,930
<u>Less</u>: Personal allowance	6,475
Taxable income	14,455

Income tax

	£
Tax borne @ 20%	2,891.00
<u>Add</u>: Tax deducted from payment	50.00
Tax liability	2,941.00

4.2

	(a)	(b)
	£	£
Total income	47,980	47,980
<u>Less</u>: Payment £1,280 × 100/80	1,600	
Net income	46,380	47,980
<u>Less</u>: Personal allowance	6,475	6,475
Taxable income	39,905	41,505

Income tax

(a)	(b)		(a)	(b)
37,400	37,400	@ 20%	7,480.00	7,480.00
2,505	4,105	@ 40%	1,002.00	1,642.00
39,905	41,505			
		Tax borne	8,482.00	9,122.00
		<u>Add</u>: Tax deducted from payment	320.00	
		Tax liability	8,802.00	9,122.00

Paul's tax liability is reduced by £320 if he makes the payment. The cost of the payment to him is therefore only £960 (payment £1,280 less reduction in tax liability £320). In effect, the gross payment of £1,600 is reduced by tax relief at 40% (£640), leaving £960 as the cost to Paul.

4.3

	£
Total income	6,465
Less: Payment £20 × 100/80	25
Net income	6,440
Less: Personal allowance (restricted)	6,440
Taxable income	nil

Income tax

Tax borne	0.00
Add: Tax deducted from payment	5.00
Tax liability	5.00

4.4

(a) 23%   (b) marginal rate   (c) 10%   (d) marginal rate.

4.5

(a) The donation is deemed to be made net of 20% income tax. Charities are not liable to income tax so the charity concerned recovers a further £240 (£960 × 20/80) from HMRC, making the donation worth £1,200 in total. Furthermore, if the basic rate had still been 22%, the charity would have recovered tax of £270.77 (£960 × 22/78). Therefore transitional relief of £30.77 is available from HMRC.

(b) If the taxpayer does not pay income tax for 2009-10 of at least £240, the income tax liability for the year will be increased to exactly £240.

(c) The taxpayer's basic rate band for 2009-10 is extended by £1,200. If the taxpayer pays income tax at the higher rate, this extension will have the effect of moving up to £1,200 of income from the higher rate to the basic rate, resulting in a tax saving of up to £240 (20% × £1,200).

4.6

	£
Business profits	23,900
Less: Personal allowance	9,165
Taxable income	14,735

Income tax

Tax borne @ 20%	2,947.00

Notes:

(i) The grossed-up donation is £350 (£280 × 100/80) and the tax deemed deducted is £70.

(ii) Adjusted net income is £23,550 (£23,900 − £350). This is £650 over the income limit, so the personal allowance is £9,165 (£9,490 − 1/2 × £650).

(iii) Raj pays income tax of far more than £70 so there is nothing more to be done.

4.7

	Total £	Non-savings £	Dividends £
Employment income	42,455	42,455	
UK dividends £3,780 + tax credit £420	4,200		4,200
Total income	46,655	42,455	4,200
Less: Personal allowance	6,475	6,475	
Taxable income	40,180	35,980	4,200

Income tax due

Non-savings income	: Basic rate	35,980	@ 20%	7,196.00	
Dividend income	: Ordinary rate	1,820	@ 10%	182.00	
	: Upper rate	2,380	@ 32.5%	773.50	
		40,180			
Tax liability				8,151.50	
Less: Tax credits on dividends				420.00	
Tax payable				7,731.50	

Notes:

(i)   The basic rate band is extended by a grossed-up donation of £400 (£320 × 100/80) to £37,800 (£37,400 + £400).

(ii)   Geoffrey is not entitled to MCA (he and his wife are too young).

(iii) Tax paid under PAYE would also be deducted.

Chapter 5

5.1

The property income assessable in 2009-10 (i.e. the income accrued for the year) is £8,200 (£8,000 × 9/12 + £8,800 × 3/12). The amount actually received is not relevant.

5.2

	£	£	£
Rents received £220 × 48			10,560
Less: Expenses allowed in full:			
Advertising		35	
Repairs to furniture		50	
Apportioned expenses:			
Council tax	1,400		
Gardener's wages	1,040		
Insurance	230		
$\dfrac{48}{52} \times 2,670$		2,465	
Wear and tear (see below)		927	3,477
Property income			7,083

Note:

The wear and tear allowance is 10% of (£10,560 – (£1,400 × 48/52)) = £927.

5.3

(a) Premiums received in relation to the granting of long leases (i.e. leases of more than 50 years) are not assessable to income tax.

(b) £12,000 – (49 × 2% of £12,000) = £240.

(c) £12,000 – (19 × 2% of £12,000) = £7,440.

5.4

The income tax assessment on the landlord is £12,300 (£15,000 – (9 × 2% of £15,000)). Therefore Jasper will be allowed an annual deduction from his trading profits of £1,230 for each of the ten years of the lease.

5.5

All three flats pass the 140-day test. However, Flat 1 does not pass the 70-day test and so will not be regarded as a furnished holiday let unless it can be averaged with one or more of the other flats. Possible averaging claims are:

(a) Flat 1 with Flat 2. This is no use since the average number of days let is only 68.

(b) Flat 1 with Flat 3. This is no use since the average number of days let is only 69.

(c) Flat 1 with Flat 2 and Flat 3. This is beneficial since the average number of days let is 70.

Chapter 6

6.1

	Total	Savings	Dividends
	£	£	£
BSI £15,772 × 100/80	19,715	19,715	
UK dividends £36,468 + tax credit £4,052	40,520		40,520
Total income	60,235	19,715	40,520
Less: Personal allowance	6,475	6,475	
Taxable income	53,760	13,240	40,520

Income tax due

Savings income	: Starting rate	2,440	@ 10%	244.00	
	: Basic rate	10,800	@ 20%	2,160.00	
Dividend income	: Ordinary rate	24,160	@ 10%	2,416.00	
	: Upper rate	16,360	@ 32.5%	5,317.00	
		53,760			

Tax borne	10,137.00
Less: Tax deducted at source and tax credits	7,995.00
Tax payable	2,142.00

6.2

	Total	Non-savings	Savings	Dividends
	£	£	£	£
Retirement pension	9,026	9,026		
Bank interest £384 × 100/80	480		480	
UK dividends £585 + tax credit £65	650			650
Total income	10,156	9,026	480	650
Less: Personal allowance	9,640	9,026	480	134
Taxable income	516	0	0	516

Income tax is due of £51.60 (£516 @ 10%), less tax credit on dividends of £51.60, leaving a tax liability of zero. Anne cannot claim payment of the remaining £13.40 of the tax credits but she is entitled to a refund of the £96 tax deducted at source from her bank interest.

Note:
The ISA interest is exempt from tax.

6.3

See text.

6.4

See text.

6.5

	Total £	Non-savings £	Savings £
Retirement pension	18,370	18,370	
NSB interest	60		60
BSI £3,784 × 100/80	4,730		4,730
Total income	23,160	18,370	4,790
Less: Personal allowance	9,360	9,360	
Taxable income	13,800	9,010	4,790

Income tax due

Non-savings income	: Basic rate	9,010	@ 20%	1,802.00	
Savings income	: Basic rate	4,790	@ 20%	958.00	
		13,800			
Tax borne				2,760.00	
Less: Tax deducted at source				946.00	
Tax payable				1,814.00	

Notes:

(a) Bernice reaches her 65th birthday during 2009-10 and is therefore entitled to the personal allowance of £9,490 for the year. However, her income exceeds the income limit by £260, so the allowance is reduced by £130 to £9,360.

(b) Any PAYE tax deducted from the pension will be subtracted when calculating tax payable.

Chapter 7

7.1

See text.

7.2

The basis of assessment for employment income is the receipts basis. The assessable income for 2009-10 is therefore £30,850 (£27,500 + £3,350).

7.3

(a) 15p per day would be exempt. The remaining £1.85 per day would be taxable.

(b) Free meals in the company canteen are exempt if available to all employees.

(c) Removal expenses of up to £8,000 are exempt if reasonable and incurred on first taking up an appointment or transferring to a new location.

(d) Long-service awards made in cash are taxable.

(e)   A gift made in a personal capacity (rather than for services rendered) is exempt so long as it is reasonable in amount.

(f)   The mileage allowance is exempt since it is less than the standard figure of 40p per mile for the first 10,000 miles. The employee has an allowable expense of £250 (2,500 @ 10p).

7.4

(a)   Not generally allowable since not incurred in performing the duties of the employment. But see the text for exceptions to this rule in the case of site-based employees, employees undertaking business journeys from home and employees who are seconded to a temporary place of work.

(b)   Allowable so long as necessarily incurred.

(c)   Allowable if relevant to the employment.

(d)   Allowable.

(e)   Not allowable, even if worn only at the office. A suit provides warmth and decency and is therefore not purchased exclusively for the purposes of the employment.

(f)   Not allowable unless reimbursed or paid out of a specific entertaining allowance. The expenses must also be wholly, exclusively and necessarily incurred.

7.5

For the purpose of deciding Kim's classification it is necessary to take into account all of her earnings (valued as if she were a P11D employee) and to ignore expenses other than the pension contributions. This gives total earnings of £9,450 (95% of £7,000 + £1,000 + £1,800) which exceeds £8,500 so Kim is a P11D employee.

7.6

The applicable percentage is 30% (15% + 12% + 3%) so the assessable car benefit is £5,640 (30% of £18,800. There is a further assessable fuel benefit of £5,070 (30% of £16,900).

7.7

The first £28,250 (£30,000 – £1,750) of compensation is exempt from tax.

(a)   £12,000 is less than £28,250 and is therefore exempt from tax.

(b)   £29,000 exceeds £28,250 so the excess of £750 is taxable.

Chapter 8

8.1

Subject matter; length of ownership; frequency of transactions; supplementary work; reason for sale; motive.

8.2

Expenditure must be incurred wholly and exclusively for the purposes of the trade.

8.3

(a) allowable so long as the salary is commensurate with the work done

(b) not allowable when computing trading profits, but relieved under the Gift Aid rules

(c) not allowable (capital expenditure)

(d) allowable so long as the diaries carry a prominent advertisement for the business

(e) allowable

(f) not allowable (fails the duality test)

(g) not allowable (related to capital expenditure)

(h) probably allowable as a trade subscription

(i) not allowable (food, drink or tobacco)

(j) allowable (relates directly to trading).

8.4

(a) add £45   (b) add £15   (c) no adjustment required.

8.5

(a) (i) Disallow 15% × £2,940 = £441.

   (ii) The allowable amount is given by:

$$£2,940 \times \frac{£12,000 \; + \; 1/2(£21,000 \; - \; £12,000)}{£21,000} = £2,310 \text{ (so disallow £630)}.$$

(b) The amount assessed on the landlord is (£15,000 – (14 × 2% of £15,000)) = £10,800. So the amount allowable in each year is £720 (1/15th of £10,800) and the amount to be disallowed each year is £280 (£1,000 – £720).

8.6

	£	£
Net profit for the year		6,960
Add: *Disallowed expenditure*:		
Proprietor's salary	10,400	
Cost of new heating system	3,800	
Telephone (1/4th of £880)	220	
Motor expenses (1/5th of £3,250)	650	
Entertaining	520	
General provision for bad debts	200	
Loss on sale of non-current asset	70	
Depreciation	2,500	18,360
		25,320
Less: *Non-trading income*:		
Rents receivable	1,200	
Bank interest receivable	80	
Profit on sale of non-current asset	310	1,590
Trading profit (before capital allowances)		23,730

Chapter 9

9.1

(a) 2009-10   (b) 2009-10   (c) 2011-12   (d) 2010-11

9.2

(a)

2007-08	Actual		1/7/07 to 5/4/08
2008-09	12 months to a/c date in year 2		y/e 30/6/08
2009-10	CYB		y/e 30/6/09
2010-11	CYB		y/e 30/6/10

There is an overlap period between 1 July 2007 and 5 April 2008.

(b)

2007-08	Actual	1/7/07 to 5/4/08
2008-09	Actual	6/4/08 to 5/4/09
2009-10	12 months to a/c date in year 3	1/5/08 to 30/4/09
2010-11	CYB	y/e 30/4/10

There is an overlap period between 1 May 2008 and 5 April 2009.

(c)

2007-08	Actual	1/7/07 to 5/4/08
2008-09	First 12 months	1/7/07 to 30/6/08
2009-10	CYB	y/e 30/4/09
2010-11	CYB	y/e 30/4/10

There is an overlap period between 1 July 2007 and 5 April 2008. There is another overlap period between 1 May 2008 and 30 June 2008.

9.3

				£
2007-08	Actual	1/1/08 to 5/4/08	£27,300 × 3/18	4,550
2008-09	Actual	6/4/08 to 5/4/09	£27,300 × 12/18	18,200
2009-10	12 months to a/c date in year 3	1/7/08 to 30/6/09	£27,300 × 12/18	18,200

There is an overlap period between 1 July 2008 and 5 April 2009 (9 months). The overlap profits are $9/18 \times £27,300 = £13,650$.

9.4

(a)

2007-08	CYB	y/e 31/1/08
2008-09	CYB	y/e 31/1/09
2009-10	End of previous basis period to date of cessation	1/2/09 to 31/5/09

(b)

2007-08	CYB	y/e 31/1/08
2008-09	CYB	y/e 31/1/09
2009-10	End of previous basis period to date of cessation	1/2/09 to 31/3/10

(c)

2008-09	CYB	y/e 31/1/09
2009-10	12 months to normal a/c date	1/2/09 to 31/1/10
2010-11	End of previous basis period to date of cessation	1/2/10 to 30/4/10

9.5

The basis period for 1996-97 was the 24 months to 31 July 1996. Transitional overlap relief relates to the period from 1 August 1996 to 5 April 1997. The relief is $£15,900 \times 8/12 = £10,600$.

The basis period for 2009-10 is the year to 31 July 2009, so trading income for 2009-10 is £600 (£11,200 − £10,600).

Chapter 10

10.1

	Main pool £	Allowances £
y/e 31/3/10		
WDV b/f	10,300	
Additions (ineligible for AIA or FYA)	8,000	
	18,300	
Disposals (£3,000 + £4,000)	(7,000)	
	11,300	
WDA @ 20%	2,260	2,260
	9,040	
Additions qualifying for AIA (£600 + £400)	1,000	
AIA @ 100%	1,000	1,000
	-	
WDV c/f	9,040	
Total allowances		3,260

10.2

	Main pool £	Motor car (40% p.u.) £	Allowances £
y/e 30/6/10			
Additions (ineligible for AIA or FYA)		15,000	
WDA @ 10%		1,500 × 60% =	900
Additions qualifying for AIA	50,000		
AIA @ 100%	50,000	-	50,000
Additions qualifying for FYA	37,000		
FYA @ 40%	14,800 22,200		14,800
WDV c/f	22,200	13,500	
Total allowances			65,700

Notes:

(i) WDA for the car is calculated at 10% because the car has emissions in excess of 160g/km.

(ii) Allowances are maximised if £6,600 of the £50,000 AIA is set against the cost of the machinery bought in May 2010 (which is ineligible for FYA). The remaining AIA of £43,400 is set against the cost of the other machinery acquired in the year (£80,400) leaving a balance of £37,000, all of which is eligible for the 40% FYA.

The adjusted trading profit is now £24,000 (£89,700 – £65,700). Trading income for the first two tax years is as follows:

Year	Basis period	Workings	Trading income
			£
2009-10	1/7/09 to 5/4/10	£24,000 × 9/12	18,000
2010-11	1/7/09 to 30/6/10		24,000

The overlap period is 1 July 2009 to 5 April 2010. Overlap profits are £18,000.

10.3

	Main pool	Special rate pool	Allowances
	£	£	£
y/e 31/12/09			
WDV b/f	178,400		
Additions (ineligible for AIA or FYA)		13,700	
Disposals	(1,600)		
	176,800		
WDA @ 20%	35,360		35,360
WDA @ 10%		1,370	1,370
	141,440		

		Main pool	Special rate pool	Allowances
Additions eligible for AIA	50,000			
AIA @ 100%	50,000	-		50,000
Additions eligible for 40% FYA	47,300			
FYA @ 40%	18,920	28,380		18,920
Additions eligible for 100% FYA	11,600			
FYA @ 100%	11,600	-		11,600
WDV c/f		169,820	12,330	
Total allowances				117,250

Notes:

(i)   The Peugeot motor car is allocated to the special rate pool because it has emissions in excess of 160g/km.

(ii) The motor van is allocated to the main pool. Total additions to the main pool are £97,300 (£82,800 + £14,500). Deducting the AIA of £50,000 leaves expenditure of £47,300, all of which was incurred between 6 April 2009 and 5 April 2010 and is therefore eligible for the 40% FYA.

(iii) The very low emission car attracts a 100% FYA.

(iv) Capital allowances on the two private use cars are £4,530 (see below).

(v)   Total capital allowances for the year are £121,780 (£117,250 + £4,530).

	Toyota (50% p.u.) £		Saab (50% p.u.) £		Allowances £
y/e 31/12/09					
WDV b/f	18,200				
Additions (ineligible for AIA or FYA)			29,300		
Disposals	(15,000)				
Balancing allowance	3,200	× 50% =			1,600
WDA @ 20%			5,860	× 50% =	2,930
WDV c/f			23,440		
Total allowances					4,530

10.4

	Factory £	Allowances £
y/e 5/4/08		
Cost	57,500	
WDA @ 4% of £57,500	2,300	2,300
WDV c/f	55,200	
y/e 5/4/09		
WDA @ 3% of £57,500	1,725	1,725
WDV c/f	53,475	
y/e 5/4/10		
WDA @ 2% of £57,500	1,150	1,150
WDV c/f	52,325	

Note:

The cost of the factory (excluding land) is £80,000. The cost of the offices is more than 25% of £80,000 and so IBAs are available only on the cost excluding the offices, i.e. £57,500.

10.5

(a)

	Building £	Allowances £
y/e 31/12/01,02,03,04,05,06 & 07		
Cost	45,000	
WDA @ 4% of £45,000 for 7 years	12,600	12,600
Residue of expenditure	32,400	

Note:

No WDA may be claimed by Francesco for the year to 31 December 2008 (i.e. the year in which the building was sold).

(b) The residue of expenditure is £32,400. The tax life of the building ends on 31 January 2026, giving an unexpired life of 17 years 6 months on the date of the purchase by Maria. She may claim an annual WDA of £32,400/17.5 = £1,851, multiplied by the appropriate percentage.

Maria's first period of account (1 July 2008 to 5 April 2009) is nine months long and falls wholly within tax year 2008-09. Therefore she will receive IBAs for that period of £1,851 × 9/12 × 75% = £1,041. IBAs for the year to 5 April 2010 are £1,851 × 50% = £926.

10.6

Giles' allowances are:		£
year to 5/4/08	£30,000 × 4%	1,200
year to 5/4/09	£30,000 × 3%	900
year to 5/4/10	£30,000 × 2% × 6/12	300
Pam's allowances are:		
1/5/09 to 31/12/09	£30,000 × 2% × 3/12	150
y/e 31/12/10	£30,000 × 2% × 95/365 + £30,000 × 1% × 270/365	378

Chapter 11

11.1

(a) £nil.

(b) The loss will be carried forward and set against the first available profits of the same trade.

(c) The loss may be set against her total income of 2009-10 and/or 2008-09. If she makes a claim against total income of 2009-10 only, any unrelieved part of the loss may be carried back and set against profits of the same trade for 2008-09, 2007-08 and 2006-07 (in that order). If she makes a claim against total income of 2008-09 (or of 2008-09 and 2009-10) any unrelieved part of the loss may be carried back and set against profits of the same trade for 2007-08 and 2006-07 (in that order).

11.2

	2006-07	2007-08	2008-09	2009-10
	£	£	£	£
Trading income	-	4,710	6,210	14,810
Other income	4,800	4,800	4,800	4,800
Total income	4,800	9,510	11,010	19,610
Less: Trading losses b/f	-	(4,710)	(6,210)	(7,940)
Net income	4,800	4,800	4,800	11,670

11.3

(a)

Year	Basis period	Workings	Trading income
			£
2007-08	1/1/08 to 5/4/08	(£13,720 – £3,460) × 3/12	2,565
2008-09	y/e 31/12/08	£13,720 – £3,460	10,260
2009-10	y/e 31/12/09		nil

(b) The trading loss of 2009-10 is £9,800 (£7,980 + £1,820). A claim could be made to set this loss against total income in 2009-10 or 2008-09 or in both of these years:

(i) A claim for 2009-10 is pointless since there is no income in that year.

(ii) A claim for 2008-09 would reduce total income for that year to £460 (£10,260 − £9,800) and so eliminate the income tax liability for the year. The personal allowance would be largely wasted.

(iii) A claim for both years is pointless since a claim in 2009-10 is pointless.

The 2008-09 claim would be less wasteful if Marcus declined to claim any capital allowances in either of the first two years of trading. Trading income for 2008-09 would become £13,720 and the 2009-10 loss would become £7,980. Claiming relief against total income in 2008-09 would then leave income of £5,740 for the year, which would absorb most of the personal allowance.

11.4

The losses eligible for early trade losses relief are:

Year	Basis period	Workings	Trading loss £	Early trade losses claim
2007-08	1/10/07 to 5/4/08	£(26,850) × 6/15	(10,740)	04-05 *to* 06-07
2008-09	1/1/08 to 31/12/08	£(26,850) × 12/15 − overlap £(26,850) × 3/15	(16,110)	05-06 *to* 07-08
2009-10	y/e 31/12/09		(25,660)	06-07 *to* 08-09

If all possible early trade losses relief claims are made, total income is:

	2004-05 £	2005-06 £	2006-07 £	2007-08 £
Trading income	-	-	-	nil
Other income	15,100	15,250	16,400	8,450
Total income	15,100	15,250	16,400	8,450
Less: Early trade losses: 2007-08 loss	(10,740)			
2008-09 loss		(15,250)	(860)	
2009-10 loss			(15,540)	(8,450)
Net income	4,360	-	-	-

Notes:

(a) Personal allowances are totally wasted in 2005-06 to 2007-08.

(b) The loss incurred in 2009-10 has been only partly relieved. The remaining £1,670 of the loss (£25,660 − £15,540 − £8,450) is eligible for early trade losses relief in 2008-09 but there is no income in this year against which to set the loss. The loss will be carried forward and set against future trading profits.

Chapter 12

12.1

	Nickleby £	Copperfield £	Drood £	Total £
1/1/09 - 31/3/09 (£18,300 × 3/12 = £4,575)	1,525	1,525	1,525	4,575
1/4/09 - 31/12/09 (£18,300 × 9/12 = £13,725)	2,745	5,490	5,490	13,725
Allocation of profit for the year	4,270	7,015	7,015	18,300

12.2

	Pickwick £	Snodgrass £	Tupman £	Total £
Interest on capital	720	1,200	600	2,520
Salaries	8,000	-	8,000	16,000
Remainder (shared equally)	(1,340)	(1,340)	(1,340)	(4,020)
	7,380	(140)	7,260	14,500
Notional loss divided 7,380:7,260	(71)	140	(69)	-
Allocation of profit for the year	7,309	-	7,191	14,500

12.3

The allocation of profit for each period of account is:

	Dodson £	Fogg £	Jackson £	Total £
y/e 30/6/07 (shared equally)	8,500	8,500	-	17,000
y/e 30/6/08 (shared 5:4:1)	11,000	8,800	2,200	22,000
y/e 30/6/09 (shared 5:4:1)	14,500	11,600	2,900	29,000

Each partner's trading income is:

Dodson

Year	Basis period	Workings	Trading income £
2006-07	1/7/06 to 5/4/07	£8,500 × 9/12	6,375
2007-08	y/e 30/6/07		8,500
2008-09	y/e 30/6/08		11,000
2009-10	y/e 30/6/09		14,500

Fogg

Year	Basis period	Workings	Trading income £
2006-07	1/7/06 to 5/4/07	£8,500 × 9/12	6,375
2007-08	y/e 30/6/07		8,500
2008-09	y/e 30/6/08		8,800
2009-10	y/e 30/6/09		11,600

Jackson

Year	Basis period	Workings	Trading income
			£
2007-08	1/7/07 to 5/4/08	£2,200 × 9/12	1,650
2008-09	y/e 30/6/08		2,200
2009-10	y/e 30/6/09		2,900

Note:

Dodson and Fogg each have overlap profits of £6,375. Jackson has overlap profits of £1,650.

12.4

(a) The trading profit of £23,490 for the year to 30 September 2008 is allocated Wardle £16,443, Jingle £4,698, Trotter £2,349. The trading profit of £27,310 for the year to 30 September 2009 is allocated Wardle £19,117, Jingle £5,462, Trotter £2,731. Each partner's trading income is:

	Wardle	Jingle	Trotter
	£	£	£
2007-08 (6/12 × y/e 30/9/08)	8,222	2,349	1,174
2008-09 (y/e 30/9/08)	16,443	4,698	2,349
2009-10 (y/e 30/9/09)	19,117	5,462	2,731

(b) The untaxed interest of £2,000 for the year to 30 September 2008 is allocated Wardle £1,400, Jingle £400, Trotter £200. The untaxed interest of £2,200 for the year to 30 September 2009 is allocated Wardle £1,540, Jingle £440, Trotter £220. Each partner's untaxed interest is:

	Wardle	Jingle	Trotter
	£	£	£
2007-08 (6/12 × y/e 30/9/08)	700	200	100
2008-09 (y/e 30/9/08)	1,400	400	200
2009-10 (y/e 30/9/09)	1,540	440	220

(c) The taxed interest of £1,250 (gross) for the year to 30 September 2008 is allocated Wardle £875, Jingle £250, Trotter £125. The taxed interest of £1,360 (gross) for the year to 30 September 2009 is allocated Wardle £952, Jingle £272, Trotter £136. The gross amount on which each partner is charged to tax in 2008-09 (assuming time-apportionment between tax years) is:

	£
Wardle (£875 × 6/12 + £952 × 6/12)	914
Jingle (£250 × 6/12 + £272 × 6/12)	261
Trotter (£125 × 6/12 + £136 × 6/12)	131

Chapter 13

13.1

(a) £120,000.

(b) £3,600 (so long as at least £2,400 is paid to a scheme which operates relief at source).

13.2

She will pay net contributions of £800 per month, so obtaining relief at the basic rate. Relief at the higher rate will be given by extending her basic rate band by £12,000.

13.3

Current year contributions are 310% of those in the previous year. This exceeds 210% so spreading may be required. The excess of current year contributions over 110% of previous year contributions is £1,200,000, which is between £1,000,000 and £1,999,999. Therefore this excess must be spread over the current period and the next two periods. Tax relief on contributions of £1,060,000 (£660,000 + £400,000) will be given in the year to 30 June 2010. Relief on contributions of £400,000 will be given in each of the years to 30 June 2011 and 2012.

13.4

If Damon became entitled to payment of his pension and lump sum at the start of the pension input period, he would receive an annual pension of £120,000 (£360,000 × 20/60) and a lump sum of £270,000 (£360,000 × 60/80). The value of his pension rights at the start of the period is therefore £1,470,000 (£270,000 + (10 × £120,000)).

If he became entitled to payment of his pension and lump sum at the end of the period, he would receive an annual pension of £157,500 (£450,000 × 21/60) and a lump sum of £354,375 (£450,000 × 63/80). So the value of his pension rights at the end of the period is £1,929,375 (£354,375 + (10 × £157,500)).

Total pension input amount for 2009-10 is £459,375 (£1,929,375 − £1,470,000). This exceeds the annual allowance of £245,000 by £214,375. Therefore the annual allowance charge is £85,750 (40% of £214,375).

13.5

(a) The first lump sum absorbs 80% of the 2007-08 lifetime allowance of £1,600,000. There is no lifetime allowance charge and 20% of the lifetime allowance remains unused. The second lump sum of £400,000 exceeds 20% of the 2010-11 lifetime allowance of £1,800,000 by £40,000. There is a lifetime allowance charge of £22,000 (55% of £40,000).

(b) The first lump sum now absorbs 25% of the 2007-08 lifetime allowance. The second lump sum is less than 75% of the 2010-11 lifetime allowance and therefore there is no lifetime allowance charge on either lump sum.

Chapter 14

14.1

(a) No POAs are required because the 2008-09 liability (less tax deducted at source) was less than £1,000. A balancing payment of £440 (£1,750 − £1,250 − £60) is payable on 31 January 2011.

(b) The amount paid by deduction at source in 2008-09 (£4,390) was not more than 80% of the total liability for the year and the remainder (£2,340) was not less than £1,000. Therefore POAs are required for 2009-10. A first POA of £1,170 (one-half of £2,340) is due on 31 January 2010 and a second POA of £1,170 is due on 31 July 2010.

A balancing *repayment* of £605 (£6,580 − £4,810 − £35 − £2,340) will be due on 31 January 2011. Marie could have made a claim to pay reduced POAs for 2009-10 if she had known that the POAs based on her 2008-09 liability were likely to be excessive.

(c) No POAs are required because more than 80% of the 2008-09 tax liability was satisfied by deduction at source. A balancing payment of £3,600 (£16,110 − £12,370 − £140) is payable on 31 January 2011.

14.2

(a) Dorothy's balancing payment was not more than 28 days late so no surcharges are payable.

(b) The first POA of £12,000 was paid 27 days late, the second POA of £12,000 was paid 43 days late and the balancing payment of £4,000 was paid 21 days late. The interest payable is as follows:

	£
£12,000 × 4.5% × 27/366	39.84
£12,000 × 4.5% × 43/366	63.44
£4,000 × 4.5% × 21/366	10.33
	113.61

14.3

(a) Jabran notified HMRC of his chargeability to tax within the permitted six months and so incurs no penalty in relation to this notification.

(b) His completed tax return was due to be submitted to HMRC within three months of the issue date. He submitted the return late (but not more than six months late) and so incurs a fixed penalty of £100.

(c) The balancing payment was due three months after the issue date of the tax return. His payment was more than 28 days late and therefore he incurs a 5% surcharge.

(d) Interest is payable on the tax paid late and interest is payable on the surcharge if it is not paid within 30 days of the date of its imposition.

Chapter 15

15.1

(a) Primary : 11% × (£120 − £110) = £1.10
Secondary : 12.8% × (£120 − £110) = £1.28

(b) Primary : 11% × (£780 − £110) = £73.70
Secondary : 12.8% × (£780 − £110) = £85.76

(c) Primary : 11% × (£844 − £110) + 1% × (£930 − £844) = £81.60
Secondary : 12.8% × (£930 − £110) = £104.96

(d) Primary : nil (earnings do not exceed the primary threshold)
Secondary : nil (earnings do not exceed the secondary threshold)

(e) Primary : 11% × (£3,300 − £476) = £310.64
Secondary : 12.8% × (£3,300 − £476) = £361.47

(f) Primary : 11% × (£3,656 − £476) + 1% × (£6,000 − £3,656) = £373.24
Secondary : 12.8% × (£6,000 − £476) = £707.07

15.2

(a) Primary : 9.4% × (£120 − £110) = £0.94
Secondary : 9.1% × (£120 − £110) = £0.91

(b) Primary : 9.4% × (£770 − £110) + 11% × (£780 − £770) = £63.14
Secondary : 9.1% × (£770 − £110) + 12.8% × (£780 − £770) = £61.34

(c) Primary : 9.4% × (£770 − £110) + 11% × (£844 − £770) + 1% × (£930 − £844) = £71.04
Secondary : 9.1% × (£770 − £110) + 12.8% × (£930 − £770) = £80.54

(d) Primary : nil (earnings do not exceed the primary threshold)

Secondary : nil (earnings do not exceed the secondary threshold)

(e) Primary : 9.4% × (£3,300 – £476) = £265.46

Secondary : 9.1% × (£3,300 – £476) = £256.98

(f) Primary : 9.4% × (£3,337 – £476) + 11% × (£3,656 – £3,337) + 1% × (£6,000 – £3,656)

= £327.46

Secondary : 9.1% × (£3,337 – £476) + 12.8% × (£6,000 – £3,337) = £601.21

15.3

Mark's profit for Class 2 purposes in 2009-10 is £6,010 (£7,270 × 8/12 + £3,490 × 4/12). This exceeds the small earnings exception so Mark is liable to pay Class 2 contributions of £2.40 per week. His profit for Class 4 purposes in 2009-10 is £8,900 so Class 4 contributions are payable of £254.80 (8% × (£8,900 – £5,715)).

Chapter 16

16.1

(a) Companies are not chargeable persons, so the sale will not give rise to a CGT liability.

(b) Disposals between husband and wife who are living together are deemed to occur at a disposal value such that neither a gain nor a loss arises. So there will be no CGT liability on the gift.

(c) Gifts to charities are exempt from CGT.

(d) In general, charities are not chargeable persons and therefore disposals by charities do not give rise to a CGT liability (subject to certain restrictions).

(e) The sale is made in the course of trade. Therefore the profit arising will be a trading profit and not a capital gain.

(f) The partnership is not a chargeable person but the partners are. Any CGT liability arising on the disposal of the freehold property will be divided between them.

16.2

(a) Shares and securities are chargeable assets (apart from gilt-edged securities and certain corporate bonds).

(b) Gilt-edged securities are not chargeable assets.

(c) A table is a chattel. Chattels disposed of for more than £6,000 are chargeable assets.

(d) A chair is a chattel. Chattels disposed of for £6,000 or less are not chargeable assets.

(e) A taxpayer's principal private residence is not a chargeable asset.

(f) Motor cars are not chargeable assets.

16.3

(a) Net losses are £2,500. The annual exemption is lost and the CGT assessment is £nil.

(b) Net losses are £1,000. The annual exemption is lost and the CGT assessment is £nil.

(c) Net gains are £5,250. The unused part of the annual exemption (£4,850) is lost and the CGT assessment is £nil.

(d) Net gains are £11,550. The annual exemption of £10,100 is fully used. The CGT assessment is £1,450.

16.4

Net gains for the year are £51,200 (£62,600 – £11,400). Deducting the allowable losses brought forward of £12,800 and the annual exemption of £10,100 leaves a CGT assessment for 2009-10 of £28,300. The CGT liability for the year is 18% × £28,300 = £5,094.00.

16.5

(a) Net gains are £8,200. £1,900 of the annual exemption is lost and the CGT assessment is £nil. The losses brought forward of £4,800 remain unrelieved and are carried forward to 2010-11.

(b) Net gains are £10,700. This exceeds the annual exemption by £600, so £600 of the losses brought forward are relieved and the CGT assessment is £nil. The remaining £4,200 of the losses brought forward are carried forward to 2010-11.

(c) Net gains are £16,100. This exceeds the annual exemption by £6,000, so all of the losses brought forward are relieved. The CGT assessment is £1,200 (£16,100 – £4,800 – £10,100). There are no unrelieved losses to carry forward.

16.6

Net losses in 2009-10 are £14,200. The annual exemption is lost and the CGT assessment for the year is £nil. The net losses may be offset against the net gains of 2008-09, 2007-08 and 2006-07, in that order, to the extent that those net gains exceed the annual exemption. Relief is £nil in 2008-09, £2,800 (£12,000 – £9,200) in 2007-08 and £6,500 (£15,300 – £8,800) in 2006-07. Total relief is £9,300. The remaining £4,900 of net losses in 2009-10 cannot be relieved at all.

16.7

31 January 2011.

Chapter 17

17.1

	£	£
Sale proceeds		172,000
Less: Incidental costs of disposal:		
Auctioneer's fee	8,600	
Legal fees	500	9,100
		162,900
Less: Acquisition cost	100,000	
Incidental costs of acquisition:		
Legal fees	400	
Enhancement expenditure	5,000	105,400
Chargeable gain		57,500

(The repainting costs do not rank as enhancement expenditure).

17.2

	(a)	(b)	(c)
	£	£	£
Sale proceeds	4,950	4,350	5,780
<u>Less</u>: Deemed acquisition cost	4,500	4,500	4,500
Chargeable gain/(allowable loss)	450	(150)	1,280

17.3

	£
Sale proceeds (June 2003)	100,000
<u>Less</u>: Incidental costs of disposal	5,000
	95,000

<u>Less</u>: Part cost:
$$\frac{£100,000}{£100,000 + £500,000} \times £240,000 \qquad (40,000)$$

Part incidental costs of acquisition:
$$\frac{£100,000}{£100,000 + £500,000} \times £12,000 \qquad (2,000)$$

Chargeable gain	53,000

	£
Sale proceeds (January 2010)	520,000
<u>Less</u>: Remainder of cost (£240,000 – £40,000)	(200,000)
Remainder of costs of acquisition (£12,000 – £2,000)	(10,000)
Chargeable gain	310,000

17.4

	(a)	(b)	(c)
	£	£	£
Sale proceeds	37,500	37,500	37,500
<u>Less</u>: Market value 31 March 1982	10,000	15,000	50,000
Chargeable gain/(allowable loss)	27,500	22,500	(12,500)

Notes:

(i)   The asset's cost is ignored, since the gain or loss is computed by means of rebasing.

(ii) In case (a), Francis is taxed on a gain of £27,500 even though his total gain over the entire period of ownership of the asset is actually only £25,000 (£37,500 – £12,500).

(iii) In case (c), Francis is granted an allowable loss of £12,500 even though he has made a gain of £25,000 during his period of ownership of the asset.

17.5

(a)

	£
Deemed disposal proceeds	80
Less: Deemed acquisition cost	6,000
Allowable loss	(5,920)

(b)

	£
Disposal proceeds	120
Less: Deemed acquisition cost (November 2008)	80
Chargeable gain	40

Chapter 18

18.1

(a) Wasting chattel.   (b) Chattel.   (c) Wasting chattel.
(d) Wasting asset.   (e) Wasting chattel.   (f) Chattel.

18.2

	£
Sale proceeds	7,200
Less: Incidental disposal costs	200
	7,000
Less: Acquisition cost	2,000
Chargeable gain	5,000 (restricted to £2,000)

The gain is restricted to (£7,200 – £6,000) × 5/3 = £2,000.

18.3

	£
Deemed sale proceeds	6,000
Less: Acquisition cost	50,000
Allowable loss	(44,000)

18.4

	£
Sale proceeds	25,000
Less: Part cost: $\dfrac{£25,000}{£25,000 + £85,000} \times 38,500$	8,750
Chargeable gain	16,250

The maximum gain is (£110,000 – £6,000) × 5/3 × 25/110 = £39,394. The actual gain is far less than this so the chargeable gain is £16,250.

18.5

	(a)	(b)
	£	£
Sale proceeds	65,000	35,000
Less: Acquisition cost	50,000	50,000
	15,000	(15,000)
Less: Available capital allowances	0	15,000
Chargeable gain or allowable loss	15,000	0

18.6

	£
Sale proceeds	8,000
Less: Unexpired portion of cost $\frac{3}{5} \times £10,000$	6,000
Chargeable gain	2,000

18.7

When the lease was acquired it had a 40-year life (Sch 8 percentage 95.457%). When the lease was assigned there were 22 years remaining (Sch 8 percentage 76.399%). Therefore the computation is as follows:

	£
Sale proceeds	32,500
Less: Unexpired portion of cost	
$\dfrac{76.399}{95.457} \times £25,000$	20,009
Chargeable gain	12,491

Chapter 19

19.1

(a)	20 October 2009	200	(bought on same day)
	10 August 2009	50	(s104 holding)
(b)	1 December 2009	150	(next 30 days)
	10 August 2009	270	(s104 holding)
(c)	10 August 2009	300	(s104 holding)

19.2

There were no acquisitions on the same day as the disposal or within the following 30 days, so the disposal must have come from the s104 holding. The s104 holding is as follows:

	Number of shares	Allowable expenditure £
Acquired 29 January 1982	1,000	4,000
Acquired 13 August 1996	1,000	9,500
Acquired 4 October 2007	2,000	22,500
	4,000	36,000
Sold 26 June 2009 (700/4,000ths)	(700)	(6,300)
s104 holding c/f	3,300	29,700

Notes:

(i)   The shares acquired before 31 March 1982 are added into the s104 holding at their market value on that date.

(ii) On average, the allowable expenditure in the pool is £9 per share. The allowable expenditure deducted on the June 2009 disposal (£6,300) is equal to 700 shares at £9 per share.

The gain or loss arising on the disposal is as follows:

	(a) £	(b) £	(c) £
Sale proceeds	8,400	6,300	5,200
Less: Allowable expenditure	6,300	6,300	6,300
Chargeable gain/(allowable loss)	2,100	0	(1,100)

19.3

The 10,000 shares disposed of on 22 December 2009 are matched as follows:

(a)   The first match is against the 3,000 shares acquired on the same day as the disposal. These 3,000 shares were acquired for £24,000 and sold for £30,000 (3,000 × £10), so the chargeable gain on these 3,000 shares is £6,000.

(b)   The next match is against the 5,000 shares acquired within the next 30 days. These 5,000 shares were acquired for £55,000 and sold for £50,000 (5,000 × £10), so the allowable loss on these 5,000 shares is £5,000.

(c)   The third and final match is against 2,000 of the shares in the s104 holding. The s104 holding is as follows:

	Number of shares	Allowable expenditure £
Acquired 19 September 2003	4,000	16,000
Acquired 20 October 2005	2,000	12,000
Acquired 21 November 2007	1,000	7,000
	7,000	35,000
Sold 22 December 2009 (2,000/7,000ths)	(2,000)	(10,000)
s104 holding c/f	5,000	25,000

These 2,000 shares were acquired for £10,000 (the allowable expenditure deducted from the s104 holding on their disposal) and sold for £20,000 (2,000 × £10). Therefore the chargeable gain is £10,000.

Overall, the chargeable gain on the 22 December 2009 disposal of 10,000 shares is £11,000 (£6,000 − £5,000 + £10,000).

19.4

There were no acquisitions on the same day as the disposal or within the following 30 days, so the disposal must have come from the s104 holding. The s104 holding is as follows:

	Number of shares	Allowable expenditure £
Acquired 17 February 2001	600	900
Acquired 13 November 2005	200	400
Acquired 9 October 2009	100	300
	900	1,600
Bonus issue January 2010	225	-
	1,125	1,600
Sold February 2010 (450/1,125ths)	(450)	(640)
s104 holding c/f	675	960

The 450 shares which were disposed of in February 2010 were acquired for £640 (the allowable expenditure deducted from the s104 holding) and were sold for £1,800 (450 × £4). Therefore the chargeable gain is £1,160.

19.5

There were no acquisitions on the same day as the disposal or within the following 30 days, so the disposal must have come from the s104 holding. The s104 holding is as follows:

	Number of shares	Allowable expenditure £
Acquired 30 September 1999	2,000	1,200
Acquired 1 December 2003	3,000	3,600
	5,000	4,800
Rights issue January 2010	1,000	1,000
	6,000	5,800
Sold March 2010 (3,000/6,000ths)	(3,000)	(2,900)
s104 holding c/f	3,000	2,900

The 3,000 shares which were disposed of in March 2010 were acquired for £2,900 (the allowable expenditure deducted from the s104 holding) and were sold for £5,400 (3,000 × £1.80). Therefore the chargeable gain is £2,500.

19.6

(a) The value of the part disposed of is £6,000 (6,000 × £1) and the value of the part remaining is £12,000 (6,000 × £2) so there has been a 6,000/18,000 (1/3rd) part disposal. One-third is more than 5% and the amount received is more than £3,000, so this cannot be treated as a small capital distribution. The s104 holding is as follows:

	Number of shares	Allowable expenditure £
Acquired November 1999	6,000	30,000
Distribution March 2010 (one-third)	-	(10,000)
s104 holding c/f	6,000	20,000

The allowable loss is £4,000 (£10,000 – £6,000).

(b) The value of Yolande's shares immediately prior to the sale of rights was £600. £25 is less than 5% of £600, so the sale of rights ranks as a small capital distribution. Assuming that this distribution is not treated as a disposal, the s104 holding is as follows:

	Number of shares	Allowable expenditure £
Acquired January 2003	300	360
Distribution May 2009	-	(25)
	300	335
Sold November 2009	(300)	(335)
s104 holding c/f	-	-

The chargeable gain is £445 (£780 – £335).

19.7

Walter received 16,000 shares worth £72,000, plus £8,000 in cash, a total of £80,000. The amount received in cash is 10% of the total. This exceeds 5% and the amount exceeds £3,000. Therefore this does not rank as a small capital distribution and the situation must be treated as a part disposal. The s104 holding is as follows:

	Number of shares	Allowable expenditure £
Acquired June 2009	10,000	70,000
Distribution September 2009 (10%)	-	(7,000)
s104 holding after distribution	10,000	63,000
s104 holding (Round plc) c/f	16,000	63,000

The chargeable gain is £1,000 (£8,000 – £7,000).

Chapter 20

20.1

So long as Mohammed actually resides in both properties he may choose which is to be regarded as his PPR. Whichever property he bought and lived in first was automatically regarded as his PPR. After he bought the second property (and began residing in it) he could, if he wished, elect that this property should become his PPR for CGT purposes. He would do this if he thought that the gain arising on the disposal of the second property would exceed the gain arising on the disposal of the first property. The election would have to be made within two years of the date from which it is to take effect.

20.2

	£
Sale proceeds	163,000
<u>Less</u>: Market value 31 March 1982	21,000
Chargeable gain (before PPR exemption)	142,000

The chargeable gain (before considering the PPR exemption) is £142,000. Considering each of the three cases individually:

(a) The house is not a chargeable asset and therefore the disposal is exempt from CGT. The gain is £nil.

(b) After 31 March 1982, Melanie owned the house for 27 years and 7 months (331 months) and was absent for 48 months. There is no indication that the absence was work-related and this absence exceeds the permissible maximum "absence for any reason" by 12 months. Therefore the PPR exemption is £142,000 × 319/331 = £136,852 and the chargeable gain is £142,000 × 12/331 = £5,148.

(c) Letting relief is available and is the lowest of £5,148, £136,852 and £40,000, which is £5,148. This reduces the chargeable gain to £nil.

20.3

	£
Sale proceeds	232,000
<u>Less</u>: Acquisition cost	55,000
Chargeable gain (before PPR exemption)	177,000

Rupert's period of ownership (a total of 268 months) is broken down as follows:

(i)	1 November 1987 to 31 October 1991	48 months	Actual residence
(ii)	1 November 1991 to 31 October 1992	12 months	Working abroad
(iii)	1 November 1992 to 31 January 1995	27 months	Actual residence
(iv)	1 February 1995 to 30 April 1999	51 months	Working in UK
(v)	1 May 1999 to 31 May 1999	1 month	Actual residence
(vi)	1 June 1999 to 1 March 2010	129 months	Living with friend

Periods (i), (iii) and (v) are exempt (actual residence) and period (ii) is exempt (working abroad). Period (iv) exceeds the four-year maximum allowable for working in the UK but the remaining 3 months of this period are exempt as part of the 36 months allowed for any reason. The last 36 months of ownership are exempt but the remaining 93 months of period (vi) cannot be exempt since they are not followed by a period of actual residence. The chargeable gain is:

	£
Total gain (as above)	177,000
Less: PPR exemption:	
£177,000 × 175/268	115,578
	61,422
Less: Letting relief (lowest of £61,422, £115,578	
and £40,000)	40,000
Chargeable gain	21,422

20.4

	£
Sale proceeds	155,000
Less: Acquisition cost	37,500
Chargeable gain (before PPR exemption)	117,500

Samantha owned the house for a total of 21 years (252 months). For 7 years (84 months) the house was used partly for business purposes. The computation of the chargeable gain is as follows:

	£	£
Total gain (as above)		117,500
Less: PPR exemption:		
£117,500 × 168/252	78,333	
£117,500 × 84/252 × 4/5	31,333	109,666
Chargeable gain		7,834

Chapter 21

21.1

The allowable expenditure in relation to the porcelain is £9,850 (£10,000 in October 2000, plus £3,850 in March 2006, less £4,000 received July 2006). The computation of the gain arising in March 2010 is:

	£
Sale proceeds	23,500
Less: Allowable expenditure	9,850
Chargeable gain	13,650

21.2

The gain arising on the theft of the original necklace would have been:

	£
Disposal proceeds	14,000
Less: Acquisition cost	13,500
Chargeable gain	500

The allowable cost of the new necklace is reduced to £14,250 (£14,750 – £500). The gain arising on its disposal is as follows:

	£
Disposal proceeds	20,000
Less: Deemed acquisition cost	14,250
Chargeable gain	5,750

21.3

The gain on the disposal of the original building is computed as follows:

	£
Sale proceeds	261,400
Less: Acquisition cost	150,000
Chargeable gain	111,400

(a) £2,500 of the sale proceeds have been retained. Therefore £2,500 of the gain is immediately chargeable. The remaining £108,900 may be rolled-over against the cost of the new building, reducing its allowable cost to £150,000 (£258,900 – £108,900).

(b) £111,600 of the sale proceeds have been retained. This exceeds the gain. Therefore the whole gain is immediately chargeable and no part of the gain may be rolled-over. The allowable cost of the new building is the full £149,800.

(c) The entire sale proceeds have been spent on a replacement building. Therefore none of the gain is immediately chargeable and the entire gain may be rolled-over against the cost of the new building, reducing its allowable cost to £165,400 (£276,800 – £111,400).

21.4

The gains which could be held-over were those relating to chargeable business assets. These were the freehold (£23,500) and the goodwill (£40,000) totalling £63,500. Listed investments do not rank as a chargeable business asset, so the gain of £10,600 was immediately chargeable.

21.5

The amount of the held-over gain is computed as follows:

		£
Disposal value		215,000
Less: Acquisition cost	91,500	
Enhancement expenditure	34,500	126,000
Held-over gain		89,000

The son's deemed acquisition cost is £126,000 (£215,000 – £89,000). If he had paid his mother £150,000 for the premises, the held-over gain would be reduced by £24,000 (£150,000 – £126,000) to £65,000 and his deemed acquisition cost would be £150,000 (£215,000 – £65,000).

Chapter 22

22.1

(a) The year to 30 November 2009 is an accounting period.

(b) The period from 1 October 2008 to 31 July 2009 does not exceed 12 months and is therefore an accounting period.

(c) The period from 1 January 2010 to 31 January 2010 does not exceed 12 months and is therefore an accounting period.

(d) The 33 months to 31 August 2009 is divided into three accounting periods. These are the 12 months to 30 November 2007, the 12 months to 30 November 2008 and the 9 months to 31 August 2009.

(e) The 18 months to 30 September 2009 is divided into two accounting periods. These are the 12 months to 31 March 2009 and the 6 months to 30 September 2009.

22.2

(a) (i) Assuming that the debentures were acquired for non-trading purposes, the debenture interest receivable is a credit on a non-trading loan relationship. The gross amount of debenture interest accrued during the accounting period is aggregated with other debits and credits arising on non-trading loan relationships. Net credits are chargeable to corporation tax. Net debits are eligible for tax relief (see Chapter 26).

(ii) The income tax of £2,160 (£8,640 × 20/80) deducted at source from the debenture interest paid must be accounted for to HMRC, but the gross interest accrued during the accounting period is allowed either as an expense when computing the company's trading income or as a debit when computing the net credit or debit arising from non-trading loan relationships (depending on whether or not the loan is for trade purposes).

(b) Both items would normally be shown gross in the company's income statement.

22.3

The gross amount of interest accrued for the accounting period is a credit on a non-trading loan relationship (assuming that the securities were acquired for non-trading purposes) and will be aggregated with other debits and credits arising on non-trading loan relationships. Net credits are chargeable to corporation tax. Net debits are eligible for tax relief (see Chapter 26).

22.4

The 17 months to 30 June 2009 will be divided into two accounting periods. These are the 12 months to 31 January 2009 and the 5 months to 30 June 2009. The chargeable profits for each accounting period are as follows:

	12 months to 31/1/09 £	5 months to 30/6/09 £
Trading income (time apportioned)	300,000	125,000
Debenture interest receivable	3,600	2,000
Income from property (time apportioned)	6,360	2,650
Chargeable gains	28,700	49,760
	338,660	179,410
Less: Charges on income	12,000	-
Chargeable profits	326,660	179,410

Notes:

(a) The debenture interest receivable is allocated on the accruals basis. Interest accrues at £400 per month. In the first accounting period, interest is due for the 9 months from 1 May 2008 to 31 January 2009. In the second accounting period, interest is due for the 5 months from 1 February 2009 to 30 June 2009.

(b) The chargeable gains are allocated according to the dates of the disposals. Even though the two disposals are on consecutive days, they fall into different accounting periods.

(c) The charges on income are allocated according to the date of payment.

22.5

The chargeable profits for the year to 31 March 2010 are as follows:

	£
Trading income	1,561,400
Income from non-trading loan relationships (£19,820 + £44,670 + £23,980)	88,470
Chargeable gains	531,000
	2,180,870
Less: Charges on income	9,000
Chargeable profits	2,171,870

Chapter 23

23.1

(a) *Disposal of factory building*

	£	£
Sale proceeds		500,000
Less: Acquisition cost	300,000	
Enhancement expenditure	50,000	350,000
Unindexed gain		150,000

Less: Indexation allowance:

(i) on acquisition cost

$$\frac{213.2 - 170.5}{170.5} = 0.250 \times £300,000 \qquad 75,000$$

(ii) on enhancement expenditure

$$\frac{213.2 - 175.9}{175.9} = 0.212 \times £50,000 \qquad 10,600 \qquad 85,600$$

		£
Chargeable gain		64,400

(b) *Disposal of office building*

	£
Sale proceeds	1,000,000
Less: Acquisition cost	650,000
Unindexed gain	350,000

Less: Indexation allowance:

$$\frac{214.0 - 173.8}{173.8} = 0.231 \times £650,000 \qquad 150,150$$

	£
	199,850
Less: Rolled-over gain (£199,850 – £75,000)	124,850
Chargeable gain	75,000

£75,000 of the sale proceeds have been retained and therefore £75,000 of the gain is immediately chargeable. The base cost of the replacement building is reduced to £800,150 (£925,000 – £124,850).

(c) *Disposal of computer system*

There is no chargeable gain or allowable loss in relation to this disposal, since gifts to charity are not chargeable disposals.

The company's plant and machinery capital allowances computation for the year to 31 March 2010 will show a disposal of £500 and this will generate a balancing allowance if the computer is being treated as a short-life asset (see Chapter 10).

Gifts of used plant and machinery to a charity are allowable as trading expenses and so there will be a deduction of £500 from the company's trading profit (see Chapter 8).

(d) *Disposal of motor car*

There is no chargeable gain or allowable loss in relation to this disposal, since cars are not chargeable assets

When the car was acquired it was treated as an expensive car (costing over £12,000). A WDA of £3,000 per annum will have been given in the years to 31 March 2008 and 2009, leaving a WDV of £94,000. There will be a balancing allowance of £14,000 (£94,000 – £80,000) in the year to 31 March 2010.

(e) *Disposal of plant and machinery*

This plant and machinery is a wasting chattel. Wasting chattels are normally exempt assets but this item has been used in business and capital allowances have been claimed, so the exemption does not apply. However, the loss of £40,000 is reduced to £nil by capital allowances of the same amount.

The company's plant and machinery capital allowances computation for the year to 31 March 2010 will show a disposal of £30,000.

(f) *Disposal of shares in XYZ plc*

The disposal is matched first against the 3,000 shares acquired within the previous nine days. These shares cost £36,000 and were sold for £30,000, so there is an allowable loss of £6,000.

The remaining 5,000 shares of the disposal are matched with shares taken from the s104 holding, as follows:

	No of shares	Cost £	Indexed cost £
Bought 22 November 2002	4,000	16,000	16,000
Add: Indexation to December 2006			
$\dfrac{202.7-178.2}{178.2} \times £16,000$			2,200
			18,200
Bought 14 December 2006	6,000	30,000	30,000
s104 holding at 14 December 2006	10,000	46,000	48,200
Add: Indexation to November 2009			
$\dfrac{215.2-202.7}{202.7} \times £48,200$			2,972
			51,172
Sold 18 November 2009	(5,000)	(23,000)	(25,586)
s104 holding c/f at 18 November 2009	5,000	23,000	25,586

These 5,000 shares were sold for £50,000 so the chargeable gain arising on their disposal is £24,414 (£50,000 – £25,586).

(g) *Disposal of Government securities*

There is no chargeable gain or allowable loss in relation to this disposal, since disposals of Government securities (or "gilt-edged" securities) by a company are dealt with by means of the loan relationships regime.

Assuming that the securities were not held for trade purposes, there will be a debit on non-trading loan relationships of £5,000.

The company has total chargeable gains of £163,814 (£64,400 + £75,000 + £24,414) and allowable losses of £6,000. Therefore net chargeable gains for the year to 31 March 2010 are £157,814.

Chapter 24

24.1

FY2008   1 July 2008 to 31 March 2009   £30,000 × 9/12 = £22,500
FY2009   1 April 2009 to 30 June 2009   £30,000 × 3/12 = £7,500

24.2

(a) Profits are £287,500 (£267,000 + (£18,450 + £2,050)). This is less than the FY2009 SCR lower limit of £300,000. The small companies rate applies and the corporation tax liability is £56,070 (21% × £267,000).

(b) Profits are £1,505,000 (£1,450,000 + (£49,500 + £5,500)). This exceeds the FY2009 SCR upper limit of £1,500,000. Therefore the main rate applies and the corporation tax liability is £406,000 (28% × £1,450,000).

(c) Profits and chargeable profits are both £10,000,000. Profits exceed the FY2009 SCR upper limit of £1,500,000 so the main rate applies and the corporation tax liability is £2,800,000 (28% × £10,000,000).

(d) Profits and chargeable profits are both £1,000. Profits do not exceed the SCR lower limit of £300,000 for FY2009. Therefore the small companies rate applies and the corporation tax liability is £210 (21% × £1,000).

24.3

The company's profits are £577,000 (£536,000 + (£36,900 + £4,100)), a figure which lies between the SCR lower and upper limits for FY2009. The chargeable profits (£536,000) are taxed at the main rate and marginal relief is available. The computation is:

	£
Corporation tax on £536,000 @ 28%	150,080.00
Less: Marginal relief:	
$\frac{7}{400} \times (£1,500,000 - £577,000) \times \frac{£536,000}{£577,000}$	15,004.75
Corporation tax liability	135,075.25

24.4

(a) Company X has chargeable profits of £875,983 and profits of £908,783 (£875,983 + £32,800) for this accounting period which falls partly into FY2007 and partly into FY2008. It is necessary to apportion between the two FYs when computing the corporation tax liability. The computation is as follows:

	£	£
FY2007 (1 month)		
Corporation tax on £72,999 @ 30%	21,899.70	
Less: Marginal relief:		
$\dfrac{1}{40} \times (£125,000 - £75,732) \times \dfrac{£72,999}{£75,732}$	1,187.25	20,712.45
FY2008 (11 months)		
Corporation tax on £802,984 @ 28%	224,835.52	
Less: Marginal relief:		
$\dfrac{7}{400} \times (£1,375,000 - £833,051) \times \dfrac{£802,984}{£833,051}$	9,141.73	215,693.79
Corporation tax liability		236,406.24

Note that the question gave a figure for FII, *not* a figure for UK dividends. By definition, FII includes the tax credits that are attached to dividends. Therefore there is no need to add tax credits a second time to the FII figure of £32,800.

(b) Company Y has chargeable profits and profits of £200,000 for this six-month accounting period which falls wholly within FY2009. The SCR lower and upper limits are scaled down to £150,000 and £750,000 respectively for a six-month period and the company's profits lie between these scaled-down limits. Therefore corporation tax is due at 28% less marginal relief. The computation is as follows:

	£
Corporation tax on £200,000 @ 28%	56,000.00
Less: Marginal relief:	
$\dfrac{7}{400} \times (£750,000 - £200,000)$	9,625.00
Corporation tax liability	46,375.00

(c) Company Z has chargeable profits and profits of £428,000 for this accounting period which coincides with FY2009. Profits lie between the SCR lower and upper limits, so chargeable profits are taxed at the main rate and marginal relief is available. The computation is:

	£
Corporation tax on £428,000 @ 28%	119,840.00
Less: Marginal relief:	
$\dfrac{7}{400} \times (£1,500,000 - £428,000)$	18,760.00
Corporation tax liability	101,080.00

If chargeable profits and profits were both £328,000, the computation would be:

	£
Corporation tax on £328,000 @ 28%	91,840.00
Less: Marginal relief:	
$\dfrac{7}{400} \times (£1,500,000 - £328,000)$	20,510.00
Corporation tax liability	71,330.00

The tax liability is reduced by £29,750, which is 29.75% of £100,000. Therefore the company is subject to a marginal corporation tax rate of 29.75% (so long as profits remain between the SCR lower and upper limits).

24.5

The due date of payment is 1 June 2009 (nine months and one day after 31 August 2008). The final payment of £4,650 was made on 3 October 2009, i.e. 124 days late. The interest due is:

$$£4,650 \times 4.5\% \times \frac{124}{366} = £70.89.$$

Chapter 25

25.1

(a)   payment made net of basic rate income tax

(b)   income received gross

(c)   income received net of basic rate income tax

(d)   payment made gross

(e)   income received gross.

25.2

Return period	Tax deducted	Tax suffered	Tax deducted less tax suffered	Cumulative	Income tax payable (repayable)
	£	£	£	£	£
1/4/09 - 30/6/09	4,000	2,000	2,000	2,000	2,000
1/10/09 - 31/12/09	4,000		4,000	6,000	4,000
1/1/10 - 31/3/10		1,400	(1,400)	4,600	(1,400)
	8,000	3,400	4,600		4,600

25.3

The income tax returns for the year are as follows:

Return period	Tax deducted	Tax suffered	Tax deducted less tax suffered	Cumulative	Income tax payable (repayable)
	£	£	£	£	£
1/4/09 - 30/6/09		7,200	(7,200)	(7,200)	0
1/7/09 - 30/9/09	9,000		9,000	1,800	1,800
1/1/10 - 31/3/10		7,200	(7,200)	(5,400)	(1,800)
	9,000	14,400	(5,400)		0

The company requires an income tax repayment of £5,400. This is made by means of a reduction in the corporation tax liability for the year, as follows:

	£
Corporation tax liability for the year (21% of £240,000)	50,400
Less: Income tax repayable	5,400
Corporation tax payable 1 January 2011	45,000

25.4

(a)   See text.

(b)   See text.

Chapter 26

26.1

	y/e 31/5/07	y/e 31/5/08	y/e 31/5/09
	£	£	£
Trading profits	-	23,800	40,300
Less: s393(1) relief	-	23,800	8,400
Trading income	-	0	31,900
Less: Charges	-	-	600
Chargeable profits	0	0	31,300
Trading losses c/f	32,200	8,400	-
Unrelieved charges	400	500	-

26.2

	£
Trading income	-
Income from property	190,200
Chargeable gains	45,540
	235,740
Less: s393A(1)(a) relief	232,300
	3,440
Less: Charges	3,440
Chargeable profits	0
Unrelieved charges	20,560

26.3

The correct answer is (c). Under s393A(1)(a), trading losses may be relieved against total profits (including capital gains) of the accounting period in which the loss was incurred.

26.4

	y/e 31/1/07	y/e 31/1/08	y/e 31/1/09	y/e 31/1/10
	£	£	£	£
Trading income	62,300	22,700	73,600	-
Capital gains	-	-	-	48,700
	62,300	22,700	73,600	48,700
Less: s393A(1)(a) relief	-	-	-	48,700
	62,300	22,700	73,600	0
Less: s393A(1)(b) relief	27,300	22,700	73,600	-
	35,000	0	0	0
Less: Charges	1,000	-	-	-
Chargeable profits	34,000	0	0	0
Trade losses c/f	-	-	-	33,400
Unrelieved charges	-	1,000	1,000	1,000

Notes:

(i)   The loss may be carried back three years since it is incurred in an accounting period ending between 24 November 2008 and 23 November 2010. But only £50,000 may be carried back beyond 12 months. Therefore only £27,300 (£50,000 – £22,700) is relieved in the year to 31 January 2007.

(ii) Losses of £172,300 (£48,700 + £73,600 + £22,700 + £27,300) are relieved, leaving losses to carry forward of £33,400.

26.5

The main effects of a s393A(1)(b) claim are as follows:

(i)   Chargeable profits for the year to 31 March 2009 are reduced to £200,000 and the company pays corporation tax at the FY2008 small companies rate of 21%. Without the claim, the company would pay corporation tax at the main rate of 28%, less marginal relief.

(ii) The original tax liability for the year to 31 March 2009 would have been £211,750. This is £800,000 × 28%, less marginal relief of (7/400 × (£1,500,000 – £800,000)).

   The revised liability is £42,000 (£200,000 × 21%). This is a tax saving of £169,750. The loss of £600,000 has been relieved at an effective rate of approximately 28.29%.

   Note that an alternative way of calculating the saving is to recognise that the first £500,000 of loss relief reduces profits from £800,000 to £300,000 (the SCR lower limit) and so saves tax at the marginal rate of 29.75%. The remaining £100,000 of loss relief saves tax at 21%. So the total saving is £500,000 × 29.75% + £100,000 × 21% = £169,750.

(iii) The corporation tax refund due for the year to 31 March 2009 carries interest dating from 1 January 2010 (or the date on which the tax was originally paid, if later).

Maximum ACT set-off for the year to 31 March 2009 is reduced to 20% of £200,000 = £40,000. This reduces the scope for relief of the surplus ACT brought forward from before 6 April 1999.

Chapter 27

27.1

(a), (d) and (e) are associates, (b) and (c) are not.

27.2

The top five shareholders are Sejanus (with Apicata) 1,020 shares, Claudius (with Livia) 590 shares, Agrippa 300 shares, Cleopatra 300 shares and Tiberius 200 shares, totalling 2,410 shares. So the company is not under the control of five or fewer shareholders.

Sejanus is ranked as a director (since he is a manager and, with his wife, owns 20.4% of the share capital). So the directors are Sejanus (with Apicata) 1,020 shares, Claudius (with Livia) 590 shares, Agrippa 300 shares, Cleopatra 300 shares, Tiberius 200 shares and Gaius 200 shares, totalling 2,610 shares. The company is under the control of its participator-directors and is therefore a close company.

27.3

(a) The director owns more than 5% of the company's share capital so the loan is taxable. The company must pay tax of £3,000 (25% of £12,000) by 1 January 2011 (unless the loan is repaid before then). Once paid, this tax is not refundable until nine months and one day after the end of the accounting period in which the loan is repaid or written off. The director will be subject to income tax on loan interest calculated at the official rate. If the loan is eventually written off (wholly or partly) the director will be taxed on the amount written off.

(b) The director will be subject to income tax on a benefit in kind of £1,800. But if the ticket had been given to a shareholder who was not a director or other employee earning at least £8,500 per annum, it would have been treated as a distribution. The cost of the ticket would have been disallowed in the company's accounts and the shareholder would have been charged to income tax as if he or she had received a dividend of £1,800 (tax credit £200).

Chapter 28

28.1

(a) They are associated companies and so they share the small companies rate upper and lower limits.

(b) The transfer pricing legislation applies to transactions carried out at artificial prices between group companies, though small and medium-sized companies are generally exempt from this legislation.

(c) They also form a 75% group so trading losses and other items may be surrendered by a group member to any other group member.

(d) Chargeable assets are transferred between the three companies on a no-gain, no-loss basis.

28.2

	£
Trading profits	220,000
Income from non-trading loan relationship	6,000
Income from property	4,000
Charges	(17,000)
Chargeable profits	213,000
FII (£27,000 + £3,000)	30,000
Profits	243,000
Small companies rate lower limit (£300,000 × 1/3)	100,000
Small companies rate upper limit (£1,500,000 × 1/3)	500,000

	£
Corporation tax on £213,000 @ 28%	59,640.00

Less: Marginal relief:

$$\frac{7}{400} \times (\text{£}500{,}000 - \text{£}243{,}000) \times \frac{\text{£}213{,}000}{\text{£}243{,}000} \qquad 3{,}942.25$$

	£
Corporation tax due	55,697.75

Note:
Small companies rate limits are shared between Alpha Ltd, Beta Ltd and the other active subsidiary.

28.3

Base Ltd has current year trading losses of £90,000 and excess charges of £1,000, giving a total of £91,000. But Apex Ltd has chargeable profits of only £73,000 (£120,000 – £42,000 + £7,000 – £12,000) so the maximum group relief that may be claimed is £73,000.

28.4

A1 Ltd owns at least 75% of A2 Ltd and A2 Ltd owns at least 75% of A3 Ltd, of which A1 Ltd (indirectly) owns more than 50%. Therefore A1 Ltd, A2 Ltd and A3 Ltd form a capital gains group. A2 Ltd does not own at least 75% of A4 Ltd, so A4 Ltd is not a member of the group, even though A1 Ltd does (indirectly) own more than 50% of its ordinary share capital.

28.5

The amount of PP Ltd's loss which is available for group relief is £84,000 (£96,000 less a potential s393A(1)(a) claim of £12,000). This is shared between the consortium members as follows:

	QQ Ltd	*RR Ltd*	*SS Ltd*
	£	£	£
Share of PP Ltd's available loss	26,880	29,400	19,320
Chargeable profits	59,000	47,000	14,000
Maximum group relief claim	26,880	29,400	14,000

Chapter 29

29.1

(a) The value of the supply is £340, VAT charged is 17.5% of £340 = £59.50 and the consideration for the supply is £399.50.

(b) The value of the supply is £333.20 (£340, less 2%), VAT charged is 17.5% of £333.20 = £58.31 and the consideration for the supply is £391.51.

(c) VAT chargeable remains at £58.31 but the consideration for the supply is £398.31.

29.2

(a) Lorna must register since her taxable turnover exceeds the registration threshold.

(b) Mike must register since his aggregate taxable turnover exceeds the registration threshold.

(c) No-one need register. The partnership of "Pat and Phil" is not the same person as "Phil" so the turnover of the two businesses is not aggregated.

(d) The taxable "person" in this case is the company (not the shareholders) and therefore the company must register.

29.3

(a) She is not a taxable person, may not register for VAT and cannot reclaim input tax.

(b) She is a taxable person and must register for VAT. She must account for output tax and may reclaim input tax.

(c) She is a taxable person and must register for VAT unless granted an exemption by HMRC. If she registers she may reclaim input tax. If she is granted exemption she will not be able to reclaim input tax but she will avoid the administrative burden associated with VAT registration.

29.4

See text.

Chapter 30

30.1

See text.

30.2

See text.

30.3

(a) Books are zero-rated. No input tax has been paid and so none may be reclaimed.

(b) Input tax was not deductible when the car was purchased so this is an exempt supply. No output tax is charged on the sale of the car and therefore none has to be accounted for.

(c) The supply of a used commercial building is exempt unless the seller elects for the "option to tax". If this is the case (and assuming a standard rate of 17.5%) output tax of £200,000 @ 17.5% = £35,000 must be accounted for.

30.4

Input tax reclaimed is £799 × 7/47 = £119.00. Output tax of £60.02 (the scale figure for this type of car) must be accounted for.

Chapter 31

31.1

	Value before AE	AE for 2009-10	AE for 2008-09	Value after AE
	£	£	£	£
Gift to grandson (exempt as a small gift)	-	-	-	-
Gift on marriage (£3,000 – £1,000)	2,000	2,000	-	-
Gift to husband (spouse exemption)	-	-	-	-
Gift to relevant property trust	10,000	1,000	3,000	6,000
Gift to Labour Party (exempt)	-	-	-	-
	12,000	3,000	3,000	6,000

31.2

(a) exempt   (b) chargeable   (c) PET.

31.3

The total of transfers brought forward in the seven years to date is £281,000, leaving £44,000 of the nil-rate band to set against the current transfer.

(a) If the trustees pay the tax, the gross value of the transfer is £80,000 and the IHT due is £44,000 @ 0% + £36,000 @ 20% = £7,200, payable on 30 June 2010.

(b) If Nicholas pays the tax, the net value of the transfer is £80,000. The gross value and the tax due are as follows:

	Net £	Gross £	Tax £
£44,000 grossed up @ 0%	44,000	44,000	0
£36,000 grossed up @ 20%	36,000	45,000	9,000
Totals	80,000	89,000	9,000

The tax due is £9,000, payable on 30 June 2010.

31.4

The value of each gift after deduction of exemptions is as follows:

		Value before AE	AE for current year	AE for previous year	Value after AE
		£	£	£	£
2004-05	Daughter (£500,000 – £5,000)	495,000	3,000	3,000	489,000
2008-09	Relevant property trust	500,000	3,000	3,000	494,000

Lifetime tax liability

The gift to Martha's daughter was a PET, so no lifetime tax was payable. The lifetime tax on the gift to the trust was £45,500, payable on 30 April 2009 and calculated as follows:

	Net	*Gross*	*Tax*
	£	£	£
£312,000 grossed up @ 0%	312,000	312,000	0
£182,000 grossed up @ 20%	182,000	227,500	45,500
Totals	494,000	539,500	45,500

Tax liability on death

(i) *Transfer made on 31 August 2004*

The gross value of this transfer is £489,000 and there were no other chargeable transfers in the seven years ending on the date of the transfer. Tax due at death rates applicable on 1 January 2010:

	£
£325,000 @ 0%	0
£164,000 @ 40%	65,600
	65,600
<u>Less</u>: Taper relief (5-6 years) @ 60%	39,360
	26,240
<u>Less</u>: Lifetime tax paid	0
IHT payable by daughter on 31 July 2010	26,240

(ii) *Transfer made on 1 June 2008*

The gross value of this transfer is £539,500 and previous gross chargeable transfers in the seven years ending on the date of the transfer (2 June 2001 to 1 June 2008) were £489,000, using the whole of the nil-rate band. Tax due at death rates applicable on 1 January 2010:

	£
£539,500 @ 40%	215,800
<u>Less</u>: Taper relief (0-3 years) @ 0%	0
	215,800
<u>Less</u>: Lifetime tax paid	45,500
IHT payable by trustees on 31 July 2010	170,300

31.5

The quarter-up rule gives 572p + 1/4 × (588p − 572p) = 576p. Average of the highest and lowest marked bargains is 575p, so the shares are valued at 575p and the transfer has a market value of 1,000 × £5.75 = £5,750.

Chapter 32

32.1

Jean-Paul is a UK resident during 2009-10 but he is neither ordinarily resident nor domiciled in the UK. His UK income tax position is as follows:

(a)   The earnings from his UK employment are fully taxable.

(b)   If the remittance basis applies to him for 2009-10, the earnings from his Belgian employment are taxable on the remittance basis. Otherwise, these earnings are fully taxable.

(c)   If the remittance basis applies to him for 2009-10, the dividends on the Canadian shares are taxable on the remittance basis. Otherwise, these dividends are fully taxable.

(d)   The interest on UK Government securities is exempt from UK income tax since Jean-Paul is not ordinarily resident in the UK.

32.2

Normally, a person is regarded as being either resident for the whole of a tax year or non-resident for the whole of that year, but a person who leaves the UK to take up employment abroad for at least an entire tax year (as Amy has done) is regarded as resident for the part of the tax year before the date of departure and non-resident thereafter. Amy's situation is therefore as follows:

(a)   In 2007-08 she is resident until 31 December 2007 and non-resident from 1 January 2008. She will receive full personal allowances for 2007-08 to set against her income for that year. Her income for UK tax purposes after 31 December 2007 will consist only of any income arising in the UK (e.g. rents from letting her house whilst away). Her Australian salary will not be subject to UK tax.

(b)   In 2008-09 and 2009-10 she is non-resident. Her Australian salary will not be subject to UK tax and she will be taxed only on her UK income, if any. As a citizen of the European Economic Area, she is entitled to personal allowances.

(c)   In 2010-11 she is resident from 1 January 2011. She will receive full personal allowances for 2010-11 to set against her income for the year. Her income for UK tax purposes before 1 January 2011 consists only of her UK income. Once again, her Australian salary will not be subject to UK tax.

However, if Amy visits the UK for 183 days or more in any one tax year she will be resident for that year and her worldwide income will be subject to UK income tax. Similarly, she may be regarded as resident if she visits the UK for 91 days or more per annum.

32.3

(a)   90% of the pension is subject to UK income tax.

(b)   If the remittance basis applies to Cara for a tax year, only the amount of the pension remitted to the UK in that year is subject to UK income tax. Otherwise, the pension is fully taxable.

32.4

See text.

32.5

See text.

32.6

	UK	Overseas	Total
	£	£	£
Trading income	2,120,000		2,120,000
Foreign dividend			
(£57,400 × 100/82 × 100/50)		140,000	140,000
Chargeable profits	2,120,000	140,000	2,260,000
Corporation tax @ 28%	593,600	39,200	632,800
Less: Unilateral DTR		(39,200)	(39,200)
Corporation tax due	593,600	-	593,600

Notes:

(i)   The dividend is not exempt from corporation tax, since it was received before 1 July 2009.

(i)   Underlying tax relief is available since Brits Ltd owns at least 10% of the voting power of the overseas company.

(ii)   The unilateral relief given is restricted to the UK tax due on the foreign income. The remaining £43,400 (£82,600 – £39,200) of foreign tax paid is unrelieved.

Answers to review questions

Set A

Question A1

(a)

	£
Car (35% of £19,500)	6,825
Fuel (35% of £16,900)	5,915
Loan (4.75% of £5,250)	249
LVs (200 @ £4.85)	970
Nursery fees	3,405
	17,364

(b) (i) Consider a car with a lower emission rating. The car on offer has an emission rating which gives the highest possible tax charge. Each 5g/km reduction would save income tax on £364.

(ii) If the £400 contribution is made towards running costs of the car such as maintenance, insurance etc. (not towards private fuel) it will reduce the taxable car benefit.

(iii) Reduce the loan to £5,000, so that no taxable benefit arises.

(iv) Take the canteen meals instead of LVs. No taxable benefit will arise.

(v) Transfer the son to the in-house nursery. No taxable benefit will arise. Alternatively, up to £55 per week of childcare can be received tax-free if the employer contracts with an approved childminder or provides vouchers for paying an approved childminder.

(c)

	Mr Tulliver				Mrs Tulliver		
	Total	Non-savings	Savings	Divs	Total	Non-savings	Savings
	£	£	£	£	£	£	£
Salary	83,000	83,000			15,000	15,000	
Less: Pension cont.					900	900	
					14,100	14,100	
Benefit package	17,364	17,364					
BSI (× 100/80)	8,000		8,000		2,760		2,760
UK divs £4,680 + £520	5,200			5,200			
	113,564	100,364	8,000	5,200	16,860	14,100	2,760
Less: PA	6,475	6,475			6,475	6,475	
Taxable income	107,089	93,889	8,000	5,200	10,385	7,625	2,760

Income tax

Mr T	Mrs T			
37,400	10,385	@ 20%	7,480.00	2,077.00
64,489		@ 40%	25,795.60	
5,200		@ 32.5%	1,690.00	
107,089	10,385			

Tax borne			34,965.60	2,077.00

Tax could be saved by switching investments from Mr T to Mrs T, using the rest of her basic rate band, where savings income would be taxed at only 20% and dividends at only 10%.

Question A2

	Total £	Non-savings £	Savings £	Dividends £
Employment income	17,760	17,760		
Property income	3,680	3,680		
Annuity £25 × 12	300		300	
UK divs £6,750 + tax credit £750	7,500			7,500
Total income	29,240	21,440	300	7,500
Less: Personal allowance	6,475	6,475		
Taxable income	22,765	14,965	300	7,500

Income tax due

Non-savings income	: Basic rate	14,965	@ 20%	2,993.00
Savings income	: Basic rate	300	@ 20%	60.00
Dividend income	: Ordinary rate	7,500	@ 10%	750.00
		22,765		
				3,803.00
Less: MCA £6,960 @ 10%				696.00
Tax borne				3,107.00
Less: Tax credits on dividends and tax deducted at source				810.00
Tax payable				2,297.00

Notes:

1. Rents received are £6,000. Insurance is £370 (9/12 × £360 + 3/12 × £400). The wear and tear allowance is £450 (10% × (£6,000 − £500 − £1,000)) so total expenses are £2,320 (£370 + £500 + £1,000 + £450). Property income is £3,680 (£6,000 − £2,320).

2. Total income exceeds the limit for age-related allowances by £6,340 so allowances are reduced by £3,170 (£6,340 × 1/2). £3,165 is deducted from the personal allowance of £9,640, bringing it down to the lowest possible figure of £6,475. The remaining £5 is deducted from the MCA of £6,965, giving £6,960.

Question A3

The main features of the Self Assessment system which should be outlined are:

- the role of the annual tax return (with supplementary pages) and the short tax return
- the option of filing a paper return or filing the return electronically
- the optional tax calculation section of the paper return
- the fact that the tax liability is calculated automatically if a return is submitted electronically
- the deadlines for submission of the tax return and penalties for late filing
- the procedure with regard to corrections, amendments and error or mistake claims
- notification of chargeability to tax
- the procedure with regard to enquiries, discovery assessments and determinations
- record-keeping requirements
- the appeals procedure.

Each of these topics is dealt with in Chapter 1 of this book.

Question A4

If the transactions are of a trading nature, then the profits made by the partnership of Bernard and Gerald will be charged to income tax as trading income in years 2009-10 and 2010-11. The "badges of trade" will be used to decide whether they are trading, as follows:

(a) *Subject matter*. It appears that the subject matter of the transaction is of a type normally associated with a trading venture, rather than of a type more normally associated with investments or personal consumption.

(b) *Frequency of transactions*. There was only one purchase but there were several sales. The fact that sales were made to a number of different garden centres gives the impression of trading.

(c) *Length of ownership*. This was a fairly short-term venture. Most of the barrels had been sold within a few months and this again gives the impression of trading.

(d) *Supplementary work*. The barrels were sawn in half and Bernard and Gerald canvassed garden centres in the hope of finding customers. These activities constitute supplementary work and support the view that they were trading.

(e) *Motive*. It seems clear that the barrels were bought with only one view in mind - resale at a profit. This is a clear indicator of trading.

(f) *Acquisition*. The barrels were not inherited or gifted. They were purchased by Bernard and Gerald. This and all the other badges of trade combine to support the view that they were trading.

Question A5

(i)

Mr de Praet	2008-09	2009-10
	£	£
Trading income	20,000	nil
Income from property	10,000	10,000
Total income	30,000	10,000
Less: Trading losses	30,000	10,000
Net income	nil	nil

Mr de Praet's personal allowance is lost in both years. Tax savings are achieved at the basic rate. If the loss had been carried forward, there would have been no loss of personal allowances and tax savings would have been achieved at the higher rate.

(ii) An AIA of £7,360 (100% × £7,360) is available in the year to 30 June 2009. This increases the loss to £17,360. A claim to set this loss against total income for 2008-09 will leave net income of £640 (£18,000 – £17,360), so wasting personal allowances.

It would be better to restrict the capital allowances claim to £1,965. This reduces the trading loss claim to £11,965, leaving net income of £6,035 which exactly absorbs the 2008-09 personal allowance. The unclaimed capital allowances increase the WDV carried forward and so result in higher capital allowances in future years.

Set B

Question B1

(i)

	£
Sale proceeds	13,000
Less: Auctioneer's commission (8%)	1,040
	11,960
Less: Acquisition cost	1,000
Chargeable gain	10,960

The maximum gain is 5/3 × £7,000 = £11,667, so the chargeable gain remains at £10,960.

(ii)

	£
Sale proceeds	900,000
Less: Acquisition cost	566,700
Chargeable gain	333,300

£200,000 of the sale proceeds were not reinvested in the new factory. Therefore £200,000 of the gain is immediately chargeable. The rolled-over gain is £133,300. The base cost of the new factory is £566,700 (£700,000 – £133,300).

Question B2

(i) The disposal is matched first with the 1,000 shares bought in the following 30 days. These shares were sold for £4,600 and bought for £4,400, giving a chargeable gain of £200.

The disposal is then matched with 4,000 of the shares in the Section 104 holding. This holding is as follows:

	Number of shares	Allowable expenditure
		£
Bought 18 August 1997	3,000	6,000
Bought 19 September 2004	2,000	5,000
	5,000	11,000
Sold 13 March 2010 (4/5ths)	(4,000)	(8,800)
s104 holding c/f	1,000	2,200

These 4,000 shares were sold for £18,400, so the chargeable gain on their disposal is £9,600 (£18,400 – £8,800). The total chargeable gain is £9,800 (£200 + £9,600).

(ii) Sally's net gains for 2009-10 are £24,000. Deducting losses brought forward of £12,000 leaves £12,000 and then deducting the annual exemption of £10,100 leaves £1,900. CGT is due at 18%, giving a CGT liability for the year of £342.00.

Question B3

(i) The gain on the disposal of the building is:

	£
Sale proceeds	250,000
Less: Acquisition cost	112,800
	137,200
Less: "Held-over" gain	127,200
Chargeable gain	10,000

The immediately chargeable gain is the amount not re-invested (£250,000 – £240,000).

(ii) The "held-over" gain of £127,200 is deferred until the earliest of:

a. disposal of the plant

b. the date that the plant ceases to be used in Ranek's business

c. December 2018 (10 years after the acquisition of the plant).

Question B4

(a) Marlene has net gains of £4,000. These are covered by £4,000 of the annual exemption, leaving a CGT assessment of £nil. The remaining £6,100 of the annual exemption is wasted. There are no losses carried forward.

(b) Moira has net gains of £12,000. Losses brought forward of £1,900 are subtracted from these gains, leaving £10,100. This is covered by the annual exemption, leaving a CGT assessment of £nil. Losses carried forward are £6,100 (£8,000 – £1,900).

(c) Marina has net gains of £3,000. These are covered by £3,000 of the annual exemption, leaving a CGT assessment of £nil. The remaining £7,100 of the annual exemption is wasted. The losses brought forward of £8,000 are carried forward to next year.

(d) Melissa has net gains of £4,000. These are covered by £4,000 of the annual exemption, leaving a CGT assessment of £nil. The remaining £6,100 of the annual exemption is wasted. The losses brought forward of £4,000 are carried forward to next year.

Question B5

(a) *Disposal of flat*

	£
Sale proceeds	142,000
Less: Incidental costs of disposal	4,000
	138,000
Less: Part cost: $\dfrac{£142,000}{£142,000 + £130,000} \times £80,000$	(41,765)
Part conversion costs: $\dfrac{£142,000}{£142,000 + £130,000} \times £32,000$	(16,706)
Chargeable gain	79,529

Disposal of ICI shares

The chargeable gain is £37,700 (£150,000 – £112,300).

Total gains are £117,229 (£79,529 + £37,700). After deducting the 2009-10 annual exemption of £10,100, the CGT assessment for the year is £107,129. CGT due at 18% is £19,283.22.

(b) Mr More might consider the transfer of assets to Mrs More (at no gain, no loss). She could then dispose of them and any gain arising would be taxed in her name. For example, he could transfer the shares in ICI plc to her. If she then disposed of them and realised the gain of £37,700, this would be entirely covered by her losses brought forward and her annual exemption, so saving a substantial amount of CGT.

Set C

Question C1

(a) The accounting periods are the year to 31 March 2009 and the six months to 30 September 2009.

(b)

	y/e 31/3/09 £	6 months to 30/9/09 £
Trading profits (time apportioned)	260,000	130,000
Less: Capital allowances:		
£50,000 + 20% × £70,000	64,000	
20% × £56,000 × 6/12		5,600
Trading income	196,000	124,400
Income from property	20,000	10,000
Income from non-trading loan relationships:		
£2,000 + £2,000 + £1,000	5,000	
£12,000 – £1,000 + £4,000		15,000
Chargeable gains		10,000
	221,000	159,400
Less: Charges on income	5,000	5,000
Chargeable profits	216,000	154,400
Corporation tax @ 21%	43,200.00	
Corporation tax @ 28%		43,232.00
Less: 7/400 × (£750,000 – £154,400)		10,423.00
Corporation tax liability	43,200.00	32,809.00

SCR lower and upper limits for the second accounting period are £150,000 (£300,000 × 6/12) and £750,000 (£1,500,000 × 6/12) respectively.

Question C2

Quarterly accounting for income tax

Return period	Tax deducted £	Tax suffered £	Tax deducted less tax suffered £	Cumulative £	Income tax payable (repayable) £
1/4/09 - 30/6/09	-	7,040	(7,040)	(7,040)	-
1/7/09 - 30/9/09	9,000	4,400	4,600	(2,440)	-
1/10/09 - 31/12/09	10,400	-	10,400	7,960	7,960
1/1/10 - 31/3/10	-	6,160	(6,160)	1,800	(6,160)
	19,400	17,600	1,800		1,800

£7,960 is payable on 14 January 2010, but £6,160 of this is due to be repaid in April 2010.

Question C3

(a)   *Poynton Producers Ltd*

	£
Cost 1 April 2001	150,000
WDA for accounting period to 30/9/01 (4%)	6,000
	144,000
WDA for accounting period to 30/9/02	6,000
	138,000
Notional WDAs for two accounting periods to 30/9/04	12,000
	126,000
WDA for accounting periods to 30/9/05, 06 and 07	18,000
WDV at 30/9/07	108,000

(b)   There is no balancing adjustment.

(c)   The residue of expenditure is £108,000. The remaining tax life of the building is 18 years, so Sale Switches Ltd may claim an annual WDA equal to the appropriate percentage of £6,000 (£108,000 × 1/18). Allowances are as follows:

y/e 31 December 2008	(£6000 × 3/12 × 100%) + (£6,000 × 9/12 × 75%)	£4,875
y/e 31 December 2009	(£6000 × 3/12 × 75%) + (£6,000 × 9/12 × 50%)	£3,375
y/e 31 December 2010	(£6000 × 3/12 × 50%) + (£6,000 × 9/12 × 25%)	£1,875
y/e 31 December 2011	(£6000 × 3/12 × 25%)	£375

Question C4

(a)   The company has two alternatives. One alternative is to carry the loss back under s393A(1)(b) and set it against the total profits (before charges) of the year to 30 September 2008. The other is to carry the loss forward under s393(1) and set it against the trading profits of the year to 31 March 2010.

(b)   The main deciding factor is the marginal rate of corporation tax payable in the period in which loss relief is given. The marginal rate for the year to 30 September 2008 is 20.5% (20% until 31 March 2008 and then 21%). The marginal rate for the year to 31 March 2010 is 29.75%.

Therefore the better alternative is to carry the loss forward and save tax at 29.75%. The non-trade charges of £750 will be unrelieved whatever the company does.

Question C5

(a)

	£
Trading profits	170,000
<u>Less</u>: Capital allowances	32,000
Trading income	138,000
Income from property	46,000
Chargeable gains £6,400 – £1,400	5,000
	189,000
<u>Less</u>: Charges on income	20,000
Chargeable profits	169,000
FII (£14,400 + £1,600)	16,000
Profits	185,000
Corporation tax at 21% on £169,000, due 1 January 2011	35,490

(b) If the company has one subsidiary, the limits for the small companies rate are divided by two. The lower limit becomes £150,000 and the upper limit becomes £750,000. Corporation tax is due as follows:

	£
£169,000 @ 28%	47,320.00
<u>Less</u>: $\dfrac{7}{400} \times (£750,000 - £185,000) \times \dfrac{£169,000}{£185,000}$	9,032.36
Corporation tax due 1 January 2011	38,287.64

Set D

Question D1

(i)   The sale to St Oggs Inc is an export to a non-EU country and is zero-rated, even though the goods in question are normally standard-rated. HMRC may require documentary evidence that the goods have actually been exported.

(ii) Scotland is not outside the UK so the sale to Rappit Ltd is not an export and the supply is standard-rated. The value of the supply is £19,000 (£20,000 less 5%) and the related output tax (with a standard rate of 17.5%) is £3,325 (17.5% of £19,000). This is the case whether or not Rappit Ltd takes advantage of the discount offered.

(iii) The sale of the machinery is a taxable supply of goods, even though the machinery was a fixed (non-current) asset rather than stock in trade.

(iv) The hire of electrical equipment is a taxable supply of services.

(v)   Unless Wakem & Co. Ltd operates the cash accounting scheme, output tax relating to supplies of goods to Garum Furs plc will have been paid over to HMRC at the end of the tax periods in which the supplies took place. This VAT can be recovered from HMRC so long as at least six months have elapsed since the date of supply and Wakem & Co. Ltd has written off the debt in its books. If part-payment is eventually received from the liquidator, part of the recovered VAT will be repayable to HMRC.

Question D2

(a)   A Ltd controls B Ltd, C Ltd, D Ltd and E Ltd, so all five companies are associated companies.

(b)   A Ltd controls 75% or more of B Ltd, C Ltd and D Ltd so these four companies form a 75% group. E Ltd is not UK resident (or EEA-resident) and so cannot belong to the group.

(c)   The profits of E Ltd (a CFC) do not exceed £50,000, so there is no allocation of E Ltd's profits to A Ltd. The profits of £15,000 are not chargeable to UK corporation tax at all.

Both A Ltd and B Ltd will pay tax at the marginal rate of 29.75% unless their chargeable profits are reduced to the small companies rate lower limit of £60,000 (£300,000 × 1/5). Therefore the first priority when dealing with the losses of C Ltd and D Ltd is to use them to reduce the profits of A Ltd and B Ltd to £60,000 each. This absorbs £85,000 of losses. The remaining losses of £10,000 could be set against the bank interest of C Ltd or surrendered to A Ltd or B Ltd, saving tax at 21% in each case. Assuming that a Section 393A(1)(a) claim is made in relation to this £10,000, the corporation tax liability of each company is as follows:

	A Ltd £	B Ltd £	C Ltd £	D Ltd £	E Ltd £
Trading income	90,000	100,000	-	-	-
Bank interest	-	15,000	12,000	-	-
	90,000	115,000	12,000	-	-
Less: Group relief	30,000	55,000	-	-	-
s393A(1)(a)	-	-	10,000	-	-
Chargeable profits	60,000	60,000	2,000	-	-
Tax @ 21%	12,600	12,600	420	-	-

Question D3

The report should make the following points:

(a)　Employees on a nine-month contract will not be absent from the UK for a whole tax year and so, for tax purposes, these employees will be both resident and ordinarily resident in the UK throughout the nine months. Their earnings whilst working abroad will be fully assessable to UK income tax.

(b)　Employees on an 18-month contract which includes an entire tax year will be treated as non-resident for the duration of the contract. Their earnings from duties performed overseas (and any other foreign income) will not be subject to UK income tax. As non-residents, they will also not be liable to UK capital gains tax. They will, however, be liable to UK income tax on any income arising in the UK (e.g. rents from letting their homes whilst working abroad).

(c)　Employees on an 18-month contract which does not include an entire tax year will be treated as resident in the UK throughout the 18 months. Their overseas earnings will therefore be assessed to UK income tax, but double tax relief will be available.

Question D4

	UK income	Income from Z Inc	Income from X S.A.	Total
	£	£	£	£
Trading income	500,000	-	-	500,000
Dividend income	-	50,000	40,000	90,000
	500,000	50,000	40,000	590,000
Less: Charges	10,000	-	-	10,000
Chargeable profits	490,000	50,000	40,000	580,000

M Ltd, N Ltd and O Ltd are associated companies, so the small companies rate limits are divided equally between them. Each company has an SCR upper limit of £500,000 and an SCR lower limit of £100,000. M Ltd's chargeable profits are £580,000, so tax is due at 28%.

	UK income	Income from Z Inc	Income from X S.A.	Total
	£	£	£	£
Corporation tax at 28%	137,200	14,000	11,200	162,400
Less: DTR	-	14,000	2,000	16,000
Corporation tax liability	137,200	0	9,200	146,400
Maximum ACT set-off	98,000	0	8,000	106,000

(See notes overleaf)

Notes:

(i)   The foreign dividends are not exempt since they were received before 1 July 2009.

(ii)   Maximum ACT set-off is:

- UK income, 20% of £490,000 = £98,000

- Income from Z Inc, 20% of £50,000 = £10,000, restricted to £nil

- Income from X S.A., 20% of £40,000 = £8,000.

(iii) The shadow ACT arising on any dividends paid in the year by M Ltd will of course use up some or all of the maximum ACT set-off of £106,000, so reducing the scope for relieving surplus ACT brought forward from before 6 April 1999.

Index